RINTED IN U. S. A.

Problems of

Stability and Progress in

INTERNATIONAL RELATIONS

Problems of
Stability and Progress
in

INTERNATIONAL RELATIONS

by

Quincy Wright

1954
Berkeley and Los Angeles
UNIVERSITY OF CALIFORNIA PRESS

UNIVERSITY OF CALIFORNIA PRESS

BERKELEY AND LOS ANGELES

CAMBRIDGE UNIVERSITY PRESS

LONDON, ENGLAND

COPYRIGHT, 1954, BY

THE REGENTS OF THE UNIVERSITY OF CALIFORNIA

LIBRARY OF CONGRESS CATALOG CARD NUMBER: 53-11251

PRINTED IN THE UNITED STATES OF AMERICA

To

HANS KELSEN

With Respect and Affection

FOREWORD

In Professor Wright's own words at the end of the last essay in Part V of this book I have found a better foreword than I can prepare:

> We live in a critical age and will continue to do so. World government is premature and isolation is obsolete. Neither will solve our problems. We are in a small world, from which we cannot escape, and it contains shipmates such as Stalin and Mao with a capacity to scuttle it. We cannot progress toward a greater security for our way of life unless we accept this world as it is, seek to live and let live, encourage others to do likewise in its narrowing confines, and cooperate with all in trying to improve it . . .
>
> We cannot be sure that the world can be made safe for democracy, but we are certain it cannot be unless the democracies see it steadily, see it accurately, and see it whole.

In the era of the hydrogen bomb and a polarized East-West tension there are too many politicians and citizens who do not see steadily or accurately. Even more regrettably, there are too many foreign-affairs professionals, paid by society to deal with the problems of life in the world community, who do not see the whole and, therefore, not accurately, either. Thus we have self-styled legal scientists who confine themselves to the definition of power structures they reject any part in forming. We have self-nominated delegates to self-generated great debates on law versus power politics. We have the international tribunal monists, the international codification monists, and the "good old-fashioned bilateral diplomacy" monists. On the other hand, we have expansive eclectics; but they, unfortunately, chose different things to be eclectic about. In short, we have confusion—a great deal of confusion.

vii

In his "Word for Today" Edward R. Murrow once quoted someone who said: "The greatest danger of our times comes from the increasing confusion of our times." Expanded on the spare framework exposed by the extract I have quoted, Professor Wright in the essays here collected has contributed a wise, sane, intelligent view of the whole. He has combated confusion by fusion and by talking good sense, sprinkled by delightful but thoughtful references to matters rarely encountered in social science writing, such as Ohm's law and even space travel.

For the amateur, the professional, the student—for all who have interests touching or concerning the relationships of individuals and of states to the international community of today and of the tomorrow which can come only if we respond intelligently to the challenge of today—for all these Professor Wright has had a very great deal to say within these covers.

COVEY T. OLIVER

Berkeley, California
November, 1953

PREFACE

The first two papers in this volume were delivered in May, 1952, at the University of California, Berkeley, on the occasion of the retirement of Hans Kelsen, as professor of international law, at that institution. Students all over the world owe much to his precise analyses of problems in international law and organization and to the challenge offered by his "pure theory of law." In publishing this volume I wish to express my obligation to him. His acute and disinterested analyses of the problems of the world have been a continuous inspiration.

When asked to prepare the Kelsen lectures for publication, it occurred to me that they constituted a summary of ideas upon the general problem of stability and progress in international relations, which I have been expressing since the establishment of the United Nations at the San Francisco Conference in 1945. As the brief space allotted to the Kelsen lectures made it necessary to compress these ideas into rather abstract formulations, it seemed to me that a publication would interest the reading public more if those lectures were accompanied by more concrete treatments of various aspects of the subject. I, therefore, suggested that the publication be expanded to include other essays of mine, published and unpublished, which dealt with this general theme. The result is the present volume.

The Kelsen lectures contrasted the condition of a shrinking and rapidly changing world in which mankind now lives, with the human institutions and values which immediately influence individual and group behavior. Unlike these conditions, which are only slightly susceptible to human control and manipulation, institutions and values are subject to modification through information, education, and propaganda. Attitudes, opinion, and policies may be changed by appeals to experience, reason, and sentiment. The Kelsen lectures give attention to the use of science, education, organization, law, and politics as methods for bringing conditions, values, and institutions into closer harmony with one another. The essays following the Kelsen lectures further elaborate these approaches to the problem of international relations.

In section two, the progress of international organization in meeting the challenge of changing conditions, is illustrated by four essays, the first emphasizing American experience, and the other three successively appraising developments in 1946, 1948, and 1951. The changes in opinion and action during this relatively brief period indicate the dynamic condition of our world.

In section three, attention is given to international politics with special emphasis upon its psychological roots and the practicability of measuring and controlling the tensions inherent in it.

In section four, the problem of education to ameliorate the excesses of international politics and to provide the basis for more effective international organization is discussed.

Section five deals with the role of law in the international field, broadening the subject, however, considerably beyond traditional international law. The tendency of international law to outlaw war and to recognize individuals and international organizations as subjects is discussed. Special attention is given to the relation of international law, on the one hand, to sociology and science, and, on the other, to politics and national institutions.

Finally, section six discusses the dynamic influence of inventions on international relations. Other factors such as population growth, the wide acceptance of novel ideologies, and the rise of charismatic personalities have also contributed to the turbulent condition of recent international relations. The widespread use of new technologies resulting from recent inventions have, however, accentuated the influence of these factors and have themselves directly affected opinions and policies modifying international institutions and values. Special attention is given to aviation and the atomic bomb, though inventions in the field of communications, especially radio, radar, and television, may have been of no less importance.

These essays were written from 1946 to 1952 and have not been substantially altered. They consequently reflect the conditions under which they were written and suggest the considerable change which so short a period as seven years has wrought in the thinking of one observer and also upon public opinion on such subjects as the United Nations, war, human rights, and the atomic bomb. Organizations, policies, and practices have also changed, though it is still too early to say whether these changes are working toward a better adaptation of institutions and values to the conditions of the world.

It is clear that in our age of invention and widespread communication, international relations is a dynamic subject. Formulations good for all time are not to be expected. Political science must be closely related to the practice of politics and this is particularly true of that branch of political science dealing with international relations. Theoretical and practical problems are less susceptible of separate treatment than are pure and applied science in the realm of physical phenomena.

What is the outstanding problem of international relations? In the first Kelsen lecture I ventured the following formulation: "International peace and security requires a centralization of institutions of information, education, regulation and control at a rate proportional to the development of economic and cultural interdependence among the nations and of vulnerability of each to destructive attack by others." With more concrete application to the present situation, the problem, I said, "is one of institutionalizing international peace and security in the right direction, of the right type and at the right speed." We must try to make international law and organization effective whether viewed from the point of view of human values or from that of current political conditions. The idealistic and realistic points of view in international relations must be reconciled.

Through ratification of the United Nations Charter by their governments, most of "the peoples of the world" have expressed "the determination" to realize certain values, such as peace, security, justice, welfare, and freedom. Experience suggests, and the Charter asserts, that the interpretation and application of these ideals to a shrinking and rapidly changing world requires a universal legal and political organization, imposing more effective limitations upon the exercise of their sovereignty by the nation-states. But it also appears that political conditions which now prevail are characterized by ideologies of unusual diversity; by unusual vulnerability of all peoples to distant attack by military, economic, or propaganda weapons; by international tensions manifested by an arms race of unusual magnitude; and by an unusual disposition of governments and peoples to subordinate legal and moral standards to political and military objectives. These conditions have resulted in a popular demand in major countries for less limitation upon the exercise of national sovereignty. The result has been an exceptional divergence of policies and organizations which appear to be required by long-range considerations of human values from these which appear to be necessitated by short-range exigencies of domestic and international politics. There is a wide gap between the ideal and the real, between long-run and short-run policies, between the means appropriate to achieve accepted values and the probable action in response to existing conditions. Such a gap is not novel in international relations, but it has become unusually wide because of the dislocations caused by two world wars; by inventions, revolutionizing the conditions of communication, transport, and war; by the rise of revolutionary ideologies such as fascism and communism; and by changes in the location of political power reducing the importance of Europe and increasing that of America and Asia. These disturbing circumstances have occurred in the course of a single generation, and adjustment to them has not been easy. The human race has seldom faced such serious problems. When problems of comparable magnitude have been faced, as they were in Europe on the collapse of the Roman Empire in the fifth century and on the collapse of the medieval system in the fifteenth century, solutions which would combine stability with progress have seldom been found.

These essays do not pretend to offer any easy solution to this problem. Their contribution, if any, is to set forth the nature of the problem viewed from the several points of view of organization, politics, education, law, and technology. The discovery and application of reasonably satisfactory solutions will undoubtedly require a closer relationship of practical political activity and scientific thought, and a better brand of both politics and social science than has been available in the past.

With the broader and deeper understanding which will make these desiderata available, reasonable stability might be combined with reasonable progress. Men may be able to look to the future with sufficient confidence to justify rational planning of their lives and with sufficient optimism to stimulate effort in formulating and realizing such plans.

All of these essays have been published previously except the Kelsen lectures themselves and the immediately following essay "America and World Organization." The latter was presented at a symposium at the University of Chicago in 1950.

For permission to reprint articles from certain publications the author is grateful to the following: *Yale Law Journal;* World Peace Foundation, *International Organization;* American Society of International Law, *Proceedings; American Political Science Review; American Journal of Psychiatry; Western Political Quarterly;* UNESCO, *International Social Science Bulletin; Conflicts of Power in Western Culture* (Harper); American Association of University Professors, *Bulletin;* Conference of Teachers of International Law and Related Subjects, *Proceedings; Bulletin of Atomic Scientists;* the Thirteenth Conference on Science, Philosophy and Religion; American Philosophical Society, *Proceedings; Measure;* University of Illinois, *James Lectures;* and *Air Affairs.*

QUINCY WRIGHT

University of Chicago, April, 1953

CONTENTS

xiii

Part IV

Education and International Stability

Part V

Law and International Stability

Part VI

Technology and International Stability

PART I

INSTITUTIONALIZING INTERNATIONAL PEACE AND SECURITY

1

SHOULD INTERNATIONAL PEACE AND SECURITY BE INSTITUTIONALIZED?

Meaning of the Term "Institution"

The term institution or institute may bring to mind many pictures. We may think of the Smithsonian Institution, of institutional care of the indigent, of instituting a new project, of Coke's Institutes of the law, or of social institutions in general. The latter is a key term of sociology like group, society, and culture. It refers to a social arrangement of considerable permanence involving (1) a cluster of usages, customs, and rituals observed by a group of people; (2) a commitment to certain goals, objectives or values, and to coöperation for realizing them; (3) a more or less logically organized body of doctrine and symbolism, rationalizing values, beliefs and rituals; and (4) an organization or hierarchy of authority and leadership to prescribe action, interpret doctrine, and apply it to situations as they arise. Thus an institution implies in a group, uniformity in certain practices, commitment to certain values, understanding of certain ideas, and obedience to certain leaders.[1]

An institution exists subjectively in the mind of each individual of the group and objectively in observable practices, especially among the leaders of the group. It exists abstractly in a body of doctrine or ideology and concretely in rituals, observances, and actions. Anthropologists dealing with primitive people tend to emphasize the objective and concrete aspects of institutions. They speak of the institutions of matrimony, war, cultivation, magic, chieftainship, and priesthood found among such peoples. Among civilized people, on the other hand, the

3

subjective and abstract aspects of institutions are more emphasized. We speak of such institutions as the states, the churches, the universities, and the business corporations, and we think of the social or personal ends they are supposed to serve, the methods they apply to realize these ends, and the theories and doctrines they espouse. But we also think of such concrete things as buildings that house them, of courtroom proceedings, of legislative sessions, church services and sermons, of classrooms, of academic degree giving, of factory activity and so forth.

The more rigid, persistent, and coördinated are rituals, beliefs, doctrines, and organizations, the more do we have an institution. Since the members of a group may function in a number of institutions, we are more likely to speak of a value, a function, or an interest being institutionalized than of a group being institutionalized. Doubtless in proportion as individuals are associated with only one institution, as tends to be true of monks in a monastery, prisoners in a penitentiary, orphans in an orphanage, or students in a boarding school, the latter expression is appropriate.

Value of Institutions

Why do we have institutions? Are they a good thing or a bad thing? Anthropologists might regard this question as silly. They might say that institutions just are, wherever man is. He lives in institutions. He is a social animal. It would be just as sensible to ask why are there lions or sheep or human beings. The question, it is said, implies an antiscientific, anthropomorphic view of the universe.

However, institutions are susceptible of human manipulation. They are often instituted by some one, at some time and place, for some purpose. A philanthropist establishes a foundation or a mystic establishes a cult, thus projecting present purposes and insights into the future. A sociologist explains a body of hitherto unexplained practices in terms of motives, goals, and functions and gives precise meaning to them as Thrasher did to the "gang" and Wirth to the "ghetto." [2] A politician organizes a ward so he can exert power, or a promoter organizes a corporation so he can make money. A theologian or a jurist integrates a body of beliefs and symbols into a logical system, as Augustine did for Christianity, as Gaius did for the Roman law, and as Glanville and Bracton did for the common law. All of these persons are creating institutions, though, of course, they could not do it unless beliefs, practices, and persons already existed ready to be institutionalized.

Institutions are not only created, they are maintained and modified by active effort. They may be destroyed by the conscious effort of revolutionists or reformers. They may, therefore, be evaluated and criticized, not in terms of the purposes of God, but in terms of the purposes of man. In this sense the utility and the disutility of institutionalizing purposes, beliefs, and practices can be stated.

Institutions on the one hand facilitate prediction and control of social phenomena and, on the other, they facilitate adjustment to and comprehension of social phenomena.

Science is an institution to aid in prediction but most other institutions by influencing human behavior also aid in predicting it. The human mind is extraordinarily sensitive and susceptible of influence by communications from a distance or by narratives of remote historic events. Consequently the prediction of human behavior is difficult, almost impossible, unless impressions that are important are sorted out from those that are not, and are interpreted to guide attitudes and actions. Institutions, focusing attention upon values and beliefs which exist in the culture or public opinion, perform this service. They create expectations of behavior which make prediction possible for one that understands the institutionalized patterns.

Such understanding also makes possible control of human behavior. By understanding the institutions of the law, legislators, administrators, lawyers, and judges are able to act so as to bring about, within limits, desired ends. Law is a process whereby the "ought to be" of group opinion is converted into the "is" of social behavior. There is, however, considerable opportunity for dexterity in interpreting the social "ought" and demonstrating that it has been converted into a social "is." Science, in addition to facilitating prediction of natural and human processes, aids in the inventing of devices and arts for their control. Here the inventor can exercise ingenuity in converting the scientific "is" into a utilitarian "ought." [3]

Some events significant for social existence cannot be controlled, such as, for example, the succession of the seasons and of day and night. The occurrence of birth, adolescence, and death are subject only to a limited control, and the same is true of such visitations as war, famine, and pestilence among primitive peoples. By institutionalizing agriculture and family life men can foresee and adjust their activities to astronomical phenomena, sowing and reaping, sleeping and waking at the proper time. They can anticipate and adjust themselves to recurrent individual, family, and social disasters and benefits by ceremonials establishing the proper emotional response to these events. Among primitive people the number of events which appear to be in this uncontrollable class are very large; consequently institutions serve more for emotional adjustment than for effective control. As civilization advances, methods are discovered and employed for regulating or controlling an increasing proportion of the events which affect human life, and institutions increasingly function as agencies of social control.

Institutions of magic, religion, science, and ethics by creating myths, doctrines, and explanations, and by distinguishing the self from other human beings, from nature, and from the spiritual world provide a conception of the whole, and of the relation among its parts and of values, and so contribute meaning to things and events satisfying to the demands of man's rationality and self esteem.[4]

However, institutions also have disadvantages.

By making life predictable, they preserve the *status quo* and stifle new ways which might better serve human needs. They tend to perpetuate obsolete customs and to preserve ancient evils. By conserving the familiar and expected, they take from life adventure and the thrill of novelty.

By making life controllable, they tend to put control of each individual's destiny into the hands of men who may exercise this power for selfish purposes. They may, therefore, facilitate tyranny and oppression of the many by the few, of the weak by the powerful.

By facilitating adjustment, they may preserve superstitions and create an unreal universe, objectifying human wishes and preventing discovery of the actual order of nature, thus hampering progress in knowledge and technology for the advancement of human welfare.

By explaining the universe in terms of values and distinctions natural to an immature stage of human development, they promote scholasticism rather than science, tradition rather than observation. They perpetuate views of the universe unadapted to present life, and, as the gap between ancient beliefs and present knowledge widens, they tend to split the community into conservatives and progressives. Such a division may lead to sudden disruption, revolution, war, and chaos. By thwarting gradual adjustments and rigidifying beliefs, in the interest of predictability and stability, they allow inconsistencies to emerge and great lags to develop between one aspect of society and another, paving the way to sudden, violent, and destructive change.[5]

Thus while institutions are agencies of prediction, control, adjustment, and understanding, they also are agencies of rigidity, oppression, superstition, and violence. They promote stability, order, and justice for a time but often at the expense of continuous progress and with the consequence of eventual injustice and disruption.

In view of the ambivalent character of institutions they are always subject to criticism and reform. They are criticized by conservatives on the ground that present practices and procedures have departed from original prescriptions and traditional customs. They are also criticized by progressives on the ground that present practices and procedures fail to accomplish the ends and purposes which the institution proposed or which present conditions demand. They are criticized by liberals on the ground that leaders and management are corrupt, tyrannical, and inefficient or that they are serving vested interests to the neglect of the general membership. They are also criticized by radicals on the ground that their ideology is ambiguous, illogical, or obsolescent and needs to be reformulated. Sometimes it is only when institutions are criticized and perhaps on the way to disintegration or supersession, that they come to be recognized as institutions.

Institutions are made by men as instruments of human purpose, are maintained to promote human policies, are subjected to criticism, and sometimes ended by human action; yet they tend to have a life of their own. They tend to become a vested interest of their management or their adherents, and their preservation, survival, and growth tends to become an end in itself. The defensive and expansive tendency of an institution, and the interplay of function, authority, knowledge, and area of operation tends to make institutions develop in both size and integration.[6] As the ancestors of most organic forms were smaller and less complex, so most existing institutions were originally smaller and simpler. With the increase of communications among, and of the interdependence of, the people affected by an institution, its functioning seems to require an enlargement of the area of its operation, sometimes accomplished by absorption of previously independent institutions and sometimes by the grouping of many institutions under a common supervision or into a federation. Like the Jurassic dinosaurs, institutions usually keep on growing and specializing until they become so large and clumsy or so specialized and unadaptable that they do not adjust themselves to changing conditions and die. Institutional evolution like organic evolution, therefore, tends to be sympodial.[7]

This tendency may be illustrated in the field of public institutions for care of the indigent and delinquent in the United States. Local institutions have been grouped under departments in most of the states, and these have tended to come under some supervision of the federal government. At the same time institutions have tended to be functionally integrated in this field. The previously independent functions of poor relief, public hospitals, and reform of delinquents have become grouped under departments of welfare. Such developments have required increase in authority and in control of funds. Private institutions have tended to be taken over by public authority with access to taxation and legal control. A professionalization of services has usually accompanied these developments. Voluntary charity has been superseded by social service workers with professional education, adequate information, and scientific knowledge. Thus local, voluntary, and spontaneous charities have developed into universal, authoritarian, and professional institutions and, as they have done so, have become impersonal and inflexible and have sometimes served ends remote from those originally designed.[8]

This discussion of institutions suggests that institutionalization cannot in itself be regarded as either good or bad. It is a process which has within it seeds of progress and decay, of liberation and enslavement. Institutions must be guided by continual thought if they are to serve real values of real people with real knowledge in a real world. The problem is not one of institutionalization or chaos, but of the right direction, the right kind, the right amount, and the right speed of institutionalization. Continuous appraisal and measurement are necessary if institutions are to serve rather than to enslave mankind. The tendency of institutions to become juggernauts must never be forgotten.

International Institutions

What is the bearing of all this on problems of peace and security? Men want both peace and security, and the world has not been without institutions to promote these ends. Sovereign states are institutions to provide security for their members. Diplomacy has been an institution to settle intergroup disputes and to serve national interests. War has been an institution to confine intergroup violence to defined periods of time, defined methods, defined groups, and defined areas. International law has been an institution with principles, rules, and procedures to regulate national policy, diplomacy, and war, to minimize violence, and to secure the existence of states. Churches have been institutions to give both peace of mind and peace among peoples. Many other institutions have influenced international relations—international banks, international commerce, international education, international communication, international travel. All of these activities have characteristic practices, purposes, vocabularies, and varying degrees and types of organization entitling them to be called institutions.

International peace and security have been institutionalized, but the institutions in this field have been widely criticized. The sovereign state has tended to expand and solidify, and the larger states have tended to bring smaller neighbors under their protection until the world is threatened by an arms race between two leading powers, each becoming, or in danger of becoming, a "garrison state," destroying the liberty of its citizens, subjecting them to intolerable taxation, and preparing for mutual destruction.

Diplomacy has been an agency of these states, but with the progress of industrialization and propaganda, and with the development of an ideological split and a bipolar world, the courtesies of earlier times have been corrupted into vituperation, human interests have been subordinated to the effort to increase the power position of the respective great powers, and the earlier limitations of law and morality have been ignored or repudiated.[9]

War has tended to depart from earlier limitations, to utilize the latest achievements of science, to become universal and total, and to threaten destruction of human life, social institutions, historical monuments, and economic wealth in unparalleled measure.[10]

On the other hand, international law, churches, economic and educational institutions have become subordinated to the requirements of national sovereignty, diplomacy, and war. They have ceased to be independent institutions in many places and have become incapable of criticizing the political and military institutions which absorb so much of human attention.

New institutions have therefore been suggested—the United Nations, the specialized agencies, a new international or world law emphasizing the outlawry of war and the rights of man, and UNESCO, a universal center of international education, developing a discipline of international relations, and an ideology of internationalism. It is hoped by their advocates that these institutions may moderate the trend toward garrison states and absolute war, may focus attention on the dignity of the human individual, may liberate him from the institutions which would destroy him, and may give him peace with justice and security with freedom.[11]

There are, however, those who fear that these new institutions may prove more dangerous than those they would supersede. The United Nations, if it develops strength to achieve its purposes, might, it is said, substitute a more remote and universal tyranny for the national, mutually limiting, tyrannies of the states.[12] By inducing widespread ratification of general treaties, if not by acquiring direct legislative power on matters such as labor regulation, agricultural development, education, and civil rights, the United Nations and the specialized agencies, might, it is said, encroach on the domestic jurisdiction of states and impose regulations upon peoples alien to their cultures and traditions.[13] The new international law, by outlawing war, through distinguishing the aggressor from the victim and instituting police measures against the aggressor, might, it is said, convert local wars into universal wars. By protecting the rights of man, economic and social as well as civil and political, and by providing for the punishment of international offenses, that law might, it is feared, submerge national sovereignties in a world sovereignty in which local variation would disappear and the influence of the individual on the government and law which control him would be reduced to the vanishing point. The new international education, it is said, might destroy local and national loyalties, absorb cultural diversities into an inhuman and artificial world culture, stultifying the competition among cultures necessary for progress and the traditional loyalties necessary for adjustment, satisfaction, and realization of personality.

When one views the feebleness of these new international institutions, spending less than one-twentieth of one per cent as much as do national states and attracting only two or three per cent as much attention in the leading newspapers, these fears seem exaggerated.[14] Yet, these new institutions have roots deep in the past. They stem from ideas of natural law, of cosmopolitanism, and of human brotherhood emerging in the classical periods of all great civilizations—Confucian, Hindu, Jewish, Socratic, Christian, and Moslem. They also have support from many persons engaged in commerce, communication, science, and education in the recent past. Consequently, whether one looks to the "inner direction" of conscience or the "other direction" of contemporary opinion,[15] these universal institutions find support. They have grown since the age of discoveries with the practices of general conference, of international arbitration and conciliation, and, especially in the past century, with the formation of numerous international unions, with the system of the Hague conferences, with the League of Nations, and with the United Nations and its specialized agencies. This growth has proceeded through processes of coördination and assimilation, and has been at an accelerating pace. Such institutions have steadily become more universal, more penetrating into all functions of human society, more efficient, and more important in human attention. If that progress continues the complexion of the world may be greatly altered in course of time. At the present time, it must again be emphasized, the importance of these universal institutions, compared to national institutions, can easily be exaggerated.

The development of these universal institutions has in fact been paralleled by the development of national institutions. The world has been institutionalizing itself at the same time in opposite directions. It has been moving toward universalism and toward nationalism at the same time, but today nationalism is still ahead so far as attention to symbols and power of institutions are concerned. From the material point of view of economic interdependence, of effective and abundant communication, and of vulnerability of each people to influences military, economic, and propagandistic from the most remote quarters, it may indeed be said that one world exists. From the point of view of symbolic loyalties and institutional effectiveness, this is far from true.

Evaluation of International Institutions

By viewing steadily the conditions of the world and the needs of man, can these institutions national, international, and universal be effectively criticized? Can we describe the institutional changes which might maximize peace with justice and security with freedom? I am not now discussing the probability that such changes might be effective, nor the means for making them so, but only the possibility of describing changes in existing institutions which might contribute to these ends.

It is necessary to distinguish conditions which cannot be changed but may be predicted, from institutions which can be controlled even though their development is difficult to predict. This distinction is not absolute. There are conditions important for human society quite insusceptible of change by human effort, such as the rotation of the earth on its axis, the revolution of the earth around the sun, and the inclination of the earth's axis—conditions which assure the alternation of night and day, the succession of the seasons, the dominant movements of the atmosphere and the oceanic currents, and the differential temperatures of the poles and the equator. The main geographic features of the earth's surface, the distribution of mineral deposits and soils, and the biological characteristics of the human organism are also relatively uncontrollable conditions, but the social importance of these conditions varies greatly with developments in the fields of technology, agriculture, transportation, medicine, eugenics, and population control.

Some institutional arrangements, such as the characteristics of the major nations of the world and the culture of the peoples, including systems of values, beliefs, and techniques, are rooted in individual attitudes and skills and in the opinions prevailing in communities. They limit the range of choice, of policy, and of structural change by governments and resemble conditions, astronomic and geographic, in that their persistence over long periods of time can be predicted within moderate margins of error. The modification of these institutions by human action can normally proceed only slowly. Yet revolutionary situations arise presenting opportunities for choice, control, and guided, but rapid, change in these basic social conditions.

On the other hand political and other leaders make decisions with important consequences, and political and other groups develop policies and change the forms of their organization. Many institutional arrangements present such opportunities for choice. Alternatives are imagined among which men may choose through rational consideration of ends and means. The frequency of such opportunities for choice perhaps marks the difference between civilized and primitive societies. The form and activity of the latter are in large measure a consequence of the physical and cultural conditions under which they live. Civilizations, on the other hand, are undergoing continual change as a result of rational and organized human effort to achieve desired goals. Among civilizations, reason plays a greater role; necessity, custom, and caprice a lesser role.

Recognizing that the difference between what are called predictable conditions and controllable institutions is relative, I want to emphasize two trends, significant for international peace and security, which are so insusceptible to change by conscious effort that they should be regarded as conditions which policy and opinion should accept and to which they should seek to adjust. These conditions may be called the shrinking world and the changing world. Both of these conditions flow from the slight probability that advances in scientific knowledge and technological inventions will be forgotten, and the high probability that each increment of science and technology will provide a basis for further knowledge and invention. The result of these probabilities is that human society as a whole tends to progress in science and technology at an accelerating rate.

The most superficial view of human history verifies this proposition. While states have risen and fallen, while civilizations have developed and decayed, while religions and value systems have flourished and declined, while centers of civilization have moved from one area to another, yet, taking human society as a whole, there has been continuous and accelerating progress in knowledge and control of nature. Accurate, generalized, and verified information, whether about planetary motions, falling objects, the functioning of bodily organs, atmospheric pressure, chemical, electrical, genetic, or nuclear reactions, while often censored and sometimes obliterated in local areas, has not been forgotten by the human race as a whole. Instead, such knowledge has tended to spread and to breed new generalizations, observations, and experiments so that the progress of science has accelerated. Similarly, human inventions—the wheel, fire, the domestication of animals, written language, the clock, mathematical systems, the sailing ship and the compass, wind and water mills, gunpowder and the rifle, steam and internal combustion engines, electric lights and motors, the telegraph, the telephone, the radio, the television, the airplane, the tank, and the atomic bomb have never been entirely lost. They have suggested new inventions, and, especially, through the utilization of advancing science, have resulted in an astonishing acceleration whether measured by the frequency of new patents, by available energy per capita for productive purposes, or by the transformation of forms of human living.[16]

The consequence has been that the world has shrunk at an accelerating pace in the sense that the transmission of information, persons, and materials from one place to another on the earth's surface and the transformation of the earth's resources to human uses have become more possible and more rapid, and the resulting utilities more abundant. As a result every human group has become more dependent on distant human groups for the requirements of life, has become more vulnerable to propaganda, economic and military attack from a distance, and has become more attentive to happenings in distant areas. Modern man cannot be isolated in a local area as could his primitive ancestors. Since the age of discoveries, bringing all the continents into continuous contact with one another, and since the acceleration of the progress of science and invention stimulated by these discoveries and by the renaissance of classical culture in Europe, peoples of the world have become materially interdependent. It is unlikely that efforts of defense or self-sufficiency can produce an artificial isolation for any group as effective as the natural isolation which ignorance, incapacity, and geographical barriers imposed upon primitive groups or pre-Columbian civilizations.

Another consequence of the progress of science and technology is that the world has changed ever more rapidly.[17] Technology once introduced in a community undermines traditional beliefs and ways of life, as modern technical-aid administrators came to realize through experience and the tutelage of anthropologists. The acceleration of science and technology and the increasing contacts among people with different traditions, value systems, and institutions have meant that change has gone on more and more rapidly in all these fields. Where earlier the moral ideas, social practices, and technical skills which a man learned from his parents would last him for life, now he must continually readjust his behavior, his techniques, and even his conscience to the changes he sees about him. He is forced to move from the "inner direction" of conscience to the "other direction" of opinion. Communities are governed less by custom and religious precept from the past and more by legislation and administration looking to the future.

It is of course possible that the politically separated segments of the world will shoot themselves to pieces in an atomic war, that science and technology will disappear, and that the survivors will pull themselves out of the ruins, fighting with stones and spears as H. G. Wells once pictured. I do not think that this is probable. I think we should assume that, whatever is done in the fields of politics and institutional change, men and nations are going to be faced by a world shrinking and changing at an accelerating rate. It would appear wiser to adjust policies and institutions to these conditions than to repeat the performance of King Canute when faced by the tide or of Chanticleer when faced by the rising sun. If the goal is a minimizing of human misery, violence, and frustration, such an adjustment requires universal acceptance of values essential to the peaceful coexistence of diverse peoples in such a world and suitable universal institutions to maintain these values. Acceptance of some universal values does not preclude great diversity in cultures and value systems among different groups. The effective functioning of such universal institutions does not preclude much variety and self-determination in local and functional institutions. Nor is it possible to define either universal values or universal institutions which will be good for all time. The problem is that of continually modifying institutions and values so that they will remain in stable relationship to a changing world. Such a task implies that institutions are not rigid but are themselves dynamic equilibria continually adapting themselves to new conditions.

My point is that we would do better to apply rational and manipulative skills to our institutions and values than to use our skills in a probably futile effort to halt the shrinkage and change of the world. Something might, it is true, be done to retard the latter tendencies. Knowledge and technique might be localized, science and invention might be censored and discouraged, barriers might be erected against communication and trade, political hatreds might be fanned to facilitate such frustration of scientific and technological progress. All of these efforts are being made today, as they have been made in past periods in history, but in spite of them science and technology have on the whole progressed. Today major efforts are in the opposite direction. The specialized agencies of the United Nations, national programs of technical aid, and informational broadcasting and exchange of persons accelerate the natural tendency toward a shrinking and changing world. In the Soviet area, in spite of efforts to regulate scientific knowledge by political opinion and to minimize communication and trade with the non-Soviet world, literacy, education, communication, science, and technology appear to be advancing and anxieties about what is going on outside appear also to be increasing.

The natural tendency of science and technology suggested by analysis, by the general trend of human history, and by the immediate tendencies of policy and action indicates that we must accept the shrinking and changing world as a condition and adjust our institutions and our values to it, if we wish to promote international peace and security.

I therefore venture the following formulation: International peace and security require a centralization of institutions of information, education, regulation, and control at a rate proportional to the development of economic and cultural interdependence among the nations and of vulnerability of each to destructive attack by others. Since we must anticipate that that interdependence and vulnerability will increase, each nation must prepare to subordinate in some measure its peculiar institutions and values to universal institutions and values if it wishes to save them at all. The form and rate of such subordination is important. Premature, sudden, and excessive subordination may be as serious for peace and security as delayed or overgradual subordination. Any nation, including our own, will refuse lightly to abandon any of its traditional values. Nations require time to be convinced that some modification of their values, beliefs, and institutions is in the national as well as the world interest.

Our problem is one of institutionalizing international peace and security in the right direction, of the right type, and at the right speed. This implies that efforts to modify institutions and values must be guided by measurements of the rate at which the world is shrinking and changing. In my next lecture I will discuss some of the methods by which this might be done and by which better adjustments of the institutional to the material world might be effected.

2

HOW CAN INTERNATIONAL PEACE AND SECURITY BE SUITABLY INSTITUTIONALIZED?

In my first lecture I sought to distinguish between the relatively intransigent conditions of a shrinking and changing world to which policy, institutions, and action must be adapted, and the relatively controllable policies, institutions, and values which can be consciously modified and adjusted. I have assumed that we want international peace and security, though I have qualified this statement by adding international peace with justice and international security with welfare. These additions may appear to make the originally ambiguous statement so susceptible of divergent interpretations that it means nothing at all. This suggests the importance of the problem of interpretation which I will deal with later.

Here I want to note that I think the additions I propose must be read into the phrase "international peace and security" which occurs in the Charter of the United Nations in many places. The word *justice,* which did not appear in the Dumbarton Oaks draft, was inserted in the Charter in several places at the San Francisco Conference, particularly in the statements of purposes and principles.[1] While the word *welfare* occurs only in Article 14, I think the idea may be implied from the purpose of promoting coöperation to solve international problems of an economic, social, cultural, and humanitarian character and to promote respect for human rights;[2] from the considerably greater elaboration of this purpose in describing the functions of the Economic and Social Council and the Trusteeship Council at San Francisco; and from the development of the specialized agencies both in number and in activities. *Peace* I interpret in this context as the settlement of controversies between nations without violence; *justice* as settlement of such controversies giving equal weight to the interests of all the parties; *security* as conditions making attack or fear of attack upon the territory, the culture, or the institutions of a state improbable; and *welfare* as a high level of production per capita and a wide distribution of economic, cultural, and social advantages.

These values may be divided into those which welcome change and those which fear change. The first may be called *progress* and the latter *stability*. The relative weight given to progress and stability as social values frequently divides parties and opinions into liberals and conservatives. The United Nations Charter does not side with either party. It recognizes both the conservative values of peace and security and the liberal values of justice and welfare. It may be that adjustment to conditions of a shrinking and changing world requires modification of these values. That is not, however, the design of the Charter. That design, as stated in the preamble and Article 1, is rather to modify institutions, laws, policies, and actions so that the realization of these values can be maximized under conditions of a shrinking and changing world.

Certain principles and procedures, however, suggest a design of preserving certain institutions such as sovereign states in a position of legal equality, the domestic jurisdiction of those states, and the dominant position of the greatest of them.[3] The first and the last of these institutions are inconsistent with one another. States cannot be both equal and unequal in their sovereignty. Other principles and procedures contemplating the elimination of war as an institution in which the belligerents are equal and other states are neutral, the international protection of human rights, and the authoritative functioning of the United Nations itself,[4] appear greatly to modify these institutions, so far as they are realized. It seems clear that if basic conditions are changing, it is unlikely both that fixed values can be realized and that established institutions can be maintained. There must be flexibility somewhere. If institutions remain rigid, resisting change, and if social energy increases, demanding progress toward the realization of values, tensions will rise threatening war and revolution, menacing to both stability and progress.[5] So far as existing institutions and the values asserted by the Charter prove irreconcilable with each other and with the compulsive requirements of a shrinking and changing world, the Charter seems to prefer its values to the maintenance of existing institutions but this again raises a problem of interpretation. Are peace and human rights more important in the scheme of the Charter than sovereignty and the great power veto?

We are dealing with many variables. The change through time of some of these variables can be measured with greater accuracy than that of others, the change of some can be predicted more precisely than that of others, the change of some can be more easily controlled than that of others. Our knowledge about the measurement, prediction, and control of these variables is at the present time empirical, incomplete and inaccurate. Those which might be controlled cannot be, under present conditions of democracy, without wide popular understanding and support. Under present conditions of national sentiment they cannot be controlled effectively without institutions of broader competence than now exist. Furthermore such controls can hardly be applied rationally unless competing values are continually interpreted in the light of changing circumstances. I propose therefore in this lecture to discuss (1) the new knowledge, (2) the new education, and (3) the new institutions which appear to be essential if the problem of international peace and security is to be dealt with successfully, and (4) the standards of interpretation which might keep the relevant variables in suitable relation to one another.

A Science of International Relations

Few would doubt that we need more knowledge about international relations, but opinions differ on what kind of knowledge and where to look for it. Doubtless curiosity, seeking to establish new relationships, to clarify motivations and intentions involved in incidents of recent and more distant history, to discover methods for measuring changes, or to identify types of change that can be measured may, in international relations as in the natural sciences, stumble upon something important.[6] But the field of international relations is so complex, the types of information that have some relevance are so varied and numerous, and the cost of assembling sufficient data is usually so great, that it seems wisest to formulate hypotheses based upon a preliminary analysis of the situation in order to narrow the field of investigation and to reduce to manageable proportions the data to be assembled for the purpose of testing hypotheses.

Institutions seeking to promote international peace and security may function in the short run to regulate the policies of groups which at the moment dominate the scene, to regulate the procedures they utilize, to regulate the forces at their disposal, or to regulate their political relationships in order to maintain equilibrium and prevent sudden or violent change. In the long run such institutions may function to establish new groups, new procedures, new forces, and new relationships better adapted to maintain international peace and stability, under the conditions of an ever changing world. The distinction between activities looking to the short run and those looking to the long run corresponds to the distinction between tactics and strategy. Tactics is the art of utilizing the forces at a given time and place to the best advantage while strategy deals with a problem of longer range—arranging the time and place of encounter and the forces to be assembled there to achieve a maximum advantage. The two are never wholly distinct. Tactics has an eye to the strategic plan and strategy is limited by tactical possibilities. Both are related to the policy of even longer range which gears the strategy of campaigns into the relatively permanent policies of national security and prosperity.

The tactics of peace has to accept the existing states with policies dominated by the symbols of nationalism and sovereignty. It may be assumed that each government will design its policies in order to maximize its security and that increase of its relative power position will be a major factor in that design. Diplomats may negotiate alliances, nonaggression agreements, settlements of disputes, or limitations of armament to stabilize the situation. They may, however, in doing so, have in mind strategic changes in the situation. Wholly new powers may be brought into the system as when British Foreign Minister Canning, "called the new world into existence to redress the balance of the old." [7] New procedures may be established, such as collective action under the United Nations. New forces may be employed as, for example, economic controls and propaganda may be added to military power. New relations may be established as by the grouping of many states in regional arrangements or by the wide acceptance of new conceptions of international law or politics. An even broader strategy may look to more radical changes. Old entities may be combined in federations or empires or split into a larger number of states. New procedures of international adjudication, international legislation, and international administration may be introduced parallel to or even superseding bilateral diplomacy. New forces may be created through winning widespread loyalty to new symbols such as human rights, economic welfare, social justice, or the world community, in a measure displacing loyalties to historic states and nations. New relations may be established as of the individual to the world community and to individuals of other nations, displacing the exclusiveness of the relation of states to states or governments to governments, characteristic of the international system since the Peace of Westphalia. [8]

What is most important to know for those operating a regulatory institution if they are to conduct their tactical, strategic, and political activities so as to promote international peace with justice and international security with welfare?

For the short-run or tactical problem they should know who are at the centers of power, what policies they are pursuing, how much power is at the disposal of each, and under what limitations each acts. With such information, the art of diplomacy can employ persuasion, threat, combination, and the building of counterforce to reduce the prospects of successful aggression, to direct attention to aims other than aggression, and, in general, to maintain the balance of power. This kind of information is not easy to obtain and depends upon efficient intelligence services and much concrete experience with human nature. Generalized scientific knowledge can hardly be a substitute for such concrete information.

Long-run or strategic planning, however, depends upon a calculation of changes during a period of years or decades, and scientific formulations may be useful. In this connection the distinction between symbols and technologies seems particularly relevant. The first provide a measure for changes in institutions and values, the latter for changes in conditions, vulnerabilities, and interdependencies. In my first lecture I discussed the irreversible movement of natural science and technology, introducing new means of transport and communication and new means of destruction and influence increasing the interdependence and mutual vulnerability of widely separated peoples. I also discussed the lag of institutions and values behind these movements, tending to produce maladjustment and violent change. The strategy of peace would be assisted by calculations of the relative rate of change in both symbols and technologies in the various parts of the world. For this purpose, the concept of "distance" between human groups and especially between states may be useful.

Technological and scientific distances between pairs of states have obviously been declining but at different rates. Continuous measurement of changes in the frequency and abundance of communication, transport, and travel between pairs of states and the relative rate of scientific and technological progress in the various nations provide a basis for estimating the rate at which such distances are changing, and thus for appraising the condition of the material world and its probable future. Less continuous have been the changes in social and political symbols which attract attention and stimulate reactions of friendship or hostility, coöperation, or conflict among peoples and groups. Symbols of nationalism such as sovereignty, the flag, the United States,

France, or patriotism, and symbols of internationalism such as the United Nations, the World Court, conciliation, international law, or peace represent values, suggest identifications, provide motivations, and maintain institutions. Appraisals of attitudes toward, and opinions about, the symbols of each state in the publics and governments of the others, provide a basis for estimating changes in social and psychic distances between states.

While technological conditions and social symbols may in time react upon one another, they do develop independently in considerable measure. Science and technology steadily shrink the world but the values and loyalties of people tend to cluster around symbols of historic groups and institutions—the nation, the state, the church, the family—established by custom and tradition and incorporated in conscience and personality. Symbols and loyalties are the cement of groups and the source of their power. Those who control such symbols may utilize science and technology to achieve their values and goals. Only rarely do groups voluntarily abandon or modify symbols and loyalties to achieve better adjustment to the changes wrought by science and technology.[9]

As I have noticed, a major cause of social tension is to be found in the lag of the symbolic structure of human society behind its technological conditions, and the lag of social and psychic distances behind technological and scientific distances. Consequently surveys of changing distances and of changing attention to social and political symbols, and measurement of the direction, intensity, continuity, and consistency of individual attitudes toward these symbols and of opinions about them would be of great assistance in strategic planning for international peace and security.

This is not the place to elaborate on the methods which may be employed for surveying and measuring these variables, material and symbolic. Statistics of trade, finance, communication, population, and armaments of more or less accuracy can be assembled and manipulated to indicate changes in the relevant material variables. Attention, interests, attitudes, and opinions have been surveyed and measured by the content analysis of documents and the analysis of responses of samples of the population to questions or questionnaires. The comparative judgment of experts has also been useful in measuring distances.[10]

Attempts have been made to analyze the relation between these variables and to verify the results by application of actual measurements. It appears for example that if the technological and strategic distances between states are shrinking more rapidly than their psychic and social distances, tensions rise.[11] It also appears that political tensions tend to increase with economic and moral progress increasing social energy, and with social and institutional rigidity increasing resistance to change.[12]

A quantitative science of international relations is only on the threshold of development, but the point I want to make is that its further development appears to be a condition for the effective institutionalizing of international peace and security. International institutions may exert regulative influence in the right direction but only if they have adequate guides to make it certain that their efforts at a given moment are in the right direction and are neither too little nor too much. Quantification is the essence of any problem of regulation. It is not to be anticipated that in the field of international relations quantitative guides can be found with the degree of precision of those by which engineers regulate the flow of water through a hydroelectric system, of those by which aviators chart their courses to avoid turbulent areas, or even of those by which central banks regulate the discount rate and the purchasing power of currencies, but even a slight degree of accuracy would be superior to that by which statesmen now regulate their policy of armament building, alliance, commercial control, and international propaganda.[13]

International Education

The conduct of international relations has been in the hands of a limited number of rulers, ministers, and diplomats. Only recently have legislative bodies and public opinion exerted any great influence in this field. That influence, however, has been increasing and, as Elihu Root once said, if the people are going to conduct foreign relations they ought to know something about the business.[14]

The consequence has been a multiplication of courses in international relations in colleges and universities, numerous private organizations in the field, a tremendous printing and distribution of documents by foreign offices, programs of exchange of persons, and international agencies like UNESCO actively engaging in widespread international education.

This activity has undoubtedly tended to reduce the freedom of statesmen in conducting foreign policy. Once public opinion is instructed and invoked, whether by a democratic leader or a dictator, it presents a certain inertia to sudden change. Even the Soviet peoples have to be prepared for a change of the party line.

It also seems probable that education and propaganda in international affairs has strengthened nationalism and made conciliation more difficult. Parliaments are usually more nationalistic and belligerent than executives, and people than parliaments, because they are less aware of the risks. Although the people want peace, that want is abstract and less influential than their insistence that the nation shall be recognized, secure, and victorious.[15]

So long as the basic structure of international politics is that of national sovereignty and power rivalry, the price of survival is efficiency in the game of power politics. Consequently people and governments are together in focusing international education upon the nation, its rights, its power, and its policy with less attention to the claims or potentialities of other nations or of the world. With such education, it is anticipated that national morale will be assured and legislative support will be forthcoming for policies of alliance, however risky, or rearmament, however expensive. But governments may find themselves prisoners of the opinion which such education has generated and incapable of pursuing more conciliatory policies when the occasion calls for it.

It would appear that if international education is to contribute to the institutionalization of international peace and security, the character of that education should be changed. It should rest upon an understanding of the complex relationships between the various variables involved, particularly those of technological progress and symbolic loyalties, those of changing distances between states, and those of political tension, economic progress, and social resistances. In short, education should deal with the science of international relations rather than with national policies and their achievement. The people should be in a position to judge the long-run effects of policies.

This implies that education should proceed from a world point of view. Instead of the student conceiving his nation as surrounded by a jungle of hostile or friendly nations, he should conceive his world as faced by problems of hostility among its parts and of poverty among its peoples solvable only by a suitable adaptation of values, symbols, and policies to changing conditions.

Such a point of view can hardly emerge unless it is introduced simultaneously everywhere, and that implies a universal center of coördination and research. UNESCO was established to be such a center and has contributed much to the understanding of the problem. Progress, however, in such education cannot be rapid unless tensions are reduced, international communications increased, and requirements of national defense moderated. The current unwillingness of the Soviet Union to collaborate in the work of UNESCO or the other specialized agencies militates against the rapid achievement of these conditions.

Thus international education implies parallel progress in developing a science of international relations and in establishing international institutions of universal scope giving greater assurance that international peace and security will be maintained. But the capacity of international institutions to function effectively depends upon a widespread support of their symbols in individual attitudes and world opinion. Except as people believe in the United Nations, the World Court, the specialized agencies, the protection of human rights, the punishment of international crime, and the maintenance of international law, these institutions cannot function efficiently. International education must, therefore, have as one task the increase of favorable attention to the symbols of the world community. But it must always be realized that attempts to press such education when the symbols of nationalism are powerful are likely to result in reaction developing dangerous oppositions between certain of the states and the world community, parallel to that between certain of the states and the federal government on the eve of the American Civil War. International education can only progress gradually through an integration of national and world loyalties which grows out of an understanding of the processes at work and creates conviction that such integration is in the interest of the nation itself.[16]

International Institutions

Institutions, as has been pointed out, exist objectively in a hierarchy of authority defined by law and procedure, and subjectively in the minds of individuals and in the opinions current in the group. The establishment of subjective conditions suitable for effective international institutions requires international education convincing people of the value of such institutions and providing symbols about which attention and loyalty can center. Since such education requires institutions for its elaboration and coördination, international institutions and international education must proceed together.

In the building of such institutions the educational problem is primary. The United States could not have been built without the propaganda activities of Sam Adams and Tom Paine and the educational activities of John Adams and Thomas Jefferson. The League of Nations could not have been established without the activities of the League to Enforce Peace, the League of Nations Union, many other private organizations, and the official pronouncements of President Wilson, Prime Minister Lloyd George, and other statesmen. Minds must be prepared for change, or agencies to effect such change will wither before they are started.[17]

The problem of constitutional structures is, however, by no means unimportant. A constitution must incorporate sentimentalized symbols identifying itself with the attitudes and opinions of the group within which it is to function; a statement of goals and purposes establishing fundamental objectives; a body of logically related juristic symbols establishing formulae defining rights and limitations, so that the whole seems rational and consistent with the symbolic identifications and with the goals and purposes; and an operational structure establishing authorities and stating their powers and procedures. The major problem in the art of constitution building is to make the sentimentalized symbols and general purposes sufficiently ambiguous so that different views can be included and adaptation to new circumstances can be possible, and at the same time to make law and procedure sufficiently precise to guide action.[18]

The ambiguities and inconsistencies in the United Nations Charter [19] indicate that its makers performed the first of these tasks admirably.

The preamble which was the joint work of General Smuts and Sir Charles Webster [20] has an inspirational tone bringing together the slogans accepted by the United Nations during the war: salvation from the scourge of war, human dignity, the equality of nations, justice, international law, social progress, and larger freedom as "determinations" of "we the peoples of the United Nations."

Article 1 of the Charter states purposes in more precise language but not so precise as to prevent interpretation and adaptation.

Article 2 states the fundamental principles of the Charter, requiring both sovereign equality of states and capacity of the United Nations to demand every assistance from its members in the actions it undertakes in accordance with the Charter, both freedom of members from the United Nations in the exercise of domestic jurisdiction and obligation of members, and indeed of nonmembers, to observe the principles and prescriptions of the United Nations.

The remainder of the Charter is largely concerned with operative prescriptions and procedures for the principal organs. Principles concerning the welfare of peoples which are not self-governing, their self-determination, human rights, and international economic and social coöperation are, however, interlarded, forming part of the doctrine mainly set forth in Article 2. The prescriptions are not free of ambiguity, especially in the relations of the Security Council and the General Assembly, and in the relation of the powers of the United Nations concerning collective security and the rights of the members concerning individual and collective self-defense.

I am not in any sense criticizing the Charter because of its inconsistencies and ambiguities. A precise document would have suffered two inconveniences. First, it could never have been adopted and, second, if by a miracle it had been adopted, it would have proved incapable of functioning for any length of time in a changing world. Fortunately such precision is beyond the capacities of the ordinary language in which international instruments are drafted. There is always room for different interpretations and, as Professor Kelsen has pointed out, often no interpretation can be regarded as absolutely right.[21] Even if the operational clauses appear precise in their terms, the symbolic preamble and the broad assertions of purposes and principles provide ample opportunity for supplementing, complementing, or modifying their apparent meaning.

The Charter has in fact within its terms potentialities of at least five quite different types of organization.[22]

The first line of the preamble ("We, the peoples . . .") and the repeated emphasis upon individual rights look toward a *world federation* in which the central agencies act directly upon individuals.

The dominant position given the great powers in the Security Council, the broad discretionary powers given that body, and the obligation which its decisions impose on all members, opens the door for a five-headed *world empire* if the Big Five would be able to unite. It has been pointed out, especially by citizens of the smaller states, that the continued liberties of these states are dependent upon the continued division of the great powers.[23]

The improbability of such unity, the limited powers given the Assembly, and the broad reservations of equal sovereignty, domestic jurisdiction, and self-defense by the members suggest a continuance of *balance of power politics* in which the great powers will play a major role both within and without the United Nations.

Skeptics who emphasize the veto vote in the Security Council and the consequent lack in any of the organs of the United Nations of powers which are both authoritative and operative, look upon the Charter as primarily an affirmation of *moral principles* with a forum for their discussion.

Most writers, however, look upon the United Nations as an *international organization* within which states have undertaken definite obligations and responsibilities and which provides mechanisms for future coöperation to stated ends.

As the United States Constitution had within it up to the Civil War potentialities both of a united nation and an alliance among sovereign states with powers of nullification within each, so the United Nations Charter has within it potentialities of world federation, world empire, power politics, unsanctioned moral commitment, and international organization. The latter concept, most widely accepted, represents a position of unstable equilibrium among the other possibilities.

These extraordinary ambiguities and possibilities of divergent development, render the problem of Charter interpretation of the greatest importance. The future of the United Nations is not determined by the Charter but by what is made of it as history progresses.

Interpretation of the Charter

The problem of interpretation divides into two problems: Who shall interpret, and what standards shall be applied?

I cannot examine either of these questions in detail. Others, including Professor Kelsen, have done that authoritatively and comprehensively. I do not believe, however, that the last word has been said. "The life of the law," as Justice Holmes remarked, "has not been logic: it has been experience." [24] I anticipate that the Charter will develop new means and standards of interpretation as experience increases and conditions change. This is as it should be.

The Charter leaves the door wide open for any organ, or even for the members individually, to interpret it. I hope the authority of the members will not be widely accepted. It is a principle of international law that no party can give a definitive interpretation to a treaty, and this should apply all the more to a constitution such as the Charter.[25] The majority of the people of the United States refused to tolerate the claim of a state of the union to nullify the Constitution. If a treaty or constitution means any commitment at all, it means that the members are precluded from definitive self-interpretation. I see no reason why this should not apply to the provisions concerning domestic jurisdiction and self-defense as well as to all other articles of the Charter. In principle only international agreement or international authority can finally determine the validity of a state's claim that a matter is essentially within its domestic jurisdiction or that it is exercising an inherent right of individual or collective self-defense.[26]

It also seems to me that the characterization of the International Court of Justice as the principal judicial organ of the United Nations,[27] the obligation of parties to a dispute before the Court to comply with its decision,[28] and the assumption of the optional clause of the Court statute that "the interpretation of a treaty" should be submitted to the Court,[29] make it clear that the Court's interpretation of the Charter is authoritative for parties to disputes before it on this subject and should be regarded by other states as of greater weight than interpretations by any other body. Advisory opinions are doubtless of less formal authority, but it would seem that on the whole the Court is the most authoritative body for interpreting the Charter.

This does not mean however that it is desirable that the Court interpret all articles of the Charter. The Supreme Court of the United States has recognized that some clauses of the Constitution are of a political character and should be interpreted by Congress or the president.[30] The International Court of Justice might similarly hold that some clauses of the Charter should be interpreted by political organs of the United Nations.

Judicial interpretation, because of its authority, its precision, and the rationalization inherent in the judicial process, closes the door to future development more than does political interpretation. The hesitancy of the political organs of the United Nations in asking opinions of the Court may, therefore, have merit. Some may think that the General Assembly might well have been even more cautious in this regard.[31] A balance between the precision which facilitates action and the ambiguity which facilitates progress should be preserved. The practice of political interpretation by the General Assembly and the councils may have much to commend it.

Such political interpretations are seldom explicit and almost never involve consideration of the standards adopted. The majority takes the action deemed expedient in the circumstances, indicating that it regards its actions as in accord with the Charter, but with a minimum of argument. Pushed to the extreme this would render the Charter a legal nullity and might encourage states in ignoring recommendations which they regard as *ultra vires*. Some appreciation of standards of interpretation is important but those standards should not be too precise.

There has been discussion of the merits of "effective interpretation" which gives weight to the purposes of the organization and "restrictive interpretation" which assumes that states cannot be presumed to part with their sovereignty or limit its exercise.[32] The first standard permits any organ to act when necessary and proper to carry out the purposes of the Charter unless explicitly forbidden or unless the proposed action is clearly contrary to the general intentions of the instrument. This principle of liberal interpretation was frequently asserted by Chief Justice Marshall as applicable to the Constitution of the United States [33] and was doubtless responsible for the adaptation of that instrument to a rapidly changing situation, although it may also have contributed to the emergence of an exaggerated movement of "states' rights" eventuating in civil war. The standard of restrictive interpretation forbids any organ to act except in accord with procedures explicitly provided and on matters explicitly within its competence. Such a standard was behind the states' rights movement in the United States.

It can be said that the organs of the United Nations have followed the standard of effective interpretation rather consistently. Certain states have, however, asserted the restrictive standard on occasion and have utilized it to justify their ignoring of resolutions of United Nations organs. Doubtless the principle of effective interpretation is essential if a constitutional document such as the Charter is to grow and adapt itself to new conditions. It must, however, be applied with discretion, or the United Nations may tread upon vested interests and prerogatives, and stimulate revolts perhaps disrupting the institution. I will discuss briefly four general problems of the United Nations in which standards of interpretation have been important.

The first problem may be thus formulated: Should the United Nations confine its activity to coördinating the national policies and settling the controversies and conflicts of its members or should it develop a policy of its own and attempt to subordinate the policies of its members to that policy? The difference is clearly one of degree. Even if the United Nations confined its activity to coördinating the policies of its members it would be manifesting a minimum policy of its own, namely, a policy of ameliorating conflicts, settling controversies, and maintaining peace among its members. The issue is, to how great an extent should the United Nations seek to formulate general policies, observance of which would be likely to prevent conflicts, controversies, and wars from arising? On the one hand it may be said that preventive policies formulated in advance necessarily seek to plan and control the future and consequently limit the independence of those subject to the policies. It may be said, on the other hand, that an ounce of prevention is worth a pound of cure. The United Nations would be too late to be influential if it had to wait until a crisis had arisen.

There can be no doubt that the Charter contemplates planning and recommendation with a view to preventive action especially in the field of armament regulation, the organization of United Nations policing forces, the development of international law, promotion of economic and social welfare, promotion of culture, education, health, and respect for human rights, and the development of self-government in territories which are not self-governing. It is also clear that so far as the members have by the Charter undertaken obligations in these matters, they are bound irrespective of obligations under other instruments.[34]

It is true, however, that the Charter itself imposes few obligations in these fields other than that the members consider recommendations and contribute to their making through participation in debate in the organs of the United Nations. Obligations to discuss and consider are not obligations to accept and apply. Perhaps Article 56 by which the members "pledge" themselves "to take joint and separate action in cooperation with" the United Nations to promote economic and social progress and respects for human rights, and Article 87 which authorizes the Trusteeship Council to "take action" in conformity with trusteeship agreements, are exceptions. In general the members do not assume specific obligations or confer legal powers on United Nations organs for *preventive* action. Their major obligations under the Charter or in respect to actions taken by United Nations organs are set forth in Article 2 and more precisely in Article 25 and Chapters VI and VII. These obligations concern the stoppage of hostilities and the settlement of disputes likely to endanger the maintenance of international peace and security. It is true the Security Council may take some preventive action in these fields because of its competence to deal authoritatively with "threats to the peace" [35] and "to investigate situations which might lead to international friction or give rise to a dispute." [36]

Obviously these powers could be expanded to a comprehensive and detailed formulation of policy or law of preventive character, but apparently a somewhat restrictive interpretation of "threats" and "situations" was intended.[37]

The intent of the Charter was apparently to provide facilities for coördinating the policies and settling the controversies and conflicts of its members. But it was assumed that the process of coördination and pacific settlement might lead to general conventions which could be considered formulations of United Nations policy binding on all the members which ratified. It is thus clear that the development of an authoritative United Nations policy was not precluded, but, because of the need of wide individual ratification by the members, it was assumed that such a development would not be very rapid.

There is, however, an issue concerning the influence of "recommendations." The General Assembly and the councils, within their respective fields, can make recommendations on any matter within the broad purposes of the Charter. This growing mass of recommendations might be said to constitute a United Nations policy. Even though members are not under a legal obligation to observe these recommendations, they may be under a moral or political obligation which would be effective in proportion as a public opinion giving support to the United Nations develops within each member state.

One particular field where the problem under consideration is important concerns the relation of collective security action under Articles

39–50; of collective self-defense and regional arrangements under Articles 51–54; and of recommendations for the maintenance of international peace and security under Articles 10–14. It is clear that only the Security Council can take authoritative action in the name of the United Nations as such to deal "with threats to the peace, breaches of the peace, and acts of aggression." The Charter states a policy involving investigations, determinations, provisional measures, economic measures, and military measures planned and operated through a Military Staff Committee and a United Nations Command under Security Council decisions. It is also clear that the procedure of the Security Council, involving the great-power veto, has rendered these provisions useless against a great power and that the actual development of events has generally rendered them useless for any purpose. The effectiveness of these provisions in initiating the United Nations operation against aggression in Korea was exceptional because of the voluntary absence of the Soviet Union from the Security Council. As a consequence the United Nations has sought to achieve the same result by coördinating the policies of the members through regional arrangements, collective self-defense arrangements, and General Assembly recommendations. There can be no doubt that such recommendations, contemplated by the Uniting for Peace resolution of November, 1950, are not "action" of the United Nations in the sense of Article 11, paragraph 2, of the Charter. They are recommendations for the coördination of the policies of states and regional groups, but from them a United Nations policy may emerge which will be effective in most emergencies. It seems certain that any member utilizing any forces in accord with such recommendations would not be acting in a manner "inconsistent with the purposes of the United Nations" in the sense of Article 2, paragraph 4, of the Charter. It cannot be said that the organization of collective security policies through General Assembly recommendations violates the Charter, although it undoubtedly is a procedure different from that contemplated at San Francisco.

Experience suggests that the United Nations should go slowly in formulating its own policies and should aim rather at coördinating the policies of its members. It should be aware, however, that through such coördination, United Nations policies will develop in time. A suitable standard of interpretation should assume that the members are equal sovereign states and are free to pursue their own policies except so far as they have assumed international obligations. They are, however, bound to make genuine efforts to coördinate their policies through United Nations discussions and recommendations in order to achieve the purposes of the United Nations. Only custom and supplementary agreements can develop firm United Nations policies obliging its members beyond their commitments in the Charter itself.

A second problem of interpretation concerns domestic jurisdiction. Should the United Nations assume that it is competent to act so far as necessary to achieve its purposes or should it refrain from interfering with the domestic jurisdiction of the members? This problem is similar to that which has just been discussed and is in fact identical, except so far as a distinction can be made between the foreign policy and the domestic policy of a state. Article 2, paragraph 7, of the Charter permits of quite contradictory interpretations. If the word "intervention" in that paragraph includes "recommendations" as well as authoritative decisions, most of the Charter provisions concerning the functioning of the General Assembly and the Economic and Social Council would be abortive. The recommendations which these organs are authorized to make generally concern matters of domestic jurisdiction. If, on the other hand, "intervention" is construed literally to mean only authoritative interference, then Article 2, paragraph 7, would have almost no influence at all, since it would permit all organs to recommend on all matters within the purposes of the United Nations, and it would not prevent "intervention" in the only field in which authoritative action is provided by the Charter, namely, in "the application of enforcement measures under Chapter VII" expressly exempt from the limitation of Article 2, paragraph 7, by its own terms. With this complete ambiguity, interpretation of Article 2, paragraph 7, has varied tremendously in accord with who did the interpreting. When members have disliked Assembly recommendations, they have asserted that they were contrary to Article 2, paragraph 7, but when the Assembly has wished to make a recommendation it has discovered no restriction in that article whether the recommendation concerned the use of force by, or the economic or social policy of, members.[38]

Difficulties have also arisen concerning the interpretation of the phrase, "matters which are essentially within the domestic jurisdiction of any state" in Article 2, paragraph 7. Legally there should be no difficulty. The World Court has said that every matter is within a state's domestic jurisdiction except so far as the state's discretion is limited by an international obligation. It has made no distinction in principle between matters of foreign policy and matters of domestic policy but in practice, matters of foreign policy are more likely to be regulated by international obligations than are matters normally considered domestic policy. The critical distinction, however, depends not upon the subject matter, but upon the existence of an international obligation. The interpretation and application of an international obligation is in the Court's opinion never a matter of domestic jurisdiction. It is within the sovereign power of a state to make treaties on any subject it wishes provided it does not encroach upon a right of a third party protected by international law.[39] Consequently by assuming obligations by treaties, states restrict their domestic jurisdiction. It is clear, therefore, that no claim of domestic jurisdiction can impair the treaty-making power of a state or the competence of United Nations agencies to "intervene" in the interpretation and application of treaties, so far as the competence of these organs extends to the subject matter involved.[40] Since the United Nations Charter is a treaty, so far as members have undertaken obligations by the Charter, the matter is not within their domestic jurisdiction. They have undertaken to carry out "decisions" of the Security Council in accordance with the Charter.[41] Consequently such decisions cannot be resisted on grounds of domestic jurisdiction. On the other hand a recommendation does not impose an obligation. Consequently while members cannot object to the organs of the United Nations making recommendations on matters which the Charter puts within their competence, the making of the recommendation in itself does not withdraw the matter from the member's domestic jurisdiction. It is not, therefore, legally obliged to observe the recommendation.

From the point of view of international law the matter is clear and would not deserve attention were it not that in the United States a movement has developed suggesting that the proposed Covenant of Human Rights deals with matters normally within the domestic jurisdiction of states and, therefore, it would be improper and ought to be unconstitutional for the United States to enter into such a covenant.[42] Clearly the United States as a sovereign state is competent to make treaties in this field as it has on numerous occasions in the past. The issue is one of policy, not of law. And it would seem most undesirable to hamper American policy by imposing such constitutional limitations upon the treaty-making power.[43] I of course recognize that there are constitutional limitations on the treaty-making power, including the guarantees of individual rights. No human-rights covenant could limit such guaranteed rights and the proposed text makes it clear that there is no intention of doing so. Its purpose is to establish a universal minimum of individual freedom leaving each state free to give more freedom by its own law.

From the political point of view it may be recognized that because of the differences of culture, the usual unfamiliarity of distant authority with local conditions, and the more effective control of local governments by public opinion, it is preferable that legislation should be local or national if possible, and international only if necessary. The interdependence of the nations, however, presents difficulties to local legislation in an increasing number of fields. Narcotic drugs, for example, cannot be controlled except on a world-wide basis. Thus national policy has increasingly recognized the necessity of international legislation if national interests are to be promoted. It is likely, therefore, that in our shrinking world international legislation will develop and correspondingly the domestic jurisdiction of states will shrink. We may expect that the United Nations will prove a suitable instrumentality in the process of developing international legislation, although it is likely that for a long time the process will require ratification by the states to be bound.

Another problem of interpretation concerns the relation of law and politics in the settlement of international disputes. Should the United Nations prefer legal or political settlements? The insertion of the words "justice" and "international law" in the Charter as limitations upon the discretion of the Security Council and other organs in making decisions or recommendations for the settlement of controversies was in response to the fear of small states that their rights might be ignored in possible "appeasements" of potential aggressors. Recognition of the general rule that members should submit legal disputes to the Court in Article 36 and of the obligatory character of the Court's decisions in Article 94 had a similar intention. However the Charter gives a priority to political settlements. The obligation to submit to the Court depends on the consent of the parties by acceptance of the optional clause, by acceptance of a general treaty obligation, or by acceptance of a specific *compromis.* In the absence of such consent the dispute must be settled peacefully but the Charter shows no preference as between "negotiation, inquiry, mediation, conciliation, arbitration, judicial settlement, resort to regional agencies or arrangements, or other peaceful means" chosen by the parties.[44] If none of these methods are effective and international peace and security are threatened, the matter must go before the United Nations. It may be dealt with by the Security Council or if that body fails to function, by the General Assembly, but in either case political considerations can be expected to play a major role. Only rarely have advisory opinions been sought from the Court although the Assembly passed a resolution urging more frequent use of this procedure.[45]

Is this desirable? Doubtless a system which gave a state final power to demand a judicial determination of any controversy would make for rigidity and preservation of the status quo, although a wise court may, as the Supreme Court of the United States has illustrated, bring about a good deal of peaceful change.[46]

On the other hand a system which gave final authority to political bodies intent on keeping the peace would be likely often to sacrifice justice for peace, especially when the peace is threatened by a powerful state.[47] Furthermore a system which provides no compulsory international forum unless international peace and security are threatened may give an advantage to the truculent. It seems doubtful whether any general standard of interpretation can solve this problem. It is a matter which the political organs should themselves solve by exercising wise discretion to request an advisory opinion or to recommend a judicial settlement by the parties when the total situation indicates no sufficient reason for important changes of the status quo.

A final problem of interpretation concerns the values which international institutions should support. Should the United Nations seek to develop universal values or should it rather encourage mutual toleration of national values? Advocates of world government and cosmopolitanism are so impressed by the shrinking of the material world and the need of a unified moral world to regulate it, that they believe politics, education, and propaganda should coöperate to create universal standards of value before it is too late. Nationalists on the other hand believe culture and values to be indigenous growths involved in local conditions and traditions and incapable of artificial creation. Consequently they believe that the most that can be expected is mutual toleration and perhaps respect by each group for the culture and values of others.

On this issue the United Nations has taken a middle ground. While recognizing that diversity of cultures exists and is probably desirable, it assumes that peace implies coexistence, toleration, and mutual respect. These terms themselves imply some values which should be accepted by all states. Toleration is only possible if people are willing to subordinate the immediate expansion of the values they believe in, to the superior value of a spirit of toleration. Mutual respect is hardly possible unless such respect is regarded as a value superior to the destruction of a value system deemed inferior. Peace is not possible unless its maintenance is considered by all a value superior to the forcible expansion of an ideology, a religion, a way of life, a national interest, or any other value with which it may be confronted. States seized with a missionary zeal for the spread of an ideology which they deem of absolute value can hardly "practice tolerance and live together in peace with one another as good neighbors" as called for by the preamble of the Charter.[48]

The preamble, the purposes, and the principles stated in the Charter constitute a value system which the members of the United Nations have accepted, and this system is elaborated by the Universal Declaration of Human Rights, accepted in 1948 by the United Nations General Assembly without dissent, the Soviet bloc abstaining. These purposes and principles might be coördinated into a philosophical system but the expediency of such an effort may well be questioned.

The discussions in UNESCO concerning its philosophy indicated that premature formulation would be undesirable even if possible [49] and a philosophical effort initiated by UNESCO, to state the philosophy underlying the Universal Declaration of Human Rights, has indicated far greater agreement upon the specific rights than upon any philosophical foundation for them.[50]

While it is doubtless true that human communication and commerce, and the expansion of technologies and knowledge tend to produce a common culture including both beliefs and evaluations, it is also true that the expression of these values is likely to differ because of the differences in the symbol patterns in different areas. This is a field in which natural development is to be preferred to artificial stimulation.

I conclude that the institutionalization of peace and security can proceed through the development of a science of international relations, through more extensive education in that science, and through the development of the international institutions which exist, but that the key task is that of interpreting the powers and functions of these institutions so that their authority will develop in pace with the opinion necessary to support it. A suitable standard of interpretation should read the texts with a proper balance among the purposes stated, the reserved rights of the members, the procedural restrictions upon the organs, and the requirements of the situation at the time the interpretation is made. Institutions cannot develop if they are tied to obsolete conditions and opinions, however influential these may have been in their making, nor can they develop if they ignore limitations and procedures which protect vested rights of minorities. A developing institution continually balances rights of the past and aspirations of the future with requirements of the present.[51]

In particular I believe that the United Nations should seek to coördinate the policies of its members, should recognize the value of local and national control of matters which can be regulated by such agencies, should urge legal settlement of controversies unless broader considerations of justice and policy require peaceful change, and should promote mutual respect among diverse cultures and value systems, permitting

universal cultural standards to develop gradually and naturally as contact and the dissemination of knowledge provide the basis.

In the institutionalization of international relations, deliberation,
balance, awareness, and timing are virtues. Too much haste in centralization is likely to arouse local or regional oppositions leading to
nullification and war. Interpretation of the problem as that of achieving a goal rather than that of balancing opposing goals may encourage
intransigence among groups whose coöperation is necessary for success.
Concentration on the long run at the expense of the short run, on efficiency at the expense of compromise, on the general interest at the expense of particular interests, on organization at the expense of the opinion which sustains it, is dangerous, as is concentration on the opposite
of each of these alternatives. Awareness of all aspects of the immediate
situation and of its universal implications is essential. Recognition of
the critical moment when opinion is ripe for action is the essence of
all statesmanship, particularly of that greatest task of statesmanship—
the institutionalizing of international peace and security.

PART **II**

PROGRESS IN

INTERNATIONAL

ORGANIZATION

3

AMERICA

AND WORLD

ORGANIZATION

The United States has had an ambivalent position in regard to international organization. On the one hand its federal system, its attitude toward law, and its ideals of peace and justice have urged it to develop international organization. But, on the other hand, the circumstances of its achievement of independence, its geographical position, and the tradition of foreign policy linked with the names of Washington and Monroe have urged it to be suspicious of supranational institutions and especially those in which European nations participate. It has loved national independence and disliked the maneuverings of power politics. Through most of its history the circumstances of geographical separation and British sea power have made a policy of isolation better adapted to these desires than participation in international organization.

It is to be observed, however, that the idea of a universal system which would preserve peace with justice has never been entirely absent from American thought and action. This was manifested in frequent reference to international law made by early American statesmen and jurists. They considered it a system which every state must observe as the price of the continued recognition of its independence.[1] This attitude was even more clearly manifested in the practical application of international law through the submission of controversies to international arbitration. As early as 1796 certain controversies with Great Britain were submitted under clauses of the Jay treaty. Matters as important as the Maine boundary (1830), the Alabama claims (1871), and the Bering Sea fisheries (1894) were similarly submitted during the nineteenth century along with nearly a hundred others with most of the countries of the world. A certain suspicion, however, was evident in the reluctance of the United States to enter into commitments to arbitrate future disputes, and especially in the Senate's refusal to approve ratification of the Olney-Pauncefote all-out arbitration treaty with Great Britain in 1897 although it had been endorsed by the titular leaders of both parties, Presidents Cleveland and McKinley, and was supported by an active public opinion.

The idea of a universal system of peace and justice was also manifested in the forward position which the United States took after the Civil War in promoting permanent institutions for coöperation in matters deemed nonpolitical, such as postal and telegraphic communications, elimination of the slave trade, maintenance of maritime quarantines, and even regulation of armaments and the rules of war. The Rush-Bagot agreement of 1817 disarming the Great Lakes was a rare and enduring instance of successful disarmament, and the American position at the Hague Conference of 1899 was more advanced than that of most European powers in respect to arbitration, disarmament, and international law. American ambivalence was to be observed, however, on this occasion in reservations relating to the Monroe Doctrine and the policy of nonintervention in European affairs.

Interest in international organization was also manifested in policies relating to Latin America and the Far East. The policy of isolationism was directed primarily toward Europe. It did not prevent the administration of John Quincy Adams from urging United States participation in the Panama Congress summoned by Simon Bolivar with the object of organizing the American nations for mutual defense and coöperation. Isolationist sentiment, it is true, especially as manifested in the attitude of Senator Thomas Hart Benton of Missouri, hampered American participation; and the will to coöperate with Latin America was not established until sixty years later, when Secretary of State James G. Blaine initiated the series of inter-American conferences and the permanent administrative body which came to be known as the Pan-American Union. In the Far East also, the United States coöperated with the European powers, even in military expeditions, with the view to opening Japan and China to trade during the 1850's and 1860's. After some reaction toward independent action in the Far East, such coöperation was renewed in the Hay notes of 1899 on the Open Door and in the joint intervention to suppress the Boxer movement and rescue the besieged legations in 1900.[2]

Finally, it is to be observed that neither the Farewell Address nor the Monroe Doctrine urged policies of *permanent* aloofness from *general* international coöperation. Washington urged the avoidance of alliances with any *part* of the European world while the institutions of the United States were *still immature* and suggested that in the meantime temporary alliances would be adequate. He was not urging a permanent policy, but a policy for the years immediately ahead and his policy did not have general international organization in mind. In fact, various utterances of Washington suggest that a universal system for maintaining peace and justice was a development to which he looked forward.[3]

The long period of comparative peace from the Battle of Waterloo to the end of the nineteenth century, broken in an important way for the United States only by the Civil War, turned American attention to the West and to domestic affairs, and induced interpretations of the Farewell Address and the Monroe Doctrine as calling for neutrality in European quarrels and abstention from the European system and from general conferences or organizations of a predominately political character. This was manifested by the policy of the United States in making peace with Britain independently in 1814 and refusing participation in the system of alliances which developed from the Napoleonic wars; in declaring the Monroe Doctrine independently rather than in collaboration with Great Britain as urged by Canning; in dealing independently with the problems of the Barbary pirates and the Danish Sound dues; in refusing to ratify the Berlin Act of 1885 concerning the development of Central Africa although participation in the conference and signature of the act had been authorized by President Arthur; and in emphasizing the Americas as a distinct sphere of political activity in the various applications of the Monroe Doctrine in the nineteenth century, especially in that concerning the boundary dispute between Great Britain and Venezuela in 1895.

In 1900 therefore the policy of the United States can be summed up as one of neutrality, political isolation, and coöperation in nonpolitical matters in respect to Europe; of arbitration, disarmament, and nonpolitical coöperation in respect to Canada and Great Britain; of somewhat qualified willingness to coöperate with the powers in the maintenance of common political and commercial interests in the Far East; and of permanent coöperation, especially in legal and economic matters, with the Latin American nations among whom, because of its relative power and resources, the United States could be certain of a predominant position. Opposition to general international organization was by no means manifest, but public opinion undoubtedly supported policies of avoiding political entanglements with Europe, and the Congress, especially the Senate, was more opposed to international arbitration and political coöperation than was the executive. In spite of some internationalist interpretations of policy and occasional vigorous actions by the executive, the American people were in sentiment and policy self-centered, secure, aloof, and suspicious of the maneuvers of the great powers and of political collaboration with them.

The period from 1900 to 1950 has marked a change which can only be characterized as revolutionary in regard to international organization. The United States is today the leading member of the United Nations and of the dozen specialized agencies associated with it. The United States contributes nearly two-fifths of the budget of these organizations and has declared repeatedly that support of their authority is its first policy. It has taken an active part in the solution of disputes within the United Nations concerning Syria, Iran, Greece, Palestine, Indonesia, Kashmir, and Korea, and has contributed weapons of war and fighting men in several instances, notably to stop invasion of the Korean Republic by North Korean forces in the summer of 1950. The explanation of this change may be indicated by an examination (1) of the alterations of the conditions of world politics, (2) of the movements of American opinion, (3) of the modifications of American foreign policy, (4) of the development of American participation in international organization and (5) of the solution of certain national and international constitutional problems during this momentous half-century.

The Conditions of World Politics

The United States was recognized as a great power after its victory over Spain in 1898. Japan was similarly recognized in 1905 after its victory over Russia. These events meant that a system of international politics which had been European for centuries had become world-wide. This universal character of international politics was augmented by a series of inventions. The development of oceanic cables and, later, radio greatly accelerated the abundance and timeliness of world news. The development of ocean and rail transportation and the invention of the airplane greatly increased the abundance of trade and travel and the rapidity of movement of goods and persons. Utilization in war of air-borne high explosives culminating in the invention and dramatic employment of the atomic bomb, created a universal vulnerability to sudden attack from any point of the world. The development of economic controls and propaganda as instruments of international policy no less important than diplomacy, war, and threats of war blurred the distinction between war and peace. The practical shrinking of the world consequent upon these changes has meant that every people, and particularly those like the Americans previously sheltered from the main center of power by oceans, has become the prey of continuing anxiety about military, economic, propaganda, and fifth-column attacks organized in remote areas. The facts of technology were antipathetic to the theory of isolation.

Coupled with these changes were changes in the position of the powers. The United States had depended for its security more than most Americans realized upon the British navy controlled by a government, which, while Americans did not always like it, they at least understood and which was generally favorable to policies of commercial freedom, human rights, national self-determination, and democracy which the two countries inherited from the ideas of John Locke and other British philosophers of the seventeenth century. The only serious diplomatic problems of the United States during the nineteenth century were with England itself. After the Treaty of Ghent and the Rush-Bagot agreement the two countries preferred in general the policy of live and let live at the two sides of the much disputed boundary separating Canada and the United States.

The twentieth century saw the decline of the position of the British navy through the development of rival navies in Germany, Japan, and the United States itself, through the invention of the airplane and the submarine rendering the British Isles vulnerable to blockade even if protected by a dominant surface navy, and through the general deterioration in Britain's financial, economic, and power position resulting from the growth of industrial power elsewhere and the losses consequent upon two world wars.

As Britain shrank in power, first Germany and then Russia rose, both of them countries with ideologies and political practices radically different from those of the United States. The philosophies of Hegel, Nietzsche, and Karl Marx lying behind German and Russian political thought and action were very different from the philosophies of Locke, Burke, Bentham, and Jefferson upon which Anglo-American thought and action rested. The American public felt itself vulnerable to attacks from these continental powers and realized that it could not rely on the British navy to keep them at arm's length. The United States therefore participated in two world wars against Germany and became the leader in the cold war against Russia. By the force of events the United States moved from the role of the youngest and least influential of the powers to that of the greatest in the world, while the world itself became increasingly bipolar, unstable, and insecure. Changes in respect both to vulnerability and to power position developed from history, technology, economy, and resource distribution, and the United States government could hardly have avoided its new situation by any steps of policy.

The Movements of American Opinion

American opinion lagged behind the development of events and conditions. Americans were, it is true, attracted by the forward policy of Theodore Roosevelt—often characterized as "imperialism"—in Panama, in the Caribbean, in the Far East, and in the Portsmouth and Algeciras conferences, and by his active naval building. But it fell away from Taft's "dollar diplomacy," and after Wilson had repudiated "imperialism," that attitude did not revive when Coolidge temporarily took over Nicaragua. Franklin D. Roosevelt's withdrawal from quasi protectorates in the Caribbean and from the right of intervention to protect nationals in Latin America, and his active Pan-Americanization of the Monroe Doctrine were popular both in Latin America and in the United States. American opinion turned away from imperialism in the second and third decades of the twentieth century as it had in the period following the Civil War after the active pursuit of "manifest destiny" in the 1840's and 1850's.

The public was also lukewarm toward Taft's internationalism looking toward all-out arbitration treaties and toward Wilson's crusade for the League of Nations. Secretary Stimson's efforts to coöperate with the League of Nations in the Manchurian episode drew insufficient support, as did the efforts of President Franklin Roosevelt and Secretary Hull to enlarge collaboration with the League. During the interwar period, both imperialism and internationalism appeared to be subordinated to a policy of complacent isolation and storm-cellar neutrality.

Hitler's attack on Poland, however, led to widespread anxieties and to the verbal battle within the United States between the America First Committee and the Committee to Defend America by Aiding the Allies. Victory of the latter led first to Lend Lease and then to active participation in the war. The almost universal support for the Fulbright and Connally resolutions, calling for American participation in a political international organization, and the almost unanimous support of the United Nations Charter by the Senate, suggested that isolationism was dead. It had apparently been superseded by active internationalism, but there were voices calling for "an American century." "Imperialism" might be in abeyance capable of being aroused by the exigencies of the cold war with Russia. The popular movement for world government in the 1940's, although it appeared to be "internationalism" with a vengeance, could also turn toward "imperialism" if, abandoning universalism, it devoted attention to union of the Western nations, among whom the United States was predominant, for more actively pursuing the cold war.

Modifications of American Foreign Policy

The foreign policy of the United States has been obliged, during the last fifty years, to compromise between the requirements of world conditions and the inhibitions of a lagging American opinion. Presidents Theodore Roosevelt and Taft urged policies of defense and expansion in the Caribbean and the Far East, policies of all-out arbitration, policies of active interest in areas such as Morocco which divided the great powers of Europe, and policies to develop the Hague system into an organization for disarmament, judicial settlement, international legislation, and even, as Theodore Roosevelt suggested in his Nobel peace-prize address, for collective security. These initiatives were, however, always discounted by the prevailing isolationism of opinion.

When Wilson came into office, he inherited the isolationist viewpoint of his only Democratic predecessor since the Civil War, Grover Cleveland, and stood for neutrality and political aloofness from the European war, while the United States profited by insistence upon "freedom of the seas" and trade with belligerents subject only to the international-law limitations of contraband, blockade, and unneutral service. This policy was, however, accompanied by a more active effort to collaborate with Latin American countries. Eventually, with the threat of German victory, Wilson attempted to mediate peace and, when that had failed and Germany had renewed submarine warfare, he urged entry into the war and permanent international collaboration to maintain the territorial integrity and independence of all nations after the war had been satisfactorily ended. Wilson was undoubtedly in advance of his countrymen and particularly of the Senate in perceiving that the United States could no longer rely upon the British navy for security. He followed Theodore Roosevelt in urging an American navy second to none and suggested a League of Nations so constituted that the United States and Great Britain acting together could control it through dominating the seas. The League of Nations was a skillful combination of American idealism and power politics, but neither the Senate nor the American people understood it, and Senator Lodge was able to prevent American participation by mobilizing the political interests of the Republican Party, the traditional isolationism of American opinion, the Anglophobia of the Irish and the Germans, and the Senate's fear that such participation might augment the power of the president and weaken its own constitutional position. The rejection of the Covenant and the political victory of the Republican Party which, contrary to its earlier tradition, had got itself committed to isolationism, resulted in a general opinion justifying the return to that policy. The American people were in a mood to abandon both the imperialism of Theodore Roosevelt and the internationalism of Woodrow Wilson, but the conditions were too strong for them. The interwar period was marked by actual American participation in international organization and world politics, but in a manner which was half-hearted, belated, and ineffective. Presidents found it necessary to conceal from an isolationist public opinion the real significance and necessity of what they were doing.

This period began with the Washington Conference of 1921 which stabilized naval armaments among Great Britain, the United States, and Japan by the 5-5-3 ratio, but without sanctions to curb Japan, other than the four-power treaty and the nine-power treaty calling for consultation in the event of disturbances to the status quo in the Pacific islands and China respectively. These agreements were supplemented by the London treaties of 1930 and 1936 manifesting decreasing coöperativeness by Japan and finally renunciation by that country of the whole system of naval disarmament.

The Washington Conference was followed by American participation through "unofficial observers" in the various conferences looking toward settlement of the reparation- and war-debts problems which had hampered European recovery. These negotiations culminated in the Dawes and Young plans named after two American statesmen who participated unofficially and in a funding of the war debts owed the United States. The result of these settlements was a system in which the Western Allies received reparations from Germany, to be in considerable measure transmitted as war-debt payments to the United States while the United States continued its high protective tariff. The keystone of the system was the continuance of large American loans to Germany which permitted that country to pay reparations and also permitted the United States to continue to export more than it imported. This system, the insanity of which was recognized by most American economists, contributed to the collapse of 1929, the subsequent moratorium on all international payments, and the rise of Hitler.

Another development of the period was American coöperation with the League system in legal, technical, and armament matters. President Harding proposed that the United States become a party to the World Court statute, but though renewed by all subsequent presidents, this initiative came to nothing because the Senate attached reservations which were unacceptable to the European states. The United States did, however, send representatives to League conferences and commissions on economic, social, health, and other "nonpolitical" matters and collaborated in armament discussions after 1926. It sent official representatives to the general armament conference of 1932. Both Presidents Hoover and Roosevelt made constructive suggestions, but the rise of Hitler, the unwillingness of France to recognize German armament equality, and the unwillingness of Great Britain and the United States to make political guarantees resulted in failure of the conference.

The Kellogg-Briand pact, springing from the outlawry of war movement, initiated by Salmon O. Levinson of Chicago, marked an American initiative to augment the general confidence which had grown from the Locarno agreements of 1926. Its originators conceived it as a change in international law abolishing war in the legal sense of hostilities in which the participants are legally equal and the nonparticipants are impartially neutral. Such an abolition of legal war would have the effect of depriving an aggressor during hostilities and after it, of the advantages which lawful belligerents normally gained by war.[4] Others conceived the pact as a moral incentive to peace and a popular mobilization against war, others as the beginning of a system of sanctions by differential embargoes, and others as a step toward American entry into the League. The pact actually achieved only the first purpose. It did not prevent hostilities, nor did it bring America into the League but it did justify the Stimson Doctrine, American discrimination in favor of the allies before entering World War II, and the policy of treating Germany and Japan not as lawful belligerents but as law violators whose leaders were war criminals.[5]

American collaboration with the League was stimulated by the Kellogg pact though the proposal for incorporation of the terms of the pact in the Covenant failed. The United States entered the field of political collaboration with the League when American representatives sat with the Council in the Manchurian episode in 1931. Unfortunately Secretary Stimson, though he appreciated the need of active collaboration, was persuaded, in the early stages of this affair, that the Japanese civil authorities would get control of their military if their faces were saved through avoiding positive League resolutions. After the Japanese had occupied all of Manchuria, Briand who had given leadership to the League was dead, the British were lukewarm, and Stimson was confronted by an isolationist public opinion and a pacifist president. Stimson could do little but announce that the United States would not recognize the fruits of aggression. Coöperation among the powers did induce Japanese withdrawal from Shanghai in the spring of 1932, but there it ended. Japan ignored League resolutions incorporating the Stimson Doctrine and settled down to occupation of its puppet state of Manchukuo, presently extended to North China.[6]

The victory of the Democrats in 1932 did not greatly alter foreign policy, although Franklin D. Roosevelt had fought on a League of Nations platform as Democratic candidate for vice-president in the campaign of 1920 and his secretary of state, Cordell Hull, had been a League of Nations advocate from the first. They confronted, as Hull sorrowfully narrated in his memoirs,[7] an isolationist public opinion, as well as the immediate problems precipitated by the depression. The policy of nonrecognition of Japan's advances in the Far East was continued and efforts were made to bring moral pressure and to persuade oil producers to engage in voluntary embargoes in behalf of China, after the new invasions of 1937. The president vigorously denounced Mussolini and Hitler for their aggressions in Ethiopia and Spain in violation of the Kellogg-Briand pact and other treaties, but Congress with popular support enacted in 1935, on the eve of the Ethiopian War, neutrality legislation which forbade discrimination against the aggressor and gave no authority to embargo raw materials essential for military activity such as scrap iron and oil. The isolationism of American sentiment was manifested in the adverse public reaction to President Roosevelt's Chicago Bridge speech of 1937 suggesting a "quarantine" of aggressors, and effective administrative action to coöperate with the League of Nations in suppressing aggression was frustrated. Even a strongly international-minded executive could do little, when faced by an uninformed and isolationist public opinion, beyond preparing for changes in that opinion which it sought to produce and which it was certain events would compel.[8]

The Nazi attack on Poland in the autumn of 1939 marked the beginning of a change in public opinion. Congress immediately reflected this change. During the president's conference with leading senators in the preceding summer, Senator Borah had said that his information indicated that there would be no war and consequently any revision of the Neutrality Act was unnecessary. But in November Congress revised the Neutrality Act to make possible aid to the European sea powers. After the fall of France and the beginning of the Battle of Britain, in the summer of 1940, opinion had sufficiently advanced to permit the president to transfer 50 destroyers to Great Britain in exchange for naval bases, and the following spring, after the Committee to Defend America had exerted a profound influence upon American opinion in favor of coöperation to suppress aggression, the Lend Lease Act was passed, openly discriminating against the aggressor powers. In spite of the fact that both the president and his Republican adversary Wendell Willkie favored an active policy against aggression, public opinion was still in such a state that by common consent, during the campaign of the autumn of 1940, neither party urged military coöperation and both continued to express the hope and expectation that a shooting war would not be necessary. These campaign statements necessitated a certain discretion by the president is giving intelligence and convoy aid to the Allies in the Atlantic and in applying against Japan the embargoes on raw materials which Congress had authorized for "conservation" purposes. Nevertheless, American participation against aggression increased until the Japanese attack at Pearl Harbor initiated the policy of all-out war and complete solidarity of the United States with the Allies which had included the Soviet Union since the preceding summer. Action to win the war was accompanied by statements of principle among the Allies which had signed the Declaration of United Nations on January 1, 1942. Pledges to establish a permanent organization to maintain international peace and security were made by the great powers at the Moscow, Teheran, and Yalta conferences, and the actual establishment or reëstablishment of general organizations on labor, agriculture, postwar relief and rehabilitation, aviation, and general security were effected at conferences at Philadelphia, Hot Springs, Atlantic City, Chicago, and San Francisco from 1943 to 1945.

The policy, in large measure initiated by the president of the United States, was to build the United Nations step by step from the common experience of war as the United States itself was built from such an experience of the states from 1775 to 1783. The Declaration of United Nations initiated a process which culminated in the ratification of the Charter which emerged from the San Francisco Conference in 1945. The United Nations grew from a war alliance to a permanent constitutional organization. It was not a part of the peace with participation of neutrals and, in limited degree, of the enemy as had been the League of Nations. The nations united in the war assumed that they constituted so large a part of the world's population that they were competent to organize the world as a whole and to persuade or compel the small number of neutral and enemy powers to accept the organization which they established. This theory was stated in Article 2, paragraph 6, of the Charter by which "The Organization shall ensure that states which are not Members of the United Nations act in accordance with these Principles so far as may be necessary for the maintenance of international peace and security." The character of the United Nations as a constitutional act organizing the world was further illustrated by the preambular statement beginning: "We the peoples of the United Nations." This bold statement, reminiscent of the Constitution of the United States although the word "peoples" is in the plural while it is in the singular in the Constitution, was not entirely realized because the end of the preamble and the final articles employed the traditional terms of treaty in respect to the making and ratification of the instrument. Furthermore, substantive provisions declare that the organization is based on the principle of "the sovereign equality of all its Members."

A careful scrutiny of the Charter, however, indicates that it attributes legal powers to the Security Council and various responsibilities to the organization as such, as would a Constitution. It is, in fact, transitional between a treaty among sovereign states and a constitution of the world, exhibiting characteristics of each and, indeed, some characteristics consistent with the conception of a world empire governed by the five great powers. They alone enjoy a veto on decisive actions but, if united, they can in the interest of peace and security take measures, if two of the nonpermanent members of the Security Council concur, of revolutionary significance.

The difficulties of achieving agreement among the great powers have, however, prevented the development of this latter possibility and have protected the smaller states from appeasements. At the same time, the difficulties of agreement have prevented the United Nations from developing the organic character which was intended. Progress in that direction has been registered in the handling of a number of political disputes particularly that concerning Korea, in the later stages of which agreement was facilitated through the voluntary withdrawal from participation by the Soviet Union and its satellites. The inherent difficulty, however, of maintaining an organic political union which is universal and consequently is not organized for defense against an external enemy has been exhibited. The United Nations faces the problem of reconciling universality, which is essential if the organization is to maintain peace, with capacity to make decisions rapidly and effectively to maintain peace in particular emergencies. The difficulty of developing such a capacity in a universal organization, in which political differences inevitably develop among the great powers, has suggested to many that the United Nations should frankly become a union of democracies excluding the Soviet Union and its satellites from membership. A move in that direction was taken in the agreement of 1949 organizing the North Atlantic states in a defensive alliance. Proposals for developing this alliance into a true federation have been actively supported in the United States Congress and elsewhere.

In contradistinction to this tendency, the secretary-general sought to maintain the universality of the United Nations by creating conditions, especially admission of representatives of the Communist government of China by the organs of the United Nations, which might end the voluntary abstention of the Soviet Union from participation in United Nations activities. This abstention which began in the winter of 1949 extended to all organs in which representatives of the Nationalist government of China continued to function but was ended by the return of Soviet representatives after the Security Council had acted in the Korean affair in the summer of 1950.

The differences between the United States and the Soviet Union, which have so hampered the functioning of the United Nations, began soon after the Yalta Conference when the Soviet Union began to establish Communist governments in the countries of eastern Europe, contrary to the obligations of the agreement emerging from that conference. These differences increased after the surrender of Japan in September of 1945, the division of Korea, as well as of Germany and Austria into zones of occupation by the Soviet Union and the Western powers, and the failure of the great powers to administer the coöperative policy which was anticipated in these areas.

The United States continued to assert that strengthening the United Nations as the major instrument of peace and security in the world was its leading policy to which other policies, such as the Truman Doctrine, the Marshall Plan, the Rio de Janeiro pact, the North Atlantic pact, military aid to Western Europe, and the technical-aid program were contributory. The latter policies, however, although formally permissible under the Charter, soon developed into measures of cold war against the Soviet Union. The United States often reported action under these policies to the appropriate organs of the United Nations and declared that their continuance was in general subject to termination on adverse United Nations action. But in spite of this, the trend has been to subordinate the strengthening of the United Nations to victory in cold war. The issue in a sense involves genuine internationalism against American imperialism. The final results of the Korean episode, in which the United States acted as an agent of the United Nations and its forces fought under a United Nations flag, may determine the future of these two facets of American policy. These results may also determine whether the United Nations is to be a universal agency to maintain peace and security primarily through conciliation and adjustment, or is to be a more limited agency employing force to forward the principles of democracy and freedom against the opposition of the Communist powers, or, as attempted by the General Assembly's "Uniting for Peace" resolution in November, 1950, is to synthesize the two tendencies.

American Participation in
International Organization

The fifty years since 1900 have been marked by an intensification of international organization and an increased American participation. The Hague system, developed through the conferences of 1899 and 1907, relied upon voluntary arbitration, disarmament, and codification of international law, but its brief existence did not permit a very great development in any of these fields. Achievements in the field of disarmament were notably lacking. The League of Nations added positive obligations to engage in sanctions against aggression and permanent institutions of international coöperation. The United Nations advanced a step further by conferring upon its organs legal powers to determine the aggressor and to take effective measures against aggression, thus constituting it an organic union in legal principle. Its weakness lies in procedures which give each great power a veto on major decisions in the Security Council, but the capacity of members to act through the vetoless General Assembly and to bind themselves by supplementary agreements—organizing "collective self-defense"—has made it much more than an agency of adjustment and conciliation.

With the growth in the political authority of the world community to preserve international peace and security, registered by these changes in its basic constitution, has gone an even more impressive development of institutions to facilitate coöperation in matters of common interest. The international unions in existence in 1900 employed a personnel of a few score individuals and cost the nations a few hundred thousand dollars a year. The League system, with the Permanent Court of International Justice and the International Labor Organization, employed many hundreds of people and cost the nations several million dollars a year. The United Nations system with its specialized agencies employs thousands of people and costs over a hundred million dollars a year. The personnel and budget of international organization is still pitifully small in comparison with the aggregate national budgets of the nations. States still spend only about one dollar for international organization to every thousand they spend for domestic purposes including military defense. Nevertheless, the proportion is rising. During the League period the ratio was only about one to eight thousand.[9]

The United States participated in the Hague system, and while it did not formally participate in the League of Nations, it did actually coöperate, after the Locarno period, in nonpolitical and disarmament activities and was embarking upon collaboration in political action in the Manchurian episode. Its participation in the United Nations system has been unqualified and has predominated in financial contributions, in taking active initiatives, and in maintaining United Nations responsibilities. Its most important action in all these aspects of participation has been in introducing and gaining general consent (with the exception of the Soviet bloc) to resolutions in June, 1950, for implementation of collective security in Korea and in November, 1950, for improving procedures and implementing collective security in the future. The latter resolution entitled "Uniting for Peace" was initiated by Secretary of State Acheson in the General Assembly in September, 1950. It followed in large measure the proposal made in May, 1948, by the Commission to Study the Organization of Peace and introduced in the Senate on July 8, 1949, by Senators Thomas of Utah and Douglas of Illinois. The latter proposal went further and suggested a supplementary treaty under Article 51 of the Charter by which Assembly recommendations on collective self-defense, if concurred in by three principal powers, would become legally binding upon the parties to that treaty. The resolution adopted by the General Assembly on November 2, 1950, did not add to the obligations of the members of the United Nations but organized procedures to facilitate rapid action by the General Assembly on the basis of adequate information and the availability of sufficient forces to stop aggression. This resolution also recognized the need for social and political as well as legal and police action by reëmphasizing the economic and humanitarian objectives of the United Nations, by urging more effective fulfillment of its Charter responsibilities by the Security Council, and by recommending continuous consultation among the great powers.[10]

This resolution tended to move the United Nations, which has functioned primarily as an agency of conciliation and coöperation among its members, in the direction of a universal society equipped to implement its basic principles against the opposition of any member. Continued progress in this direction will depend on further developments in the realms both of world constitutional law and world public opinion. In both of these lines of progress the practice and policy of the United States will certainly be important.

Constitutional Problems

Its active participation in the United Nations has involved important constitutional and organizational problems in the United States itself. Outstanding is the problem of coördinating action at the national level without frustrating coördination at the international level. If international organs are to function, the representatives of states must be free to be influenced by the discussion and to commit their countries to international policies as a result of these discussions. This, however, may mean that representatives of a particular state, such as the United States, will make commitments in different international agencies which are inconsistent with one another and inconsistent with policies developed by national organs. On the other hand, complete coördination of policy at the national level leaves delegates with such rigid instructions, after all interested national agencies have been consulted, that there is little possibility of compromise as a result of discussion in the international organs. Nothing is so frustrating as an international conference of delegates who are so rigidly bound that discussion means nothing and agreement is impossible. The problem is inherent in confederations, and increases in difficulty of solution in proportion as the subject matter within the competence of the confederation increases in scope. The difficulty of solving this problem is one reason for the tendency of confederations and international organizations either to break up or to develop into federations in which the central organs have conclusive powers in a delegated field resting, not on many national public opinions reflected in the instruction of delegates, but in a world public opinion which can be appreciated by representatives of the various nations as public discussion of each issue proceeds. Edmund Burke pointed out the radical difference between an instructed delegate and a representative free to discover and to contribute to realizing the general interest.[11] In the present situation, American nationalists and imperialists seek to coördinate policy at the national level, utilizing the organs of the United Nations as instruments to win wider adherence to these policies. American internationalists and federationists on the other hand favor the alternative policy by which efforts at national coördination are minimized and representatives in the organs of the United Nations and the specialized agencies have wide discretion to discover and to develop a world public opinion on the subjects within the competence of the international organization, and to accept policies in accordance with that opinion.

Another problem concerns the increasing influence of Congress on international organization because of the increasing budget requirements of these organizations and the large share of the budget borne by the United States. Although the United States pays nearly two-fifths of the budgets of the United Nations and the specialized agencies, it is still not bearing its fair share if judged by capacity to pay. Congress, however, tends to set limits to the total American appropriation for each organization and, if the American ratio remains fixed, this sets limits to the total budget of the organization. Such a situation is undoubtedly unhealthy for international organization. The general conference of each organization should determine the scope of the organization's activity and the size of its budget, but the American Congress is unlikely to accept this position while the United States pays so large a share of the budget and yet has only one vote among fifty-odd in the conference of the international organization. This situation might be remedied by a weighting of votes, as is provided in the international bank, the international fund, and a few other international organizations, so that the members who contribute more will have a larger voice in the determination of the budget and the appropriation of funds from it. Even with such a situation, however, since the instructions to United States representatives are given by the president, the Congress might not be satisfied. The United Nations and some of the specialized agencies have therefore considered the possibility of independent sources of income such as a tax on international postal and telegraphic communication.[12] Such a development would move the United Nations in the direction of federation.

Somewhat similar are the problems concerning American participation in the use of force by the United Nations. The Charter calls for special agreements by the members with the Security Council to earmark defined forces for policing purposes. Congress, in the United Nations participation act, authorized the president to make such agreements with the consent of Congress. None have been made, however, because of the inability of the Western powers and the Soviet Union to agree on proper quotas. If such agreements were made, undoubtedly the president would be constitutionally competent to utilize forces so earmarked with the consent of Congress without further congressional authorization.

The question has arisen, however, especially in connection with the Korean situation, whether in the absence of such agreements, the president can respond to the Security Council request for forces without specific congressional authorization. The members are committed by Article 2, paragraph 5, of the Charter to give the United Nations every assistance in any action it takes in accordance with the present Charter and, under Article 25, to accept and carry out the decisions of the Security Council in accordance with the present Charter. Under Article 39, the Security Council is obliged to determine the existence of any threat to the peace, breach of the peace, or act of aggression and to make recommendations or to decide what measures shall be taken to maintain or restore international peace and security. The General Assembly can make recommendations on such matters if the Security Council neglects its duties (Articles 10, 12). Article 43 contains a specific obligation of the members to contribute forces, assistance, and facilities provided in the special agreements made with the Security Council, but it does not impair the general obligations of the members "to take effective collective measures for the prevention and removal of threats to the peace and for the suppression of acts of aggression or other breaches of the Peace" (Article 1) or to take appropriate measures to assist the Security Council in carrying out its decisions.

It has been established in American constitutional law that while the president cannot declare formal war, he has authority as commander-in-chief of the army and navy in time of peace as well as war, to utilize the armed forces to the extent necessary to suppress domestic insurrection, to defend the territory or citizens of the United States, and to fulfill the international obligations of the United States.[13] Many precedents exist of independent presidential action of this type, although Congress has sometimes objected, especially when forces of considerable magnitude have been used. The instances include hostilities against the Barbary pirates, hostilities against American Indians, landing forces in the Caribbean, interventions in Mexico, participation in international expeditions in Japan and China in the mid-nineteenth century, and in the Boxer affair in 1900, and most important of all, the president's initiation of large-scale hostilities to suppress rebellion in the South by military and naval action.[14] Congress did not act to recognize the existence of Civil War until several months after the initial hostilities, but the Supreme Court held that the president was competent to use forces to suppress insurrection and that war existed by the fact of such insurrection from the moment of the first hostilities, thus permitting capture of neutral vessels at sea under international law.[15]

Under this theory of his powers, President Truman authorized armed forces to go to Korea to assist the United Nations and the Korean Republic to drive North Korean forces back to the 38th parallel. This was done in pursuance of explicit resolutions of the Security Council, approved by the required vote, although the representatives of the Soviet Union were voluntarily absent, and China was represented, not by the Communist government which controlled the mainland of China, but by the Nationalists whose control extended only to the island of Formosa. While the president's authority was challenged by some members of Congress, the prevailing view in that body supported it.[16] In constitutional theory the president is in a better position to fulfill military commitments to the United Nations than to fulfill financial commitments. If, however, military action becomes of considerable magnitude, congressional support is necessary to appropriate for the conduct of such operations.

The weakness of an organization which has to rely on the voluntary contributions of force by its members has been appreciated in all confederations and leagues. The United States itself suffered from this situation during the Revolution and also during the War of 1812. For the land operations of this war the federal government relied in the main upon the clauses of the Constitution and acts of Congress which authorize the president to call forth the militias of the states to suppress insurrection, repel invasion, and enforce the laws. Embarrassment was felt when certain New England states, which were in general opposed to the war, refused to respond to such calls. Subsequently the United States has relied less upon the militia clause than upon the clauses of the Constitution which authorize Congress to provide armies.[17]

The problem faced by the United Nations in Palestine, following the assassination of Count Bernadotte, resulted in the employment by the secretary-general of several hundred police guards to protect and assist the United Nations mission. The General Assembly approved the practice and authorized the secretary-general to maintain a permanent field service for such purposes. Although small, this may constitute the beginning of an independent United Nations police force which would reduce the need for calling upon the members for special forces to aid missions engaged in investigation, conciliation, or plebiscite administration in various parts of the world. Large forces required for actual military operations could not in any immediate future be provided in this manner but in principle, it would seem that the United Nations is competent to acquire and utilize such forces provided the General Assembly votes the necessary appropriation.[18]

International organization, marking a transition from diplomatic negotiation to parliamentary democracy, also faces a dilemma between the secrecy necessary for success in the first and the publicity necessary in the second. A diplomatic bargain cannot be made if negotiators are bound by rigid instructions or are limited by a vigorous public opinion behind initial proposals. It was difficult for the United States to recede from the Baruch proposals on atomic energy, or for Russia to recede from the Gromyko proposals. Diplomacy requires give-and-take between groups that are opposed to one another in most matters, suspicious of one another's motives and intentions, and above whom there is no embracing and effective public opinion. Secrecy is therefore the essence of diplomacy, at least until the agreement is completed. President Wilson had to recognize that the "openly arrived at" part of his formula stated in the Fourteen Points "open covenants openly arrived at" could only mean that the process of negotiation, as well as the results, should be published, but only after agreement was reached.[19]

Parliamentary democracy, however, requires publicity and debate because its essence is the support of public opinion which cannot be either discovered or guided without publicity.

The General Assembly and the Security Council of the United Nations, as well as the other councils and the organs of the specialized agencies, generally conduct their debates in the open. But since the oppositional relations which do actually exist among members, militate against the development of a world public opinion, private diplomatic negotiation is often essential, especially on political matters among the great powers. A compromise has been suggested by the General Assembly in urging that the Big Five seek by private conference to reach agreements which might avoid the excessive use of the veto in Security Council meetings.[20]

In the San Francisco Conference such meetings in Secretary of State Stettinius's pent-house apartment undoubtedly facilitated agreement in the open sessions of the conference, although the indefatigable press usually succeeded in giving early publicity to these transactions, often to the discontent of some of the delegates. As an excuse, the agencies of the press, which were very numerous at that conference, said that since the Charter would require ratification by parliaments, particularly by the United States Senate, it must command the support of a universal public opinion or it would not be ratified. The argument was perhaps supported by the speedy general ratification of the instrument, but in this case, major agreement had been reached among the principal powers at the preceding conference at Dumbarton Oaks, the proceedings of which were, and remain, confidential.[21]

Undoubtedly at its present stage, confidential negotiation must accompany open debate in international organizations which deal with political matters. The principles of the two are however conflicting. World organization cannot achieve its goal of peace with justice through law unless it develops a world public opinion which can be relied upon to support the decisions of the organization even when they appear to neglect or oppose the immediate interests of certain states. The fundamental problem is that of merging many distinct and national publics into a world public with a common opinion on many matters. The procedural rules concerning instructions, voting and secrecy, and the basic control of the powers of the purse and of the sword must reflect the existing structure of public opinion or the organization will not function. The sentiment of nationalism is still stronger in the minds of most people than that of internationalism, and very much stronger than that of cosmopolitanism. Consequently, national public opinions are more powerful than world public opinion, and world institutions must be agencies of conciliation and adjustment rather than agencies of authority and power—they must be diplomatic rather than parliamentary.

Conclusion

The problems of America and world organization involve numerous complexities and contradictions. These problems can only be solved if public opinion in the United States and elsewhere merges to some extent in a world public opinion insistent that the aims of the Charter shall be fulfilled, even if national traditions centering on sovereignty and international procedures centering on the veto have to be modified. Parallel with such a development in the realm of public opinion, officials of the United Nations, of the United States, and of other nations must labor continuously and intelligently to solve day-by-day problems of coördination, administration, and policy. International organization must be geared into national governments. Both are complex and have developed from different traditions, but the possibilities of coördination are great if attention is paid to the problem of the moment, and distant goals of organization and power are approached only step by step and often circuitously. Political institutions that are sufficiently complicated to be viable, adaptable, and effective grow by precedent and interpretation rather than by the elaboration of long-run plans and action to realize them.

Philosophy and argument concerning long-run requirements of world institutions, such as are indulged in by advocates of world federation and world government, may be useful to broaden the horizons of individual attitudes and public opinion. Politics and administration in the work of existing institutions are, however, more important. They make such institutions function to maintain international peace and security, to enlist the coöperation of governments toward common purposes, and to win the general confidence necessary if the United Nations is to become a symbol of high value in world opinion.

4

ACCOMPLISHMENTS

AND EXPECTATIONS

OF WORLD

ORGANIZATION

Nature of the World Community

Every community and particularly the world community has many parts, each of which, in our dynamic age, is continuously changing. Attempts to define these parts, to describe the processes of change, to measure rates of change, and to analyze the influence of changes upon the relationships of the parts and upon the life of the community as a whole are likely to appear dogmatic and unreal. Communities, like all living things, resist mechanical division and abstract definition. Life implies both coöperation and opposition among parts of the living thing [1] and involves processes the functioning of which gives unity to the whole.[2] But these parts and processes cannot be identified and separated by sharp definitions. The geographic areas, temporal oscillations, and functional processes of communities are in continual flux. Permanent boundaries are possible only when life has ceased.

Nevertheless, both politicians and social scientists persist in assigning major social and political ills to "disharmonies," "maladjustments," or "lags," implying that different parts or processes of a community can be examined independently and their changes compared with one another.[3] We are painfully aware that the policies of different nations

From *Yale Law Journal*, LV (August, 1946).

conflict. We can easily perceive that the different regions and areas of the world are unequally developed technologically and politically. Culture in some areas appears to be centuries behind that in others. Taking the world as a whole, it has been suggested that natural science has outstripped political science, that a twentieth-century technology is beyond the capacities of Neanderthal human nature to manage,[4] that political nationalism is out of harmony with economic interdependence,[5] that political myths are maladjusted to economic realities,[6] that reactionary ideologies are in conflict with revolutionary utopias.[7]

Among the many possible analyses of the processes which maintain a community as a whole, that which distinguishes its technology, its science, its opinion, and its organization seems well adapted for studying world politics. Sociologists characterize a community by the abundance of communication among its members (which in large communities usually varies with its progress in technology), by the degree of similarity of its members (which in the traits important for civilization varies with its progress in and diffusion of knowledge), by the degree of harmony among its members (which usually varies with the homogeneity of its public opinion), and by the capacity of the community to act as a unit (which is likely to vary with the degree of centralization of its organization).[8]

Within the world community there are very considerable local differences. The processes of technology, of science, of opinion, and of organization are changing at different rates and even in different directions. Furthermore, the rates and directions of change differ in different areas. Tensions because of such lags and disharmonies have been world-wide, tending to world war. They have also been international, tending to international war, and intranational, tending to civil war.

With this order of thought, the definition of these processes of the world community and the measurement of the rate and direction of their changes, generally and locally, may provide a basis for predicting the future of world politics and also for controlling it.[9]

Trends of Technology and of Opinion

Difficulty arises, however, because certain of these processes appear to exhibit little continuity or trend in their changes, but vary spasmodically and unpredictably. This is less true of technology and science than of opinion and organization. Men have always been inventing and utilizing devices for communicating, for transporting persons and things, and for transforming natural resources to human purposes. They have also been employing methods and ideas for discovering regularities, for predicting the future, and for controlling nature. Nations, civilizations, and even the human race as a whole have advanced progressively and cumulatively, and at an accelerating rate in these processes of technology and science. One generation has built on the shoulders of its predecessors. There have been setbacks in this progress in local areas following the death of nations and civilizations. Technology and science retrogressed in Europe in the Dark Ages and in China in the Age of Warring States, but in general man has moved steadily forward in his capacity to eliminate space, to utilize his natural environment, to recall his social past, and to understand natural phenomena.[10]

Opinions and organizations, however, have exhibited much less continuity. There is today a wide diversity of religious beliefs, moral codes, political philosophies, and economic theories. History discloses little continuity in the acceptance and interpretation of such standards. While cumulative development of social ideals can be traced in the opinions of large groups over long periods, as for example the ideals of humanity, liberty, tolerance, and reasonableness since the Renaissance,[11] history as a whole records the rise, decline, and recurrence of social ideas and institutions.[12] Ideas of social equality have been succeeded by ideas of social inequality, ideas of liberty by ideas of obedience, the idea of a universal god by the idea of many national gods. Ideas of rationalism and humanism have been succeeded by ideas of irrationalism and self-interested expediency, ideas of free economic enterprise by ideas of centralized economic organization, ideas of a world community under law by ideas of ceaseless struggle between nations and groups. Social experiments have seldom been so conclusive that apparent failures will not be tried again under new conditions or that apparent successes will not be abandoned when conditions change. Such changes have usually been accompanied by considerable social violence.

Revolutionary Transitions

This apparent unpredictability of changes in opinions and organizations may be a consequence of their dependence both upon ancient traditions and upon contemporary conditions of science and technology. Continual adaptation of social opinions and organizations is necessary if man is to take advantage of new inventions and discoveries. Institutions and organizations, however, depend so much on custom and habit for their smooth functioning that such adaptation causes social disorder. Furthermore, men acquire an emotional attachment to traditional beliefs and institutions.[13] There is, consequently, a tendency for opinions and organizations, ill adapted to the present conditions of science and technology, to persist until their obsolescence becomes so obvious to many that change takes place with revolutionary violence. In his *Study of History,* Arnold J. Toynbee has illustrated this process in the transition from one civilization to another usually with "dark ages" between, and in the transition in the structure of each civilization from a heroic age of pioneering conflict, to the troublous times of a progressively less stable balance of power, followed by a period of a universal state, and then that of a universal church which may contain the germs of a new civilization as the old civilization declines and falls.[14]

To avoid the violence of transitions, which has sometimes caused retrogression for several centuries in the progress even of science and technology, the lag of opinions and organizations behind science and technology should be narrowed. Such a narrowing is not likely to prove practicable, however, unless men show a greater willingness than they have in the past to abandon traditional opinions which cannot be realized under existing conditions, and to modify historic institutions and organizations based upon such obsolete opinions. Furthermore, continuous adaptation of opinions and organizations to contemporary material conditions necessarily destroys their adaptation to the customs of human society and the habits of individual human minds. A compromise is consequently necessary which can be effected only by a continuing effort of education and information. In the present dynamic age when the steam engine, the telegraph, the radio, the airplane, and nuclear fission have followed each other in rapid succession, education cannot be effective in promoting this adaptation if it seeks to demonstrate eternal truth or historic tradition. Instead it must develop a sense of responsibility in every individual to think things through in the light of the present and the probable future.[15]

The accomplishments and failures of past efforts at world organization should, therefore, be judged by their success (1) in meeting the political and economic problems arising from the impact of new discoveries and inventions on customary modes of thought, and (2) in changing those modes of thought to modes of thought better adapted to contemporary conditions.

Organizations and institutions have often attempted to effect such adaptations not by changing traditions but by changing conditions to the more primitive situation in which the traditions arose. While an adaptation might be effected in this way, and in fact has been in "dark ages," it may be assumed that that form of adaptation is not desired by many people in the contemporary world and would not be practicable in the long run. The clock of science and invention cannot be permanently turned back. Eventually opinions and organizations must be adapted to advances in science and technology although there are usually many choices in the form of that adaptation.

The Organization of Modern Civilization

Modern civilization, which began in Europe with the discovery of new continents and the rediscovery of ancient civilizations at the time of the Renaissance, has experienced several periods characterized by distinctive types of organization and opinion. It began with a continuance of the religious tradition of medieval Christendom, tinctured by notions of objective science and cultural relativity and politically disorganized by the struggles of national monarchies equipped with firearms in war, the printing press in peace, and Machiavellian policies at all times. After the Reformation and the Thirty Years' War, the concept of balance of power among sovereign territorial states guided the policy of princes and became the political organization of Europe.

The American and French revolutions and the recognition of Latin American, Asiatic, and African states made the state system world-wide and reduced the influence of the European and Christian tradition in the opinion which sustained that system. These revolutions developed the ideas of individual liberty and equality which had been latent in the ideas of the Renaissance and the Reformation. They also had an important influence in developing ideas of nationalism and internationalism.

The concept of a concert of the great powers was practiced after the Napoleonic wars as a means for preserving the balance of power. After the nationalistic wars of the mid-nineteenth century, international administration of technical services, the codification of international law, and the international arbitration of disputes of a legal character gave a certain reality to internationalism so long as the balance of power remained comparatively stable under the influence of British sea power and finance. At the same time the idea of self-determination of nationalities, the protection of national minorities, and the emancipation of dependencies gave a renewed vigor to the concept of nationalism as it had been expounded by Mazzini.

The League of Nations sought to give harmony and form to these diverse tendencies. Accepting the basic structure of national territorial states, it sought to encourage peaceful change in the direction of national self-determination, emancipation of colonies, and freedom of trade, and to adjust controversies by arbitration, conciliation, or consultation within the theory of international law which recognized the sovereign independence of states. The League of Nations, therefore, depended primarily on the influence of reason and persuasion. An element of power, however, existed in the predominance of the concert of great powers with permanent representation in the Council and in the anticipation that the United States and Great Britain, who together controlled most of the world's sea power and available finance, would be able to exercise a leadership and to bring effective pressures of an economic character to support the resolutions of the League's Council and Assembly. In form, Article 16 of the Covenant recognized the equality of states and left it to each state to appreciate its obligations to engage in sanctions against a state which resorted to war in violation of its covenants, but it was anticipated that the reality of Anglo-American solidarity in the use of sea power and finance would give practical effect to these provisions.

The abstention of the United States from the League and the growing importance of the Soviet Union, not an original member of the League, eliminated this expectation, and the League was in practice reduced to an instrument for formulating opinion and facilitating persuasion. World politics reverted to power politics but without the capacity of Great Britain alone to maintain the balance which had preserved stability during the nineteenth century.

Nevertheless, the successes of the League in applying the techniques of pacific settlement in many cases, in developing international administrative services in many fields, and in educating peoples to the need of even more effective international organization laid the foundation for new effort and during the 1920's created a considerable hope that a long period of peace might be expected. The economic collapse and the rise of aggressive governments during the 1930's shattered this hope, but the experience with the League and with World War II eliminated policies of isolationism even in the United States and the Soviet Union. The need of international coöperation both for security and for prosperity was recognized in nearly all countries.

In the meantime, however, the material conditions of the world had changed through the development of inventions and practices which had the effect of increasing international communication and transport, governmentalizing economies, concentrating military, political, and economic power, and augmenting the vulnerability of all peoples to the destruction of war. The form of international organization which might have been adapted to conditions of 1920 was not adequate to meet conditions of 1945. It may even be doubted whether the organization of the United Nations, which took form before Hiroshima, is adequate to the conditions of the atomic age.

Transitions in the Form of World Organization

Although history is continuous and some form of organization always regulates the relations of peoples in contact with one another, forms of organization may undergo relatively rapid transition at certain periods usually characterized by war and violence. Such transitions may be accelerated and become turbulent because of an inherent contradiction between the mode of organizing security and prosperity which has existed and that which new conditions require.

As an illustration, systems of states regulated by an equilibrium of power can hardly move gradually into a system of states regulated by law because the functioning of the two systems calls upon states to behave in manners which are mutually contradictory. Stability through power politics can only result if each state maintains its own defenses comparably with that of its neighbors, maintains the freedom and the capacity of its government to act rapidly and decisively, and promptly joins in temporary alliance or common action to decrease the relative power of a state which is becoming so powerful as to threaten its neighbors. Power must be the dominant criterion. If other considerations enter into the policy of any state of importance in the balance, the stability of the entire system will be impaired.[16]

On the other hand, stability through law can only result if each member of the community limits its defensive measures to those which the law permits, subordinates its policy to the general law, and utilizes the procedures of the general law for determining, protecting, and modifying its rights. Law must be the dominant criterion. If other considerations predominate in the policy of states or groups of states, too large to be controlled by the agencies of law enforcement for the community as a whole, the stability of the entire system will be imperiled.

International Justice and Preventive War

It is clearly impossible for states to be guided predominantly at the same time by precepts both of power and of law. The difficulty was recognized by the early writers on international law in discussing the justice of war to preserve the balance of power. Beginning with the Spanish Dominican Francis of Victoria in the sixteenth century, the classical writers recognized that war was not justified except against a state that violated the law.[17] Yet a state might dangerously increase in power without violating the law. Alberico Gentili at the Court of Queen Elizabeth, thoroughly versed in Italian balance-of-power politics and quoting with approval the opinion of Lorenzo de Medici "that the balance of powers should be maintained among the princes of Italy," denied as a jurist "that it is just to resort to a war of this kind as soon as anyone becomes too powerful" because a prince may "have his power increased by succession and election." "Will you assail him in war," writes Gentili, "because his power may possibly be dangerous to you? Some other reason must be added for justice's sake." [18]

Hugo Grotius in the midst of the Thirty Years' War elaborated the same point.

> We have said above that fear with respect to a neighboring power is not a sufficient cause. For in order that a self-defense may be lawful it must be necessary; and it is not necessary unless we are certain, not only regarding the power of our neighbor, but also regarding his intention; the degree of certainty required is that which is accepted in morals.
>
> Wherefore we can in nowise approve the view of those who declare that it is a just cause of war when a neighbor who is restrained by no agreement builds a fortress on his own soil, or some other fortification which may some day cause us harm. Against the fears which arise from such actions we must resort to counter-fortifications on our own land and other similar remedies, but not to force of arms. [19]

Samuel Pufendorf [20] and Christian Wolff [21] similarly distinguished the expediency from the justice of wars. Emmerich Vattel, writing realistically in the midst of the Seven Years' War, emphasized the importance of maintaining the balance of power, but added:

> . . . Since war is only permissible in order to redress an injury received, or to protect ourselves from an injury with which we are threatened, it is a sacred rule of the Law of Nations that the aggrandizement of a State cannot alone and of itself give anyone the right to take up arms to resist it.
>
> Supposing, then, that no injury has been received from that State, we must have reason to think ourselves threatened with one before we may lawfully take up arms. Now, power alone does not constitute a threat of injury; the will to injury must accompany the power. It is unfortunate for the human race that the will to oppress can almost always be believed to exist where there is found the power to do so with impunity. But the two are not necessarily inseparable; and the only right which results from the fact that they ordinarily or frequently go together is that first

appearances may be taken as a sufficient proof. As soon as a State has given evidence of injustice, greed, pride, ambition, or a desire of domineering over its neighbors, it becomes an object of suspicion which they must guard against.[22]

Vattel then speaks at length of the duty of the state to take precautions proportionate to the risk and to take advantage of even the "smallest wrong" by an overpowerful state to make demands, but if the "powerful state is both just and prudent in its conduct and gives no ground for complaint," force cannot be used against it though counter-alliance may be appropriate. Such a balancing of power by diplomacy, Vattel considers both legitimate and prudent. If this fails and the balance of power becomes disturbed,

> the safest plan . . . is either to weaken one who upsets the balance of power, as soon as a favorable opportunity can be found when we can do so with justice, or, by the use of all upright means, to prevent him from attaining so formidable a degree of power. To this end all Nations should be on their guard above all not to allow him to increase his power by force of arms, and this they are always justified in doing.[23]

If the disturbance of the balance is due to the construction of fortresses or increase of armament by a state, attack upon that state is not justifiable unless there is evidence of intended perfidy. The only remedy is defensive military preparation and alliances, policies likely to lead to armament races which are both expensive and dangerous to the peace.[24] Vattel's difficulty in reconciling the expediency of preventive wars to maintain the balance of power with the injustice of wars undertaken merely for that purpose is clear, and his extended advice by no means solved the difficulty.

Nineteenth-century writers generally followed Vattel's lead, although they somewhat changed his terminology. They recognized the political expediency of maintaining the balance of power while insisting that armed intervention merely for that purpose is not legally permissible.[25]

To summarize, international lawyers have agreed that if states consistently follow the precepts of the balance of power, they will weaken law as an instrument of security. If, however, they follow law in all circumstances, the balance of power is likely to become so disturbed that the security of all will be imperiled, assuming that the world community lacks effective processes of law enforcement. Consequently, the sanctions of law must become adequate all at once if law is to be substituted for the balance of power.

If they are not adequate, subjects of the law will not abandon the right of self-help, or if they do abandon it will become victims of their own confidence in an inadequate system as did Ethiopia and Czechoslovakia [in the 1930's]. If the force of a State is adequate to defend its own right, it will also be sufficient in some cases to defy the law. Consequently an unorganized balance of power system contains no guaranty against lawlessness. As a result of these circumstances, the establishment of a system of international sanctions, assuring that the power behind law is greater than the power of any law-breaker or any probable combination of law-breakers, cannot take place gradually. Unless such sanctions are made sufficiently powerful all at once, they may be worse than useless.[26]

The Organization of Security and of Prosperity

Probably the same dilemma exists between an economic system regulated by free-market processes and an economic system regulated by central planning. The first fails to assure prosperity if government operation and regulation of industry become so great that basic price adjustments cannot be made through the market. Central planning, however, cannot assure prosperity if so large a sphere of economic activity is left to free enterprise that a comprehensive plan cannot be administered. A government cannot plan more than a small fraction of the national economy and maintain a free-enterprise system at the same time.

The suggestion, however, that there is an incompatibility between the balance of power and world law as bases of security, and also an incompatibility between free enterprise and government planning as the basis of prosperity, should not be understood to imply that there is any incompatibility between world law and free enterprise. In fact the reverse may be true. There may be an incompatibility between world law and highly governmentalized economies.[27] Law functions best when the natural and artificial persons who are its subjects are relatively weak in comparison with the community as a whole.

The difficulty of the situation lies in the fact that governments, even if they realize the incompatibilities between different systems of security and of prosperity are not entirely free to choose the system which they, and the public opinion under which they function, desire. Conditions of technology and science may be such that even with the fullest support of opinion and the most suitable organization, a policy, perhaps feasible under other conditions, cannot be made to work. What is practicable depends on both conditions and opinions. But conditions genuinely [28] imposed by technological and scientific advance are so difficult to alter that opinions must be adjusted to them.

There is, it is true, always a considerable range of choice among policies either of security or of prosperity, and in general this range probably widens as science and technology advance, but at the same time science and technology establish conditions difficult to alter which impose important limits upon the range of choice. Europe could not be a world in itself after Columbus. The horse and buggy age was gone after Henry Ford. The Wright brothers greatly reduced the influence of sea power in the history of the future. Since Hiroshima, no city can feel secure during war. A security system which relies heavily upon geographical distance and geographical barriers is today obsolete.

Evaluation of Recent Systems of World Organization

With these considerations in mind, attention may be given to the three systems of world organization which have been attempted since the Napoleonic wars: (1) balance of power under the Concert of Europe conducted by the British Empire, (2) balance of power under the League of Nations, and (3) balance of power under the United Nations.

The first of these systems appears to have worked the best.[29] It kept comparative peace for the century between the battles of Waterloo and the Marne, whereas the League of Nations kept the peace for less than twenty years, and opinion seems divided whether the United Nations has kept it even that long.

This comparison, however, does not mean that the British system was best in an absolute sense, only that it was best relative to the conditions which it faced. It failed in 1914 and was not completely successful during the twenty years of nationalistic wars in Europe, the Americas, and Asia from 1850 to 1870.[30] This system rested on a widespread opinion which acquiesced in the dominance of British sea power and finance, in the British theory of economic and civil liberties, in the functioning of the great power concert in Europe, and in the principles of international law supporting territorial sovereignty, localizing wars, and regulating intergovernmental relations not directly related to national security. The adequacy of this system was destroyed by the diminution of the influence of Britain's sea power consequent upon the invention of the submarine and the airplane and the rise of American, Japanese, and German sea power; by the diminution of the influence of British liberalism consequent upon the rise of rival centers of finance and industry, the diffusion of socialistic theories, the increasing political influence of labor, and the increasing control of economies by governments and international cartels; by the serious disturbance to the equilibrium in Europe consequent upon the development of German military and industrial power, the weakening of the independent position of the Habsburg monarchy faced by dissident nationalities, the corruption of tsarism in Russia, the static condition of the French population, the rise of non-European great powers, and the increasing influence of democracy on the conduct of foreign policy; and by the agitation for self-determination in Eastern Europe, in Asia, and in the colonies consequent upon the diffusion of European military and industrial techniques and European ideas of liberty, equality, and nationality. Under these conditions Britain in the twentieth century was unable to maintain the equilibrium of Europe and of the world as she had during the nineteenth century.[31]

The nineteenth-century Pax Britannica was more successful in dealing peacefully with international problems as they arose than in educating opinion to the need for change. It was in large measure an automatic and static system which lacked processes for peacefully adapting itself to the new conditions of the twentieth century.

The League of Nations, established after a world war had emphasized the need for change in world organization, was intended by its founders to carry on the nineteenth-century system by adding American sea power to British, committing the United States to economic liberalism and international coöperation, restoring European equilibrium by German, and eventually general, disarmament, extending and coördinating international coöperation in nonpolitical matters, and drawing the teeth of nationalism by accepting its main theses: self-determination of nationalities, gradual liberation of colonies, and international protection of minorities.[32] While the main assumptions of international law were accepted, the League, particularly after it was buttressed by the Pact of Paris, in principle eliminated the legitimacy of aggressive war and of neutrality.[33] The League was an effort gradually to supersede the balance of power by effective international law, utilizing the experience of the international unions and the Hague conferences. It might have effected the transition sufficiently rapidly to be successful if the United States had accepted it. Without American support the system of security in the interwar period was less a League of Nations system than a balance-of-power system without the balancing activity of predominant British sea power.[34]

The situation of 1945 was radically different from that of 1920. The power of Britain and the importance of sea power itself were greatly reduced. War equipped with air power, rockets, and atom bombs was far more destructive than ever before. Power was more concentrated, and the hands in which it primarily resided—the United States and the Soviet Union—were less similar in their economic organization and social outlook than were the two greatest powers of the earlier period, the United States and Great Britain. Faith in liberalism had declined in the face of the immediate success of Soviet totalitarianism. Thus the tensions of the world, politically between nationalism and internationalism and economically between free economy and governmentalized economy, were tremendously augmented. Technology and science had made enormous advances. Opinions and organizations were less adapted to these advances than they were after World War I.[35]

Reviewing the situation in the light of human history as a whole, it appears that conditions are present which have in the past led to the termination of systems of power equilibrium. The number of great powers has been reduced, the relative superiority of these powers over the lesser powers has increased, war techniques have become more destructive, the contacts of states have become closer, and economy has become less free. In past civilizations such conditions have frequently led to conquest of the entire area of the civilization by one state. The equilibrium of power has sometimes been superseded by the universal state.[36]

The United Nations

With these considerations in mind, it is not to be anticipated that the system which worked in the nineteenth century under British hegemony or the system which might have worked in the 1920's through the League of Nations will work today. Will the United Nations be more adequate? Its Charter relies upon a balance of power among the "superpowers" permanently represented in the Security Council, upon the capacity and will of those powers to preserve the peace among the lesser states so long as they maintain their solidarity, upon the development of economic and social coöperation through autonomous organizations coördinated by the General Assembly and the Economic and Social Council, upon processes of gradual self-determination of colonies through the Trusteeship Council, and upon the development of methods for protecting human rights and fundamental freedoms. The United Nations, therefore, combines aspects of several different systems of political organization. It may be considered a world empire governed by the great powers as a unit. It may be considered a balance of power among the great powers. It may be considered a world federation organized in the General Assembly and the Economic and Social Council. Finally, it may be considered an ethical system depending upon the self-restraint of states in respecting the principles of sovereign equality, territorial integrity, political independence, nonintervention in domestic matters, abstention from aggression, and pacific settlement set forth in the first chapter of the Charter.

The Charter has been criticized as attempting to combine incompatible systems of power and of law. Probably the Achilles heel of the United Nations is its dependence upon the maintenance of a stable balance of power among the permanent members of the Security Council. That equilibrium, primarily between the United States, Britain, and Russia with the first two frequently acting together, has not shown signs of stability up to date. In principle it is difficult to see how an equilibrium between only two centers of power can be stable. In general, the stability of a political equilibrium increases with the number of relatively equal states contributing to that equilibrium. In such a situation, the possibility of small weights being moved to one or the other side of the balance makes for stability. If the world is divided into two great power combinations, no such equilibrating device exists, and the moment one or both of the combinations consider war inevitable or probable, that one against which time appears to be running is likely to begin hostilities.[37]

The world is not yet committed to a two-power structure. Britain and France maintain independent positions. China may develop sufficient independence to engage in power politics. Some of the lesser states have successfully resisted absorption in the sphere of any superpower. The conditions, however, are far less favorable to a stable equilibrium than they were in the nineteenth century or even in the interwar period.[38]

In this situation statesmen have been temporizing, attempting to reach agreements on one point after another without marked success. It does not seem likely that such measures will create confidence and security unless in the long run they tend to develop organizations and opinions better adapted to the conditions of science and technology in the modern world. These conditions appear to be such that a balance of military power cannot be stable and will become progressively less stable as the techniques of nuclear fission spread to all great powers.

Federation or Empire

It may be that the price of stability will be a rapid transition to a system which can give security through adequately enforced world law. That is the contention of the numerous organizations urging world federation.[39] Perhaps the same thought is in the minds of those who suggest that a preventive war may become necessary.[40] The federalists, however, seem not to realize sufficiently the barriers which the present state of opinion and of organization in the world offer to their proposal.[41] The advocates of preventive war have not sufficiently realized that security by that means implies universal conquest and assumption of the burdens of world empire by the victor.[42] Furthermore, it does not seem likely that the United States, at least, could find support in its own public opinion for initiating a war which international law and numerous political pronouncements of the United Nations would brand as aggression and would consider sufficient grounds for criminally indicting the responsible officials of the aggressor government.

In spite of these obstacles it may be that the only alternatives actually before the world are a form of world federation or of world empire. It does not seem likely that a stable balance of power can be restored. It is even less likely that there will be such a firm and universal acceptance of ethical or legal norms that force will be controlled by self-restraint. In democratic countries the choice of federation, emphasizing consent, as opposed to empire, emphasizing coercion, is logical and obvious. Critics of the present state of world organization in democratic countries are likely to evaluate a system of world politics as bad if it depends on "power politics" or is directed by "pressure groups" and to evaluate a system as good if it rests upon "law" and is guided by "world public opinion." President Wilson summarized the aims of the United States on July 4, 1918, as, "The reign of law, based upon the consent of the governed and sustained by the organized opinion of mankind." That summed up, he thought, the objectives of the Fourteen Points and of his other war speeches. It may also be said to sum up the Atlantic Charter and the other United Nations declarations of World War II. That opinion, however, is by no means realized in the United Nations Charter. Perhaps the "federalists" are right in believing that a world organization which realized the Wilsonian opinion would be better adapted to the material conditions of the world than is the organization which exists.

However that may be, power politics is today the basis of the world's political organization, and the number of states which can actively participate in that game is small. The world is moving toward two great centers of power, the United States and the Soviet Union, each bringing the lesser states in its neighborhood under its protection and producing points of insoluble disagreement where those great regions meet in China, Korea, Germany, the Balkans, and the Middle East.

Pressure groups of universal character such as the Communist party, the Catholic church, the great business cartels and combinations exercise a certain influence. In fact, the International Labor Organization is constitutionally constructed to develop such pressure groups in the economic field representing capital and labor. The influence of such pressure groups, however, in view of the present control of armaments by states, is likely for a considerable period to be small in comparison with the influence of the great states. Pressure groups are more likely to be agencies of the principal actors in power politics than checks upon them, although the influence of supranational pressure groups wielding great blocks of opinion within the states themselves cannot be entirely discounted.

International law, as interpreted in the nineteenth century, emphasized the territorial state as the exclusive subject of that law, and emphasized the sovereignty of such states including the rights to make war, to remain neutral, to refuse to settle disputes by judicial procedures, and to veto the application of international legislation to itself. It assumed the success of power politics in maintaining a stable equilibrium. It could not give security through law. International law must be reinterpreted in the spirit of its great founders of the sixteenth and seventeenth centuries, if it is to provide security for the members of the world community under present conditions. It must outlaw aggressive war, require pacific settlement, eliminate the liberum veto on international legislation and sanctions, and recognize the individual as subject to liabilities and entitled to rights under its rules. The latter is particularly important if the world community is to accept the democratic theory that the state is for man, not man for the state, under material conditions which make the entire world a comparatively small neighborhood.[43]

Such a reinterpretation implies, however, a world opinion prepared to subordinate the nation to the world in the fields regulated by international law and to support a world organization able to enforce that opinion. Such a world public opinion is today a hope rather than a reality. The only publics that have effective opinions are national publics and, to a limited extent, certain supranational pressure groups. The problem of world organization is the problem of creating an opinion, permeating the public of every important nation, prepared to subordinate immediate national interests to world law.

The Problem for Statesmen

The world is at a cross road. Conditions will no longer permit a stable balance of power. Opinion will not yet permit a stable world federation. The drift may be, as it has been in similar situations in past civilizations, toward a new world war which might eventuate either in a world empire or in such complete destruction that technology and science would decline in a new dark age. The only rational solution appears to be temporizing adjustment of security problems through skillful diplomacy which carefully distinguishes the essence of national opinions which cannot be safely compromised from lesser issues where accommodation is possible, while within the United Nations and its subsidiary organizations federalism is built as rapidly as possible.[44] The United Nations represents the limit to which present world opinion will go in the direction of world federation. It must not be sacrificed because it is not perfect. Rather it must be the foundation on which to build as evolving opinion permits.

The Charter itself directs the United Nations to reach down to the individual through the protection of individual human rights and cooperation in promoting universal human interests. The Nuremberg trial suggests the further possibility of promoting world federalism by establishing the responsibility before an international tribunal of individuals for crimes against the law of nations. The Department of State's report on the international control of atomic energy and the statement of the American representative on the United Nations Atomic Energy Commission suggested direct administration of one universal interest through an authority functioning within the territory of all states.

Through the development of such practices, the United Nations might assume a more federal character than it now has. Furthermore such practices might develop a world opinion aware of the necessity of giving the United Nations a degree of authority and power able to develop law to meet the needs of the contemporary world and to create a sense of security among all peoples, nations, states and governments under that law.

These proposals recognize the inconsistency between the measures necessary to maintain equilibrium among the great powers within the United Nations in order to gain time, and the measures necessary to develop a world opinion which will permit the United Nations to become a government able to develop and maintain world law. It is idle to talk of a world state without a world state of mind. It is idle to talk of security through law when there is no world state. It is idle to urge governments to abandon primary reliance upon their own power when world law cannot give them security. It is unlikely that the use of national power in preventive war would create conditions favorable to the development of a world state of mind. Conquest is more likely to lead to empire dependent upon force than to federation dependent upon consent.[45]

The statesmen of the world are faced by the dilemma that they cannot organize a stable balance of power and they cannot rely on law for security. The people do not want to submit their national sovereignties either to world empire or to world federation. The dilemma is one which is difficult to solve by abstract logic and will have to await the logic of history. Conditions and opinions are out of harmony. It belongs to statesmen to utilize the opinions that exist in order to create what stability they can under existing conditions while they strive to educate opinion to broader horizons. They must judge from moment to moment how far they can go in balancing power without stultifying the law of the United Nations, how far they can go in subordinating national opinion to that law without risking war. In that task a day-by-day analysis of the state of opinion in each of the superpowers and in the world as a whole might be an important guide. It is unlikely that without quantitative measurements of opinion statesmen can keep the ship of world peace in the narrow course between the rocks of national opinions buttressed by the sovereignty of states and the whirlpool of a still inchoate world opinion not yet aware of itself in a world which rapidly shrinks as technology and science advance.

Tasks for the United Nations

The General Assembly and the Security Council may by their resolutions give some evidence of the state of opinion, but more precise evidence is needed. The direction, intensity, homogeneity, and continuity of the opinions of each important public toward other nations and toward the United Nations and its policies can be measured and such measurement might well be undertaken by the Secretariat. For this purpose it would be necessary to collect systematic samplings of opinions expressed in the press, in questionnaires, and in elections at frequent intervals.[46] If the opinions of the important publics were known in all their dimensions, the agencies of the United Nations might circulate information to conform those opinions more closely to world conditions. This, however, would only be possible if United Nations debates, resolutions, and documents were assured free and immediate access by radio and press to every important public. If iron curtains continue to isolate opinion in any great area of the world, statesmen will lack the only guide which could keep them from steering into disaster, and such opinions may depart further and further from the conditions of the world.

The United Nations may, as already suggested, bring itself into direct contact with the people of the world by international coöperation in matters of common interest such as health, communication, commerce, education, and standards of living; by promoting universal respect for fundamental human rights and individual responsibility for fundamental human duties; by administering directly vital human interests like atomic energy; and by disseminating abundant information concerning its policies and problems. By such activities the United Nations may in time transform itself into a federal order. In the meantime it must carry on programs of opinion measurement and analysis among all the major publics of the world for the guidance of diplomacy, both within and outside the Security Council. With such information, statesmen may be able to maintain an unstable and hazardous balance of power until the peoples of the world by becoming accustomed to the functioning of the United Nations are prepared to support improvements in its structure and powers.

5

TRENDS IN THE

EVOLUTION OF THE

UNITED NATIONS, 1948

In discussing in 1948 developments regarding the United Nations, an earnest advocate of world government might label as significant any steps which would move the United Nations either toward or away from world government, while an American nationalist might consider activities of the United Nations significant if they either forwarded or frustrated American policies. Accepting, however, the value system of the United Nations Charter, developments may be considered significant so far as they influence the probability of war, the security of fundamental human rights, respect for international justice, and the advancement of social and economic welfare. These criteria are vague, but they do exclude criteria flowing from values peculiar to any nation, religion, race, or economic class. Further, most of the peoples of the world have subscribed to them by permitting their governments to ratify the United Nations Charter.[1]

The first of these values is generally considered most important. Consequently, the most significant developments concerning the United Nations are those which tend to preserve peace, to create confidence that peace will be preserved, and to direct attention to international organization as a means to preserve peace. Developments with an opposite effect are perhaps of equal consequence, though the optimism of humanity may turn people's attention less often to retrogression than to progress. Therefore, one cannot disregard trends toward war, belief

---

From *International Organization*, II (November, 1948).

in the imminence of war, and discouragement with the United Nations as a means of peace.

The success of the United Nations depends not merely on the institutions and procedures which encourage coöperation, but on the will of states to coöperate. Diplomats and generals can be instruments of coöperation among governments that want to coöperate, and the United Nations Security Council and General Assembly can be instruments of opposition among governments that wish to oppose one another. Some institutions, it is true, tend to stimulate and encourage coöperation while others have a reverse effect. It is well to bear in mind that any analysis of international organization must include both the institutions of international life and the disposition of the states or peoples to use them. *Opinion* is no less important than *machinery*.

We will, therefore, consider international events, particularly those of the years immediately following World War II, for their effect upon the opinions and attitudes of peoples or governments, and for their influence upon the actual machinery of international coöperation, either to promote or to hamper progress toward the objectives of the United Nations.

The Development of Public Opinion

Public opinion concerning the United Nations has been particularly affected by ten events. The failure of the United Nations to organize an effective control of atomic energy or to establish forces for the maintenance of international peace and security, the frustrating use of the veto in the Security Council, and the continued lack of agreement among the powers concerning peace with Germany, Austria, and Japan, have had great influence while the formation of the European Recovery Program and the development of regional security arrangements in the American, Western European, Soviet, and Arab areas have also been affective in public thought. The assumption by the General Assembly of a positive initiative in political matters, together with the persistent activity of the United Nations in dealing with the problems of the Balkan-Greek frontier, Palestine, Indonesia, Kashmir, and Korea have drawn considerable notice, as have the progress made in developing a declaration of human rights and the initiative of the Trusteeship Council in hearing petitioners from or sending commissions to several trust territories, particularly Togoland, Samoa, Ruanda-Urundi, and Tanganyika.

Many other things have occurred in the United Nations commissions, in the specialized agencies, in the General Assembly, and in the councils, but these ten events seem to have been outstanding in making the headlines and in influencing opinion about international organization. The influence of many of them has been unfavorable to international organization and to confidence in the long continuance of peace. Public opinion polls indicate that, in the United States, the outlook has progressively become more pessimistic since the signing of the United Nations Charter in San Francisco. Dr. Stephen White, reviewing on the third anniversary of Hiroshima, the history of efforts to control atomic energy, concluded:

> This, then, is the unfortunate history of three years. The fears have been intensified, for they were based on realities. The hopes have faded, for it is clear today that they were essentially unreal. The atom bomb was born in time to make a bad situation immeasurably worse.[2]

Public opinion polls in 1945 showed that 40 per cent of the American people thought the United States would be involved in war in a generation; this opinion was held in 1946 by 60 per cent, in 1947 by 70 per cent, and in early 1948 by 76 per cent. During the same period the optimistic opinion on the subject sank from 48 to 15 per cent; it is also significant that the number who had no opinion on the subject sank from 18 to 9 per cent. The expectation that the United States would get into another war within ten years has risen from 49 per cent in 1946 to 54 per cent in 1948. A similar increase in pessimism is shown in opinion polls concerning the Soviet Union. The proportion who think Soviet aims are aggressive rather than defensive has increased from 58 per cent in 1946 to 77 per cent in 1948, and the proportion who believe that the United States should adopt a firmer policy toward Russia has increased during the same period from 50 to 72 per cent of those queried. Those who favor preparation for war or actual war against Russia have increased from 21 to 50 per cent, while those who have confidence in conciliation or in doing nothing have declined from 28 to 9 per cent.[3] Anxiety in regard to war and to Russia probably reached a high point with the Berlin blockade controversy during the summer of 1948.

While knowledge about the United Nations has been increasing (in the spring of 1948 about 80 to 95 per cent of the population were found to know about it in Brazil, Great Britain, France, Canada, Mexico, Sweden, Switzerland, and the United States) 25 to 40 per cent in those countries thought the organization had only a poor chance of maintaining world peace. Western Europeans were most skeptical and Americans most optimistic. Of the latter, 67 per cent thought the United Nations had a fair to good chance of preventing another war.[4]

The declining confidence in the United Nations has been evidenced by American initiation of the European Recovery Program outside of the United Nations, and by the development of regional arrangements as primary defense agencies. The Rio de Janeiro and Brussels agreements, organizing security in the Americas and in Western Europe, have little connection with the United Nations other than the allusion to the permission given for collective self-defense by Article 51 of the Charter. The Arab League has declared itself a regional organization under the United Nations, but in the matter of Palestine has acted independently. The Soviet "regional arrangement" has been established by unilateral action of the Soviet Union without reference to the United Nations, and in the Czechoslovak case possibly in definite violation of Charter provisions.

The failure to provide security forces for the United Nations and the influence of the veto on the work of the Security Council have unquestionably reduced confidence in the ability of the United Nations to protect states against aggression. The increase of national armaments and the activity of movements for world government thus manifest a decline in confidence in the United Nations as an agency of security. In March, 1948, 63 per cent of those who responded to the poll favored a world conference in 1950 to revise the United Nations Charter while 13 per cent opposed such a conference and 24 per cent had no opinion on the subject. It is surprising that confidence in this revolutionary step to supersede the United Nations by world government commanded a considerably larger approval among college graduates than among those with less education.[5]

As some compensation for this decline in confidence in the United Nations, note may be taken of the proposal of the secretary-general[6] to increase the number of police guards within his staff for use in aiding missions of the United Nations, and the actual use of some of the Lake Success guards in Palestine. Also, increased initiative by the General Assembly in the political field has somewhat offset the discouragement, caused by the veto, about the progress of the Security Council. This was especially notable in the creation of the Interim Committee of the General Assembly, which may give that body a continuity of activity, and in the General Assembly's intervention in the Palestine and Korean situations. The former has apparently indicated the General Assembly's capacity to bring political changes through mobilizing public opinion, although not, it is true, entirely peacefully. The latter incident indicated the possibility of Assembly consideration of problems directly related to the settlement of the war, in spite of the intention apparently manifested by Article 107 of the Charter to leave these problems to the principal powers. The experience has suggested to some that the General Assembly might break the deadlock over peace with Germany, Austria, and Japan. The transfer of discussions on the Berlin crisis to the Security Council in September, 1947, suggests that the peace settlements may be considered by this body also.

The General Assembly's political activity may have stimulated the Security Council to manifest energy and ingenuity in dealing with the Indonesian and Kashmir cases, thus arousing hope that it might, in spite of the veto, develop procedures capable of dealing with difficult political controversies.

Apart from these circumstances, which have cast a ray of hope in the otherwise gloomy valley of opinion concerning the efficiency of the United Nations to preserve peace, the activities mentioned have contributed something to other objectives of the United Nations.

The success of the Geneva conference of December, 1947, and of the Commission on Human Rights in drafting a declaration and a covenant of human rights; the success of the Geneva conference of May, 1948, in drawing up a convention on freedom of the press (without however achieving agreement of the Soviet bloc); the success of the Economic and Social Council in formulating a convention on the crime of genocide; and the vigorous activity of the Trusteeship Council in dealing with petitions from the people of Togoland and Samoa in a way to forward self-government for these peoples—these events have given hope for further progress in the field of fundamental human rights. United Nations achievements in this field may possibly have contributed to the strong stand taken by President Truman in favor of federal legislation better to maintain human rights in the United States.[7]

Other achievements of the United Nations, particularly the promotion of respect for international justice and the advancement of social and economic welfare, have attracted less attention. Important but less dramatic activities of the United Nations and its specialized agencies, including General Assembly proposals for the establishment of an International Law Commission, international social coöperation such as the wide control over narcotic drugs, and the activity of the International Court of Justice in one case (Corfu Channel) and one advisory opinion (qualifications of applicants for membership in the United Nations), have generally been almost completely ignored.

Summing up, it appears that events of the three post-World War II years and particularly those of 1948 have made public opinion less sanguine of the efficacy of general international organization. As a consequence, government policies have tended to implement major national interests by self-help or regional arrangements. Nevertheless, opinion has not been altogether disillusioned. In the United States, the majority still believes that the United Nations may in time progress toward its objectives of securing peace, promoting human rights, developing international justice, and contributing to social welfare. This long-run opinion was manifested by the generous, though somewhat belated, loan by the United States to assure construction of the United Nations headquarters in New York City.

Development of United Nations Machinery

The events affecting the machinery and procedures of the United Nations, though less spectacular, may prove no less important in the long run than the circumstances affecting public opinion and national policy. Increased efficiency of the mechanism can affect the disposition of governments to use it and of peoples to support it; such a disposition can reciprocally affect the efficiency of the mechanism. The subjective and the objective aspects of the United Nations may thus reciprocally influence one another in a rising spiral of peace, security, justice, and welfare through organized effort.

Twelve recent developments affecting the efficiency of the United Nations may be mentioned. The practice of the General Assembly in making recommendations on political changes and war problems, the provision for the continuous operation of the General Assembly through the Interim Committee, and the tendency of the General Assembly and the Security Council to ignore pleas of domestic jurisdiction designed to oust their competence have been noteworthy, as have been the recognition that the agenda of the Security Council can be determined by a procedural vote, and the Interim Committee's proposals for a considerable extension of the use of procedural votes in the Security Council. The use of Secretariat guards in Palestine and the extensive utilization of Article 51 of the Charter in security arrangements may well have important consequences, together with the emerging pattern of political rather than juridical interpretation of the Charter and the extensive employment of investigating commissions by the General Assembly, the Security Council, and the Trusteeship Council. Failure to achieve universal membership in the United Nations, the inability of the Military Staff Committee to function as an advisory body, and the practice of constituting United Nations commissions by representatives of governments rather than individual experts have been important on the other side of the ledger. The recognition of the autonomy of the specialized agencies and the emphasis given by the United Nations and the specialized agencies to the development of a world public opinion behind international organization should also be pointed out.

These events, however, manifest an encouraging flexibility in the functioning of the United Nations. The major problem has been the incapacity of the United Nations to act because of the veto of the great powers in the Security Council. This procedural arrangement might not have been serious, had there not been vigorous political differences between the American and Soviet blocs to stimulate Soviet use of the veto. Although the League of Nations Council required unanimity to make decisions, the political differences of the members of that Council seldom prevented agreement on a resolution. The diplomatic procedures of prior confidential consultation, the drafting skill of rapporteurs assisted by officials of the Secretariat, and the avoidance of votes until agreement was assured proved adequate to achieve a decision in most cases. In contrast, the organs of the United Nations, which in general do not require unanimity and whose principal members have been divided by political differences which did not appear soluble by confidential discussion, have tended to proceed more like parliamentary bodies and less like diplomatic conferences. The result has been frequent votes and, in the Security Council, frequent vetoes. The Security Council has been unable, because of the veto, to make recommendations on several important matters including control of atomic energy and conventional armaments, the establishment of security forces, the admission of a number of applicants for membership in the United Nations, and the determination of aggression. There has been somewhat less difficulty in making recommendations on political disputes.

Practice has tended to evade the veto by greater utilization of the General Assembly. This has been made possible by acceptance of the thesis that matters can be removed from the agenda of the Security Council by a procedural vote. Also, the General Assembly has been strengthened by the establishment of the Interim Committee, which has given it practical continuity of operation. Though established for only a year, the committee has recommended its own continuance, and it seems probable that the General Assembly will concur in this recommendation. Contrary to the expectations implied by the Charter provision which gives the Security Council primary responsibility in the maintenance of international peace and security, the General Assembly has originally or by reference dealt with political controversies almost as much as has the Security Council. It may be that in some cases where the General Assembly has not actually acted, the possibility of transfer has facilitated the solution of such disputes by the Security Council itself. There the policy of not counting a great power abstention as a veto has also been of considerable assistance in overcoming the difficulties of the veto. Further moderation in the use of the veto has now been proposed in an elaborate report on the subject prepared by the Interim Committee of the General Assembly.[8]

Transfer to the General Assembly, however, has not been able to solve the problems of the veto on applications for membership, on atomic energy control, on armament regulations, and on security police. For these difficulties, other devices have been proposed. An advisory opinion of the International Court of Justice was obtained in an attempt to discourage the use of the veto on the admission of new members. The court held that a nation could not properly base its vote against admission of a state on grounds other than those stated in the Charter. The increased use of Article 51 of the Charter [9] has compensated to some extent for the failure of the members to contribute military contingents to the United Nations. The General Assembly has made recommendations on atomic energy control and on the regulation of conventional armaments, but in view of the necessity of great power agreements to implement such recommendations, no progress has been made.

Practice has tended to confirm the view, vigorously expressed by the small and middle-sized powers at San Francisco, that the great power veto should be either eliminated or restricted. Most students of international organization agree that the Security Council ought to be able to make decisions on political problems rapidly and that such decisions ought to be supported by all of the great powers. These two *desiderata* may however conflict with each other. Doubtless elimination or restriction of the veto would make it easier for the Security Council to reach decisions promptly, yet it was argued at San Francisco that the veto was necessary to assure support for important decisions by all of the great powers. However, while the veto provision means that a positive decision of the Security Council will always have the support of all the great powers, it also means that a practical decision not to act at all, which may be equally important, can be compelled by only one power over the vigorous dissent of all the others. The veto may therefore have impaired rather than buttressed the unity of the great powers.

A minority with power to frustrate tends to be an intransigent minority. But a majority with power to act sometimes tends, under conditions which make unanimity desirable for all, to be a magnanimous majority. Furthermore a majority, especially an overwhelming majority, does not take frustrations easily, particularly if the situation is such that failure to act at all will be disastrous. Such a majority seeks means of evasion, the employment of which may tend to break down the spirit of unity.

While the utilization of the General Assembly, of agreements for collective self-defense under Article 51, and of regional arrangements, when the Security Council has proved impotent because of the veto, are "constitutional" and have been in many cases valuable manifestations of United Nations flexibility in devising means for achieving its ends, they hardly make for great power unity. Furthermore, technically and apart from the veto, the Security Council is in many respects a better body to deal promptly and effectively with political controversies than are the General Assembly or special conferences constituted in accordance with Article 51 or with regional arrangements. These considerations suggest that both the *desiderata* mentioned—capacity to reach decisions promptly and maintenance of great power unity—might be forwarded if the great power veto could be eliminated or severely restricted in Security Council procedure.

Another significant circumstance affecting the efficiency of the United Nations concerns the composition of its commissions. The experience of the League of Nations manifested the great value of commissions which brought together individual experts to examine problems from a technical and a universal point of view, and the representatives of governments with instructions drawn up from national points of view. The combination of universal idealism and national realism proved remarkably effective, particularly in the field of armament regulation. Here no progress at all was made by the League so long as the advice of the Armaments Commission, established by the Covenant and composed of military representatives of the principal powers, was utilized. The Assembly, consequently, created a temporary mixed commission and this body, in which individual civilians and military men conferred, presented valuable analyses of the problem and initiated constructive work. With this experience it is not surprising that the Military Staff Committee of the United Nations, composed of the chiefs of staff of the principal powers, has proved incapable of functioning as an advisory body on security and armament problems. A chief of staff, whose job is to see that his country is in a military position to withstand any probable attack, cannot be expected to take the world point of view necessary to advise on security forces and armament regulation best adapted to prevent any country from committing aggression, and to enable the United Nations to maintain international peace and security. The point of view of the chief of staff is necessarily oppositional rather than coöperative, except under circumstances in which his country is actively engaged in coöperation against a common enemy.

The general political situation of the world in 1948 militates against achievement in the field of security agreements and armament regulation in the near future. It may be anticipated, however, that even if a more propitious situation should develop, a different body will have to be established to advise on these matters. The Military Staff Committee might be confined to its proper function of serving as a general staff in case United Nations forces are actually employed. It can serve as an operative agency to implement military policies already decided upon, as did the combined chiefs of staff during World War II. But it can hardly serve as an advisory agent to formulate such policies.

The Military Staff Committee was established and its composition determined by the Charter itself. The Economic and Social Council was, however, free to determine the composition of other commissions. It is unfortunate that it decided, under pressure from the Soviet Union,[10] to compose the commissions of representatives of governments rather than of individual experts. Doubtless experience will devise practices to ameliorate this error, and it may be that in course of time the Economic and Social Council will make a different decision. The General Assembly has not followed the practice of the Economic and Social Council and has constituted two committees, the Advisory Committee on Administrative and Budgetary Questions and the Committee on Contributions, with individual experts. This decision resulted in the continued service of Jan Papánek of Czechoslovakia on the first of these committees, after the government of Czechoslovakia had been taken over by the Communists and Mr. Papánek had ceased to represent it. The fact that the Communist Czech government objected to this situation did not necessarily mean that Mr. Papánek's services had ceased to be valuable to this committee.

Another evidence of flexibility in the United Nations is to be found in the restricted use of the International Court of Justice in interpreting the Charter. The political agencies of the United Nations have in practice interpreted the Charter themselves, notably in controversies concerning the domestic jurisdiction reservation in Article 2, paragraph 7. This ambiguous provision could have been interpreted to bar consideration of almost all questions by United Nations organs. On the other hand, it might be held that matters ceased to be domestic when placed within the competence of United Nations agencies. In this category are all matters threatening or disturbing international peace and security; all matters concerning the promotion of higher standards of living, full employment, conditions of economic and social progress and development; the solution of international economic, social, health, and related problems; international cultural and educational coöperation, as well as promotion of universal respect for, and observance of, human rights and fundamental freedoms.[11] If all these matters are withdrawn from the field of domestic jurisdiction, the reservation would be reduced to practically nothing. Furthermore, all that the reservation prohibits is "intervention" in matters that are essentially within the domestic jurisdiction of any state. If a literal interpretation is given to the word "intervention" there would seem to be no prohibition against recommendations, conciliation, or other action not involving threats of force. Furthermore, if "intervention" is used in the narrow technical sense the only authority to "intervene" accorded the United Nations by the Charter is the authority to apply enforcement measures provided in Chapter VII of the Charter. Strangely enough, it is precisely these measures which are explicitly permitted by Article 2, paragraph 7, even though they interfere with domestic jurisdiction. In view of these ambiguities, it is not surprising that the trend of practice has been to avoid efforts to interpret Article 2, paragraph 7, and simply to ignore pleas of domestic jurisdiction. The Assembly, for example, has made recommendations concerning South African treatment of Indians in its territory, and concerning the Franco government in Spain, and the Security Council has made recommendations on Dutch treatment of Indonesians in spite of pleas of domestic jurisdiction.

This disposition to interpret the Charter in favor of the legal competence of United Nations organs has been paralleled by attempts to increase their practical competence through the use of visiting commissions. The General Assembly, the Security Council, and the Trusteeship Council have all used such commissions, developing a practice frequently utilized by the League of Nations Council. The League Council, however, never authorized the Permanent Mandates Commission to make investigations within the mandated territories, and the practice of the Trusteeship Council of the United Nations is a distinct advance in this respect.

The enlargement of the competence of the United Nations has not implied more centralization. In fact the United Nations is a less centralized organization than was the League of Nations. This flows from the relatively independent position of the three councils in contrast to the single council of the League of Nations, and from the preservation of the autonomy of the specialized agencies in the agreements establishing their relationships with the United Nations. Although these agreements generally respect the autonomy of the specialized agencies, some of them envisage the possibility of more centralization through budgetary control.

The failure of the League of Nations to develop a world public opinion, insistent upon observance of the Covenant by governments, has often been cited as the reason for the League's inability to stem the tide of extreme nationalism initiated by the Fascist powers. The League, it is true, made efforts to meet the problem through the Committee and Institute of Intellectual Cooperation and the Committee on the Education of Youth on the Aims and Purposes of the League, and tried to give publicity to its meetings and documents. The United Nations has given much greater attention to this problem. It has attempted to increase the volume of international communication through maintenance of human rights, especially freedom of expression and communication; it has attempted to prevent subversive and disintegrating propaganda, to define "war mongering" and to enjoin states to prevent it; it has attempted to promote higher standards of education with a broader understanding of international relations through the activities of UNESCO; and it has attempted to provide an abundance of information about the activities of the United Nations itself through radio, news releases, and other public relations activities.[12]

This field of activity is highly controversial and the Western emphasis upon freedom and abundance of communication has often clashed with the Soviet emphasis upon prevention of subversive and disintegrating communications. Approaches toward reconciliation have, however, been made. Because the laws of even the most liberal countries qualify freedoms of speech and press by forbidding libel, slander, and utterances constituting a clear and present danger to the public order, a reconciliation of these opposing viewpoints may prove possible.

The experience of the United Nations through the three years since its establishment has tended to make it a more efficient agency. It has progressed more in the development of adequate mechanisms and procedures than in its ability to command the support and confidence of peoples. This suggests that if a more favorable political atmosphere could be erected through peace settlements with Germany, Austria, and Japan, and through amelioration of the active rivalry between the United States and the Soviet Union, the United Nations would provide the technical equipment to maintain such a peace.

The Most Significant Developments

Comparing the two lists of events which have affected the development of the United Nations, it is clear that they are not entirely unlike. There are, however, a considerable number of circumstances of long-run importance in building the United Nations which have not attracted public attention, and failures predominate on the list dealing with opinion, while constructive action is evident in the list dealing with machinery. The second list shows the practical efforts, not usually highly publicized, to overcome the failures which have impressed public opinion. Thus the failure to organize international control of atomic energy, while not directly countered, was probably in part responsible for the European Recovery Program and development of regional security arrangements in the Americas and in western Europe. The frustrating influence of the veto in the Security Council has led to the political activity of the General Assembly, the establishment of its Interim Committee, the practice in Security Council voting of not counting abstentions, and the regulation of its agenda by procedural vote. The failure of the Military Staff Committee and the Security Council to create United Nations armed forces has led to the utilization of Secretariat guards and the development of security arrangements under Article 51 of the Charter. The protracted failure to conclude peace with Germany, Austria, and Japan has induced the United Nations to take action in the cases of Korea and the Berlin blockade and has probably influenced the formation of regional security arrangements. Finally, the general discouragement of opinion concerning international organization may have stimulated United Nations organs to act energetically where there was hope of success, as in the matters of human rights and trusteeship.

Considering the period as a whole, the vitality of the United Nations has been shown by the flexibility of its organs in finding new procedures and new bases of authority, when other methods have proved inadequate. There has been a disposition to interpret the Charter liberally, on the assumption that its operative provisions are designed to achieve the purposes stated, even if the domestic jurisdiction of states, the principle of sovereign equality, and the veto enjoyed by the great powers in the Security Council seem to deter such achievement. In this respect the attitude of the organs of the United Nations in dealing with the Charter has resembled that of John Marshall in dealing with the Constitution of the United States.[13] The trend has been toward liberal rather than restrictive interpretation.

The General Assembly has sought to make itself the town meeting of the world. As was to be expected it has been used as a sounding board for propaganda, but it has attracted interest and given leadership to what may become a world public opinion, even under the inauspicious conditions of the present day. Soon after Pearl Harbor and before the United Nations came into existence, the present writer expressed the following opinion:

> It is the "natural" tendency of governments to deal with immediate issues of war and peace by methods which make the general world structure less stable. The result has been the perpetual recurrence

of war in the world. Statesmen have, when confronted by crises, usually turned the rudder the wrong way if their object was to bring the world to a harbor of political stability.

In this sense peace may be considered artificial and war natural. The ships of state have for so large a proportion of the time been tossed upon stormy seas that even the broadest characteristics of a peaceful port elude the imagination of statesmen. What are the characteristics of that port? Can it be sufficiently identified so that if the desire is present, progress can be made toward reaching it? What sort of a structure, to change the metaphor, should the engineers of peace try to build in order to increase stability? [14]

The experience of the past years confirms this opinion. National statesmen have usually acted so as to augment anxiety and decrease the expectation of peace. International organization in the subjective sense has retrogressed. On the other hand, officials of the United Nations and to some extent the representatives of the nations acting in United Nations agencies may have contributed to strengthening international organization in the objective sense. The immediate problem of statesmen, to maintain their power position in a divided world, has conflicted with the long run objective of the United Nations to supersede the condition of power politics by a regime of law and to bring into being a situation in which international coöperation will play a larger role. The problem of the time is that of reconciling the short-run and long-run objectives.[15]

In 1942, the writer, recalling the experience of the League of Nations, suggested eight lines of advance toward a more effective structure and functioning of peace. These included the extension of the investigational and educational competence of world institutions; the maintenance of balance between political procedures and legal procedures in dealing with international controversies, between international executive and legislative power, and between regional and universal responsibilities; and the organization of fair world representation. The definition and punishment of world crimes, the development of a sentiment of world citizenship, and creation of a public opinion which accorded high value to human rights and world welfare [16] were also considered necessary. To the observer evaluating those criteria today, the United Nations Charter seems to mark some advance on the League of Nations Covenant, and the procedures developed through the United Nations experience indicate further progress.

The United Nations and its associate organizations have emphasized, more forcefully than the League of Nations, the investigation of facts and the education of peoples toward awareness of world interrelationships. Especially in the discussion of human rights, international law, domestic jurisdiction, and Charter interpretation, the need to balance legal by political procedures has been recognized, though a great deal remains to be done in this field. The United Nations Security Council has provided an opportunity for a better balance between international guarantees against the violent overthrow of the status quo, and international procedures for the peaceful change required by justice, even though the veto has prevented the full realization of this opportunity. And the General Assembly has shown that its recommendations may exert an important influence in bringing about political changes contrary to established legal rights, as in the Palestine case.

Also, the United Nations Charter emphasizes the principle of universal, as opposed to regional, responsibilities for security and change, an emphasis justified by modern inventions shrinking the world and increasing the range of attack. In actual practice, of course, regional arrangements have been somewhat more emphasized because of the incapacity of the Security Council to act rapidly.

It should be noted, too, that the United Nations, although committed by the Charter to the principle of sovereign equality of states, has been able to a limited extent to adapt representation to the actual interests and capacity of the group. The composition of the Security Council has been a step in this direction through the special position given to the great powers, while the representation in United Nations organs given to the specialized agencies leads further in this direction. In the specialized agencies themselves, in some cases, there is considerable departure from the principle of equal representation of states. The problem, however, of representation of interests other than these of states is one which demands attention.

The United Nations has been engaged, too, in defining crimes against the world community, and has considered the expediency of tribunals for the prosecution of such crimes, although little progress has been made other than through the precedents established by the International Military Tribunal at Nuremberg, by the Charter under which it acted, and by the subsequent tribunals charged with further enforcement of its principles. Cultivation of a sense of world citizenship has been the primary aim of UNESCO, and the services of many of the specialized agencies, as well as United Nations activity in promoting respect for human rights, may tend to develop a sense of direct relationship between the individual and the world community. Studies of the basic conceptions underlying the notion of human rights have also been stimulated by UNESCO, but these studies have indicated the great variety of philosophical standpoints and have made it clear that a unity of opinion even in the broadest aspects must be a matter of growth rather than of construction. The task, the importance of which is exceeded only by its difficulty, is one of developing a philosophy of world welfare which recognizes the value of great diversities, of continual change, and of opportunities for self-determination of individuals and groups, within a unity which springs from a common humanity and a single shrinking world.

There is no cause for excessive optimism on either the state of the world or of the United Nations. The successes of the United Nations have not kept pace with the deteriorating influence of great power rivalries, failures to make peace with the major enemy nations, and disagreements over atomic energy control. But in the widespread studies of the Secretariat, the economic and social commissions and the specialized agencies, data for building a world public opinion exists. Such an opinion has been stimulated by the General Assembly debates, and in lesser degree by the procedures of the Security Council and other organs in dealing with particular controversies and situations. There are consequently grounds for hope that a moral solidarity commensurate with the world's material unity may be achieved before disaster occurs.

6

COLLECTIVE SECURITY

IN THE LIGHT OF THE

KOREAN EXPERIENCE

The action of the United Nations in Korea has been interpreted on the one hand as the most significant and successful application of collective security in world history,[1] and, on the other hand, as evidence that collective security cannot work and must be abandoned.[2] These different interpretations may be accounted for partly by the differing attitudes toward collective security of those that made them, but partly by the different periods during the course of the Korean episode at which they were made. We are still in the midst of that episode, and consequently it would be premature to make a final appraisal of the efforts of the United Nations to frustrate the aggression of North Korean forces across the *de facto* boundary of the Korean Republic early in the morning of June 25, 1950.

In the writer's opinion it will never be possible to appraise the operation as either an unequivocal success or an unequivocal failure. In this the operation is like most other major political actions. The American Civil War, for example, was from the point of view of the North a policing operation and it was not wholly successful. It cost many lives, much destruction, and dissensions which continue in American politics nearly a century after the event. Nevertheless, it did carry out its purpose of preventing secession and preserving the Union, and it created conditions which permitted the American people to live for many years in unexampled prosperity and security.

From *Proceedings of the American Society of International Law*, 1951.

97

In Korea the duration of active fighting, the losses of life, and the destruction visited upon Korea already preclude denominating the operation an unequivocal success. The objective of collective security is to deter aggression, or if aggression occurs, to restore international peace and security at a minimum of human cost. That cost has already been large. Nevertheless, the operation has prevented aggression from being immediately successful and may already have deterred other contemplated aggressions. It may in the long run prove to have greatly strengthened collective security and the capacity of the United Nations to function in this field.

I will not, therefore, attempt to appraise the success or failure of the Korean affair as a whole. I propose rather to consider the lessons which may be learned from it for the future. As the United States incorporated lessons from the Civil War in constitutional amendments, government practices, and popular opinion, so the long-run influence of the Korean affair can best be appraised in the changes which it may initiate in the procedures and practices of the United Nations and in the opinions and policies of its members.

Some general changes in United Nations procedure have already been indicated by the Uniting for Peace resolution adopted by the General Assembly on November 3, 1950,[3] and other changes are to be expected. Doubtless of greater importance will be the impact which the Korean affair has upon public opinion in the world and especially within the principal nations, but of this it is still too early to speak with confidence. The course of that affair throws light on some of the conditions of opinion and national policy which are requisite if collective security is to operate effectively.

I propose to comment on ten commandments which I think flow from the world's experience with collective security since the establishment of the League of Nations, and particularly from the Korean experience. Six of these have to do with the legal and political organization and action of the United Nations, and four with the opinions of peoples and the policies of governments.[4]

Writers on collective security have generally emphasized that, if it is to work, there must be international organs and procedures (1) for rapidly acquiring and making available authentic information on the occurrence of aggression or on immediate threats thereof, (2) for rapidly and authoritatively deciding upon the occurrence of aggression and the measures to be taken, and (3) for mobilizing force adequate to stop aggression with a minimum of actual fighting.

Information

The first of these requirements was fortunately present when the Korean episode began. The United Nations Commission for Korea was at this time in Korea and was able to report to a special session of the Council on June 25 that "the present situation is . . . a threat to international peace." This report did not clearly indicate that North Korea was the aggressor, and the Yugoslav representative in the Security Council thought further information was desirable before action. Nevertheless, the Security Council was convinced by evidence from other sources and unanimously (Yugoslavia abstaining) "noted with grave concern the armed invasion of the Republic of Korea by armed forces from North Korea." On the following day reports from the United Nations Commission in Korea stated, "judging from actual progress of operations, the northern regime is carrying out well-planned, concerted, and full-scale invasion of South Korea," and "South Korean forces were deployed on wholly defensive basis in all sectors of the parallel" and "were taken completely by surprise." [5]

On subsequent events in Korea, including the intervention of Chinese forces in November, the United Nations was kept informed by its high command in Korea.[6]

The relative sufficiency of the information available at the outbreak of the Korean affair was fortuitous. Consequently, the Uniting for Peace resolution of the General Assembly provided for a Peace Observation Commission of fourteen members. The commission is authorized to maintain observers in disturbed areas and to serve as a continuing intelligence agency for the United Nations on collective security problems. This commission may greatly increase the probability that the political organs of the United Nations will in the future have the necessary information on which to base decisions concerning collective security.

Decision to Act

The Security Council on June 25, 1950, "determined that this [North Korean] action constituted a breach of the peace"; "called upon the authorities in North Korea to cease hostilities forthwith, and to withdraw their armed forces to the 38th parallel," and also "called upon all members to render every assistance to the United Nations in the execution of this resolution and to refrain from giving assistance to the North Korean authorities." [7] This decision was prompt and, in my opinion, adequate, although it has been attacked on the ground that the Soviet Union was absent from the meeting and that China was not properly represented.[8]

The opinion of most commentators and the previous United Nations practice indicate, however, that neither abstention nor absence of a permanent member of the Security Council constitutes a veto.[9] It is also clear that the decision of the Security Council to accept the representative of the Nationalist government to represent China was legally within its power,[10] even though the Communist government had at the time a claim to be considered the *de facto* government of China.[11]

The ability of the United Nations to act thus promptly was, however, due to the voluntary absence of the Soviet Union, a circumstance which might not recur. Incapacity of the Security Council to function after the return of the Soviet representative in August, 1950, emphasized the importance of searching for other procedures.

The Uniting for Peace resolution met the difficulty by providing for emergency sessions of the General Assembly in case aggression had occurred or was threatened and the Security Council was unable to function because of lack of unanimity among its permanent members. Such a meeting could be summoned within twenty-four hours on request of seven members of the Security Council or of a majority of the members of the United Nations. The General Assembly was authorized to make recommendations to members for "collective measures," including the use of armed force.

This resolution has been attacked on the legal ground that the General Assembly cannot make recommendations unless the Security Council has by a procedural vote eliminated the question from its agenda (Article 12 of the Charter) or has by a substantive vote requested the General Assembly to make a recommendation (Article 11, paragraph 2; Article 12) and that it cannot make recommendations on "questions on which action is necessary," in any case (Article 11, paragraph 2). The practice of the General Assembly and reasonable interpretation of its powers (Articles 10, 11, 14) in the light of the general purposes of the United Nations indicate, however, that it can make "recommendations," although not "decisions," on any question when the Security Council is not in fact "exercising the functions assigned to it" by the Charter (Article 12, paragraph 1) and that it is competent to determine that fact so far as its own actions are concerned.[12] These functions of the Security Council include the obligation to determine "the existence of any threat to the peace, breach of the peace, or act of aggression" (Article 39). The General Assembly might well hold that failure of the Security Council to discharge this obligation in a reasonable time justifies it in making recommendations. While it may not "take action by air, sea or land forces" as may the Security Council (Article 42), it can make recommendations for action to the Security, Economic and Social, or Trusteeship Councils; to the secretary-general; to regional arrangements; to specialized agencies, or to member or nonmember states (Articles 10; 11, paragraph 2; 14; 60; 66; 85; 98).[13] The Uniting for Peace resolution provides for a Collective Measures Committee to recommend to the General Assembly before September 1, 1951, effective measures for collective security action.

It was anticipated that these developments would enable the United Nations promptly to make the necessary finding of facts and to recommend suitable measures to maintain collective security; but considerable delay occurred after the United Nations command in Korea had reported on November 8 that units of the Chinese Communist forces had been in hostile contact with United Nations forces.[14] The issue raised by this new aggression was placed on the agenda of the General Assembly on December 4 after the Security Council had failed to pass a proposed resolution because of a Soviet veto. The General Assembly, however, was unable until February 1, 1951, to pass a resolution finding the Chinese Communist government to have engaged in aggression.[15] The motives influencing the action of the Chinese Communist government and the political expediency of seeking conciliation raised issues on which members of the United Nations differed. This episode, like earlier experiences of both the League of Nations and the United Nations, indicates that the determination of aggression can never be entirely automatic. The Assembly, however, in this instance proved more effective than did the Security Council.[16]

Police Forces

When the North Korean aggression occurred, the United States had forces of considerable size in Japan and was prepared to use them in support of the Security Council's "call" of June 25. There has subsequently been a discussion whether this resolution provided an adequate basis for action and whether the president of the United States was constitutionally competent to act. But on neither of these points does there seem to be serious ground for legal question. The use of the word "call" in this resolution imports an obligation for members to act within their capacities, and the president as commander in chief has authority to utilize the armed forces which Congress has provided in fulfillment of international obligations of the United States.[17]

The Security Council's resolution of June 27 "recommended" that members of the United Nations "furnish such assistance to the Republic of Korea as may be necessary to repel the armed attack and to restore international peace and security in the area." Sixteen nations have responded to this recommendation by contributing to the United Nations forces in Korea. Others have made offers which have not been accepted.[18]

Appreciation that similar favorable circumstances might not occur in the future and realization that the agreements contemplated by the Charter for placing forces at the disposal of the United Nations (Article 43) were not likely to be made because of Soviet intransigence, induced the Assembly to recommend in the Uniting for Peace resolution that members voluntarily earmark forces for United Nations service. Subsequent discussion in the Collective Measures Committee, established by the Uniting for Peace resolution, have added the suggestion of a permanently embodied "United Nations Legion" for this purpose.[19]

The extent to which these proposals will equip the United Nations with forces adequate to give preventive as well as remedial effectiveness to collective security measures remains to be seen. At least the Korean experience has initiated a movement which may prove of major importance.

While the Korean experience has created a consensus on certain juristic procedures and on military steps for making collective security more effective in the future, progress has been less satisfactory in regard to political steps. That experience suggests that United Nations organs (4) should make precise and authoritative declarations of policy concerning the scope and purpose of collective measures; (5) should control whatever military action is undertaken within the intention of such declarations; and (6) should conduct careful negotiations to prevent policing action from spreading into general war.

United Nations Policy

The initial policy of the United Nations in regard to Korea was clearly expressed in the Security Council's resolutions of June 25 and 27, 1950—to compel North Korean forces to withdraw behind the 38th parallel. The Security Council's resolution of July 31 added to this policy by providing for relief for Korean citizens. After this, the Security Council was unable to function on the Korean matter because of Soviet obstruction, but the matter continued to be discussed until finally removed from the agenda of the Security Council on January 31, 1951, to remove any technical doubt of the capacity of the General Assembly to deal with the matter. The Soviet representative concurred in this resolution because he considered that all of the action of the Security Council on the matter had been illegal.[20]

The General Assembly's policy in the matter has, however, been far from clear. It had before it a full report of its commission in Korea when its fifth session opened in September, 1950, and it did not hesitate to consider recommendations on the matter, although the Security Council was still seized of the problem. The General Assembly considered that the actual failure of the Security Council to function permitted it to make recommendations without violating the restrictions of Article 12 of the Charter.[21]

The June resolutions of the Security Council having been substantially achieved by October when the North Korean forces had been forced back of the 38th parallel, opinions differed upon the next step. Should the United Nations purpose of uniting all Korea, expressed by the General Assembly long before the June aggressions occurred, be carried out by military means or should conciliation be attempted to end hostilities and to prevent Communist China from intervening?

The first of these policies seems to have been tacitly accepted by the General Assembly on October 7, 1950, by a vote of 47 to 5, with 7 abstentions. The resolution referred to Assembly resolutions of 1947, 1948, and 1949, with the "essential objective of establishing a unified, independent, and democratic government of Korea," and recommended that "all appropriate steps be taken to ensure conditions of stability throughout Korea." Restoration of peace, withdrawal of troops, elections, and economic rehabilitation were contemplated, and a commission of seven states "for the Unification and Rehabilitation of Korea" was authorized to proceed to that country, superseding the United Nations Commission for Korea.[22]

On this basis, the United Nations High Command in Korea extended operations into North Korea. This resulted in large-scale Communist Chinese intervention and important reverses for the United Nations. Nevertheless, on December 1 the General Assembly provided an administrative agency to implement the policy of reconstruction in Korea.[23]

On December 14, the General Assembly felt "that immediate steps should be taken to prevent the conflict in Korea spreading to other areas and to put an end to the fighting in Korea itself, and that further steps should then be taken for a peaceful settlement of existing issues in accordance with the purposes and principles of the United Nations"; consequently it authorized the president of the Assembly to appoint a three-man "cease-fire" committee. This committee, supported by the voluntary twelve-power Arab-Asian group of nations, initiated negotiations with the Chinese Communist government, without much success.[24] On January 13, however, a resolution was approved by the Political Committee of the General Assembly reaffirming the policy of a unified, independent, democratic Korea, and proposing a "cease-fire," interim arrangements, and negotiations by a body including the United States, the United Kingdom, the Soviet Union, and the Chinese Communist government, to deal with political issues, including the status of Formosa and representation of China in the United Nations.[25] The Chinese Communist government's response to this resolution was variously interpreted as willingness to continue discussions or as outright rejection. The United States, although it had supported the resolution, took the latter view and urged a resolution declaring that the Chinese Communist government was engaged in aggression in Korea and affirming the determination of the United Nations to continue its action in Korea to meet the aggression. This resolution noted that "the Security Council, because of the lack of unanimity of the permanent members, had failed to exercise its primary responsibility for the maintenance of international peace and security with regard to the Chinese Communist intervention in Korea." It was approved by the General Assembly on February 1, 1951, after rejection of Arab-Asian proposals looking toward further efforts at conciliation. The vote was 44 to 7, with 9 abstentions. Only three of the Arab-Asian states voted for the resolution. The resolution, however, included provisions affirming the policy of bringing about a cessation of hostilities and achieving United Nations objectives in Korea by peaceful means.[26]

After passage of this resolution, hostilities continued, with increasing demand by the United Nations High Command in Korea to extend air operations into the "privileged sanctuary" of Chinese territory.[27]

United Nations Control

The divergencies of opinion in the General Assembly were reflected in the Assembly's resolutions, which looked, on the one hand, toward vigorous enforcement of the policy of an independent, united, democratic Korea and suppression of all aggression, and, on the other, toward convincing the Communist government of China that no aggression against it was intended, and offering to conciliate with that government by negotiating on major political issues, such as Formosa and Chinese representation in the United Nations. This duality of objectives would not have been objectionable, in fact would have been desirable, had a political committee of the General Assembly been able to interpret policy as the situation developed for the benefit of the High Command in Korea. The lack of such a liaison, however, left the United Nations High Command a considerable discretion on political as well as military decisions.[28]

The United Nations had not itself appointed a commander-in-chief of its forces, but the Security Council, by a resolution of July 7, 1950, had requested the United States to designate a commander and to provide it with reports of operations. It also authorized the use of the United Nations flag concurrently with those of the participating nations. General MacArthur, appointed to this position by the president of the United States, and long accustomed to making political decisions in connection with his administration as Supreme Commander for the Allied Powers in Japan, was not a man likely to subordinate his opinions to the nuances of policy as indicated by debate in the General Assembly, or even as indicated by the opinions and instructions of the president, the secretary of state, and the joint chiefs of staff.[29]

It seems likely that if the United Nations had had more direct relationship with, and more effective control of, its commander in the field, collective security would have worked better. The Charter contemplated such control through the Military Staff Committee "responsible under the Security Council for the strategic direction of any armed forces placed at the disposal of the Security Council," and also for the working out of "questions relating to the command of such forces" (Article 47, paragraph 3). That committee, however, could not function in the circumstances because of the presence on it of the Soviet chief of staff. It became clear, as it should have been at San Francisco, that an effective Military Staff Committee would have to be appointed with reference to the particular operations in order to exclude representatives of states participating in aggression, or favorable to the aggressors. The Collective Measures Committee will undoubtedly consider the need for a procedure for establishing such a committee whenever the system of Assembly control, contemplated by the Uniting for Peace resolution, is in operation.[30]

United Nations Diplomacy

The United Nations sought to arrange a "cease-fire," accompanied by offers of political negotiation, particularly after intervention by the Chinese Communists in November, 1950, and all of its resolutions, as noted, looked in the direction both of military enforcement and political conciliation. If a more astute policy had been followed before entry of the Chinese forces, the result might have been more satisfactory. Collective security will not work if every policing operation initiates a world war—the danger that it may do so has, in fact, been the main criticism of collective security.[31] Effective negotiation, with the object of localizing the operation and preventing the aggressor from gaining allies, is essential.[32]

Collective security is not world government in the sense of central authority able to declare and enforce law in all emergencies. Until world opinion is more unified than it is likely to be for a long time, collective security must rely upon a balance of power which maintains such general stability that a localization of policing actions is possible. The United Nations must be able to contribute to maintaining such an equilibrium of power by effective political action parallel with its legal and policing action to suppress aggression. Collective security must, in other words, be thought of as a stage in the evolution of international relations halfway between unorganized diplomacy, seeking to maintain the balance of power, and world government, enforcing a general rule of law upon individuals as well as governments, throughout the world community.[33]

If the United Nations is to function in this way, it should have at its disposal a political committee sufficiently small to be operable and able to begin functioning at the same time as the policing operation or even before. The Charter, of course, anticipated that the Security Council itself would serve this purpose and Chapter VI provides procedures. It would appear that under circumstances when the Security Council cannot function, such a committee should be appointed by the Assembly from members selected with reference to the particular operation.[34]

The General Assembly, it is true, had at its disposal the Commission for Korea, which gave valuable information on the outbreak of hostilities, and in the October resolution it appointed a seven-power commission, followed in the December 1 resolution by an administrative agency; but these were concerned only with the unification and rehabilitation of Korea. The three-person "cease-fire" commission was not established until December after the intervention of the Chinese Communists. During the earlier stages of the operation, there was no United Nations body in touch with the Chinese Communist government instructed to ascertain the actual state of its anxieties, the actual division of its opinions, the nature of its intentions, and the inducements which might be requisite to prevent its intervention. It is possible that for these purposes an individual conciliator, found to be effective in the Palestine dispute, would be preferable to a committee.

In addition to the United Nations agencies and procedures necessary to make collective security work, certain conditions of opinion and policy among the peoples and governments of the world are no less essential. These include (7) general belief in the possibility of peaceful coexistence among states of diverse culture, ideology, and government; (8) general acceptance of some common standards of value and goals of effort; (9) general acceptance by the leading governments of the policy of collective security; and (10) manifestation of a public opinion among the peoples of the principal states in support of that policy. These conditions are by no means established today.[35]

Coexistence

It is doubtful whether the general public of either the Soviet Union or the United States believes that the two systems of Soviet Communism and American democracy can continue to exist together for an indefinite future. Each appears to believe that the other is bent upon aggression and conquest. There is evidence of Soviet expectation, based upon Marxist theory, that eventually the Communist system will triumph in the world. There is also evidence that the Soviet government is prepared to contribute to the realization of that expectation by the use of armed force or the stimulation of its satellites to use such force when such action is not accompanied by too much risk. There is further evidence, again based upon Marxist theory, that the Communist states believe that the leading capitalist states will eventually succumb to internal contradictions and revolutions, and that, in the last throes of their dissolution, they will seek to destroy Communist states by external aggression. No one can question that there have been utterances on the democratic side of the "Iron Curtain" which, when magnified, may tend to convince Communist leaders both in Moscow and Peiping that they are about to be the victims of military aggression.

It should be realized, however, that the time and the manner of realization of the expectations by each of these systems that the rival system is to disappear are important. If neither the Soviet countries nor the democracies anticipate the triumph of their system for centuries, coexistence of the two systems may be rationally believed in for all purposes of practical politics, which ordinarily deal with a time span of less than a decade, and seldom more than a generation. Furthermore, if each expects its system to triumph by peaceful adoption or spontaneous revolution, the continuance of coexistence depends on the efficiency of each system within its sphere, rather than upon the balance of power. Finally, even if each system is willing to employ force to exterminate the other, a balance of power, mutual fears of the retaliatory capacity of weapons possessed by the other, and the operations of collective security may maintain peaceful coexistence for a long time. But whatever the theory, it does not seem likely that either system will in fact be exorcised in any foreseeable future. Consequently, peaceful adjustment to coexistence seems to be more rational than belligerent resentment against conditions which are deplored but cannot be mended without risk of worse ills.[36]

People may, in time, achieve a degree of sophistication which will recognize that the coexistence of different competing systems contributes to human progress more than would a uniform world based upon one system.

Universal Standards

A world-wide opinion which accepts coexistence may in time tolerate that condition, and from such toleration, appreciation of some common values may develop. Only on the discovery of such values and the development of coöperation to achieve them can an atmosphere prevail in which collective security can be relied upon. It is not to be anticipated that all peoples will hold all values in common. Variety and competition are to be expected and are desirable, but collective security cannot work unless at least some values, for example, that stability is preferable to instability, are generally accepted.

It is the effort of the United Nations, through the Economic and Social Council, the Human Rights Commission, the International Law Commission, and the specialized agencies, to develop common interpretations of the values stated in the Charter and other instruments which have been formally accepted by most of the states, and to coöperate in efforts to realize those common values.

The sparseness of information crossing the Iron Curtain and the refusal of the Soviet government and its satellites to participate in many of the specialized agencies or other coöperative activities in the United Nations hamper the growth of common values. Amelioration of this situation may occur in time. Efforts to bridge the gap by radio and other information programs too rapidly may, however, stimulate reactions and increase, rather than diminish, the barriers to free communication among the peoples of the world.[37] It is probable that the fate of collective security rests in the long run upon the growth of toleration, mutual understanding, and the appreciation of some values common to all in a world of much diversity.

National Policy in Reference to the United Nations

The president and the secretary of state of the United States have frequently stated that national security is to be gained under present conditions primarily through collective action organized by the United Nations. Such a policy implies a willingness to be influenced by discussion in the United Nations, to give due weight to the views of others, and to accept decisions and recommendations resulting from established procedures, even though, in some instances, they do not conform to the position taken by the American representative. Such a policy is the reverse of one which treats the United Nations as an instrument of national policy. The latter policy is tempting, especially to powerful states, but unless the temptation is resisted, it will destroy the United Nations and the system of collective security. Moderation is a virtue less likely to be found in powerful governments than in individuals, because governments are influenced by the public opinion, which they build or which they must follow, to regard the policy supported by that opinion as an absolute value.

In democracies like the United States, in which public opinion springs from many sources other than government policy, the problem is one of exceptional difficulty. The government cannot ignore public opinion in such a democracy and continue to govern. On the other hand, public opinion is likely to be inadequately informed on the conditions of the world and on the requirements of a policy which will promote the interests of national security. Consequently, observance of public opinion in foreign policy may lead to national disaster. Governments in a democracy, therefore, are faced by the extraordinary difficulty of continually reconciling the requirements of foreign policy disclosed by the cables and by international consultations with the demands of public opinion influenced by party politics and by the natural proclivity of the public to view the interests of foreign governments with suspicion and of their own government without perspective.[38]

National Opinions

The basic condition for the success of collective security is, therefore, the development of national public opinions based upon considerations wider than the nation. If the peoples believe sufficiently that national security depends today on world stability, and that collective security is the best means for assuring that stability, the basic condition for its success will have been established. Such a condition, however, involves a degree both of understanding and of responsibility unusual in the masses of the voting population and unlikely to be achieved unless general education and current information about international affairs are considerably improved.

The representative of a democratic government cannot pursue a policy of collective security within the United Nations unless the people who vote understand the requirements of that policy, particularly that prompt action with adequate force must follow upon findings by international agencies. Protracted legislative debate upon the expediency of fulfilling collective security obligations in a particular emergency will provide a green light to the aggressor and will destroy both the preventive and remedial effect of collective security. For this reason, collective security implies broad executive authority to fulfill treaty obligations, especially those involving military commitments. A democracy, it is true, implies legislative control of the budget and hence of the size of the military establishment available for use, but it does not imply inadequate executive authority to use the forces that the legislature has provided in the fulfillment of collective security obligations.

There is undoubtedly a problem of gearing constitutional divisions of power into international obligations, but in the United States the problem is one of politics rather than of law. The American Constitution makes treaties the supreme law of the land, and the capacity of the president, as commander-in-chief, to fulfill military obligations is amply supported by both practice and judicial precedent. Whether the president should in fact seek the approval of Congress for large-scale troop movements so far as time will permit is a problem not of law but of political expediency.[39]

The representatives of a democracy will also be unable to pursue a policy of collective security if the public, however understanding it may be of the issues involved, lacks a sense of responsibility to discharge the obligations of treaties and to achieve the value of world stability. If the public is more interested in party advantage or in expanding national power than in national security, world stability, and the integrity of treaty obligations, the government will find great difficulty in pursuing a policy of collective security. The hampering influence of disuniting attacks from irresponsible senators, from organs of partisan opinion, and from overloquacious generals in the field upon the pursuit of a policy of collective security by the United States was evident during the years 1950 and 1951. This experience illustrates the extraordinary difficulty of conducting foreign policy under conditions of democracy in times of international tension short of war.[40]

The United Nations operation in Korea has suffered not only from continued intransigence of the Soviet government and its satellites, but also from imperfect understanding by the American people of the requirements of collective security and from a general irresponsibility of the public under the influence of party politics and emotional instability. It is clear that if collective security is to succeed, the United Nations must be able to rely not only upon a general public opinion throughout the world which places a high value upon the United Nations and the success of its collective security operations, but also upon a public opinion in the principal nations ready to support the decisions made by United Nations organs.

I believe that collective security can work, and that the Korean experience has much to teach on each of the ten points I have referred to. The United Nations must be assured sufficient information, must be able to make rapid decisions, and must have sufficient forces to implement them. It must formulate its policies clearly, control its agents, and localize policing operations by careful diplomacy. Peoples must believe in the coexistence of diverse systems and in some universal standards. National policies must support the United Nations and national publics must support such policies.

Institutions grow by experience, by action, and by adaptation of custom and opinion to that experience and action. If the people of the United States and other countries wish it, the Korean experience can be a milestone in the progress of the United Nations toward a stabilization of international relations which would permit an extension of the rule of law throughout the world.

PART III

POLITICS

AND INTERNATIONAL

STABILITY

7

POLITICAL SCIENCE

AND WORLD

STABILIZATION

Few persons who look at the world thoughtfully are complacent. It is difficult to believe that the balance of power will become more stable. Quite the contrary! A degree of bipolarity in world politics has been reached which compels each of the opposing groups to bend its efforts to bring the remaining neutrals into its orbit and to augment its power. If the war which each regards as a possibility should come, each wants to be sure that it will not be the loser. The race in atomic weapons and armaments of all kinds is on and experience suggests, as in the rivalries between sections before the American Civil War and the rivalries between alliances before World War I, that such a race will eventuate in war.

There is no balancer in a bipolar world, nor are there uncommitted powers which may cast their lot on one side or the other in a crisis. The process of nucleation about the two poles makes prediction of the power potential of each more and more feasible. It becomes increasingly clear to one side that time is with it and to the other that time is against it. Under such circumstances each expects war and it can be anticipated that the side which becomes convinced that time is against it will start the war. Fortunately there are still many unknown variables in the present situation. No precise calculation is yet possible, though it may be in the course of a few years. However, if war comes, there are few

From *American Political Science Review*, XLIV (March, 1950). *Presidential address delivered at the annual meeting of the American Political Science Association, December, 1949, in Washington, D.C.*

who doubt that atomic weapons would be used and that the human race would face disaster.

But if few people expect a stable balance of power, the number who anticipate effective world government is even less. There is not, nor can there be, an external enemy against which the world as a whole can organize itself in defense. The differences of culture are so great that a sense of solidarity throughout the world's population is slow in developing. Traditional insistence upon national sovereignty and traditional loyalty to national governments resist modification even though reason suggests that common defense against the disaster of war is expedient. While inventions in the fields of communication and transport, and interdependence in commerce and security make for one world, the actual sentiments of peoples have been moving toward more exclusive loyalty to their nations, more insistence that their governments exercise totalitarian control over law, defense, economy, and even opinion. Materially the world community steadily becomes more integrated, but morally each nation gains in solidarity and the split in the world community becomes wider. Under these conditions, people await with a blind fatalism the approach of atomic war. Disaster seems as inevitable as in a Greek tragedy. Has the science of politics anything to offer in this situation?

The Meaning of Politics

Politics may be defined as the art and practice of achieving group ends against the opposition of other groups. It implies that a practitioner of the art has identified himself with one state, one nation, one party, one government, or one group of some kind and is seeking to achieve the ends of that group against the opposition of other groups. Conflict is its essence. People engaged in politics are engaged in a battle, if not of bullets then of ballots, if not of armies then of rhetoric, if not of strategy then of persuasion. There have always been people who dislike conflict in any form. Their vision of the perfect human society is a City of God in which there is perfect harmony, or a communist society in which there are no classes or groups and where all differences are co-ordinated. There are others who do not regard politics as an evil, but who look upon conflict and competition as conditions of progress and as means for realizing the better life. To liberals, a continuous competition of ideas in a free market place of discussion is a better society than one in which the dead hand of unanimity has eliminated freedom and personality.

Political scientists assume, not only that politics is always to be with us, but also that it is a positive value. It is usually recognized, however, that there should be limits to the methods used. Discussion, most would say, is better than assassination. Parties are better than concentration camps. Vituperation in the General Assembly of the United Nations is better than war. Politics, therefore, should not only seek to gain the ends of one party; it should seek to keep the methods which it uses from degenerating. War, insurrection, assassination, terrorism, though frequent methods of politics, are also evidence of the failure of politics. Politics implies that men struggle to achieve their values, but they also struggle to prevent methods from sinking beneath the dignity of man. In the latter struggle, men engage in politics as members of the universal society of humanity faced by the opposition of any lesser group which attempts to justify barbarous means by ends which it considers noble.

The Meaning of Science

Science is the process of systematizing observation and thought, and of formulating propositions the truth of which is tested by their capacity to predict and to control. Science is primarily contemplative, while politics is manipulative. Science is motivated by curiosity rather than by utility. It progresses when it ignores values, as Bacon suggested when he said that final causes are barren. This is true of pure science. Applied science, however, assumes certain values and seeks formulae to control events toward their achievement, thus contributing to the arts.

Political science as a pure science, therefore, should seek to devise formulae to predict how political conflicts are likely to turn out. What new political conflicts are likely to develop? What groups are likely to become important? What methods are likely to be used? What goals are likely to be striven for? In short, political science should seek to devise formulae to predict those aspects of group behavior centering on tension, struggle, and conflict.

As an applied science, political science may assume the values of a particular group and seek formulae useful in achieving those values. Most of political science has been of this type. It has asked for example: What are the ends of the United States internally and externally? What type of organization, what methods of administration, what principles of law, what legislation, what foreign policy will contribute to achieve those ends? As an applied science, however, political science may also assume values above the parties in the political struggle. Values of the most general type, such as human personality, general welfare, civilization, human progress may be assumed and formulae sought for keeping the political struggle from utilizing methods which would frustrate these higher values. There are always men who, whether their group be state, church, or business, become so wedded in the heat of politics to their ends that they conceive them as justifying any means. There are always others who, however committed they are to particular group ends, believe that there are limits and bounds to the means which can properly be employed. Such an appreciation is certainly one of the signs of civilization. Machiavelli thought of applied political science in the first sense. He advised the prince how to build the power of his group and through the use of that power to achieve his ends. Erasmus, writing at the same time, thought of applied political science in the second sense: How can the struggles of politics be kept from getting too violent, too oppressive, too monopolistic, too anarchic? What arrangement will assure that politics operates with reasonable respect for human personality, for civilization, for justice, for welfare—all values which most men, upon reflection, will recognize?

Neither in its pure nor in its applied aspect has political science become so exact a science as physics or even biology. We cannot ignore the circumstances which hamper such development. The methods of science imply, first, exhaustive analysis of a situation or problem so that all its elements may be described as constants or measured as variables, or perhaps treated as parameters which, though actually varying, can be taken as constants over periods of time and over areas of space. Second, scientific method implies the search for relations among those constants and variables which are persistent and as independent as possible of particular times and places. So far as relations are independent of time, they can be anticipated in the future and thus make prediction possible. Finally, science implies continuous testing and self correction. No scientific formulation is absolute. Science does not envisage the world as a body of immutable laws, but as congeries of regularities and irregularities which may appear increasingly regular as the process of scientific formulation continues. The scientist seeks to make his formula as general as possible, but he anticipates that every formula will in time yield to new observations.

As James B. Conant has remarked, the test of a good scientific theory is the stimulus it gives for new investigation which will in time produce a better theory. While science seeks generalizations, independent of time and space, it recognizes that all generalizations are in fact dated and located. The Newtonian law of gravitation was the best that could be said in seventeenth-century England. Much better can be said on the subject today, and if science continues, we can expect still better in the future. The mind that demands absolute and eternal truth is not adapted to science. Science has no place for doctrinaires. While eighteenth-century rationalism was associated with contemporary developments of science, there can be no doubt that science has considered concrete observations as more real than any generalizations. Its philosophy is nominalism and relativism.

Science and Politics

In this aspect science resembles politics. Both are pragmatic and relativistic. Absolutists like Hitler and Stalin seek to eliminate politics by subordinating all parties to one, and to eliminate science by subordinating all investigators to the party line. Both science and politics assume the virtue of free competition of ideas and policies in the market place of discussion. They accept the concept of free speech enunciated by Mr. Justice Holmes.

But while acknowledging this resemblance between science and politics one must be aware of the difficulties of making scientific generalizations about political behavior. Political situations and problems are so complex that they cannot be exhaustively analyzed. They depend upon information rather than upon energy. New information from distant or remote places, from ancient history, or from the other side of the world may at any moment inject itself into a political situation in a way which could not be anticipated. As the means of communication, as the recording of history, and as the advance of science itself proceed, the complexity of political situations becomes greater and the possibility of exhaustive analysis less. Any formulation of constants and variables in a political situation is therefore necessarily incomplete. Unknown or hitherto nonexistent factors are likely to be influential and to frustrate the best documented expectations. Even the known conditions in any society are so complicated that it is usually wisest to confine particular formulations of political science to limited areas and periods within which it is reasonable to assume that the general conditions of opinion, of attitude, and of culture will not change. These conditions are the parameters of most generalizations in political science, making such generalizations imperfectly transferable from one country to another or from one civilization to another.

A particular difficulty arises from the advance of science itself. Planets and atoms are not influenced in their behavior by the generalizations of Newton or Einstein, but human beings are influenced in their behavior by the predictions of political science. The continuous stream of new political knowledge affects the behavior of the society which is the subject matter of that knowledge. Consequently generalizations made in political science may make or break themselves in accordance with the influence they exert upon the groups and persons whose behavior they seek to predict or control. As impartial analysts, political scientists must, therefore, include as a variable in their equations this "feed back" of the developing science itself upon the behavior which the science generalizes.

As citizens, political scientists must take cognizance of the influence which their generalizations will have upon the values to which they are committed. This is true even of physical scientists. The atomic scientists have appreciated that as citizens they should hesitate to place dangerous weapons in the hands of immature politicians. The problem is, however, even more serious in political science. Valid instruction on how man may be manipulated to achieve political ends may aid tyrants to destroy human dignity and freedom.

Closely related to this consideration is the fact that controlled experiments, and even certain types of investigation, are inhibited by the moral and democratic principle that man is an end, and should not be made a means to any end, even the end of scientific advance. The West was properly shocked at the disclosures at Nuremberg of the extent to which Nazi medical scientists had used human beings as guinea pigs. Communist social scientists are utilizing human guinea pigs on an even larger scale. The entire Communist state may be regarded as a huge human experiment to test methods by which men can be induced to conform to a plan imposed upon them.

These considerations suggest that political science and political practice must, as maintained by Mannheim, go hand in hand. Provisional conclusions of political science have to be tested by political practice, but in free and democratic societies, the only practices which are permissible are those which all the available evidence indicates will make toward the good society. In such a society practices can only be accepted which are supported mainly by consent and which require coercion only in rare cases. Consequently commitment to values and application of scientific generalizations must proceed together. The objectivity of the natural sciences which means that the scientist, as such, dissociates himself from human values, is impossible in political science. The political scientist cannot experiment to see whether the methods which, according to scientific prediction, will destroy a society with his values or produce a society with different values, will really do so. He can only experiment in maintaining the values in which he believes, and he cannot experiment at all until he has persuaded the people who will be involved that these values are sound and that his prescriptions for maintaining them are reliable.

I have perhaps expanded too much on the nature of politics and science. I justify myself by the observation that both terms are controversial. One finds persons who assume that politics can be neither wise nor efficient unless the politician is guided by absolute values. There are likewise persons who associate science with a view of the universe as an absolute system of unchanging laws. To such persons, what I have to say may sound like nonsense. But if political science means what I think it does, I believe it can contribute to improving the present unsatisfactory state of the world.

Responsibilities of Political Scientists

Doubtless there are many American citizens and many officials in the Department of State and the Department of Defense who look to political science for advice on how to make sure that our side will win. I have no doubt that political science can give such advice on matters of organization, administration, and strategy. But as citizens of this country and of the world, I think political scientists should consider whether and to what extent they should give that advice.

They are faced by the same problem which faced the atomic scientists in contributing the atom bomb to our war effort. There is only too much reason to anticipate that concerted and effective efforts to assure that the United States would be in a position to win if a war should break out will encourage equally concerted efforts on the part of the advisers of the Soviet Union to make sure that the Soviet Union will win. The consequence is likely to be a war in which both will lose. I do not mean by this to dissuade political scientists from a reasonable interest in national defense. I certainly do not want the United States to lose if a war should occur. The question is, however, whether as political scientists we should not place prime emphasis upon means whereby the political struggle can be moderated and developed in such a way that neither side will lose. Victory by the United States after an atomic war would certainly not be of any particular advantage either to us or to the world. If, therefore, we are considering whether political science can do something to improve the present unsatisfactory situation of the world, we must raise our sights somewhat higher than national victory. What can political science do to increase the probability that the political struggles going on in the world will utilize only methods consistent with human dignity and human progress?

I believe that more general education in political science would be one such contribution. It is my experience that such an education tends to develop a spirit of moderation and to qualify the natural human disposition toward doctrinairism and intolerance. It is hard to see how a political scientist can be either a Nazi or a Communist. The spirit of compromise and relativism inherent in political science, the appreciation of the relativity of means to ends and of ends to means can, I think, be a protection against absolutistic beliefs whether of the right or of the left, of the church or of the state.

Political science can also, I believe, contribute to an understanding of the nature of the world community. Political scientists understand the role of the external enemy—the "out-group"—in creating the solidarity of the state, and they consequently appreciate that the world community, necessarily lacking such an "out-group," must differ from lesser political communities.

Political scientists also understand the role of common culture, common religion, common history, common language, and common nationality in contributing to the solidarity of the state. They realize that the world community, with its tremendous variety on all of these points, must be different from the national state. Recalling the history of crusades and aggressions seeking to establish a universal religion, a universal culture, or a universal ideology, they anticipate that this variety will continue for a long time. They therefore tend to conceive the problem of a world society as adjustment of the diverse rather than conversion of all to uniformity.

Conversant with the history of political constitutions, political scientists appreciate that political machinery which works is always a compromise between effectiveness and acceptability. Rationally perfect utopias that would alter the traditional practices of people and step upon innumerable vested interests are not likely to win sufficient acceptance to be given effect except through methods of mass coercion. The problem is not only to win consent of the leaders, but also to win consent of the masses who are to be governed. That consent is affected by numerous factors other than the logical perfection of a proposed constitution.

The political scientist therefore who remembers his Burke, as well as his Rousseau, is likely to envisage the improvement of the world's constitution, not as action to realize a plan, but as a process of development. Action to realize a plan assumes, in proportion as the plan is detailed and comprehensive, that politics has been eliminated within the community. A plan is a prescription for realizing a goal. Those engaged in implementing it assume that both the ends and means which it prescribes have ceased to be controversial. Their problem is, therefore, administration, not politics. Politics exists only when ends or means are controversial. Consequently, politics implies that all plans are temporary, limited, and flexible, that new plans continually emerge, have their day, and succumb to other plans as new parties come into power. Action to realize a plan implies the persistence of one party at least for the period of time for which the plan is made. Such action involves compulsion and denial of freedom in proportion as the community is large and heterogeneous, and as the plan is comprehensive in the aspects of life it covers and precise in respect to goals, methods, and timing. Political scientists, therefore, are likely to be skeptical of planning in proportion as the plan is long in duration, wide in area, comprehensive in coverage, and precise in means, ends, and timing. Consequently they think of the world order not as a plan but as a developing process, and they are willing to take one step at a time anticipating that if one step in the right direction is taken it will be easier to win sufficient consent for the next step. The cold war has arisen because inconsistent plans for the world as a whole have emerged from different capitals. The effort to plan for a group as lacking in solidarity and integration as the world community results in the elaboration by many parties of many universal but inconsistent plans. Efforts to realize them all means global war.

Political science may contribute not only to the development of attitudes of moderation but also to the encouragement of ingenuity in proposing practical compromises. Perhaps the most important of such compromises is that between the policies which are suggested for the realization of our national values and those which are appropriate to realize the values of a stable and peaceful world order. More concretely the problem can be posed: Shall we utilize the United Nations for the purpose of forwarding American policies? Or shall we make the development and effectiveness of the United Nations the first consideration of American policy? I do not quarrel with the effort to realize democratic values and human rights through the United Nations. Such values are the essence, not only of American democracy, but also of the United Nations. But if the United Nations is utilized as a means for augmenting our prestige and power above that of the Soviet Union, we may be weakening the United Nations itself.

Debates in the United Nations provide many opportunities for discovering common values which are shared by all its members. There are values which are shared by the people of the United States and the people of the Soviet Union and, wherever the political process discloses them, political invention may devise coöperative efforts for achieving them. The barriers to communication across the Iron Curtain, the failure of direct contact among peoples at each side of it, the doubt on each side of the reliability of information from the other side, the refusal of the Soviet Union to join UNESCO and other of the specialized agencies present obstacles to understanding and coöperation. These obstacles make it all the more important to utilize the United Nations to the utmost. Political conflict is always less dangerous when the parties engaged in it are also engaged in political coöperation. The political scientist can contribute by continually recalling that the national policies of the United States are relative to the world policies of the United Nations, that these policies may at times appear to be conflicting, and that compromises must be made, if a world is to develop that is at the same time sufficiently varied to be progressive and sufficiently stable to be peaceful.

Levels of Political Investigation

Political scientists should be particularly adept at drawing attention to the different levels at which political problems may be examined. As between the United States and the Soviet Union, the bipolar rivalry seems implacable. If one fixes his gaze at this level, the impression of fateful tragedy is difficult to avoid. But both of these great groups are composed of many subgroups, themselves composed of men and women. If no solution can be found at the international level, perhaps it would be well to focus attention at the sociological or the psychological level. May not the developing hardness, integration, solidarity, and implacability of these great structures be reduced? May not the United States and the Soviet Union simultaneously soften and pacify through changes in the relations of the subgroups or in the minds of the men and women who compose them? May not both Americans and Russians become more world citizens and less nationalists? The difficulty of the problem lies in the necessity that it be solved simultaneously in both countries. A softening United States would be smashed by a hardening Soviet Union, but if both softened simultaneously, communication between the populations would be easier, understanding would be facilitated, coöperation would increase, tensions would diminish, and war would be less likely.

The hardness of these huge structures rests on the exclusiveness and intensity of the loyalties of the masses of their populations, and these loyalties are exaggerated by widespread expectations of inevitable victory or of inevitable war. In exclusive and intense loyalties there is danger for, as the psychoanalysts tell us, such loyalties can develop only if ambivalent feelings are resolved by displacement of hate upon an "out-group." An individual with many divergent loyalties may often live in quandary and sometimes in unhappiness. If some of the divergent loyalties are intense he may even become frustrated and either aggressive or neurotic. We must conclude that in a good society loyalties are neither exclusive nor excessively intense. A group composed of men and women each with many loyalties, which are so moderate that conflicts among them can be compromised in each individual mind, is less dangerous and more stable than a group, each member of which maintains an exclusive loyalty to his group, building its power, hardening its policy, converting it from a rational association into an irrational mob eager for the blood of the "out-group" selected as a scapegoat.

It was this insight, as well as appreciation of the civilizing influence of the contact of different ideas and cultures, that induced Lord Acton, in the heyday of nationalism and long before the time of Freud, to regard "the theory of nationality as a retrograde step in history." "States," he said, "in which no mixture of races has occurred are imperfect; and those in which its effects have disappeared are decrepit. A state which is incompetent to satisfy different races condemns itself; a state which labors to neutralize, to absorb, or to expel them, destroys its own vitality; a state which does not include them is destitute of the chief basis of self government."

In our complicated world each human mind must continually synthesize the claims of family, nation, church, business, cultural associations, local community, and world society. That is the meaning and price of liberty and peace in a diverse but shrinking world. A world with millions of small conflicts in the minds of individuals and in the discussions of small groups is likely to be more peaceful and prosperous than a world divided into two opposing groups each of which commands the exclusive, intense, and blind obedience of its population.

The Picture of a Free and Peaceful World

The political scientist can contribute to attitudes of moderation and formulae of conciliation. Can he also contribute a picture, however vague, of the complex of values and relationships which might ameliorate the tensions of diverse and conflicting nations and alliances in the world? If men must be world citizens as well as national citizens, what picture of the world can command some of their loyalties, however diverse their cultures, economies, and governments?

A picture will not command interest unless some relationship among, and some organization of, its parts is evident to the observer. So the picture of a peaceful and progressive world must include much world communication linking its parts and some world organization realizing its purposes. There cannot be one world unless each people can and does talk to every other, and unless there is some system, however decentralized, by which decisions, authoritative for all, can be made on matters vital to all. All political scientists recognize the roles of communication and organization in the design of a good society. Do they also recognize that some uniformity of tone and some unity of idea are as necessary in a good society as they are in a good picture? In a peaceful and progressive world some behavior patterns must be standardized and some objectives must attract the coöperation of all.

Doubtless there is a universal human nature, deriving not only from biological drives which man shares with lower animals, and from common experiences which all have encountered in infancy, but also from certain necessary relations of the individual to society which all adults and all cultures must take into account. To assure a maximum satisfaction of these demands of human nature is the object of constitutional bills of rights and the Universal Declaration of Human Rights promulgated in 1948 by the General Assembly of the United Nations. The abstract terms of the latter instrument must be applied to concrete situations and its meaning must be widely understood if it is to assist men everywhere spontaneously to understand one another.

If, however, emphasis is laid only upon what men have in common the variety of the world will be lost. There must also be an understanding, a tolerance, and even an appreciation by each people of the distinctive aspects of the cultures of others. Each must recognize, not only that all cultures, however much they differ, spring from a common human nature, but also that all, by their very diversity, have something to contribute to the world. Such an appreciation is difficult to achieve because people tend to be parochial minded. Each culture tends to judge others by its own values. But variety must enter into the picture of the world which every man carries in his mind, if the actual world is to be peaceful and desirable.

There must be more than understanding, tolerance, and appreciation for other cultures. There must be some loyalty to the whole. Men must synthesize national loyalty with world loyalty and this is hardly possible unless the world, in addition to symbolizing the common elements in mankind, is symbolized by something as concrete as the United Nations. But such a symbol cannot long inspire loyalty unless it represents active and effective coöperation for specific ends which all people regard as valuable. It cannot be anticipated that the diverse people of the world will agree upon ultimate ends. Such ends are the final synthesis of an individual's experience. In proportion as groups become large and people diverse, differences among individuals in regard to ultimate ends are to be anticipated. Coöperation for limited and temporary objectives which all deem of value is, however, possible and such coöperation can ameliorate the political struggles which develop around differences in regard to values of higher level.

Men must picture the world as a varied population with symbolic unity, the parts of which are related by systems of communication and organization, and the members of which are standardized in some patterns of behavior and are coöperating to realize some common objectives. But above all they must see that the picture is moving. New inventions, technologies, and ideas are continually changing it. The processes of communication, organization, standardization, and coöperation are changing at different rates. Tension and perhaps war occur when development of one part, one system, or one process gets too far ahead or too far behind the others. Continuous measurement of rates of change and intelligent interventions to accelerate here, or retard there, are required, if the dynamic equilibrium is to be stable, and if the human drama is to be satisfying to the participant-observers.

A community varied, interesting, and deserving of affection; a society active and effective in achieving particular policies, vague in ultimate ideals and values; a dynamic equilibrium resulting from complex relationships of coöperation and opposition; a process by which the inertia of history, and the aspirations and inventions of genius continually interact to create the future—this may be the best meaning to attribute to "one-world."

In the task of understanding, developing, and regulating such a dynamic, complex, stable, and peaceful world, political science needs the coöperation of the other social disciplines—psychology, sociology, economics, geography, anthropology, law. All of these have been coming together in a new discipline of international relations, but the science of politics is at the heart of this discipline. That science rests upon the assumption that conflict and coöperation are both of the essence of human society and are necessary for stability and progress. Its investigations contribute to the practice of the art of politics at all levels—local, national, and world. Its students tend to manifest the virtues of compromise, tolerance, balance, and sanity, which our world, distracted by the peddlers of nostrums and utopias, sorely needs.

8

SOME REFLECTIONS

ON WAR AND PEACE

War has been a subject of human interest as far back as any records can be found. A vast literature exists treating the subject from the technical and strategic point of view designed to instruct on how to win wars. An equally extensive literature exists from the legal point of view attempting to inform statesmen, generals, and the common man on the circumstances in which, and the methods by which, wars may be justly begun, and how they may be properly conducted. There is an even larger literature of history and belles-lettres recounting the motives, causes, and circumstances of wars in the past, or stimulating the reader's emotions and sentiments to favor or oppose a particular war, or war in general. More recently social scientists have sought to utilize all these materials in formulating propositions useful for predicting or controlling war. I will discuss some of the approaches that have been made to this end.

Prediction and Control

We may first distinguish formulations aimed at predicting war from those aimed at controlling war. The distinction, however, is less easy to maintain than is that between pure and applied science in the physical realm. This is true because the conscious efforts men make to control war play a large role in estimating its probability, and men's knowledge of the causes of war plays a large role in the effectiveness of efforts to control it. In other words, the applied science and the pure science are so interdependent that they can hardly be distinguished. This is true

From *American Journal of Psychiatry*, CVII (September, 1950).

of the social sciences generally, but particularly of the field of international relations where opinions and stereotypes, though often "erroneous," constitute the "reality" of the subject. Failure to act wisely to preserve peace is an important cause of war and widespread understanding of the causes of war is an important condition of peace.[1]

This interrelationship of the processes of prediction and control has become closer with the shrinking of the world through modern inventions. Among the thousands of primitive tribes that once inhabited the world, the occurrence of war was a function of human drives for dominance, sex, revenge, and territory; of the mores of each particular tribe giving social form and sanction to these drives; of the frequencies of contact among tribes; and of the frequency of occurrences that called for an activation of tribal mores by revenge or war. Among the most primitive tribes war had the character of a ritualistic or formal response to appropriate stimuli rather than of a rational action to acquire power or economic resources. Under these conditions the occurrence of war was like the collision of molecules in a gaseous mixture. No molecule could do much to control the frequency or intensity of such collisions though a mathematically inclined molecule by a proper use of statistical averages might be able to predict the frequency of collisions of different intensity under given conditions.[2]

With the advance of civilization, human groups have become larger, their behavior has become less rigidly controlled by custom, their relations with other groups have become more extensive, and their action has been in larger measure governed by rational adaptation of means for the accomplishment of conscious group ends. Since the geographical discoveries at the end of the fifteenth century, all parts of the world and all civilizations have been brought into continuous contact with one another. The advances of science and technology have increased contacts of all kinds by developing means of rapid global communication and transport, by increasing population and knowledge and by making all peoples vulnerable to military, economic, and propaganda attacks. These conditions have resulted in an embryonic world community of which all peoples are members in the sense of economic and political interdependence although they may be only vaguely aware of it. Under these conditions, war resembles rebellion in a state. The frequency or intensity of its occurrence in the future cannot be calculated from statistics of the past because the number of instances under like conditions are too few, but it might be controlled by better political and social organization, better education and legislation, better administration and adjudication. All the social sciences can contribute to such improvements.[3]

Change in the character of war has been proceeding with accelerating speed. The inventions of the airplane, the radio, and the atomic bomb in our generation have made the twentieth century in this respect more different from the nineteenth than the nineteenth was from the second. Our job today is less to calculate the probability in a given number of years of a given state being at war, of war occurring between a given pair of states, or of general war occurring, than to create conditions that will prevent war from starting or to devise procedures that will nip it in the bud. If war gets underway it is, under modern conditions, very likely to become world-wide and to threaten the existence of civilization.

Power Politics

In the nineteenth century wars arose because of disturbances of the balance of power. The system of power politics changed from a purely European to a world-wide system with the development of the power position of the United States and of Japan at the end of the century. A balance of power may be described as a situation in which any state that attempts aggression will be confronted by a spontaneous coalition so powerful as to make the success of its enterprise extremely doubtful. Such spontaneous coalitions tend to develop because each state wishes to continue to exist and appreciates that if it permits a neighbor to become overpowerful, its security will be prejudiced. Consequently, it tends to join others to suppress any one of the states in the system that is threatening to become overpowerful.[4]

The balance of power functioned in the nineteenth century because Great Britain, with a relatively invulnerable position, a dominant navy, a developing economy, a liberal economic policy, and no imperial ambitions in continental Europe, was able to act as balancer. Britain tolerated the wars of Italian and German unification in the mid-nineteenth century and the minor wars of nationalism in the Low Countries and the Balkans. It participated only in the Crimean War to check Russian expansion. The really serious wars of the century were the civil wars in the United States and China in the mid-century and the Lopez War in the Plata area in which Brazil, Argentina, and Uruguay joined to check the expansive disposition of the Paraguayan dictator, practically exterminating the population of Paraguay in the process.[5]

Reference to these wars suggests that the balance of power was not so perfect as to convince nationalist movements, whether aimed at the integration of nations or the disintegration of empires, that they could not be successful. There was, in fact, a general opinion among the great powers that such wars were sometimes desirable. In the century between Waterloo (1815) and the Marne (1914), however, there were no efforts by any of the great powers to follow the paths of Charles V, Louis XIV, and Napoleon seeking to realize the medieval idea of universal empire.

The relative stability of the nineteenth century was shattered by the weakening of the British position; by changes in military technology and the world's economy; by the entry into the system of non-European powers unfamiliar with the nature of power politics; by the increased control of economies by governments reducing the ameliorating influence of free international trade; by the rise of democracy increasing the political influence of industry, agriculture, and labor, with economic and social demands, inconsiderate of the requirements of international politics; and especially by the shrinking of the world, making it less possible to localize wars and more dangerous to enter into them. There was no experienced balancer. The pressure for change was greater. The capacity of government to guide foreign policy by balance of power considerations was reduced. Policies of aggression by some were assisted by policies of neutrality by others.[6]

The wars of the twentieth century can be interpreted as transitional, from a system of world order based on the individual policies of sovereign states thinking of their own security and prosperity in preserving the power equilibrium, to a system of world order organizing collective efforts to maintain an equilibrium, recognized as a common interest of all. It has been discovered, however, that organized efforts, even though institutionalized as in the League of Nations and the United Nations, will not be reliable unless such a consciousness of world citizenship exists that governments can retain domestic support even if they appear to ignore immediate national interests when necessary to carry out international obligations of collective security. So long as people think as nationalists, exclusively loyal to their states whose sovereignty they cherish, governments, especially governments dependent upon popular support, cannot be relied upon to observe obligations of collective security. A world society resting upon a world public opinion does not yet exist in which reliable institutions of world government can be established.

The result of this disharmony in the needs seen by statesmen and the opinions entertained by peoples has been two world wars of unprecedented destructiveness, and threats of a third that would be fought with atomic weapons. The overwhelming power of the United States and the Soviet Union makes the present power equilibrium extraordinarily unstable. It rests, as Churchill has said, upon mutual fears springing from the realization of the suicidal character of atomic war.

It seems unlikely that the nineteenth century system of power equilibrium can be restored. There is no potential balancer and there are too few great powers to coalesce effectively against aggression by either of the greatest powers. The problem is to prevent war between Russia and the United States in the short run while efforts proceed to create sufficient consciousness of world citizenship among the people of all nations to make possible world institutions able to prevent war and administer justice. The long-run problem is hampered by the isolationist policy pursued by the Soviet Union. It seeks to prevent its people from communicating or trading with the noncommunist world and from coöperating in the specialized agencies of the United Nations. Consequently the conditions of technology and communication that would naturally hasten the development of a world society are prevented from functioning between the two halves of the world. The sparse contact of Soviet representatives with others in the United Nations tends, by the mutual vituperation that it engenders, rather to divide than to unite the world.[7]

The problem is difficult, but not hopeless. Understanding of the nature of *international tension,* of *intergroup negotiation,* of *social organization,* and of *political education* may help toward solving both the short-run and the long-run problems. Here social science may aid statesmanship.

Tensions

International tensions develop from rivalry between groups so independent that they can rely only on self-help for survival. These tensions increase with the progress of moral and material preparations by each for defense. In this progress, war seems more and more inevitable to each. The process of irritation, retaliation, and counter-retaliation that has augmented the cold war between Russia and the United States since the Yalta Conference of 1945 illustrates the point.

There are, however, the more fundamental problems: Why should international rivalries exist at all? Why have they arisen between one pair of states, rather than another?

The latter question can usually be answered by reference to history, geography, and politics. Two states may be rivals because there is a historic feud between them that has been periodically alimented by war and new injuries, renewing the spirit of revenge and of mutual hatred. Each generation accepts the feud as natural and inevitable through the versions of national history taught in the schools. Such feuds existed between France and England for centuries, between France and Germany, between England and Ireland, between England and America, between England and Russia, between China and Japan. Feuds seldom exist except between states that are so situated geographically that they can easily injure one another by invasion or blockade. They also seldom exist unless the general political situation permits each the luxury of feuding without rendering itself vulnerable to some other state or without endangering the loss of a needed ally. England dropped its feuds with France, America, and Russia, and they reciprocated when each began to fear Germany more. France and Germany seem likely to drop their feud if each fears the Soviet Union more. Japan and China might have become friends in the same way had not China become communist. England dropped its feud against Ireland when it saw the need of American friendship, but Ireland continues to feud because it feels protected by America.[8]

The situation of the power equilibrium as a whole also exerts an important influence upon the location of rivalries. With the shrinking of the world, this influence becomes more important than that of particular grievances of the past. Systems of power politics tend to polarize about the two most powerful states in the system and that tendency becomes more manifest as the general tension level rises and as the world shrinks through inventions. The two polar states become the principal rivals. Others arrange themselves around these poles in varying degrees of union, protection, alliance, and friendship, fading out into a buffer zone of states that hope to remain neutral. The shrinking of the world tends to diminish the area of this zone.

The question remains, why should rivalries between states exist at all? The answer is to be found less in the external grievances of the states than in their internal composition, conflicts, structure, and policies and in the structure of the supercommunity of which they are all members.

Grievances arise because a state, by accident, negligence, or design, at some time acted in a way that another regards as injurious or dangerous. The closer states are in relation to one another; the more they are financially and commercially interdependent; the more nationals of one are in the territory of another; the more internal overcrowding is believed to require an extension of markets or of sources of raw materials; the more fears of attack are believed to require external bases, strategic areas, strategic materials, or alliances; the more likely are grievances to arise. States in close proximity, and nearly all states in the present shrunken and interdependent world are very close to all others, will almost certainly have some grievances against others. It is the continuous business of diplomacy and the United Nations to deal with these grievances. Most of them are dealt with peacefully, but sometimes diplomacy and international organization fail. Any grievance may baffle devices of pacific settlement and become serious if it occurs between states that are already rivals. In such circumstances, it may become a test of strength and neither will yield one jot or tittle of its claim to the other. We are, however, inquiring, why do rivalries arise in the first place? If they didn't exist, it would seem that grievances could be dealt with peacefully. Grievances, therefore, are not the cause of rivalries but rather rivalries cause grievances to endanger the peace.

Rivalries seem to arise in part from the internal condition of each state requiring it to find an external enemy to support its internal solidarity. This need originates in psychological processes. Tensions start in the individual human mind [9] because of frustrations and ambivalences consequent upon the early training of the child for social life. Discharge upon parents of the aggressive impulses that arise is suppressed. External scapegoats become the target of hatred and aggression. Furthermore, repressed antisocial feelings may be projected upon others. The more widely the social group expands, the more suppressed aggression exists among its members, the more necessary is an "out-group" to serve as a scapegoat if the solidarity of the "in-group" is to be preserved. This need may be less in a free society, where much internal competition, conflict, and rivalry are possible for the discharge of aggressions, than in an authoritarian society that insists on severe discipline and rigid internal order.[10]

This theory is supported by the fact that, among primitive societies, war seems to serve the primary function of manifesting the unity of the in-group and providing a scapegoat for the discharge of antisocial feelings and actions which, if discharged internally, would disintegrate the group. In many of the small islands of the Pacific, the sparse population is divided between two hostile groups, each of which constitutes an out-group for the other.[11]

This psychological cause of rivalry, tension, and war might be reduced by systems of education, especially preschool education, that would occasion less ambivalence and frustration than is usually the case today, by systems of economy that would distribute production more equitably, and by systems of society and politics that would give greater assurance to all of opportunities for social advance and recognition. Especially important would be social conditions permitting more of the existing aggressions to be discharged harmlessly in party politics, business competition, or sports, or to be discharged symbolically in artistic, literary, or other cultural activity.[12] While the Marxist theory that class rivalries are the sole cause of external aggression is grossly oversimplified, undoubtedly social, economic, and political conditions within the state and tensions in the minds of individuals that arise because of these conditions are an important source of international rivalry, tension, and aggression. If these conditions are not ameliorated among all important states, some will continue to feel the need of an external scapegoat to preserve internal solidarity. To expect universal reform of social conditions is, however, utopian. In a shrinking world where population presses on resources and the speed of social change assures much maladjustment within all societies, it is not to be expected that all serious internal tensions can be avoided. Social reform and education can, however, do much to reduce international rivalries.

This leads us to a second cause of rivalries—the necessary oppositions within a system of sovereign states. So long as states are looked upon as independent of one another and consequently obliged to engage in the maneuvers of power politics if they are to continue to exist, each state will oppose whichever neighbor it believes most likely to attack it. That state will become the scapegoat for displacement of hatreds and projection of aggressions; thus rivalry will develop. Only as states become united in alliances or other supergroups do they cease to be potential enemies and, where contacts are close and power equal, present rivals.

The reasons that have through history led to the subordination of related clans to tribes, of tribes to states, and of states to federations, so that larger areas of coöperation and of authoritative adjudication of disputes have been established, continue to operate, until today the subordination of all states to a world society organized in a world government is urged. Such a society, however, can have no out-group to organize against and consequently it differs from all lesser federations. The process of union, therefore, has tended to stop with the world divided into two groups, each an out-group to the other as in the Pacific islands referred to. Such a bipolar system is the least stable and most dangerous type of power equilibrium. Among large civilizations of the past—Egypt, Mesopotamia, China, India, Rome, Christendom, Islam—such equilibria have usually been ended by a universal conquest or by unsuccessful attempts at such conquest ending in anarchy and disintegration of the civilization. The process in these historic civilizations, however, is not precisely parallel to that which the world faces today because, large and isolated as they were, those civilizations always had barbarians or rivals on their periphery. Though Arnold Toynbee refers to the Roman Empire as a "universal state" it was actually organized against barbarians across the Rhine and the Danube and against rival empires in the Orient. A really universal society must permit the discharge of tensions in the individual human mind and in lesser and larger groups of all kinds within that society itself. It must, therefore, be very flexible and very complex. It must have systems of education that develop some common values and a tolerance of much variety. It must attempt to identify as targets of aggression, not human out-groups, but abstract ideas such as war, disease, social discrimination, and political oppression. The adversary of a universal society, as of universal religions, must be an abstract devil, not a tangible enemy. The difficulty of effecting such a substitution is indicated by the tendency of world government movements to become North Atlantic federation movements with the very tangible Soviet Union as adversary. Peace in our age, however, requires a genuine world society to absorb within itself the tensions that individual human minds and all lesser groups must discharge somewhere.[13]

Negotiations

The development of such a society takes time, and the vast populations under Soviet rule are subjected to conditions of discipline, oppression, and terror in which tension is probably very great. Amelioration of this condition is, however, hampered by the Iron Curtain and the continuous fear for their positions and lives of the Soviet elite inducing them to direct the animosities of the vast monolithic society toward the non-communist world, which is made a universal scapegoat. Sentiments of enmity are reciprocated. As the arms race proceeds, the lines become hardened and the rivalry increases.

What action might the United States take to modify this situation? War, sabotage, preparedness, containment, economic development, political declaration, communication of information, and negotiation are possibilities. Changes may take place within the Soviet Union through internal causes, such as difficulties of succession, revolution, or changes of policy. But the methods referred to seem to constitute the principal possibilities of action by which the United States or other Western countries might influence the situation. None of them, however, is very promising.

The initiation of preventive or aggressive war would probably be suicidal and in any case impossible for democracies. Efforts at assassination or sabotage within the Soviet Union would probably be unsuccessful, might precipitate war, and would be even more against the principles of democracy than war. Policies of preparedness and containment have been pursued but they have led to an arms race and an augmentation of tensions, and they might lead to war. They are

necessary as defensive precautions but they should not develop programs of a size or character to encourage Soviet belief that the United
States intends to attack. Economic development becomes a means of
preparedness or containment if the Soviet states are excluded and it
requires negotiation if they are to participate. Declarations of pacific
intention are certain to be construed as propaganda in an atmosphere
of rivalry. The transmission of informational, educational, and even
propaganda materials is permitted by the Soviet Union in limited
quantities and under strict Soviet censorship. Such efforts without the
consent of the Soviet Union, as is possible by radio or distribution of
printed material, are looked upon by the Soviet government as sabotage
and have led to Herculean efforts at radio jamming, to counterblasts
of propaganda, to closer drawing of the Iron Curtain, and to worsen-
ing relations. It is possible that more skillful efforts to transmit information could bring better results even if initiated by single nations. It
is even more possible that the United Nations might be able to influence the Russian people directly if it had the resources. But it seems
doubtful that such efforts, unless they are consented to by the Soviet
government itself, can do much to relieve tensions except in a very long
time. Thus the main hope of improving relations lies in negotiation.

Negotiation among rivals whose relations are, in general, hostile can
succeed only if there is (1) careful and confidential exploration to determine areas in which there is a genuine common interest or a genuine
willingness to bargain, (2) scrupulous limitation of detailed discussion
to these areas, (3) realization that agreements will not be reliable unless
self-executing in the sense that they are expected to last only as long
as there is a mutual interest in observance. It is assumed that the parties
differ in most of their views of the future. Consequently agreements
are not sanctioned by a general solidarity of interest, by commitment
to common principles, or by a sense of good faith. Finally there must
be (4) realization that agreements will not be reliable unless they have
been genuinely understood and accepted by the highest authorities of
each state. Negotiations that assume general opposition between the
parties have a resemblance to cartels, armistices, and other agreements
made between active belligerents. The rules of war that govern the making of such agreements insist on precision in observance of formalities,
expression of terms, and duration of agreement, and termination on
notice if duration was not specified or without notice if violated by the
other party.[14]

Negotiation even between friendly states differs from legislation
within a state or federation, the members of which are assumed to be
committed to general coöperation. Negotiation requires secrecy because

the publics behind the negotiators, being suspicious of one another, would manifest opinions and insist upon positions preventing concessions and compromises essential to agreement. Legislation, on the other hand, since it is designed to give formal force to the prevailing public opinion, requires continual publicity. If broad international commitments for coöperation are made sincerely, as was hoped to be true of those undertaken in the United Nations Charter, the publics of nations tend to be merged in a superpublic and negotiation may tend toward legislation. It is clear, however, that no such general and sincere commitment for coöperation actually exists in the relations of the Soviet and the West.

Because of the needs of secrecy and of limiting the agenda, negotiation requires limitation of the parties to those whose power position makes their consent indispensable. To democracies, however, committed to democratic principles, nationally and internationally in the United Nations, this requirement presents difficulties. Secret explorations or negotiations between the United States and the Soviet Union would probably be viewed with alarm by other countries that think their interests may be sacrificed for peace. Such negotiations might be regarded as an abandonment by the United States of the progress made toward development of a world public opinion and world democracy in international relations through the United Nations.

Because of the rigidity of the Soviet system, negotiation with subordinates bound by rigorous instruction is usually fruitless, but negotiation at the top level cannot be initiated without public knowledge, which would mean that failure to achieve results might increase suspicions and tensions and make the situation worse than it was before.

In view of these considerations, the prospects of successful negotiation are not good. Discussions either at top level or at lower levels may, however, be a means of exchanging information. Mutual knowledge of the intentions of each of the countries with reference to the other may, in itself, reduce tensions, provided those intentions are not of a belligerent character, as is probably the case. Observers have generally concluded that neither the United States nor the Soviet Union has any intention of making war on the other. The danger arises because of excessive tensions inducing miscalculation or irrational action, or because of mistaken belief by one that the other is about to strike, inducing it to act in order to gain the advantage of the initiative. Such misinformation is quite probable on the part of the democracies because of Soviet secretiveness and on the part of the Soviet government itself because of the tendency of the agents of a dictatorship to report what is agreeable to their superiors, rather than what is the fact.[15] Each side discounts statements given in public discussion as, for example, in the organs of the United Nations, because it interprets them as propaganda. It is possible that private discussions might convey accurate information which would be believed. This appears to have been the case in the discussions at Teheran and Yalta.[16]

Organization

Tensions may be reduced through unilateral action by the United States, especially in economic development and in suitable preparations with an eye to defense and avoidance of provocation, and through discussions and negotiations between the United States and the Soviet Union, especially to improve mutual information, to discover areas of mutual interest, and to achieve reliable agreements within those areas. These appear to be practicable steps toward creating conditions of peace. Steps looking to a more distant future lie in the orbit of international organization and political education. Clearly if such efforts extend only to the Western powers, they will be looked upon by the Soviet Union as designed to strengthen the power position of those powers and will augment the arms race. To lay foundations for permanent peace, they must be universal in scope.

The United Nations Charter establishes an international organization formally accepted by both the Soviet Union and the United States. This organization has possibilities of development, but is not now able, because of the veto, to deal authoritatively with disputes or to prevent aggression so far as Soviet-American relations are concerned. The United Nations can deal and has dealt with a number of other disputes and situations effectively, such as those on the Balkan-Greek frontier, in Indonesia, and in Palestine. It is still struggling with the Kashmir and Korean problems.

The United Nations also provides for coöperation among its members on social and economic problems and for the development and maintenance of respect for fundamental human rights and for the development of attitudes and opinions throughout the world suitable for peace. The Economic and Social Council, the Human Rights Commission, UNESCO, and the numerous other commissions and technical agencies have produced many reports and passed many resolutions. They have influenced national action by many states. They have also drafted, and gained some adhesions to, certain agreements in these fields. This work, however, is hampered by the refusal of the Soviet Union to join the technical agencies and the uncoöperative attitude it has taken toward most of the work of the Economic and Social Council and the commissions.

A great deal of attention has been given to the scientific study of international organization—the machinery and procedures by which it can function most effectively, the conditions of opinion that make its functioning possible, and the processes of reciprocal action and reaction between machinery and opinion by which it can be strengthened. Historical studies of federations, confederations, and leagues suggest that efforts to strengthen the machinery in advance of the development of conditions and opinions that will assure general consent may lead to secession and war. Failure to develop the machinery when economic conditions and public opinion are ripe for it may also lead to war. The problem is to develop organization and opinion step by step in relation to one another. The histories of Swiss and American confederations, of the Holy Roman Empire, the Germanic Confederation, and the German Empire; of the Holy Alliance, the League of Nations, and the United Nations are illustrative and deserve detailed study and analysis, which cannot, however, be attempted here.[17]

Education

People are not by nature world citizens. Art must make them so if a stable, just, and prosperous world order is to develop in the shrinking world. The people of the world, therefore, need to be politically educated to understand the nature of the world, to tolerate its varied cultures, governments, and economies, to accept the principles and procedures essential for the functioning of international institutions capable of settling disputes and preventing violence, and to subordinate loyalties to, and the immediate interests of, their nations to those principles and procedures. Such education, particularly as it refers to attitudes and loyalties, must begin at a very early age. At higher levels it involves extensive knowledge and understanding of the culture and history of the peoples of the world and comprehension of the values and institutions to which the peoples of the world must be committed, if a world point of view is to be effective. The methods of political education have been extensively studied, but they cannot be dealt with here.[18]

Sociologists analyze the development of societies by distinguishing the processes of extension and intensification of communication and exchange throughout the group, of the development of loyalty to the group as a whole, of the assimilation by the members of the group of some common values, and of the organization of the group so that it can act in certain matters as a unit. These four processes interact upon one another and this interaction contributes to education for citizenship in the group.[19]

In the world today, the process of political education for citizenship in the world as a whole is hampered by the Iron Curtain. The people at the two sides are being educated to citizenship in different worlds, one with its center in New York, and the other with its center in the Kremlin. If abundant communications from both centers were received by people everywhere, these conflicting ideas might be accommodated and perhaps in time assimilated. Loyalty to one world manifesting some of the characteristics of each of these two worlds might develop. Some common standards of value might be universally accepted and an organization of the human race able to achieve the purposes that nearly all states have formally accepted in the United Nations Charter might emerge. Such a development is being worked for continuously in the United Nations, but the process cannot be rapid. Until tensions have been sufficiently reduced to permit of more abundant transnational communication, relations between the United States and the Soviet Union will depend primarily upon intergovernmental discussions and negotiations proceeding on the assumption that the two worlds are in most points opposed. As areas of common interest are discovered, tensions may be reduced and the commitments to cooperate for comprehensive purposes, formally accepted in the United Nations Charter, may permit the reciprocal processes of international organization and political education to build firmer foundations of peace.

9

THE NATURE OF CONFLICT

War is a species of conflict; consequently, by understanding conflict we may learn about the probable characteristics of war under different conditions and the methods most suitable for regulating, preventing, and winning wars.[1]

In the legal sense, war has been considered a situation during which two or more political groups are equally entitled to settle conflicts by armed force. Its essence is the legal equality of the parties and the obligations of impartial neutrality by outsiders. In this sense, the Kellogg-Briand pact and the United Nations Charter have eliminated war. Procedures have been established to determine who is the aggressor if hostilities occur, and all states have bound themselves not to be neutral but to assist the victim of aggression and to give no aid to the aggressor.[2]

In the sociological sense, which is the sense of ordinary usage, war refers to conflicts among political groups carried on by armed forces of considerable magnitude. The street fight of two small boys, the forensic contention in a law court, the military suppression of mob violence in the state, the collision of two automobiles, and the combat of two stags are not war; but they are conflict. Perhaps an analysis of the broader concept will help better to understand the lesser.[3]

Conflict and Inconsistency

Conflict is sometimes used to refer to inconsistencies in the motions, sentiments, purposes, or claims of entities, and sometimes to the process of resolving these inconsistencies. Thus, if it is said that the values of the communist and democratic systems are in conflict, it may mean that it is impossible for a person rationally to believe in these two systems at the same time; or it may mean that some process of propaganda,

From *Western Political Quarterly,* IV (June, 1951).

education, synthesis, or war is going on for reconciling them or for superseding one by the other. The two meanings are not necessarily identical, because inconsistent systems of thought and action may co-exist in different places for long periods of time. However, as contacts increase and the world shrinks under the influence of new inventions, such inconsistencies tend to generate processes of reconciliation or super-session and thus to constitute conflict in the second sense of the term.

The word conflict is derived from the Latin word *confligere* meaning to strike together. Originally, it had a physical rather than moral con-notation, though the English word has both. In the physical sense of two or more different things moving to occupy the same space at the same time, the logical inconsistency and the process of solution are identical. For example, the logical inconsistency of two billiard balls being in the same place at the same time is resolved by the conflict which results in their rolling to different positions.[4]

In an analysis of conflict, as used in the sociological sense and in ac-cord with the etymology of the word, it seems best to limit its mean-ing to situations where there is an actual or potential process for solv-ing the inconsistency. Where there is no such process, conflict does not seem to be the proper word. If used to describe mere differences or inconsistencies in societies or value systems, it may induce the belief that peaceful coexistence is impossible. Where such differences have ex-isted violent conflict has sometimes been precipitated when none was necessary. An example may, perhaps, illustrate this terminological dis-tinction. Islam began a career of conquest in the seventh century with the thesis that it was the only true faith and was necessarily in conflict with all other religions. This was represented by the doctrine of the *Jihad,* or perpetual war of the "world of Islam" with the "world of war." According to Majid Khadduri,

> The world of war constituted all the states and communities outside the world of Islam. Its inhabitants were usually called infidels, or better termed, unbelievers. In theory the believers were always at war with the unbelievers.[5]

Belief in the *Jihad* induced continuous attacks by the Arabs upon the decadent Roman Empire and rising Christendom during the seventh and eighth centuries, and resulted in extensive Moslem conquests in the Near East, North Africa, and Spain. Christendom, however, re-acted militantly in the Crusades of the eleventh, twelfth, and thirteenth centuries, turning on Islam with the doctrine of papal sovereignty of the world. The Ottoman Turks then took the leadership of Islam, and during the fifteenth, sixteenth, and seventeenth centuries were almost continuously at war with Christian Europe, conquering Constantinople, the Balkans, and Hungary, as well as most of the Arab countries. Turkish power then waned, and eventually the Ottoman Empire broke up into national states, as did the Holy Roman Empire. Today Christian and Moslem states coexist and coöperate in the United Nations. Both the *Jihad* and the Crusades are things of the past. When, as a political measure, the Ottoman sultan, after entering World War I on the German side, proclaimed the *Jihad* on November 16, 1941, his action was repudiated by the Arab leader, Hussein Ibn Ali, of Mecca, who had entered the war on the Allied side.[6]

Similarly, the identification of religious differences with conflict led to a century and a half of war between Protestants and Catholics in the sixteenth and seventeenth centuries, ended by the Peace of Westphalia which recognized the sovereignty of territorial states and the authority of the temporal monarch to determine the religion of his people if he wished. Since then Protestant and Catholic states have found it possible to coexist peacefully.

These bits of history suggest the question whether the inconsistency of democracy and communism makes conflict between the Western and the Soviet states inescapable. May it not be possible for communist and democratic states to coexist, even in this technologically shrinking world, as do Moslem and Christian states, Protestant and Catholic states? The answer may depend on the policy pursued by the governments or other regulatory agencies, rather than on the ideologies themselves. In 1858 Lincoln thought that, "A house divided against itself cannot stand. A government cannot endure permanently half-slave and half-free." Three years later, however, in his first inaugural, he asserted that he had "no purpose, directly or indirectly, to interfere with the institution of slavery in the States where it exists. In your hands, my dissatisfied fellow citizens, and not in mine," he said, "is the momentous issue of civil war. The government will not assail you. You can have no conflict without being yourself the aggressor." Coexistence in the Union of diverse institutions of North and South then seemed to him possible. The Civil War occurred, and eventually emancipation was proclaimed. Some historians, however, think that emancipation could have been achieved peacefully if war had been avoided for ten years longer. They are not certain that "the inevitable conflict" really was inevitable.[7]

Historically, radical differences of religion, ideology, or institutions have tended to induce conflict. They do not, however, necessarily do so, nor does conflict if it occurs necessarily eliminate the differences. Consequently, it is unwise to identify inconsistencies of opinion with conflict. Coexistence of inconsistent opinions may, in fact, be an essential condition of human progress. It is through the contact and competition of differing opinions and methods, and the eventual synthesis of thesis and antithesis that history is created.

Conflict and Tension

It depends on the policies of governments whether inconsistencies of social ideologies develop into conflicts, but these policies are likely to be influenced by the amount of social tension which the inconsistencies have generated. Social tension has been defined as the condition which arises from inconsistencies among initiatives in the structure of the society.[8] Ideologies accepted by different groups within a society may be inconsistent without creating tension; but if initiatives or actions are taken by individuals or groups in accord with those inconsistent ideologies, and if these actions lead to contact, tension arises. The degree of intensity of tension tends to increase with decreases in the social distance between the groups and with increases in the amount of energy behind them. If the groups with inconsistent ideologies are in close contact, that is, if the society is closely integrated, the tension will be great. If the society is loose (as was, for example, the world society during the nineteenth century) such initiatives originating in different and widely separated nations may create little tension. It is also true that if the groups or nations within the society from which the inconsistent initiatives emerge are small and weak, tension will be less than if they are great and powerful.[9] In the present world of decreasing social distances, initiatives emerging from such different and inconsistent ideologies as democracy and communism, respectively supported by such great powers as the United States and the Soviet Union, can be expected to cause great tension.

Tension is more likely to develop into violent conflict if it is intense and if regulatory arrangements are ineffective.[10] The United Nations is a more effective regulatory arrangement than was the system of diplomacy of the nineteenth century, but tensions are so much greater today that serious conflict is more probable. Once conflict develops, the process by which anxiety and power accumulate in each of the conflicting groups tends to result in war.

The phenomena of inconsistency, tension, conflict, and war within a society may thus be considered distinct, but they constitute a series in which each succeeding term includes those that precede. In war, each inconsistent value system has integrated itself in order to maintain its position against the other; tensions have risen, the situation is recognized as conflict, and open violence is used or projected.[11] Relations of logical inconsistency in social ideas or institutions are likely to generate tension, which in turn leads to conflict and frequently to war.[12]

However, this progress is not inevitable. Social inconsistencies can coexist without tension, and tension can exist for a long time without conflict, just as conflict may be resolved without war. If regulatory procedures such as diplomacy, mediation, conciliation, consultation, arbitration, and adjudication are available and efficiently operated, then accommodation, adjustment, and settlement may be achieved at any point and the process stopped. If, however, tensions rise above a certain level, these procedures are likely to prove ineffective.

Conflict and Competition

Conflict, defined as opposition among social entities directed against one another, is distinguished from *competition* defined as opposition among social entities independently striving for something of which the supply is inadequate to satisfy all. Competitors may not be aware of one another, while the parties to a conflict are. *Rivalry,* halfway between, refers to opposition among social entities which recognize one another as competitors. Conflict, rivalry, and competition are all species of *opposition,* which has been defined as a process by which social entities function in the disservice of one another. Opposition is thus contrasted with *coöperation,* the process by which social entities function in the service of one another.[13]

These definitions are introduced because it is important to emphasize that competition between organisms is inevitable in a world of limited resources, but conflict is not; although conflict in some form—not necessarily violent—is very likely to occur, and is probably an essential and desirable element of human societies.

Many authors have argued for the inevitability of war from the premises of Darwinian evolution—the struggle for existence among organic species from which only the fittest survive. In the main, however, this struggle of nature is competition, not conflict. *Lethal* conflict among individuals or groups of animals *of the same species* is rare. Birds and some mammals monopolize nesting and feeding areas during the mating season and fight off intruders of the same species. Males of such polygamous species as seals, deer, and horses fight other males to maintain their harems. Social animals, such as monkeys and cattle, fight to win or maintain leadership of the group. The struggle for existence occurs not in such combats, but in the competition among herbivorous animals for limited grazing areas, and for the occupancy of areas free from carnivorous animals; and in the competition among carnivorous animals for the limited supply of herbivorous animals on which they prey. Those who fail in this competition starve to death or become victims, not of attack by their own, but by other species. The lethal aspect of the struggle for existence does not resemble human war, but rather the business of slaughtering animals for food, and the competition of individuals for jobs, markets, and materials. The essence of the struggle is the competition for the necessities of life that are insufficient to satisfy all.[14]

Among nations there is competition in developing resources, trades, skills, and a satisfactory way of life. The successful nations grow and prosper; the unsuccessful, decline. It is true that, because nations are geographically circumscribed and immovable, this competition may induce efforts to expand territory at the expense of others, and thus lead to conflict. This, however, is a product of civilization. Wars of territorial conquest and economic aggrandizement do not occur among animals of the same species or among the most primitive peoples. They are consequences of large-scale political and military organization and of legal relations defining property and territory. Even under conditions of civilization, however, it cannot be said that warlike conflict among nations is inevitable, although competition is.[15]

Conflict and Coöperation

Lethal conflict among individuals or groups of the same species, or war in a very general sense, is not a necessary factor of either animal or human life. Most psychologists seem to be in agreement on this.[16] However, opposition—both in the sense of conflict and of competition —is a necessary factor of human society no less important than coöperation. A society has been defined as a group manifesting sufficient coöperation internally and sufficient opposition externally to be recognizable as a unity.[17] This definition raises the question: Can there be a *world* society unless contact is made with societies in some other planet to which it can be opposed? It is perhaps premature to say there cannot be a society existing without external opposition and manifesting itself only by the coöperation of its members to achieve common ends. It would be difficult to discover such an isolated society among either primitive or civilized peoples; but, even in such an isolated society, there would be internal opposition because a society implies that its members have interests of their own as well as common interests, and in these individual interests they not only compete but also, on occasions, conflict.

Communism seeks, like the ant colony, completely to subordinate the individual to the society and thus to eliminate all oppositions within it. In a communist society—whether through heredity, education or central control—all divergent initiatives of individuals and subgroups have been destroyed and all are, in theory, in complete harmony. There is no historic illustration of such a society, and it is probably inconsistent with the psychological characteristics of man. Among colonial insects guided by instinct, it is perhaps possible; but among man, having taken the road of reason, which is a function of the individual human mind, such a complete subordination of the individual to the group is impossible.[18] Human societies exist by the coöperation of individuals and subgroups, and the existence of the latter implies that they have some initiative, some autonomy. They cannot exist unless each defends some sphere of freedom. Such a defense implies conflict. A society in which there was no internal conflict would be one in which no individual or subgroup could formulate its own purposes and act to achieve them. A society of that character would be an entity guided by a single purpose and a single method. In short, it would not be a society at all. It would not even be a machine, because in a machine gears and other parts are opposed to one another. It would rather be an undifferentiated mass moving toward a single goal—perhaps more like an inflamed mob than any other social manifestation.[19]

Democratic societies, in accepting human rights, freedom of association, and a multiplicity of political parties, have institutionalized opposition. They regard it as no less important than coöperation. In England, "His Majesty's Loyal Opposition" is an essential feature of parliamentary government, and its leader gets a salary from the Consolidated Fund. American party leaders recognize an opposition party as an essential, though sometimes unpleasant, feature of the Constitution.

Psychologists have suggested that the ability to consider conflicting alternatives of action at the same time distinguishes man from the animals. This mental conflict creates the possibility of choice, thus permitting man to escape the necessity of following a single course of action to which minds incapable of such internal conflict are bound.[20] The hesitancy of a man, suddenly faced by a wild bull and by the choice of fleeing to a fence, taking to a tree, or facing the animal and dodging may save his life, provided he chooses rapidly and adequately. In the field of politics, the democratic state, within which the opposition of parties continually suggests alternatives of policy, has possibilities of choice and progress denied to the one-party state. The same is true in the economic field. Competition among many firms offers the consumer choices that may be denied the citizen under a totally planned economy.

Too severe and enduring conflicts in the individual mind may create neuroses, and overintense conflicts can disrupt societies. Even democratic societies must keep their internal oppositions within bounds, or they will become anarchies. In general, they prohibit fraud and violence. The competition of business firms must be by fair methods, and the conflict of political parties must avoid violence. Although a society cannot exist without competition and conflict, and cannot progress without a good deal of both, it can exist without violence and war. However, even in the best regulated societies, eternal vigilance is the price of avoiding these disruptive manifestations of opposition.

Types of Conflict

As already noted, conflict can take place among different sorts of entities. *Physical conflict* by which two or more entities try to occupy the same space at the same time must be distinguished from *political conflict* by which a group tries to impose its policy on others. These two types of conflict can be distinguished from *ideological conflicts* in which systems of thought or of values struggle with each other, and from *legal conflicts* in which controversies over claims or demands are adjusted by mutually recognized procedures.[21]

War in the legal sense has been characterized by the union of all four types of conflict. It is manifested by the physical struggle of armies to occupy the same space, each seeking to annihilate, disarm, or capture the other; by the political struggle of nations to achieve policies against the resistance of others; by the ideological struggle of peoples to preserve or extend ways of life and value systems; and by the legal struggle of states to acquire titles, to vindicate claims, to prevent violence, or to punish offenses by recognized procedures of regulated violence.[22]

Is this identification of different sorts of conflict in a single procedure expedient? Might it not be wiser to deal with legal conflicts by adjudication; ideological conflicts by information, education, and persuasion; political conflicts by negotiation or appeal to international agencies, such as the United Nations Security Council or the General Assembly, leaving to armies only resistance to armed aggression? Such discrimination is the objective of the United Nations, as it was of the League of Nations before it, the Hague system before that, and of customary international law even earlier. Practice has indicated that such a segregation of the aspects of conflict is difficult to achieve, but the effort should nevertheless be made.[23]

Tendency of Conflict

It has been emphasized by Clausewitz that there is a tendency for conflict to become war, and for war to become total and absolute in proportion as the parties are equal in power and determination, and are unaffected by outside influences. This tendency has four aspects—the unification of policy, the garrison state, total war, and the bipolar world.

The legal claims of the state come to be conceived as inherent in the value system and way of life of the people. These claims come to be formulated as national policy, and armed forces are developed as the only certain means of achieving this policy. Policy in the legal, moral, political, and military field becomes integrated at the national level.

This integration of policy, and of military preparation to maintain it, tends to integrate the state. Public opinion and moral values, as well as economic life and the maintenance of law and order, are placed under central authority; institutions of deliberation, freedom in the formulation and expression of opinion and the exercise of individual rights are subordinated to the demands of national policy, of military preparation, and of national loyalty. The garrison or totalitarian state emerges in which the individual is in a large measure subordinated to the group.[24]

In such unification of the state, restraints on war tend to be abandoned. These restraints have existed because of the presence of religious, moral, aesthetic, economic, and legal opinions and interests that are independent of the government and have been influenced by similar opinions in outside countries. Once all elements of the state are united behind the national policy and the effort to achieve that policy by war, internal and external influences for moderation cannot penetrate the crust of the gigantic war machine in motion. War becomes unrestrained and total.[25]

Integration, however, does not stop with the nation, since alliances and coalitions are formed until the entire world is drawn in on one side or the other. Absolute war is fought in a bipolar world. There are no neutrals, and the forces of the world, concentrated at two strategic centers, lunge at each other in unrestrained fury, each demanding total victory and the annihilation or unconditional surrender of the enemy.[26]

This expansion of war is in fact but an aspect of the movement of conflict from the individual mind. The constitution of UNESCO declares that wars begin in the minds of men. The psychologists assert that conflict in the individual mind is a human trait. Instead of the simple sensory-motor circuit of animals, whereby a stimulus of the senses at once induces appropriate action developed in the instincts or the experience of the animal, the circuit is interrupted in man at the seat of consciousness in the brain. Here ideal alternatives of action are set against one another, their advantages considered, and eventually a decision is made and action proceeds on the chosen course. Sometimes, however, decision fails; and the indecision gives rise to ambivalence, especially when each of the conflicting alternatives is highly charged emotionally. Such conditions are characteristic of the child who loves his mother as the source of his material comforts and yet, at the same time, hates her because she disciplines him to teach him the requirements of social life. To escape this ambivalence the child displaces his hatred upon a scapegoat—perhaps the father, perhaps a neighbor's child; but the habit of displacement to solve apparently insoluble conflicts is established. As the child becomes an adult in a local group he tends to find a scapegoat outside the group so that all can be harmony within. So with consciousness of the nation, all citizens displace their hatreds and animosities upon an external enemy who conveniently serves as scapegoat. Similarly when coalitions are formed their maintenance depends in no small degree upon displacement of all sources of conflict among the allies upon the enemy. While the United States and Russia were desperately fighting the Axis, they could displace the hatreds causing differences among them on the common enemy.

The mechanism of displacement tends to enlarge all conflicts from the individual mind to the bipolar world, and the mechanism of projection tends to augment the vigor of these conflicts. Once group conflict develops, each group is stimulated by its anxieties about the other group to build its armaments and to prepare for strategic action. Its own preoccupation about the favorable conditions of attack is projected upon its antagonist. It sees every move of that antagonist as preparation for attack. This stimulates its own preparation. The enemy similarly projects his own aggressive dispositions, armaments mount, and eventually war emerges.

The tendency toward the expansion and intensification of war is further developed by the rational pursuit of balance-of-power politics. Each of two rivaling great nations seeks allies to maintain the balance, and smaller nations seek protection of one or other of the great. The number of uncommitted powers declines. Finally, all power in the world is gathered about one or the other pole. Once the world is bipolarized, each center of power anticipates war and begins to calculate the influence that time is having on its relative power position. There is a strong urge for the power against which time is running to start the fight. This may entail risk, but the risk may be greater if hostilities are postponed. Thus, psychological and political factors conspire to extend, enlarge, and integrate conflicts, and to precipitate war.[27]

Methods of Conflict

Conflict may be carried on by methods of coercion or persuasion. The former usually involves violence and has the character of physical conflict; the latter need not involve violence, though violence may be utilized as a method of persuasion, and is characteristic of political, ideological, and legal conflict.

In employing purely coercive or physical methods of conflict, each party may seek to destroy the other, to control him, or to occupy his territory. In war, the destruction or disorganization of the enemy's armed forces, communications, and sources of supply; the capture of his materiel and the imprisonment of the personnel of his forces; and the driving of the enemy from strategic points or from productive territory and the occupation of that territory are operations of this character, constituting what may be called the military front in war. These methods are also used by governments in conflict with criminals and by international organizations in operations of collective security.

Noncoercive or moral methods of conflict involve efforts by each party to isolate the other, to persuade him to change his policy, ideology, or claims, or to defeat him in accordance with the rules of the game. In war successful efforts to cut off the enemy's external trade and communications, to create an opinion opposed to him in other countries and governments, and to deprive him of allies, make for his isolation. Such efforts constitute the economic and diplomatic fronts in the war. Military methods may also contribute to such isolation—such as naval blockade and the destruction of the instruments of external trade and communication.

Persuasion may be conducted by propaganda utilizing symbols to influence the minds of the enemy's armed forces, his government, and his civilian population. In war, propaganda constitutes the psychological front. Persuasion is, of course, used in many types of conflict other than war, such as diplomatic conversations, political campaigns, and parliamentary debates.

In a certain sense, however, all methods of war, unless the total destruction of the enemy's population as well as his power is contemplated, are aimed to persuade the enemy's population and government. The object of war is the complete submission of the enemy. It is assumed that military methods aimed to destroy or control his armed forces and occupy his territories, economic measures designed to starve his population and reduce his resources, and diplomatic measures designed to destroy his hope of relief or support will, when sufficient, induce the enemy government and population to change their minds and submit to whatever terms are demanded.[28]

Defeat means formal abandonment of effort by the losing party to the conflict. It implies that all parties to the conflict have accepted certain rules and criteria by which victor and vanquished can be determined. In games such as chess, bridge, football, and tennis, defeat is thus conventionalized, although in some, such as football, the conventions may permit coercive methods resembling war, but with less violence. Chess is a highly conventionalized war in which available forces, strategies, and tactics are strictly regulated by the rules. War itself may have a conventional character. Rules of war may prohibit certain kinds of action, and custom may even decree that forces or fortified places ought to surrender in certain circumstances even though such action is not physically necessary. War among primitive peoples often has a highly conventional character not unlike a game; and in the wars of the *condottiere* in fifteenth-century Italy and the sieges of the eighteenth century, war was highly conventionalized in Europe and regulated so as to moderate losses. In most wars, the formalities of surrender instruments, armistices, and peace treaties register defeat and victory symbolically, usually after the application of military, economic, diplomatic, and psychological methods have persuaded one side that further resistance is hopeless. The degree of formality, regulation, and symbolic representation in conflicts varies greatly from games to total war. However, the extent to which war has been conventionalized at certain periods indicates possibilities of limitation and avoidance of the trend toward absolute war by means of rational considerations and suitable social organization.[29]

Under suitable conditions, war might be decided by highly intelligent generals without any bloodshed. Each would calculate the best utilization of materials and man power, the best strategy and maneuvers of armed forces both for himself and the enemy, each assuming—as in playing a game of chess—that the other would similarly calculate and would follow the plan most in his own interest. According to such calculations, victory for one side and defeat for the other might be certain, and the defeated would surrender without any hostilities. However, it is highly improbable that war will ever be so conventionalized that incalculable factors like courage, morale, faulty intelligence, accidents of weather, and new inventions can be eliminated. The party whose defeat seems certain by logical calculations may yet believe it can win because of these factors, and so will not surrender without a trial of strength unless indeed the disparity in strength is very great as in interventions by a great power in the territory of a very weak power. In the course of time, such disparity may be presented by the United Nations in its operations of collective security or international policing; but, as the Korean episode indicates, the United Nations cannot yet be certain of overwhelming power against an aggressor. Even national federations cannot always muster sufficient power to discourage rebellion, in which case their policing operations assume the character of war—as witness the American Civil War.

Consideration of the variety of methods by which conflict is conducted suggests that appraisal of national power or capacity to win wars cannot be based on any simple analysis. Capacity to win allies and persuade enemy and neutral opinion by propaganda is no less important than capacity to create a powerful war potential including the command of large armed forces. Capacity to invent and to produce, which depends upon a high development of science and technology, is no less important than capacity to plan the strategy of campaigns and tactics of battle. Perhaps most important in statecraft is the capacity to analyze conflicts, to distinguish the important from the unimportant aspects, to view the world as a whole, to appreciate the influence of time and opinion, and to synthesize this knowledge in order to forward the interests of the nation and of the world without resort to violent methods, which often destroy more than they create and which settle fewer conflicts than they initiate.

Solution of Conflicts

None of the methods by which conflict is carried on necessarily ends the conflict—unless, indeed, the conflict is completely conventionalized as in a game. Even total defeat in war may not remove the causes of conflict, and after a time the defeated may revive and renew the conflict.

A conflict is solved by *definitive acceptance* of a decision by *all* parties. In physical conflicts where all but one party are totally destroyed such decisions may be absolute; but if the conflict concerns ideas, policies, or claims, the words "definitive," "acceptance," and "all" have to be taken relatively. The rejected ideas, policies, or claims may be presented again. A decision may be accepted in a different sense by different parties. Finally, the direct parties to a controversy may not be the only parties interested. In the modern situation of widespread interdependence and general vulnerability to military and propaganda attacks from distant points, solutions of a dispute may not stand unless accepted by many states and groups in addition to the formal litigants.

In democracies, the relative character of decisions and settlements is both acknowledged and approved. In the United States, defeat of the Republicans by the Democrats in an election is accepted by the Republicans only on the assumption that they will have another chance in which the decision may be reversed. The opponents of legislation adopted by Congress often hope to acquire a majority and to repeal the law later. Democracy seeks to avoid once-for-all decisions which permanently reject certain alternatives, but rather seeks to facilitate temporary and relative decisions achieved by methods which avoid violence by keeping alive the hope of those defeated that eventually they may triumph. Only by the maintenance of such hope can minorities be persuaded to submit easily and can a spirit of tolerance be maintained.

Dictatorships that seek final decisions find it necessary to suppress minorities by force and are likely in time to be overthrown by revolution. Democratic institutions maintaining—at least to some degree— freedom of thought, expression, opinion, and association are not designed to suppress conflicts within the society but to encourage advocates of all policies, ideas, or claims to think that eventually they may win sufficient support to achieve their objectives.

Psychologists have discovered, however, that unresolved conflicts in the individual human mind may cause neuroses, incapacitating the individual for social life, or produce a displacement of animosities upon scapegoats resulting in serious social conflicts. A mature human personality is one which poses alternatives of action, reflects upon such conflicts, but eventually decides and acts, abandoning the rejected course after commitment.[30]

It may be that while the definitive settlement of conflict is a vice in societies, it is a virtue in the individual mind. A more accurate description would perhaps avoid the dichotomy between psychic and social conflicts and would recognize that sociopsychological conflict may occur at a number of different levels. It may occur in the individual mind, in small societies like families, clubs, trade unions, and corporations; in large societies like nations; and in supranational groups like alliances, regional arrangements, international organizations, and the world community. It is perhaps a safe generalization that the smaller the group, the more necessary is decision; the larger the group, the more dangerous is decision. In the world as a whole, in which differences of religion, ideology, culture, economic system, and policy exist and are to be expected for a long future, definitive decision of conflicts that may arise because of these differences seems to be both improbable and undesirable. Variety is the essence of a progressive and interesting world. However, so long as these differences exist conflict is possible.[31]

There are four ways in which social conflicts can be relatively solved: (1) by negotiation and agreement resulting in settlement or adjustment in accord with the will of all the parties; (2) by adjudication and decision in accord with the will, perhaps guided by legal or moral principles of an outside party; (3) by dictation or decision in accordance with the will of one party to the conflict; and (4) by obsolescence through agreement to disagree which may in time, as new issues arise, sink the conflict into oblivion and result in a settlement according to the will of no one.[32] It may be that while negotiation and obsolescence are least likely to result in speedy and definitive decisions, yet, for that very reason, they may be most suitable for dealing with controversy among the nations and alliances of the international community. In practice, settlement by dictation usually involves violence; and while it brings about social change and settles some conflicts, at least for the time, it is likely to precipitate new ones. Adjudication in the form of arbitration and judicial settlement has been used in international affairs; but has, on the whole, proved capable of settling only controversies in which both parties base their claims on formal principles of law and in which vital interests, such as national power and survival, and policies supported by widespread and intense public opinion, were only slightly involved.

With these considerations in mind, it is well for those responsible for the foreign policy of a nation in the presence of any conflict to ask in what degree decision is desirable, and to adjust the methods employed to conclusions on that point.

Conflict and Civilization

This discussion should indicate that conflict is a complicated subject and presents complicated problems to individuals, group leaders, and statesmen. Conflict is related to competition and to coöperation, but differs from both. There are many types of conflict—physical, political, ideological, and legal—but there is a tendency for conflict to become total and absolute, and to split the community of nations into halves which would destroy one another in absolute war. The shrinking of the modern world under the influence of new means of communication and transport, and the increasingly destructive methods of warfare culminating in the air-borne atomic bomb, have augmented this tendency, and have made war ominous for the future of civilization.

Conflict is carried on by many methods—coercive and noncoercive—

and there are various procedures for settling conflicts; but among large groups final solution of most conflicts is not to be expected, and it is probably undesirable to hope for such solutions.

It may be suggested that all champions of civilization, particularly of the American type, should earnestly and hopefully search for means to obstruct the natural tendency of conflict under present-day conditions to integrate policies, to centralize authority both geographically and functionally, to bipolarize the world, and to precipitate absolute war between the poles. It is difficult to question the existence of that tendency manifested in two world wars and in the present "cold war." It is possible to describe the psychological, technological, sociological, and political factors which account for this tendency, but it is difficult to stem the tide. Nevertheless, the effort to do so is called for by our culture and may be required for the salvation of our civilization. It is worth recalling that, when faced by conditions resembling those of today, most civilizations have begun a fatal decline ending in death to be followed, after a period of dark ages, by a new civilization.[33] Since our civilization, differing from others, is world-wide, and therefore, without the roots of new civilizations on its periphery, the situation may be more ominous.

The object of such efforts should be to diffuse conflicts by increasing the number of centers of initiative. Overcentralization is dangerous. Many small conflicts are less serious than one great conflict. Perhaps if the West were less willing to accept the alleged Soviet thesis that all communist states are necessarily satellites of the Kremlin and that all other states are necessarily in opposition to them, it would be discovered that states other than Tito's Yugoslavia have within them strong nationalist roots and resist integration into the Kremlin pattern of ideology and policy; and that states other than Nehru's India, while not wishing to become satellites of the Kremlin, may also hesitate to accept American leadership completely.

American policy, while creating situations of strength and containing Soviet expansion, might also encourage communist states to emancipate themselves from complete subservience to the Kremlin. Perhaps the national interest of China in resisting Soviet absorption of Manchuria, Mongolia, and Sinkiang is not wholly dead even in the communist government of Mao Tse-tung. Perhaps the age-old love which the Chinese peasant has for the "good earth" will check his enthusiasm for the Kremlin pattern of collective farms. It may also be that a zone of states manifesting different patterns of nationalism, and reluctant to follow blindly the leadership either of the United States or of the Soviet Union, can in time establish third, fourth, and fifth forces in the world thus multiplying centers of initiative between the two great poles and providing the conditions for a more stable equilibrium of power and a more effective international organization.[34]

Conflicts can perhaps be analyzed and certain of their aspects dealt with by nonviolent methods, thus weakening some of the urge toward unified policies and total war. Perhaps, also, a more careful examination of the roots of social and political conflict in the individual mind will suggest methods of education in personal decision making which, when widely practiced, will moderate the tendency to displace hatreds and project aggressive impulses upon scapegoats. Such education of the kind attempted by UNESCO, but up to this time rather ineffectively, might reduce the ultimate springs from which great conflicts arise.

Undoubtedly wider appreciation of the complexity of most international conflicts, of the inevitability and desirability of some conflict in the world, of the value of a broad spirit of toleration in our complex world, and of the possibilities of coexistence of divergent cultures, systems, ideologies, and policies, may offer effective obstacles to the development of the fatal tendency toward a new world war.

10

THE IMPORTANCE

OF THE STUDY OF

INTERNATIONAL TENSIONS

Meaning of Social Tension

The "tensions project" undertaken by UNESCO has a general interest for the social sciences because it constitutes an approach to their central interest. "Tension" may be regarded as one of three aspects of all societies of which the other two are structure and energy.[1]

Societies have a structure which may be more or less flexible, more or less rigid. In some primitive societies the structure regulates much of the life of the members of the society by custom and in totalitarian societies it regulates much of that life by comprehensive legislative, administrative, and police action. In free societies, on the other hand, the structure leaves a wide margin of initiative and action to individuals, to local communities, and to voluntary groups.

The energy of a society may be measured by the average quantity of mechanical energy available for each individual of the population. This quantity increases roughly at the rate at which the society produces a surplus of capital, and puts it to productive use. If the product of the activity of its members is entirely consumed day by day a society has little energy. If, on the other hand, the society's capital or potential energy grows rapidly, and this capital is put to work, the society has much energy. Social energy permits individual leisure and activity in the arts, in politics, in science, or in religion beyond the necessities for sustaining the life of the members and preserving the existence of the group.

From *International Social Science Bulletin* (UNESCO), II (Spring, 1950).

Tension may be regarded in the broadest sense as the condition arising from inconsistencies among initiatives in the structure of a society. The resolution of these inconsistencies results in decisions which regulate the utilization of the society's energy. It may be that the amount of tension in any society varies as the product of the degree of rigidity of its structure and the amount of its energy. Or stated mathematically, the rate of change of tension may vary as the product of the rate of change of structure and the rate of change of energy, thus suggesting an analogy to an electrical system in which tension or electromotive force varies as the product of resistance and current strength. Such an analogy has only the roughest application. It may suggest however that a scientific examination of social tension should avoid the assumption of common parlance that social tension is an evil which ought to be eradicated. Tension is not the germ of war, though it may be an element in the causation of war. As high electrical tension is dangerous to human life and may become so great as to destroy the structure in which it functions, so high social tensions may lead to violence or war and even destroy the structure of society. Yet without a minimum of tension an electrical system will not operate at all. So also societies will not function, much less progress, unless there is some tension within them. It is tension among inconsistent initiatives that makes possible choice, direction, and achievement of goals. Tensions contribute to the causation of war, but they also contribute to the causation of progress.

Tensions may occur within the individual human mind, and they may occur within groups and societies of any degree of magnitude. Within the world community tensions occur between nations and groups of nations. A characteristic of the present world is the grouping of nearly all nations about either the Soviet Union or the United States of America and the mounting of tensions between these two poles. As tensions increase, the energy available at each pole increases and this further augments the tensions. Tension may reach such magnitude that the confining structure of the United Nations and international law may give way, resulting in violence of unprecedented magnitude. The electrical analogy suggests that success either in rigidifying world institutions or in augmenting the surplus energy available to either group is more likely to increase than to diminish this tension.

Activity designed to maintain tensions at the right level in relation to social institutions and social energy is the art of statesmanship. This art requires the maintenance of an appropriate equilibrium and, therefore, its practitioners must attempt to analyze and to measure the important variables involved and to determine the effect of changes in one upon the others. At some times, at some places, and under some circumstances, maintenance of equilibrium may require an increase of tensions. Other times, places, and circumstances may require diminution of tensions. It is true that regulatory action may be applied, not to tensions, but to structure or to energy. Political action that changes institutions, structures and laws, or economic action that changes production, distribution, and capital accumulation, may under some circumstances be most appropriate. But the present study is concerned with the manipulation of tensions. This art depends upon knowledge of social psychology—a field which, if developed, may provide the basis for more adequate control of societies than either of the others.

Levels of Study

The character of reality varies with the level at which it is observed.[2] A house at the social level is a structure to be lived in. At the technical level it consists of boards, brick, and stone which could be rearranged into many other forms for human use. At the chemical level it is a group of atoms and molecules which by combination could be converted into very different substances which might or might not be useful. At the subatomic level it is a system of atomic nuclei and electrons separated by distances, vast in relation to the size of *these* entities. Manipulation at this level presents the possibilities of the most radical transformation. The smaller the level of observation, the greater is the possibility of radically changing the house into something else.

So with societies. If the reality of the world is viewed at the level of the Soviet and American power groups, the opportunities for manipulation to stabilize the equilibrium and to promote international peace and security are limited. If one views that reality at a lesser level, the parties, the local groups, the associations, the nations within these great power combinations, more opportunities may emerge. An understanding of the individuals within these groups and of the conflicting attitudes within the mind of each individual might suggest action, especially in the fields of education and the communication of information and ideas, which could radically alter the situation. The study of tensions within the individual human mind, and the process by which these tensions develop tensions in groups of ascending magnitude until finally they threaten the bipolar world atomic war, is of basic importance to all social science.[3] Both conflict and coöperation, both tension and energy development are aspects of every society from the family to the world. The analysis and measurement of the variables involved, the establishment of the relationship of these variables and the understanding of the processes by which they interact are the core of social science.

Many forms of analysis are possible. Few variables have been measured, few relations established, and few processes understood.

Approaches to the Study of Tensions

The influence of political and economic factors is important in any analysis of a situation. Once an organized group exists it seeks to continue its existence and to achieve its policy. This brings it into conflict with other groups that wish to absorb it, encroach upon it, or frustrate the achievement of its policies. If the groups which thus find themselves in conflict are not subject to a larger group which enforces law to prevent violence and settle disputes, such controversies lead each side to strengthen its power position by increasing its forces or the number of its allies in order to defend its existence, its interests, and its policies against any group which may threaten them. This is the situation among sovereign nations known as "power politics."

Once a system of production through division of labor, exchange, and the use of money has developed, individuals and groups become interdependent and the possession of wealth becomes a major mode of controlling the economic process to achieve desired ends. The effort to increase the wealth available to an individual or group by technological improvements in production and transportation, by expansion of markets through pricing, advertising, organizational and bargaining policies, and by control and coördination of sources of production— land, capital, labor, and managerial skill—leads to coöperation with some and opposition to others. The social consequence of the economic process is therefore similar to that of the political process, but since coöperation tends to increase wealth and opposition tends to diminish it, coöperation is the essence of the economic process while opposition is the essence of the political process.

At a superficial level these political and economic processes account for intergroup conflict. Among independent states they are difficult to distinguish. Political power may be sought as a means for increasing wealth to develop the welfare of the population, or economic wealth may be sought as a means for increasing power. State policy has always been motivated by considerations of both power and plenty, both security and welfare; the two objectives sometimes support one another and, if they conflict, one or the other may at a given moment be the primary focus of attention.

This paper, however, is concerned with a less superficial level of analysis. Why do groups exist? Why are individuals loyal to them?

Under what circumstances do loyalties shift, do old groups dissolve or become absorbed, and do new groups emerge?

On this level modern sociological thought recognizes the continuous interaction of groups and individuals, but the approach may be from one side or the other—the side of group culture or that of individual personality.

The student of culture, usually an anthropologist versed in the ways of primitive peoples, treats culture as a group phenomenon with a life of its own. Culture, he believes, exists in the minds of individual men but it has an integrated structure and a history. The relationship of each culture trait to the whole complex can be analyzed, its function in the group determined, and its origin from independent invention or from borrowing ascertained. Individuals are brought up in a culture which gives them behavior patterns, language, techniques, values, and beliefs.[4]

Thus it is said that the tendencies of individuals to be aggressive or docile, to be loyal to a particular group or to be independent, to be coöperative or competitive are phenomena of culture. The same is true of the tendency of the group to be belligerent, or peaceful, to be totalitarian or liberal, to be conciliatory or controversial. The patriotism, nationalism, liberalism, humanism, pacifism, and militarism found in varying degrees among Western peoples is thus traced to the cultural complex which emerged from the combination of classical, Christian, and barbarian ideas, greatly affected, and to some extent diffused throughout the world, by discoveries, inventions, and broadening contacts since the fifteenth century.

This mode of thought is more useful for explanation than for manipulation. A culture, as thus interpreted, is extremely difficult to change; it is the result of an unalterable history. It is an integrated complex no part of which can be changed without modifying the whole. It is transmitted as a whole by each generation of parents to their children, beginning at birth.[5] Thus change of culture seems to require early separation of children from parents and subjection of them to a new culture inculcated by institutions maintained by the elite of that culture. The cultural theory thus seems to leave no alternatives other than conservative maintenance of the entire culture or revolutionary substitution of a wholly new culture. This at least is the interpretation which the communists seem to have given to the theory of culture.

The psychologists, who approach the problem of relationship between the individual and the group from the side of the individual, do not deny the contribution which culture makes to the personality of the individual but they insist that the individual is primarily a biological organism with a hereditary constitution different from all others and that this constitution influences from the first his utilization of the cultural patterns provided by his environment. His individuality is never wholly lost in the group culture. He alters that culture by adapting it to his peculiar desires and to the new conditions imposed by scientific inventions, new technologies, new social ideas, and new contacts with outside cultures.[6] From this point of view culture is undergoing continuous though gradual change through the impact of personalities, especially those of the "creative minority," [7] or the "cultural élite" [8] and their influence can be profound if exerted in a common direction, even without resort to the revolutionary method advocated by Plato of plucking infants from the cradle and subjecting them to the State.[9]

The social psychologist, who is more likely to be familiar with persons of advanced civilization than with primitive groups, is impressed by the variation of personality and the malleability of behavior patterns through education even at later ages. He does not see culture as a solid integrated inflexible pattern among all members of a particular group transmitted as a whole to the rising generation at an early age. He sees it as a loose system of beliefs, values, standards, patterns of behavior and techniques differently interpreted and applied by different individuals and subgroups. He sees it undergoing continuous and sometimes rather rapid change through the influence of individuals, subgroups, outgroups, and supergroups.[10] Understanding of the characteristics of the individual personality which may lead to group tension and war may therefore suggest educational treatment both of the leaders and the led which can modify group cultures, and even tend to the assimilation of those cultures in that of a mere embracing group.

Psychological Theories of Tensions

From this point of view it is especially important to understand the process by which individual tensions influence tensions between nations. It would be premature to present a definitive analysis of this process but some theories may be suggested.

One theory places the concept of ambivalence at the heart of the matter. The child, faced now by benefits, now by discipline from the mother, loves and hates her simultaneously. This ambivalent situation is unpleasant and is commonly relieved by displacing the hate and accompanying aggressive tendency upon someone else. As a child's social contacts increase, the hated scapegoat must be placed outside his social group in order that internal conflict may be reduced and internal coöperation augmented. Thus the process of displacing hatreds upon the out-group continues until the world as a whole is involved. A bipolar world emerges in which the tensions in each human mind and in each lesser human group is relieved by displacement of the target of aggressive dispositions upon that group which is an out-group to all.[11] This process has been observed in small isolated islands in which the groups of primitive peoples tend to become divided into two opposing poles continually in cold or hot war with one another. It can also be observed in the tendency of political parties to polarize. The varied individuals and groups within one party displace their political animosities upon the other party, thus developing a party of sufficient size and solidarity to have a chance to win the election.[12]

With this explanation, solution of the problem of excessive social tension might be sought in methods of early child training so as to reduce the initial ambivalence in the mind requiring displacement.[13] Perhaps later education could encourage displacement of aggressive tendencies upon common enemies of humanity such as pestilence, poverty, and war itself.[14] Institutions might be modified so that instead of encouraging the process of displacement, they will encourage solution of ambivalence through decision within the individual mind or within smaller groups.[15]

Another explanation emphasizes the role of frustration. Instead of a conflict of opposing attitudes within the individual mind, it is assumed that the basic conflict is that between goals and achievements. The child lacks the technique to achieve his desires and consequently feels frustrated and reacts spontaneously with the blind and usually ineffective technique of aggression which may be directed against himself or against any supposed obstacle to his achievement. He kicks and strikes at that obstacle, whether animate or inanimate, whether in fact related to his failure or not. This tendency to aggress on frustration is instinctive and exists in adults as well as children whenever techniques are inadequate to achieve goals.[16]

This source of tensions, it is suggested, may be ameliorated by better education concerning the effective relation of means and ends, and by education directing attention to ends capable of achievement with the means at hand. Such education may reduce frustration, and may cultivate habits of rational adaptation of means to ends and of considering the relative value of different ends whether in economics, in politics, in culture, or in social relations.[17]

Another explanation emphasizes the role of stereotypes, including false identifications and personifications. The primitive mind tends to explain natural phenomena as the acts of persons and tries to combat them by attacking or placating the natural or supernatural person deemed responsible. Civilized man tends to generalize about racial, social, economic, or other groups on the basis of insufficient instances, and to attribute to all persons in the group undesirable characteristics identified with the group. This process of stereotyping, identification, and attribution tends to develop group antagonisms.[18] The people in one nation acquires stereotypes about another nation, often resulting from anecdotes about distant historical epochs, attributing to them characteristics with little or no relation to reality.

Such false beliefs and stereotypes have undoubtedly contributed to racial tension, class tension, and international tensions, and it has been suggested that they might be ameliorated by an educational process providing more adequate information and demonstrating the inaccuracy of the popular stereotypes.[19]

Finally, there are some who emphasize the influence of the mechanism of projection. An individual projects his aggressive dispositions or dominance drives upon another person with whom he happens to be in controversy. This assures him of the aggressive intentions of the other and induces him to take defensive measures to protect himself from the assumed aggression of the other. The other party acts similarly. Individual projection reflects itself in the opinions of conflicting groups. The armament race proceeds and tensions rise. The source of the projection mechanism may lie in the difference between social standards and individual impulses, between the conscience and the drives, between the super-ego and the id.[20] If instinctive drives are in conflict with cultural standards,[21] the individual refuses to recognize them in himself. Subconsciously, however, he realizes that they do exist in himself and escapes self-condemnation by attributing them to others. Group leadership seeking to solidify the group may contribute to this process. Better understanding of this psychological mechanism and better adjustment between the *mores* and the *counter-mores* in society might ameliorate this source of tension.

These various explanations of the psychological source of tensions are not necessarily alternatives. There may be a measure of truth in all, and each may be of predominant importance in certain situations. All however suggest ways in which wars, as said in the UNESCO Constitution, "begin in the minds of men." They suggest how major political, social, and economic tensions may be traced from tensions in the individual human mind, whether to conflicts of individual human attitudes with one another, to conflicts of goals and techniques, to conflicts of beliefs and realities, to conflicts of standards and drives. They also suggest methods by which "the defences of peace" may be constructed in the minds of men. This is the major objective of UNESCO.

Public Approval and Practical Effectiveness

A major practical difficulty in efforts to solve the problem of war lies in the fact that in many circumstances there is little relationship between the ease of selling a project to the public or to the appropriate authorities, and the effectiveness of the project in producing the results expected of it. This arises from the inherent tendency of the human mind to wish for and to accept simple explanations, although most situations in the social field are complex and difficult to understand. The mind tends to operate on the basis of criteria which judges all proposals as either good or bad irrespective of the circumstances and conditions of their application, while actually the effects of any proposal in producing the desired result is relative to the total situation in which it is applied. Doubtless this situation is accountable for much frustration and consequent aggression.

These points deserve further examination. The public is inclined to consider that literacy, health, wealth, democratic government, and security from invasion are absolutely good. Consequently the public tends to believe that efforts, at any time, in any place, or in any circumstances, to increase literacy, to promote public health, to increase economic productiveness, to increase popular participation in government, and to increase protection from invasion deserve support. However, from the point of view of maintaining international peace and security, these beliefs are far from being universally applicable. Let us consider each of them.

It is a common observation that when illiterate people learn to read they tend to attach an exaggerated importance to the written word, and, consequently, to become easy preys of propaganda. Today illiteracy is usually accompanied by a low standard of living, but with illiteracy there is usually little awareness of this low standard of living or of the fact that other populations have a much higher standard. Consequently, if such a population is taught to read, its members are likely to be deluged by interested propagandists with reading materials informing them of this great contrast in their condition with that of others, attributing this contrast to the malevolent motives of a suitably selected group or party, and urging prompt liquidation of that group. Such explanations may be believed and may lead to violence and war.[22]

A similar analysis may be applied to public health measures. There are areas of the world where population is extremely dense, the level of living is extremely low, and health conditions are such as to maintain an expectation of life of some twenty-five years at birth instead of sixty-five as it is in the most healthy countries. In such areas public health measures may have the immediate effect of increasing the existing overpopulation more than they increase the *per capita* productiveness of the population, and consequently of lowering the general level of living, increasing the restiveness of the population, and developing conditions in which propagandas of violence may easily be accepted.[23]

So also in regard to wealth. Introduction of foreign capital into an area of very low living standards may at first increase productiveness and average wealth, but, unless the government enforces equal distribution of the increased production, the effect is likely to be an augmentation of existing inequalities, an increase of social tension, and a tendency to displace aggressive impulses upon an external enemy. If the government seeks to enforce equal distribution it will have to curtail liberty and enterprise, thus hampering production, and unless it reserves capital from the annual production, which is difficult to do if the control is democratic, the increased production will result in an increase in population and there will be no increase in average wealth. Both of these tendencies can be observed in the development of colonies and they have often led to tensions between colonies and the mother country.[24]

In regard to democratic government, it is clear that such a government, if operated by a people wholly unprepared to understand the sources of social evils and the effects of proposed reform, may enact policies which produce chaos and result in reactions toward absolutism and tyranny. For this reason Aristotle questioned the value of pure democracy. History is full of the ill effects of premature popular institutions. Effective democracy, in the sense of popular participation in government, depends upon adequate preparation in the society of means of communication, of social understanding, of economic opportunity, and of political toleration.[25]

In regard to security from invasion, it is clear that the development of national defenses may have the effect of making attack from outside more difficult, but also may have the effect of making such an attack more likely because others interpret such preparation as intended for aggression. Some analysts have even suggested that the latter effect is certain to be greater than the former with the result that defensive preparation diminishes security by developing armament races.[26] Probably the situation is in fact much more complicated. Numerous factors have to be considered in judging the actual effect of defensive preparation upon security in a given situation. Generalizations should be made with caution, but the historical record appears to indicate that, in a large proportion of the balance-of-power wars of the last three centuries, the militarily better-prepared country initiated the war and that in about half of these wars, that state, though winning the early battles, eventually lost the war largely because its less prepared enemies were able to convince the world that they were the victims of attack and thereby to gain sufficient allies to achieve eventual victory. This seems to have been true of about two-thirds of the fifteen major balance-of-power wars during this period including the Thirty Years' War of the seventeenth century, the wars of Louis XIV, the Napoleonic wars, and World Wars I and II.[27]

If it is suggested that the proper defense against invasion is not military preparation but subordination to international government, qualifications are also necessary. Apart from the difficulty of gaining sufficient agreement upon any specific form of international government, it appears that the influence of such a government—even if established—upon peace and security is by no means simple. From 1815 to 1914 the states of the United States were united by a federal government while those of Europe were not, but the losses of life in the American Civil War were greater than in all the wars of Europe put together during that century. Other illustrations could be given suggesting that the relations between supergovernment and peace among the members is not simple.[28]

These illustrations are not intended to disparage efforts toward more literacy, more health, more wealth, more democracy, and more security, but only to indicate that the effect of such efforts on international peace and security is dependent upon the conditions and circumstances of the population, groups, and world in which they are applied, and upon the rate at which they are applied. It should also be emphasized that other values such as social welfare and justice have to be weighed against that of peace and security.

Efforts to solve the problem presented by the dichotomy of the complexity of social reality and the simplicity of mental constructs of that reality may take two forms. The first is the path of dictatorship. Government alone, it is assumed, can understand what the people need and should implement that superior knowledge through using simple slogans which the people are prepared to understand however imperfect may be their relationship to the policy actually pursued. This method, however, leaves the people unprotected from exploitation by the government, and history has shown that they usually find themselves victims of tyranny. Furthermore, tyrannical governments are peculiarly prone to defend themselves from internal sedition by finding an external enemy against whose actual or imagined invasion the entire community will unite to defend itself. This method, therefore, is dangerous both to human rights and to peace.

The second form of the effort to solve this dichotomy is the path of democracy, by which the government, however superior may be its understanding of the situation, refrains from taking any steps until the public also understands and through appropriate legislative institutions authorizes action. This method is likely to result, because of difficulties in educating the public sufficiently rapidly to understand the true complexity of the situation, in public insistence upon action, based on oversimple premises, inadequate to meet the situation. Or the public may fail to agree on any solution at all, consequently the government has to rely on traditional practices inadequate to adapt the society to the necessities of a changing world.

It seems probable that a proper solution of this problem requires continuous interaction of those who understand and those who must learn, before collective action can be taken. Furthermore, the nature of this interaction must be related to circumstances. Under certain circumstances, positive leadership and action by the government or the elite prior to popular understanding may be more necessary than in other circumstances. The problem of determining the measures to be taken and the authority to initiate them must, however, always be treated relativistically. The question must always be asked whether the population is prepared for this reform or whether some preparatory step must first be taken. Is the emergency such as to require action by those who know and have authority prior to complete understanding by the public destined to be the victims or the beneficiaries of the action taken? The questions cannot be answered unless leadership is always aware of its need of popular support and the public is always aware of its need of intelligent leadership.

UNESCO has as its field of action the world, where there are tremendous differences in the preparation of the various groups and peoples for any proposed reform, and where the number of factors involved and the complexity of their relationships is so great as to tax the understanding of the most expert social scientists and the art of the most adroit political leaders. If UNESCO is to succeed in its task, it is, therefore, of the utmost importance that the basic concept of society as a complex equilibrium be grasped by those who have authority to initiate projects and that the world public be educated to this concept as rapidly as possible.

Even while accepting this point of view, minds should be alert to the possibility that new insights into culture and psychology may simplify the problem. As an illustration one may consider the theory of health developed by Claude Bernard in the first half of the nineteenth century. In this theory the concept of equilibrium and relativity was prominent. Health was a stable equilibrium among the various systems of the body and in the relations of the whole body to its environment. Presently, Louis Pasteur discovered the influence of specific germs in causing many diseases, and medicine turned from the equilibrating process taught by Bernard to the effort to isolate and destroy specific germs. Perhaps this tendency went too far. Walter Cannon's new examination of physiological equilibria is in the tradition of Bernard. The public health movement suggests that the proper maintenance of a physiological equilibrium may produce natural defenses against the invasion of germs no less important for health than maintenance of a healthy environment.

While it may be premature to discard the possibility of discovering a controllable germ of tensions and war, yet until such discovery is made, it appears wisest to assume that tensions and wars are consequences of disturbances in a very complex equilibrium. Efforts should be devoted to analyzing, measuring, and controlling those variables which are most easily controlled so as to maintain the equilibrium.

Unesco and the Study of Tensions

The preceding discussion suggests that the study of tensions is not only central to the social sciences, but that it has a special relevance to the work of UNESCO. The purpose of UNESCO set forth in Article 1 of its constitution is to contribute to peace and security by promoting collaboration among the nations through education, science, and culture in order to further universal respect for justice, for the rule of law, and for human rights and fundamental freedoms. To realize this purpose the organization seeks to advance the mutual knowledge and understanding of peoples, to give fresh impulse to popular education and to spread culture, and to maintain, increase and diffuse knowledge, without impairing the independence, integrity and fruitful diversity of the cultures and educational systems of the member states.

The purpose of UNESCO is therefore not different from that of the United Nations itself, but UNESCO uses different means. The Security Council of the United Nations works at the political level to reduce tensions between governments, settle controversies between states, and so to balance the forces of the United Nations and the nations that successful aggression will not be practical. The Economic and Social Council and most of the specialized agencies work at the economic level to promote international coöperation for common welfare, to facilitate processes of production and distribution in the interest of rising standards of living and social justice, and to prevent unfair or coercive uses of economic power likely to augment dangerously tensions among economic groups. UNESCO, differing from both, works on the psychological level to the end that human minds everywhere may entertain and act on the bases of attitudes, opinions, beliefs, values, and skills consistent with, and promotive of, a peaceful, secure, just, and progressive world. The results of its work may be of great value to the work of the United Nations and the other specialized agencies, but the work itself is different.

One of UNESCO's problems has been to discover criteria for evaluating the numerous proposals in the fields of education, science, and culture suggested to it. Such criteria are essential if projects are to be selected which will utilize UNESCO's limited resources so as to make the greatest contribution to its objectives. Two approaches to the solution of this problem have been suggested. The first is to analyze and measure the psychological factors involved in the development of tension, insecurity, and war, and to determine the relations among these and other factors. Such analyses, measurements, and determinations may suggest methods by which some of the psychological factors can be controlled and the degree in which any one of them should be modified, in relation to the others, to maintain international peace and security. With such a theory, the probability that a proposal for educational, informational, or other action will achieve its objectives could be appraised.

The other approach is to investigate the conditions of human loyalties in the world community and their relation to movements of technology and population and to the variety of national cultures, religions, and economic systems, in order to determine what changes might permit the United Nations better to maintain international peace and security. If these changes were understood, concrete proposals for realizing them might be appraised.

Research in the social department of UNESCO has attempted to contribute to both of these approaches, though the first, followed by the "tensions project," has been given primary emphasis, as perhaps it should, since in general it follows the pure scientific method of attempting to relate causes to effects. The second approach implies in greater degree the applied science method of relating ends and means. Studies connected with the "tensions project" sought to discover and appraise the distinctive character of national cultures, ideals, and legal systems; the influence of the stereotypes which the people of one nation apply to another nation; and the effects of population changes and technological changes upon the attitudes of peoples and their relations with one another. Other studies concern the means by which attitudes can be changed and the influences which make for international understanding and for aggressive nationalism.[29]

I believe that studies of this kind aiming at description and analysis should be followed by studies which seek to measure the relative influence of different factors found to be important, and to elaborate formulae indicating the relation of changes of one variable to changes in another so that the total effect of modification of some tensions upon others may be foreseen. Experience shows that reduction of tensions among some groups may result in their amalgamation into larger blocs, and that this may result in graver tensions among these blocs, thus resulting in less frequent, but more serious wars. Such a development is not necessarily favorable for civilization or for the human race.

Proceeding from the second point of view, the social-science department has developed a project on international coöperation. Studies have been proposed on the conditions of effectiveness of types of international organization and on the process of change in the focus of loyalty in large and complex groups in relation to the incidence of insurrection and civil war. Especially significant might be studies of the evolution of federations such as the United States and Switzerland, in which loyalties to the federation have been superimposed upon earlier loyalties to the member states. It appears that in these, and perhaps in other circumstances, the development of loyalties to the supergroup resulted in the intensification of loyalties to certain of the subgroups. Citizens of the latter, feeling themselves in a minority position, were induced to revolt. These cases suggest that an effort to induce loyalties to a supergroup in the interest of peace, if not developed evenly and gradually, may by its very success precipitate reactions leading to war. A transition from small international wars to mammoth civil wars can hardly be regarded as a victory for peace.[30] Somewhat similar developments have been observed in the process of expanding communities through utilization of new inventions in the field of communications. The printing press, the telegraph, the radio made communication possible over the world, but the initial effect of these inventions was to stimulate a much more intensive communication within the nations than between nations, with the result that the sentiment of nationalism has developed more intensively than that of internationalism. These inventions, therefore, far from contributing to the social solidarity of mankind, have widened the gaps between nations and increased national egoisms and national rivalries.[31]

Historical studies of the processes thus considered might throw light upon the general process by which social solidarity has developed in larger and larger areas. We may assume that the broadening of communications and contacts will lead to the diffusion of cultures, technologies, and value systems. This will encourage increasingly comprehensive coöperation toward the achievement of common ends and the establishment of government to facilitate such coöperation, to maintain order, to enforce law, and to defend the society from external invasion. Historical analysis, however, may show that this model of the process is far from accurate. Retarded development in one area may cause temporary reversals, and the very unevenness of the process may be a major cause of wars. We need indices for measuring the rate at which the processes of communication, standardization, coöperation, and organization are proceeding, and formulae expressing the influence that excessive speed or slowness in one has upon each of the others.[32]

Studies of the kind suggested may indicate the states of mind favorable and unfavorable to international peace and security; the means for maximizing the former and minimizing the latter; and the sorts of equilibria, attitudes, and loyalties suitable for maintaining sufficient tension to promote civilization and not enough to promote war. Such studies may provide criteria for defining the scope of UNESCO's work.

The constitution of UNESCO suggests, although this interpretation is not free of controversy, that activities in the field of education, science, and culture are significant for UNESCO only in proportion as they contribute to modifying attitudes, opinions, values, loyalties, and skills, whether of political leaders, public officials, or others, so as to maintain peace and security with due regard to justice, law, and freedom. With this interpretation the tensions study and other studies in social science may provide the master guide for the whole of UNESCO's work. It may provide criteria for appraising the contribution to this objective of any proposed activity (as distinguished from research), whether that activity concerns reconstruction, education, natural science, social science, culture, exchange of persons, or mass communication.

It is not to be expected that criteria can ever be developed, the application of which will eliminate the need to exercise wise judgment. The program of UNESCO will always have to be decided upon by the representatives of the members in the general conference properly advised by the executive board and the director-general. The judgment of these agencies as to the relevance and importance of any proposed project, might, however, be more reliable if it were guided by a body of verified propositions concerning the causes and consequences of tensions, the relation of tensions at one level to those at another, the conditions of effective international coöperation, and the means of influencing attitudes, opinions, beliefs, evaluations, and skills through educational, scientific, and cultural interchange.

The "tensions project" and the other research projects in social science are only at their beginning. It is to be expected that, as they develop, all of the social sciences will be able to contribute to them. The development of international associations in the various social sciences and the consequent diffusion of knowledge in these fields from the countries in which it is most advanced to others in which the social sciences are relatively unknown can be of major importance in this connection, as well as in the promotion of understanding among different nations.

In the work of UNESCO, activities in the field of the social sciences may not be the most important, but they have a certain pioneering and guiding character. It is within the competence of the social sciences to establish the relationship between conditions of the human mind and the condition of stability, peace, security, justice, and progress in larger and smaller groups, even in the largest group of all, the human race. Some knowledge of these relationships is necessary before it is possible to appraise the effect of any given activity in the fields of education, science, and culture upon peace and security. It certainly cannot be said that because an educational activity develops individual understanding or awareness, because a scientific activity increases man's knowledge of the universe and the control of nature, because a cultural activity elevates the human spirit and creates new values, that it necessarily contributes to peace and security. It may do so, and it may also contribute to the secondary objectives of UNESCO. But an objective answer to the question whether, and in what degree, it does is not in the province of education, of natural science, or of the arts and humanities, but in that of the social sciences.

11

THE RELATION OF
UNIVERSAL CULTURE
TO POWER POLITICS

Culture and Power

Culture and power are not opposites. Culture includes all the patterns of behavior of a group, including tendencies to use political, economic, administrative, and military means to coerce other groups. These tendencies are entirely absent in few cultures, but the desire to dominate plays a greater role in some cultures than in others. Power includes all the characteristics of a group which contribute to its capacity to coerce others. Technical skills, moral unity, and efficient organization are no less important than size of territory and population, geographic barriers and bases, economic resources, industrial plants, military armaments, and strategic leadership. A group's political, economic, military, educational, and religious institutions are aspects both of its culture and of its power.

There are, however, differences. Culture looks primarily at values, power at instruments. The cultures of groups differ qualitatively and are less susceptible of quantitative comparison than the power of groups. Culture, therefore, tends to be regarded as absolute, and power as relative.

From Lyman Bryson, Lewis Finkelstein, and R. M. MacIver, eds., *Conflicts of Power in Western Culture,* Seventh Symposium on Science, Philosophy and Religion (New York: Harper, 1947).

The Classification of Cultures

There has often been a tendency to rate culture by power, but anthropologists habitually criticize that tendency. Few impartial observers would agree that Russia necessarily has a culture superior to that of Switzerland because it is more powerful. The doctrine of equality of states in international law does not imply equality in power or influence but in opportunity for self-development. It asserts that the culture of all groups recognized as states should be considered of equal value irrespective of the relative power of the states.

Attempts have also been made to rank cultures by their stage of advancement in technology and science. Men who use fire have been considered more cultured than those who do not. Men who add to the use of fire the use of agriculture, the wheel, the domestication of animals, the smelting of metals have been considered more cultured. Those who, in addition, employ writing, arithmetic, clocks, steam engines, airplanes, and nuclear energy have been considered more cultured still. Such a criterion for ranking cultures is suggested by the sequences primitive, barbarous, civilized; old stone age, new stone age, bronze age, iron age; eotechnics, paleotechnics, neotechnics. As man has been distinguished from preman by the use of speech, so civilized man has been distinguished from primitive man by the use of writing, and modern man from civilized man by the use of printing.

If applied with caution, such a ranking of cultures by their technological advance might be legitimate, although this criterion tends to confuse culture with power. Technological advance refers more to the instruments for exerting power over nature and other groups than to cultural values. The justification for this usage, if there is one, should be found in the demonstration of a relationship between values and technological advance. Does technological advance permit a realization of more values, or of superior values, or of values by more people? Obviously the question cannot be answered unless values themselves be evaluated in a value system. Technological advance has tended to enlarge human groups conscious of their identity as a group, and to increase the opportunities of the members of the group to observe, to think, and record their thoughts. Such opportunities have not always been seized, and, when they have, it is not certain that superior values have always been created or transmitted to more people, if indeed there is any consensus on what values are superior. The large element of subjectivism in all value systems urges caution in the attempt to rank values and cultures.

Culture and Opinion

The difficulty in objectively evaluating values and cultures can perhaps be avoided by discussing opinions instead of values, and public opinion instead of culture. I do not contend that opinions and values are identical. Opinions are identical neither with values nor with attitudes. They are, however, important evidences of individual values, and they may approach identity with social values and culture because only opinions can be communicated. Opinions are not only evidence of attitudes but also stimuli of attitudes in others. Groups are groups because opinions are communicated. The attitudes of the individual, the culture of the group, and the values at the root of both, are the consequences as well as the sources of opinions.

By confining discussion to opinions, one gains the advantage of avoiding the almost irresistible urge to regard values as absolute and to rate them by subjective standards which carry no conviction to others. People are more inclined to be pragmatic about opinions than about values, that is, to judge them scientifically by their consequences reduced to a consistent system verified by many observations.

Analysis and Measurement of Public Opinion

In discussing public opinion on any subject it is necessary to distinguish the *public,* the *interest,* and the *opinion.* Any human population, the members of which communicate with one another, can be taken as a public; and any issue, proposition, symbol, or idea about which they communicate can be taken as an interest. The opinion of any public concerning any interest can be measured according to its *direction* (pro or con), its *intensity* (strong, moderate, weak), its *homogeneity* (normal distribution, skew, bimodal) or its *continuity* (curve of temporal change).[1]

In applying such a system of analysis and measurement it is clear that public opinion is related to means of communication. As men have successively invented language, writing, the printing press, the postal system, the telegraph, the telephone, and the radio, publics have tended to enlarge until today there is a world public on many matters. People all over the world are talking to one another about war and peace, about prosperity and depression, about human rights and national rights, about the U.K., the U.S., the U.S.S.R. and the U.N. They are not, however, all expressing the same opinions on all these interests. There is more homogeneity and continuity on the virtues of peace and prosperity, compared with those of war and depression, than there is on the relative values of human rights and national rights. There is least unity of all on the relative value of the U.K., the U.S., and the U.S.S.R. On the latter question, and on many others, there is probably much more unity of opinion within each national public than in the world as a whole. The differences of opinion among national publics are in some cases in opposite directions and very intense.

The Characteristics of a Universal Culture

It seems to me that a study of opinions might help us in understanding culture and power in the modern world. A culture becomes stable in proportion as the population which sustains it has a homogeneous and continuous public opinion on a multitude of interests. Such a condition, which implies that the attitudes of the members of the population are relatively uniform, stable, and accurately expressed, can hardly exist if the population is continuously communicating with other populations with a very different state of public opinion. Consequently, as publics have come into contact with one another through the use of discoveries and inventions in the field of communications, all local and regional cultures have tended to become unstable and a world culture has tended to evolve. A broadening of social contacts immediately produces social chaos, ultimately a larger social cosmos.[2]

I have elsewhere tried to show that since the Renaissance there has been a tendency for the world public to accept the value of the individual, the value of humanity, the value of scientific method, and the value of tolerance. Human rights, human welfare, objective investigation, and renunciation of war are the primary aims of the United Nations, and they reflect the wide acceptance of what I have called liberalism, humanism, pragmatism, and relativism as the values of the developing world civilization.[3] I am aware that these words are susceptible of varied interpretations, and I am not concerned with their precise meaning. Like all affective words, they have different meanings for different people. Public opinion forms about symbols and propositions of vague meanings.[4] One cannot study public opinion as a fact, susceptible of analysis and measurement, if one insists that the meaning of its interests must first be clarified.

In considering the opinion of a world with many religions, nationalities, traditions, and laws, it is clear that symbols and values distinctive of a particular religion, nation, people, or state are not interests on which world opinion can unite. The individual human being, and the human race of which he is a member, are, however, everywhere. Man and mankind are not distinctive of any public. They may become universal interests. The practical values of science and the practical dangers of intolerance are evidenced in the experience of every group. The values of individual liberty, of human consideration, of scientific method, and of tolerance, are in fact given recognition in varying degrees in most of the lesser publics called religions, nations, peoples, or states. Although conscious recognition of each of these values originated in a particular culture, they have tended to become distinctive of none.

The State of Opinion and the Nature of the World Order

With this order of thought, we must think of cultures in the modern world not as isolated entities, or as steps in human progress, but as the opinions of separated, overlapping, or concentric publics, each characterized at any moment by the relative homogeneity of its opinion concerning many interests. Culture changes in time and merges in respect to certain interests in the emerging universal culture.

How does the state of culture, in this sense, influence the state of power? The power of a group in the broadest sense includes persuasion as well as coercion and is measured by all the material and political assets at the group's disposal through which it can realize its opinions, including the intensity, homogeneity, and continuity of the opinion itself. The relative power of a group can be reduced by fission into groups of diverse opinion, by confrontation with a group of superior power and opposing opinion, and by submergence of the group in a larger group whose opinion it largely shares. The state of opinion determines the publics which have power, the interests for which power will be used, and the intensity, unity, and persistence of action which are major elements of power itself.

World politics becomes power politics when the publics, characterized by sharing many opinions in common with intensity, are geographically separated groups. World politics, on the other hand, tends to become a regime of law in proportion as the opinions of the world public become homogeneous, continuous, and intense with respect to many interests.

The balance of power which tends to result from the operation of power politics becomes less stable as communications among the geographically separated publics increase, thereby decreasing their separation and augmenting the influence of universal symbols. States, influenced by pride in sovereignty, the inertia of tradition, and the hope of restoring a stable balance of power, attempt to stem the tide of a growing world opinion by isolating their national publics behind artificial barriers. If the progress of science and communication frustrates such efforts, conditions of instability and tension increase, leading to the absorption of smaller publics by larger and to increasing concentrations of power. These are utilized by the traditionalists to maintain the autonomy of distinctive publics and to prevent the growth of a universal public opinion, but the liberals, attracted by the possibilities for individual and human welfare of organizing the latter, press toward wider horizons. The world appears to be moving simultaneously in opposite directions toward more intense nationalism and toward a more coherent world opinion.

World public opinion has not yet reached a degree of homogeneity, continuity, and intensity able to maintain a regime of world law. We may, however, expect the trend toward a universal opinion to continue under the influence of more rapid and abundant world communications, of the United Nations and its subsidiary institutions laboring for human welfare and human rights, and of the universal terror of the atom bomb.

The Problem of World Politics

The problem for our generation is to regulate the method by which world politics adapts itself to this trend. We do not want to eliminate the diversity of cultures within a universal culture. We do not want to centralize coercive power in a universal empire. We do not want the destructiveness of atomic wars. To avoid these dangers, understanding and caution are necessary. During the period immediately ahead diplomacy must utilize the methods of power politics, which alone can be successful in preventing universal conquest so long as opinions remain dominantly national. But as the institutions of the United Nations, the increasing flow of communications, and the fear of atomic war develop a world opinion, institutions must be developed capable of enacting law in pursuance of that opinion and enforcing it upon individuals within the nations. Under conditions of increasing contact of states and decreasing numbers of states, we cannot expect a military balance of power to be stable. If the balance of power is unstable, we cannot rely upon a law which binds only the states as such. Under such conditions, stability requires that law govern matters of universal interest and that it operate directly upon individuals. The alternatives before the world are universal empire or universal federation. The choice depends upon the movements of world public opinion susceptible both of measurement facilitating prediction and of influence facilitating control.

Control is difficult because the methods of power politics tend to frustrate the growth of a universal opinion, and the growth of a universal opinion tends to unstabilize the equilibrium of power. Statesmen, by meeting immediate necessities, tend to frustrate the possibility of long-run stability; by working toward long-run stability they leave their states vulnerable to universal conquest. There is little hope that world government formed by universal conquest could avoid the over-centralization, the suppression of individual and local initiatives, and the violence of tyranny and revolt which have prevented empires of the past from achieving an enduring adaptive stability. Can our universal civilization effect the transition from an unstable balance of power to a regime of law with a minimum of coercion and a maximum of consent, a minimum of imperial conquest and a maximum of voluntary federation? That is the problem of culture and power in our world.

PART IV

EDUCATION AND
INTERNATIONAL
STABILITY

12

THE UNIVERSITIES

AND THE WORLD ORDER

As the universe gets larger, the world gets smaller. From the objective side, the astronomers tell us that for the last two billion years matter has been moving outward and still is. The outer galaxies are receding at about one-third the speed of light. Today some of them are over 500 million light years away from us. That is a long distance and has no significance for what I want to say except to suggest the size of our material universe and a becoming modesty in attributing importance to the affairs of this small globe on which we live. Such a perspective may help us to view terrestrial crises with a sense of humor in the realization that, if the two billion humans now parasitic upon the thin scum of organic matter which covers the surface of much of our world should destroy themselves, it may not make very much difference to the vast reaches of time and space and the innumerable galaxies, stars, and worlds which populate the expanding universe.

From the subjective side, the expansion of the universe is more important for my theme. Man's mind has been penetrating with accelerating speed the history, the structure, and the composition of the universe and of its component parts including the earth and the atom. Science has been expanding at the rate of compound interest, and with it invention, technology, and engineering have been enlarging man's capacity to release imprisoned energies, to control his environment, and to adapt the conditions of his life to his biological drives and his social aspirations.

From the *Bulletin* of the American Association of University Professors, XXXIII (Spring, 1947). Presidential address delivered at the 33d annual meeting of the association, February 22, 1947, in Boston.

The Shrinking World

Here, however, lies the paradox. The growth of knowledge has shrunk the human world. Progress in cosmogony, cosmography, and cosmology has concentrated the growing universe with all its complexities in a few human minds. Progress in history, geography, and social science has made statesmen aware of the entire world community with all its local differences, its conflicts, its trends, and its aspirations. Progress in reporting, in statistics, in transportation, in communication, in technology, and in administration has made the knowledge and experience of scientists and statesmen remote in time and space available to anyone near a library who knows how to read.

As a consequence, anyone sufficiently equipped with radio, money, food, airplanes, rockets, and atom bombs has the capacity to bring upon his fellow men in the most remote areas the persuasive or compulsive influences of propaganda, bribery, blockade, and war. The desires, greeds, hungers, and fears of men everywhere may be affected by these influences whether directed from London, Washington, or Moscow. Only isolated tribesmen in North Australia, the Pacific and Indonesian islands, in remote valleys of Asia, in the wilds of Africa, or in the forests of the Amazon are relatively free of such distant influences. As civilization spreads and economies become more interdependent, as UNESCO succeeds in its task of eliminating illiteracy, as the circulation of newspapers and the availability of radio receiving sets become more universal, the minority, now immune from sudden coercion or subtle influence by distant men, will disappear. Through technology men are escaping from the dominance of nature, from the tyranny of flood, drought, heat, cold, pestilence, and famine but, in doing so, they are imprisoning themselves in one small world. Nearly the entire two billion of them is subject to the influence and power of the few who have the "know-how" and the machinery at their disposal.

But the growth of knowledge has tended not only to concentrate power, it has also tended to increase each man's awareness of himself. In emancipating themselves from local custom, men are seeing themselves as personalities. They are no longer mere cells in a compact social organism. They are coming to know that others of their species live differently and perhaps enjoy more food, leisure, and knowledge. They are absorbing ideas of freedom and of equality. They are wondering whether they are not as entitled to guide their own lives according to their wants and aspirations as anyone else. With these thoughts they resent age old conditions of hardship and compulsion springing from local tyranny, ancient custom, or economic exploitation.

In this century the world has shrunk not only in the vulnerability of each part to influences from every other part, but also in the knowledge in each part of the conditions of every other part, and in the demands of each part that it shall not lag behind any other in realizing its desires.

Mankind as a whole has the opportunity to adapt the conditions of his life to his biological drives and to realize his aspirations. Every man is increasingly aware of that opportunity and increasingly insistent that he shall benefit by it, but most men fear that they may have to adapt their lives to someone else's biological drives or to contribute to the realization of someone else's aspirations.

While the world of man is increasingly subject to control from a few centers, wants and aspirations continue to emerge from each of the two billion examples of *homo sapiens* who ride the ranges, plough the prairies, and crowd the cities of the world. The shrinking world has tended to integration of control and differentiation of demand. Even with the most virtuous at the levers, how can control be exercised for the good of all when there are so many voices emerging from different conditions, inheriting different traditions, committed to different ideals, and demanding different solutions. Every man wants to realize the opportunities of human knowledge, but each is inclined to believe that all will benefit if knowledge is mobilized in the service of his ideals and his traditions. Though their powers are universal, men's values are local and mired in the mud of history. Power is too often untamed by responsibility to the world.

Few want to turn back the clock of science and technology. Most approve the trend toward an integration of the world so that its resources, its experience, its knowledge will be available to everyone, but they do not want to turn their backs entirely on the customs, the morals, the language, the institutions which they have inherited from their ancestors. They may resent many of the limitations of these traditions. They may want a broader sphere of individual or local self-determination. They may long for the greater freedoms enjoyed by others. But the nostalgia for familiar customs cannot be downed by the beckoning of newer freedoms. Men want security as well as adventure, and the sense of security is likely to wane as familiar conditions of life give way to unknown ideals, standards, and laws, even though the latter may carry the potentiality of greater freedom of expression and of religion, greater freedom from want and from fear.

The dilemma I am discussing is manifested in the popularity of the words "mass" and "freedom." Mass suggests the consequence of the application of modern science and technology to the conditions of human life; freedom points to the influence of these conditions upon human attitudes and aspirations.

Under the influence of mass production, mass media of communication, mass movements, and weapons of mass destruction, mankind is in danger of becoming a huge undifferentiated mass, but under the influences of free thought, free speech, free enterprise, and free education, men are demanding more individual freedom.

In a shrinking world men are aware of wider horizons as the pressure of innumerable impressions upon the individual's attention increases. He perceives more opportunities for choice, but finds himself more bound by the conditions of his life. Determination by the mass and freedom of the will are both in the ascendant. Perhaps the first dominates in Russia, and the second in America, but both affect people everywhere.

The Role of Universities

I do not see how this problem of unifying power and diversifying values, of one world and many men, can be solved except through the university. The very name suggests that it is dedicated to that problem.

Thirty-three years ago Graham Wallas saw this problem which it has taken two world wars, the devastation of a continent, the killing of tens of millions by war, war-borne disease, mass massacre, and the explosion of five atomic bombs to drive into the sluggish minds of any large number of people.

In *The Great Society,* published in June, 1914, Wallas wrote:

> We are forced now to recognize that a society whose intellectual direction consists only of unrelated specialisms must drift, and that we dare not drift any longer. We stand, as the Greek thinkers stood, in a new world. And because that world is new, we feel that neither the sectional observations of the special student, nor the ever accumulating records of the past, nor the narrow experience of the practical man can suffice us. We must let our minds play freely over all the conditions of life till we can either justify our civilization or change it.
>
> The Greek thinkers, with all their magnificent courage and comprehensiveness, failed in the end either to understand or to guide the actual social forces of their time. Our own brains are less acute, our memories less retentive than those of the Greeks, while the body of relevant facts which we must survey has been increased ten thousand fold. How are we to have any chance of success?

Wallas saw no solution except through the better organization of thought. He examined the material circumstances, the mental attitudes, and the processes of recording, manipulating and analyzing data to facilitate effective thought. While he believed that conditions could be developed to promote thought by people in many walks of life, he suggested that the university is the organization most deliberately developed to this end. He acknowledged that it has not been wholly successful. "There are hundreds of cases in which a professor's teaching spoils his thinking, and these are balanced by hundreds of others in which his thinking spoils his teaching."

This is true, but the problem is rather to improve the university than to place reliance upon the intrinsically less adapted institutions such as the government, the business corporation, or the church to provide the conditions for effective thinking on our great problem.

Freedom from censorship; freedom from the explicit directives of superior authority; freedom from pressure to produce practical results; periods of freedom from time schedules and the coercions of an operative institution; the opportunity to bring all fields of knowledge, all procedures, all varieties of data to bear upon a particular problem; and the habit of reflection, of deliberation, and of dealing with novel ideas—all of these can be provided by a university. Often they are not, but it is difficult to see how any other institution could combine them all.

I assume that these are among the conditions conducive to good teaching and research at the university level. I understand that one of the foundations is financing a study of the conditions which promote productive research. Perhaps this study will help the universities it serves.

Let us consider how the universities might apply themselves to solving this problem of narrowing the lag of a universal moral integration behind that of a universal material integration. How can the progress of the world toward social solidarity catch up with its progress toward technological unification? How can the discords which trouble all who have ears to hear be orchestrated? Tunes which have delighted local environments for millennia produced intolerable cacophonies when each is heard everywhere.

Few thoughtful people doubt that this is the supreme problem, and few advocate its solution through hampering the progress of science and technology. Discoveries and inventions once made cannot be unmade. Scientific ideas cannot be forgotten. The world has come to believe in science and invention. It cherishes the opportunities they offer for satisfying human wants. It will not tolerate the suppression of scientists and inventors, as witness the rallying of American public opinion behind the atomic scientists in their struggle with the military for civilian control of atomic energy.

There are still some people who believe the problem can be solved by political wisdom, by efficient administration, or by adequate law. All of these methods are useful, but none can solve the problem unless an atmosphere of opinion exists in the world which assures the stability of the world's constitution however controversy may develop among its parts. So long as any lesser group, be it church, people, nation, empire, federation, party, or sovereign state, regards the world as its oyster to serve its particular needs, any constitution of the world will be vulnerable. This vulnerability will continue unless the people of the world recognize that the whole is greater than the part; unless they recognize that their human commitments are prior to their professional attachments, their national loyalties, and their ecclesiastical preferences; unless they feel themselves world citizens, ready to support the limitations upon political methods, the accepted objectives of administration, and the processes of legal interpretation and change prescribed by the United Nations, however those may for the moment seem to encroach upon the interest or the autonomy of lesser groups.

The Role of Public Opinion

Why does such an opinion seem essential if our world is to become stable? What are the conditions under which such an opinion can develop?

It is clear that politics, the method of which is to organize stability by opposing one group to another, tends toward the use of fraud, violence, and other extreme procedures unless limited by a law with more power behind it than that available to any political group. Political parties within the state are always on the verge of resorting to such methods. If the state is weak, they do, and society endures insurrection and civil war. In world affairs, where there is no universal state, the threat of fraud and violence is continuous and the reality is frequent. In our age the barriers of space and the efficiency of defensive weapons, which in the past often protected lesser states from the hostilities or even the threats of great powers, can no longer be relied upon. The devastating efficiency of modern weapons, the lack of any material defense against them, the advantage of the initiative in attack, and the speed with which hostilities may begin, create little confidence in the fear of retaliation or the equilibrium of power as a means to stability. Politics unlimited by effective law gives no promise of security.

It is also clear that administration can function only where all accept the law to be administered and that such a law cannot exist unless opinion is committed to some common ends. Furthermore, administration, in proportion as it is efficient, tends to make the ends which it assumes absolute values which justify any means and which treat all other interests as subordinate. The efficient administration of a plan tends to look upon the individual and group for which the plan was made as instruments for its achievement. The larger the plan the more danger that its administration will support tyranny and hamper progress.

Law also is not able to stand alone. However intricate its pattern, however carefully the rights of the individual and the family, the autonomy of the state and the culture of the nation, the freedom of religion, of business, of labor, of agriculture, of the professions are considered in its structure and protected by its procedures and balances, law cannot withstand the strain of a rapidly changing society unless supported by a public with some common opinions about justice and a common determination to achieve justice without departing from the procedures which the law permits.

Politics, administration, and law are essential elements of stability, but they cannot be relied upon unless supported by public opinion throughout the area within which they function.

Accepting this conclusion, it is easy to assume that our problem is to mobilize the forces of education and propaganda in order to create common opinions throughout the world. If only all men were Christians, or democrats, or Confucians, or Buddhists, or Marxists our problem would be easier. But they are not. There is nothing in history, in sociology, or in psychology that justifies us in expecting that they will be in any foreseeable future. Men are in many respects alike. They have common needs for food, sex, activity, and society; common wishes for security, recognition, adventure, and response; but in their larger aspirations they differ because of particular historic traditions, particular environmental conditions, and the particular experiences of each personality. They cannot all be molded to a uniform society, and, if they could, the possibilities of further progress might be impaired. Without the stimulus of comparison, of competition, and of social experiment, science and invention might halt, and human adaptation to new opportunities might lag.

The problem cannot be solved by a common faith or ideology or doctrine or ideal. The history of the future cannot be limited by anything that could be formulated today. History has always been creative and we want it to continue to be. No generation can prescribe its destiny. It is unlikely that any opinion can integrate the world unless it is so flexible that it leaves every faith some grounds for hoping that it may survive and eventually triumph. People of varied faiths may get together in support of constitutions or laws which regulate means and instruments but leave ends and ultimates to the future.

At the meeting of UNESCO in Paris, in 1946, the Yugoslav unofficial representative, speaking for the absent Soviets, made it clear that his country would have nothing of UNESCO if it assumed "scientific humanism" as its philosophy and ruled out "dialectical materialism." It was necessary to assure him that UNESCO had no doctrine. We cannot hope for universal agreement on ultimate values and I doubt whether we should desire it. Too much unity may be as bad as too little.

The fear of excessive integration is not confined to national politicians, laissez-faire economists, or minority ideologists. Mr. Justice Brandeis made a plea against too much bigness. Professor W. E. Rappard of Geneva, at the Princeton conference on February 19, 1947, deplored the centralizing effect of the increasing cost of research. "Only the wealthiest institutions," he said, "and soon only the greatest countries can hope to engage in the most promising forms of research." His suggestion of a great international university in the League buildings at Geneva, while it might equalize opportunities, would hardly avoid the dangers of excessive integration. The philosopher Horace Kallen fears that all unification movements, whether in the fields of science, economics, government, religion, or art, tend toward totalitarianism. "They obtain," he writes, "in a wider climate of opinion which affects also free society. Its differentia is the emphasis upon 'planning.'" Rejecting "unity" and even "integration," as too restrictive of a pluralistic world, he suggests the word "orchestration" to describe the limits which relationships impose upon diversity.[1] But an orchestra does better if all the performers in addition to wanting the performance to succeed have before them music recorded with a common notation. Perhaps science and the world can best strive for unity of tools and of the particular performance rather than for a unity of ultimate ends and values.

Universities and Freedom

Can world opinion recognize the desirability of protecting all human personalities from military destruction, of enlarging the freedoms of all to the limits possible without encroaching upon the freedoms of others, of extending the benefits of science and technology for a general elevation of standards of living, and of practicing mutual tolerance? Can such an opinion be universalized without unduly restricting the future of the world or the peculiar aspirations of any? Can a constitution be erected upon such a simple consensus and if so can it prove adequate to prevent war and to facilitate coöperation throughout the world?

I do not know, but I believe if universities strive to become communities of scholars they may contribute to such a realization. In such a community each feels free to cherish his own ideals, assumptions and hypotheses; each tolerates those of others; each makes available to his fellows his methods and his conclusions; each is eager to advance knowledge in his field. To all are available accumulations of knowledge about facts, methods, and generalizations, and an atmosphere of devotion to intellectual integrity and personal toleration.

A university, while a community of scholars, is an anarchy of assumptions. It thus resembles the world which may be a community of men but remains an anarchy of beliefs. "To deny, to believe and to doubt well are to a man what a race is to a horse," said Pascal, and William James thought, "Our undisciplinables are our proudest products . . . the university most worthy of rational admiration is one in which your lonely thinker can feel himself least lonely, most positively furthered and most richly fed." "A free society," writes Horace Kallen, after recalling these statements, "is one which shelters and cherishes these divergencies, whether it be a sovereign state or an academic commmunity." [2]

The world is full of doubters and enthusiasts, of skeptics and idealists, and here again it resembles universities. Criticism is the life of scholarship and science, and criticism is next door to skepticism. But on the other hand, as President Harper once said, "If in any environment idealism reigns supreme, it is in that of the university" [3]—the presence of youth assures this.

A university, more than any other institution, is a microcosm of the world. It seems possible, therefore, that it can provide the conditions under which the problems of the latter can be worked out in thought. With the ideas available, men of affairs, driven by the will of people to save themselves, their countries, and their world, when faced by the necessities which become more obvious day by day, may build enough of the sentiment of world citizenship to permit the United Nations to function and to develop an upward spiral of world opinion and world organization, each contributing to the other.

Only if oriented to this vast task which transcends national boundaries can the universities justify themselves in our age. Harvard, Princeton, Chicago have been exploring the problems of general and specialized education. The debate continues upon whether university education should cultivate an appreciation of values or should emphasize the disinterested pursuit of scientific truth. These and other universities have been greatly expanding both education and research in the field of international relations. American university men have been prominent in recent commissions which have reported on the rehabilitation of education in Japan and Germany. UNESCO has before it projects for a world university. Research is being carried on upon the conditions of its own progress. Investigators are inventing better processes of invention and discovering improved methods of discovery. These stirrings may indicate wide appreciation of the job which universities must undertake.

American universities, alone in the world, were materially untouched by the war. Their libraries, laboratories, buildings, and staffs are functioning. It is for them to set standards of individual freedom, national development, and world citizenship. By example and suggestion they may contribute to the revival of universities elsewhere as centers from which ideas and students may radiate, planting the seeds of an informed world public opinion. Such an opinion may make it possible for the United Nations and its affiliated organizations to stabilize the world order without destroying its variety.

13

THE TEACHING OF
INTERNATIONAL LAW
IN THE POSTWAR WORLD

The first Conference of the Teachers of International Law and Related Subjects was held in April, 1914, and subsequent conferences have been held in 1925, 1928, 1929, 1933, 1938 and 1941. During these thirty-two years we have discussed the importance of instruction in international law; the means of increasing and improving that instruction; the difference in the type of instruction appropriate to undergraduate, graduate, and law students; the sources of international law and the means of making them more available, particularly State Department documents; and the vocational opportunities available to students of international law. In more recent meetings, we have discussed the teaching of international politics, international economies, international propaganda, and other subjects related to international law.

International Law and International Relations

There is, perhaps, significance in this widening of the scope of our deliberations in the last decade. Elihu Root said at the first meeting of the American Society of International Law in 1907 that broad popular understanding of international law was essential if international relations were to be conducted peacefully and satisfactorily under democratic conditions. He repeated this thought in opening the first of our conferences in 1914 when he said: "The putting of instruction in inter-

---

From *Proceedings of the Eighth Conference of Teachers of International Law and Related Subjects,* held at Washington, D.C., April 24–25, 1946.

national law in American educational institutions on a broader basis, giving it a wider scope and greater efficiency, is not a mere matter of book learning; it is not a mere matter of science. It is a matter of patriotic duty."

This statement was made a few months before World War I, but in our second meeting eleven years later the same spirit prevailed. International law, its sources and modes of instruction occupied our attention. In our meetings during the 1930's, however, other approaches to international relations were increasingly considered, and in a conference on "Teaching and Research in International Relations" held under the auspices of the New York Council on Foreign Relations in February, 1946, international law was not mentioned in the resolutions at all. This may have been partly because "international relations," which was the subject matter of the conference, was considered to be exclusive of international law, although by defining "international relations" as "the study of those social relations that transcend national boundaries" the conference seems to have given the term an inclusive meaning. With this definition, however, the conference agreed that "the 'core' of an undergraduate international relations curriculum should include international politics, international organization, political geography and diplomatic history."

I note that our own program at the present meeting is concerned as much with international politics, the United Nations, and the atom bomb as with international law.

Has the experience of thirty-two years shaken by two world wars broken the faith of American teachers in the value of international law as a subject of college and university teaching?

One should not jump hastily to that conclusion. One of the purposes of the United Nations is "to establish conditions under which justice and respect for the obligations arising from treaties and other sources of *international law* can be maintained" and the International Court of Justice is established as one of its principal organs. I have not counted college catalogues, but I do not believe there has been a diminution in the number of courses on international law or in the number of students and instructors in that field. The change has not been a decline of interest in international law but an increase in interest in other aspects of international relations. The amount of attention given to international relations in all its aspects has enormously increased, both in education and in public thinking during the last generation.

It is perhaps significant that while the League of Nations Covenant called for "the maintenance of justice and a scrupulous respect for all treaty obligations in the dealings of organized peoples with one another," the United Nations Charter seeks "to establish *conditions* under which justice and respect for the obligations arising from treaties and other sources of international law can be maintained." The problem of establishing a law-governed world is perhaps less simple than we thought a generation ago. Conditions political, economic, social, and educational we now know have to be studied, their tendencies understood, and their stabilization facilitated before we can expect international law to be observed. We cannot maintain international law directly but must first establish the conditions under which it can be maintained. It is, therefore, a sign of maturity that we realize the need of instruction in international relations in all its aspects, and are not content with international law alone.

It would, however, be dangerous to allow international law to step out of the curriculum altogether. Modern educators anticipate serious consequences if technical and professional studies entirely supersede the humanities in general education. There is always a danger in the "professional distortion."

International Law and Public Policy

I recently participated in a discussion of the role which military affairs should have in general education. A military man presented the point of view, natural for one of his profession, that we should assume that in the next war we would have no friends or allies, that we would be attacked without warning, that we would be at a disadvantage if our government was limited in its action by democratic procedures, and that we would also suffer if our industry had not been previously organized by the government in the interest of military efficiency. I raised the question whether a public opinion, moulded to accept such theses, might not consider war inevitable and might not demand that in preparation for that inevitable war we put the military ahead of the civilians and the diplomats, that we attack any potential enemy preventively, that we abandon democratic controls over military affairs, and that we governmentalize our economy in the interests of preparedness. If one may judge from history, even very recent history, countries that have accepted these theses have tended to get into war and to lose the war after they got into it.

Yet one cannot doubt but that our general staff would be failing in its responsibilities if it did not consider all of these hypotheses. The danger is that such hypotheses if presented in general education are likely to be accepted, not as hypotheses, but as inevitabilities. Policy may then be shaped in adaptation to them rather than in opposition to their realization. It is true, popular military education might be developed in a form which would not produce such results. We cannot, however, overlook the propensity of the professional military mind to assume the dominating importance of war, and to base national policy on considerations of tactics and strategy. From such assumptions the student is likely to view the world beyond the national frontiers as an enemy against which national policy must relentlessly struggle.

Perhaps it is safer to base general education, from which democratic public opinion is formed, on humanistic studies, that is, studies which contribute a broad knowledge of human nature as it has functioned in the history of different societies, and of human values as they have been exemplified in the art, literature, and social standards of all civilizations. Such studies may enable the student and citizen to view man and society on the broadest possible geographic and historical base and to deduce wise national policy from that broad base. Appropriate strategies and tactics can then be chosen to forward such a national policy in contingencies as they arise. The "art of war" instead of being a condition of existence, assumes its proper position as one among many means for achieving human ends, applicable only under particular historical circumstances.

I am not denying that constructive thought must move in both directions, from the universal to the particular, and from the particular to the universal, from the ideal to the actual, and from the actual to the ideal. It is safer, however, if man as citizen begins with the universal and the ideal, that is, with the broadest and longest experience he is capable of assimilating from his observations and readings.

It seems to me that these observations illustrate the relation of international law to the other aspects of international relations. International law examines the entire field of international relations from the universal and ideal points of view. The other aspects of international relations tend to proceed from particular and practical points of view. They are concerned with the application of means to immediate objectives and the tendencies which flow from the pursuit by independent nations of political, military, economic, social, and educational policies and strategies each in its own immediate interest. They deal, like the pure and applied sciences, with the consequences of observed activities and with the means for achieving limited ends. They are, therefore, to be contrasted with international law which seeks norms of behavior and procedures for realizing them which give consideration to more remote interests, consequences, and possibilities. International law cannot neglect the actual behavior of states in determining its norms, but it always strives to direct that behavior in order to achieve the common values held throughout the world community. International law cannot neglect precise analysis and careful weighing of evidence in formulating and applying its rules and procedures, but its technique must always be subordinate to its broad purpose. It exists neither to perpetuate the *status quo* nor to enrich its present practitioners.

There is a danger that if exclusive attention is focused on the objective analysis of world politics, the values which make our civilization worth preserving may be forgotten. We may drift into a profound defeatism leading to a decline of civilization if not to sudden disaster. I am, of course, assuming that in our day and age civilization must be thought of as universal, if it is thought of at all. It is no longer possible for a segment of the world's population to consider its civilization in any aspect other than as a part of the universal civilization which mankind has been developing since the Renaissance and the discoveries.

I am not unaware of the opposite danger that in the construction and analysis of an ideal world order, the actual condition of affairs may be overlooked and that by striving for utopia, we will become disillusioned and convinced that progress is impossible.

It is, therefore, necessary that we approach international relations with due consideration to both the general and the particular, to both the desired and the observed. We must realize, however, that in this field, more than in almost any other, opinions are the facts that make the world what it is. Attempts have been made to analyze world politics in terms of armaments and military potentials; in terms of geography and strategic positions; in terms of economic resources and techniques; in terms of races and cultures; and in terms of historical and social formations, such as nations and states. But no one of these explanations has proved adequate. International relations depend less upon these conditions than upon opinions about them. In fact these conditions are but crystallizations of opinion. Even geography and resources change their significance as changing opinion changes values and utilities. The rocks on which the determinists have sought to anchor human behavior are but sand which shifts with the waves of opinion and the tides of belief. The state of the public mind at any moment may be more or less intelligent, more or less crystallized, more or less homogeneous, but that state is the phenomenon from which international relations grow, and the state of the public mind and public opinion, however crystallized, is malleable when compared with almost any other phenomenon. Changes in the world's opinion will change the character of the world.

International Law and Education for Citizenship

Education is the mode of changing public opinion, whether that education is formal or through the hard road of experience. The values imported by general education, the analyses of conditions developed by university education and research, the policies and operations which more advanced study and responsibility suggest for maintaining a harmony between conflicting values under existing conditions—these are the stuff out of which a stable, secure, and prosperous world can be built.

Clearly, when world politics is being discussed, it is world education that is important. Education in one country cannot remake the world. Efforts must go on simultaneously and harmoniously in all countries if a world opinion, capable of giving order to the world is to result.

Can such education proceed harmoniously in all sections of the world except through the medium of international law? International law is the one objective source of universal values. There are many governments, many economies, many cultures, many philosophies, many religions in the world. There is only one international law. It is true books have been written on American international law, British international law, Soviet international law, Chinese international law; perhaps the production of such books is a sign of the disintegration of the world under the stress of nationalism and regionalism, but unless such tendencies are controlled and general opinion accepts the universality of international law, the "one world" which the atomic scientists say we must recognize will not exist in the minds of men.

International law seems then to be the best approach to the concept of the moral unity of mankind and to the foundations of our global civilization. With our studies of power politics, of economic rivalries, of conflicting propagandas, necessary as they are to understand the actual conditions of international relations, let us not neglect to cultivate the oasis of common understanding called international law.

International law, however, cannot be considered in isolation. Unless continually related to international politics it becomes unreal. Its sources and its sanctions are to be found in the conditions of international relations no less than in its own traditions and institutions. Like any system of law, international law is always in flux between the inertia of past customs and precedents, the pressures of present politics, and the attraction of ideals of the future. To neglect any of these sources and sanctions is to study a dead system, not a living and growing international law.

In our period of transition, this tension between the forces of the past, the present, and the future is extreme and we international lawyers must teach our students to understand all types of forces. The Pact of Paris, the United Nations Charter, the resolution of the General Assembly on the control of atomic energy, the resolution of the Economic and Social Council on the protection of human rights and fundamental freedoms, and the charter for the trial of major war criminals may prove to be more important sources of international law than the opinions of Sir William Scott or the Hague conventions. With a full appreciation of *all* of its sources, some of the time-honored classifications and principles of international law may be found to have fallen into the discard. We may find that the extreme deductions from the principle of national sovereignty which became current in the nineteenth century and which led to conclusions contrary to the assertions of both judges and jurists of the classical period of international law, were aberrations unsupported by the international law of today. We may have to abandon the concept that states are the only subjects of international law and to recognize rules which confer rights and impose duties on individuals directly. We may have to discard the sharp distinction between war and peace and the notion of neutrality which grew from the concept that the legal position of belligerents is equal. We may have to include all resorts to violence in international relations within the concepts of aggression, of defense, or of sanctions. We may have to recognize that the needs of international legislation and of international executive action must, under certain circumstances, override the principle that no state can be bound to a new rule without its consent. Such a development is, in fact, suggested by articles of the United Nations Charter which assert the competence of the United Nations to enforce certain of its principles against nonmembers (Article 1, paragraph 6) and the competence of the Security Council to make decisions which bind all of the members (Article 25). We may have to abandon the rule stated by the Permanent Court of International Justice in the Eastern Carelia case, and to accept the universal jurisdiction of the International Court of Justice in controversies between states on legal issues.

There will be resistance to these changes. The spirit of national sovereignty remains strong, but the force arising from apprehension of the atom bomb may prove to be stronger. The philosopher Hobbes recognized three centuries ago that individuals might exchange their natural liberty for government when conditions made the war of all against all intolerable. Grotius was of the opinion that reason, even when not driven by such extreme conditions, might establish a universal will to observe the law. The hope of Grotius has not been demonstrated by experience. It may be that the two world wars and the prospect that a third would be even more destructive to the existence of states or even of civilization itself will have established the conditions which Hobbes regarded as the prerequisite for the establishment of law.

If the public in all countries can appreciate the need of international law in the world of today and the need of continually conforming the rules of that law to the conditions of the world as it has been, as it is, and as it should be, we can perhaps have one world instead of none. To achieve these appreciations is the responsibility of the teachers of international law.

14

ON THE APPLICATION

OF INTELLIGENCE

TO WORLD AFFAIRS

One difficulty with which the world is faced is the absence, even in the minds of the wisest, of conviction concerning the direction in which movement should take place. The arguments for and against socialism and capitalism, national sovereignty and world government, individual liberty and collective will, conciliating Russia and containing Russia, are so convincing that no one who understands the problems wants to commit himself to one or the other of these alternatives.

The partisans are committed, and the masses—convinced that these alternatives state the problem—await to be told which they should select. Unable to tell them, the leaders lose prestige, with the results of partisan warfare, partisan leadership, wobbling, and universal skepticism.

May there not be in this apparently gloomy situation an opportunity for intelligence? May not the opportunity exist for educating the public to the belief that simple alternatives seldom state the whole of any social problem? Assertion of such simple alternatives is a tool of warfare, whether military, economic, or psychological. Search for a larger range of choice and exploration of the possibilities of more complex proposals is a tool of reason. May not the obvious inadequacies of the simple alternatives with which the propagandists deafen the ear provide an opportunity for enlightenment on the difference between reason and war?

Here, however, it may be said: You are committing the sin you

From *Bulletin of the Atomic Scientists,* IV (August, 1948).

describe. The contrast of reason to war is another of those simple alternatives which seeks to limit choice to policies neither of which is wholly desirable. Reason has the merit of imagining and exploring the possibilities that might be chosen, but it may permanently frustrate action. It may justify fiddling while Rome burns. War has many evils, but a firm decision and commitment to action may be the only solution to a pressing problem. It may be better to give whole-hearted allegiance to a program which may be only second or third best than to have no program at all.

There is merit in this criticism. The contrast of war and reason is itself an oversimplification. There may be possible choices different from either.

There may, for example, be commitment to a policy or principle not so absolutely as to invite war, but within the orbit of defined procedures. There may be a utilization of reason, not to the extent of investigating all the possible policies which can be imagined or the last consequence of each, but so far as time and circumstances permit. Descartes recognized that "sufficient reason" is all that can be expected for practical action, and Justice Holmes remarked that every moment we stake our lives on predictions that are far from certain.

It is the function of intelligence to break through the bonds of simple alternatives, and this applies to the often assumed contrast between understanding and action, no less than to other dichotomies. Action, which implies assault on things as they are or tend to be, implies resistance and faces some risk of war, however carefully the consequences have been explored by fallible man. Understanding, which implies investigation of all possible developments of, and interventions in, a situation also implies deliberation and faces the risk of indecision and drift while matters go from bad to worse.

Only with God and inert matter are reason and action perfectly united. God can unite them because his omniscience foresees all the consequences of action, and his omnipotence assures the triumph of his act, even though interludes of conflict with the devil may occur; but since the occurrence and results of such conflict are foreseen and provided for, it should not be called "war" but "police action."

Inert matter, on the other hand, can unite reason and action because the individual choice of each of its constituents is so small and their number is so great that the statistical principle of large numbers assures that the results of action upon it can, in considerable measure, be predicted by the application of previously formulated laws of nature. Because man has more intelligence and more freedom than the atom and less than God, his actions with respect to himself always involve risk.

He cannot, by any use of reason, avoid responsibility to appraise the risk and to decide whether the circumstances justify it.

It is not possible in the space of this article to examine fully the simple alternatives mentioned earlier, but perhaps suggestions can be made pointing the direction of other possible choices.

Freedom under Socialism and Capitalism

The value of socialism in presenting the possibility of a vertical expansion of a community's economy and in avoiding the dangers inherent in the horizontal expansion of many national economies in a shrinking world, has been mentioned by Harold Laski and others.[1] These writers, however, give insufficient attention to the danger that socialism, conducted by national governments, preoccupied with problems of defense, will utilize the possibilities of economic planning, not for welfare, but for augmenting national power as an instrument of security and economic bargaining if not of expansion. In the process the individual may be ground down by the social juggernaut, lack of incentive may restrict production, and total war may ensue. The socialisms which have been experienced in history have been state socialisms, and they have proved dangerous to liberty, prosperity, and peace.

Capitalism has the virtue that it presents the possibility of a separation of politics and economics, thus permitting each to check excesses of the other. This possibility was in considerable measure realized in the nineteenth century, to the benefit of liberty, prosperity, and peace in Europe. Mr. Anthony Eden in referring to this mentioned the danger that monopoly, abusive exercises of power, and periods of depression may grow out of capitalism, and agreed that planning for freedom is necessary.[2] He perhaps underestimated the difficulty of restoring and maintaining a free economy under conditions in which men are able both to perceive economic inequities and to use the machinery of the state to rectify them.

The separation of economy and polity is hardly practicable in a democracy unless all citizens recognize that neither liberty nor equality can be enjoyed completely without destroying the other. If democracy exaggerates its demand for equality, it tends to produce socialism, which is likely to destroy the civil liberties which are its essence. If capitalism exaggerates freedom including freedom to combine for the maintenance of wages and prices, it tends to produce monopoly which also leads to socialism.

The evils of both socialism and capitalism are so manifest that the search for alternatives in various forms of mixed economies has proceeded. Stability is the consequence, not of simplicity, but of complexity. We may expect that a pattern including both competition and coöperation may develop in which government corporations, state enterprises, free enterprises, and regulations, both national and international, will all have a role. Such a pattern may provide answers to some of the evils of both socialistic and free market economies and permit reasonable liberty without excessive inequalities. That it is difficult to permit government enterprise and regulation, sufficient to prevent private monopoly and exploitation, without destroying market freedom sufficient to regulate basic price relations, no one can deny.

National Sovereignty and World Government

The contrast between national sovereignty and world government is not new. It is, however, novel to find the leading Marxist country the outstanding advocate, both theoretically and practically, of state sovereignty, while the leading advocate of capitalism, of democracy, and of nationalism has developed within it the most powerful movement for world government, and has proposed officially, far-reaching steps for the actual control of sovereign action in the important field of atomic energy by a vetoless world authority. The cosmopolitans have become nationalist, and the nationalists have become cosmopolitan.

The contributions which particularistic nationalism and claims of self-determining sovereignty have made to the initiation of war have been recognized by most serious students of the subject. National sovereignty has also presented grave difficulties to the utilization of the world's resources for promoting human welfare. It is not surprising that the experience of two world wars and the obvious instability of a world in which national security rests on an increasingly bipolar balance of power have converted nationalism and sovereignty into terms of reproach. On the other hand, the potentialities of a world state for oppressing humanity and for frustrating progress have not escaped the attention of most thinkers.

Universal states have developed in the limited civilizations of the past, but, according to Arnold Toynbee, they have tended to degenerate, to stagnate, to oppress, and to disappear in periods of human misery which end the civilization which they sought to integrate.[3] Now that man has put all his eggs into the one basket of a developing world civilization, such a collapse would be devastating.

With national sovereignty, we may be physically destroyed by atomic warfare; with world government, civilization may be destroyed by oppression, corruption, and disintegration. Here again it is well to recall that stability is the product of complexity. The United Nations includes elements of empire, of balance of power, of federation, and of international coöperation. If the great powers agreed, they could, under the Charter, rule the world. Only because of the probability of their disagreement can the small powers hope to retain their freedom. But if the great powers do not agree, they can be controlled only by their mutual fears, and the world's peace depends upon the unreliable equilibrium of their power.

Yet the possibility, envisaged by the Charter, that the General Assembly may develop and lead a world public opinion, and provide direct protection for human rights even against national authorities, points toward federation. The moves of the General Assembly to interpret the limits of domestic jurisdiction relatively, and to assert authority when the Security Council is unable to act, suggests that the United Nations may assume a more federalistic character than the makers of the Charter probably intended.

The United Nations may develop into something different from either national sovereignties or world government. It may facilitate the development, hoped for by Mr. Dewitt Poole, of a more complex balance of power.[4] Balance-of-power systems have in the past tended, through the process of conquest of the lesser states by the greater, toward a reduction in the number of states involved, and toward less frequent but more devastating wars, until eventually a universal empire has been established through the conquest by one of all those remaining. China thus moved from the period of Confucius to the period of "warring states," ended in universal conquest by the Ts'in emperor in the third century B.C. The history of classical civilization culminating in the universal empire of Augustus was similar.

Such a course is typical historically, and perception of the ways of power makes it appear probable so long as each state must rely for security on the superiority of its own power over that of its most dangerous rival. More complex and more stable equilibria which might arise from the development of a larger number of independent centers of power cannot be expected except within the framework of a world order whereby the whole, without exercising the supreme power of a world government, yet has sufficient power in itself to prevent aggression and to give force to the law of nations.

The United Nations has the possibility of developing in several directions which would provide alternatives different from either national sovereignties or world government, and which perhaps offer more hope for the future. The difficulty of keeping sovereignty divided must, however, be recognized.

The Individual and the Group

The debates in the human rights commission of the United Nations have made it clear that the world is not prepared to accept either the individual or the group as the supreme value. The West places first the human rights to be free in the choice of religion and opinion, to be free to communicate, and to be free from oppression, whether by the group or by others. The East, on the other hand, places first the human rights to be fed, clothed, and housed by the group.

The effort to combine the two points of view in President Roosevelt's Four Freedoms has not eliminated the conflict. The group can more easily assure its members freedom from fear and from want if it directs them without regard for their civil liberties. Freedoms of opinion, communication, and activities, especially economic activities, hamper the state in its planning and direction to assure a livelihood for all citizens.

The evils of excessive individualism and excessive collectivism are evident in theory and the need and difficulty of compromise becomes manifest when efforts are made to interpret and apply constitutional bills of rights. Such applications make it clear that rights of the individual are relative to the right of the community to protect itself from "clear and present dangers" and that exercises of national power are relative to the expectations of human rights sustained by a vigilant public opinion. In these relativities, mankind, by complicated rules of law, may find alternative choices to the simple dichotomy between the individual and the state.

Conciliating and Containing Russia

Mr. Wallace and Mr. Byrnes, in the controversy which led to the former's retirement from the cabinet in September, 1946,[5] precipitated the idea that Russian-American relations must be defined in terms of the alternative of conciliation or containment. Appeasement versus toughness is another but less friendly way of expressing the idea. Mr. X has argued for containment on the ground that the Soviet state by its ideology, by its need of maintaining domestic authority, and by the requirements of a monolithic party, is irrevocably committed to the proposition that the capitalistic world is its enemy. According to this opinion, Soviet conciliation with the West is impossible. The Soviets must continually strive to conquer.[6]

If this opinion is true, efforts at conciliation are mistaken. The Soviets will understand no argument but force; consequently unless their expansion is made physically impossible, it will take place, and the balance of power will eventually be overthrown in their favor. Containment therefore seems necessary. But on the other hand, containment provides the justification for the Soviet theory that the world is their enemy. It strengthens their will to expand and stimulates them to develop the means for implementing that will. Containment of an expanding gas prepares the way for explosion.

The advocates of conciliation, therefore, argue that containment is self-defeating, and that, on the other hand, under appropriate conditions, a spirit of conciliation may be reciprocated. Examples are cited in which hostile rivals have accepted policies of coöperation.

It must be admitted, however, that such incidents have seldom occurred in the game of power politics unless both rivals have found themselves faced by a new power which they feared more than they feared one another. Britain and France were able to conciliate after Fashoda because Germany was becoming a menace to both. The West and the Soviet could conciliate during the war because both were fighting for their lives against the Axis.

An effort at conciliation between states each of which is dependent for security on its own arms and each of which fears attack by the other is likely to be interpreted as weakness or as a strategic maneuver, and to bring little favorable response. This certainly has been the postwar experience in relationships of the West and the Soviet Union.

Can other alternatives be found? Mr. Benton hoped that the Voice of America might reach behind the Iron Curtain and create there a new state of mind.[7] Mr. Burnham thought that persuasion and containment were both hopeless and urged isolation of the Soviet Union and preparation for war.[8] Others hoped that a meeting of heads of state might be effective. Stalin alone in Russia, it was thought, might be free to change his mind.[9]

Others hoped that the development of world public opinion through the United Nations [10] or the organization of the West into an overwhelmingly powerful federation,[11] or the bulding up of a third great power through union of western Europe [12] might bring the argument of facts to persuade the Soviet Union to abandon policies of expansion which might then become hopeless. Mr. Lippmann believed that if Soviet troops could be got out of Germany and Austria, the European situation would become more stable.[13] Mr. Poole thought if the Soviet Union became one of nine major centers of power, instead of one of two such centers, the world would become stable.[14]

Mr. X hoped that containment might succeed until Stalin died, when, if not before, changes within the Soviet Union might alter the situation.

Discontent, he pointed out, can hardly be absent within the Soviet structure, rich in secret police, purges, and discipline, but poor in consumers' goods, civil rights, and information about the outside world.[15]

At a later date Secretary Marshall suggested that success in building the economy of western Europe would create conditions under which the Soviet Union would see that for the time being a policy of fomenting chaos and expanding communist parties was impracticable and would change, for a time at least, to the opposite policy of establishing normal relations with the West for mutual economic benefit.[16] Such a change it was pointed out, was evident in Soviet policy in the late 1920's after conclusion of the Locarno agreements.

The Problem of Preventing War

From such suggestions as these and from further imaginative thought, alternatives better than either conciliation or containment may be found. The ceaseless search for them, even while we are pursuing one, is the path of wisdom. The world is certainly in danger from tendencies which will lead to general war unless human ingenuity devises methods of changing them.

The power system is tending to become bilateral and such a system cannot be stable. War-devastated areas are tending to deteriorate further and to afford favorable opportunities for radical propaganda. Respect for legal procedures is tending to decline, and the belief that any means can be justified by a sufficient end is tending to grow. The power of the military offensive over the defensive is tending to increase through the use of airborne superexplosives, and a universal fear of sudden and devastating attack is developing. Can anything be done to rectify these dangerous tendencies of power, economy, law, and technology?

The power equilibrium might become more stable if western Europe became an independent center of power, and if the United Nations became more powerful relative to the states, either through developing its own military contingents and its capacity to make decisions promptly, or through a general reduction of national armaments. Efforts in both of these directions are in progress.

Economic improvement in the war-devastated areas cannot be expected to proceed with sufficient rapidity without aid from the more fortunate countries. Immediate sustenance, capital replacements, technical skills, and restoration of domestic order are needed in varying degrees in these areas. Detailed local knowledge is necessary to appreciate the relationship of these needs and to plan the order of priority in supplying them. The European Recovery Program has led to the assembly of much of this information within the field of western Europe.

Respect for law implies genuine and wide-spread appreciation of the virtue of following established procedures, and is considered by many a necessary condition of civilization. Such respect is difficult to rebuild rapidly once it is impaired. Experience with two world wars and widespread propaganda of novel political and economic doctrines with religious fervor and with new means of mass communication has won many recruits to the belief that the ends thus propagandized justify any means to attain them. Only patient effort utilizing established procedures in the United Nations and in international and national tribunals, buttressed by scholarly analyses and popular education can restore appreciation of the value of law and then only if men are freed from the fear of sudden annihilation.

Reduction of the efficiency of military attack by any group is therefore an important element in political stabilization and in economic and legal recovery. By regulating the weapons available and the means for making them, the power of defense may be increased and the incentive to attack reduced. The slow progress of atomic-energy negotiations is a cause of prime concern, especially when, as was to be expected, this delay has resulted in a race between the United States and the Soviet Union, in the development of airplanes, rockets, atomic bombs, and other weapons. Limitation agreements supported by international inspection and control are essential if this race is to be stopped.

Possibly such agreements will become easier if they include a long moratorium upon the production and use of atomic energy in the large quantities which would be required for economic utilization. The atomic scientists and the economists doubt whether atomic energy can in many places in any near future, compete in price with other sources of energy. Consequently the economic loss from such a moratorium might not be great. The utilization of fissionable materials in medicine and in industrial testing requires the production of such materials only in "safe" quantities and would not be affected.

Problems in Control of Technology and Science

The problem of keeping progress in science and technology in step with progress in social opinion and organization is one that both scientists and statesmen must face more seriously than they have during the past few centuries.[17] Advances in pure science must not be in any way retarded. Scientific freedom is a major value of civilization. It should not be assumed, however, that the production of any gadget is desirable merely because it can be used for some purpose when society is not yet developed adequately to control its misuse. Technology must be distinguished from science.

Practical intelligence induces the ceaseless application of reason and imagination to find new and better courses of action. Such intelligence is wary of simple statements of problems and simple solutions. It recognizes that stability is a function of complexity, and yet that action in time, with all its risks, may be better than search, through further investigation and discussion, for a better course while the boat departs. If more practical intelligence in the disturbed state of our world cannot be beneficial, it is difficult to say what can be.

15

SYMBOLS OF
NATIONALISM AND
INTERNATIONALISM

The invitation which I received to contribute to this symposium proposed that discussion be confined to the type of symbol "which conveys representation or is charged with value significance" and that it concern itself "with the use, as well as the manipulation of symbols, in social relations, in religious, political, economic, educational, and other group activities."

Symbols of this type may be characterized as being in some degree sentimentalized, ambiguous, controversial, and changeable. They do not include such symbols as scientific names and symbols of relation such as *"homo sapiens,"* "central North America," "$+$," "$=$," "$\sqrt{2}$." These symbols have almost none of the last three characteristics mentioned. While any symbol may be sentimentalized these are not likely to be. Humanitarian sentimentalists love "man" not *"homo sapiens."* Sentimental nationalists love "the United States" not "central North America." Sentimental scientists may love "science" or even a particular scientific theory such as "Darwinism," but seldom such relations as "$+$," "$=$," or "$\sqrt{2}$."

Proper nouns, symbols representing social entities, social processes, social forces, or social relations, and especially words ending in "ism," belong to the type of symbol under discussion. In proper nouns the denotation may be unambiguous, uncontroversial, and relatively un-

Contribution to the Thirteenth Conference on Science, Philosophy and Religion, Columbia University, New York, September, 1952, to be included in a publication by that conference in 1954.

changeable but such symbols are apt to be highly sentimentalized, and to have connotations which are highly ambiguous, controversial, and changeable. Does the symbol, "United States," refer to an area on the map, to a population, to a complex of political institutions and practices, to a culture with distinctive values, beliefs, and techniques, to a test of democracy—as by implication, it appeared to in Lincoln's Gettysburg Address—or to a type of aggressive imperialism as it seems to in some utterances from the Soviet Union during recent years. Apparently the symbol, "United States," has different meanings for different people and most of these meanings incite love or hatred in degrees which vary in time and place. This symbol is therefore highly sentimentalized, ambiguous, controversial, and changeable.

Social scientists have long deplored the preponderance of these characteristics in such words as "democracy," "tyranny," "aristocracy," "elections," "proportional representation," "social progress," "social stability," "balance of power," "sovereignty," "freedom," and especially "socialism," "communism," "capitalism," "militarism," "pacifism," "imperialism," "cosmopolitanism," "nationalism," and "internationalism." Men get excited on hearing these symbols, quarrel about them, dispute on their meaning, and do so in different degree and in different manner in some times and places than in others. Social scientists have sometimes sought to give precise definition to these words or to substitute other words with no connotation in the popular vocabulary, but these efforts have not proved successful. Social scientists have not been able to emancipate themselves from the connotations of the words they find it necessary to use as have the natural scientists.

The attitudes and opinions of individuals, and the public opinion of groups, about such symbols, about their origin, the growth of their usage, and their obsolescence are the warp of culture and history, of which people, groups, their beliefs and acts are the woof. Social evolution and social revolution can be measured by rates of change of the vocabulary and of the elite of a community.[1]

Nature of Political Symbols

Certain general propositions may be made about the type of symbols we are discussing.

1. They are necessary elements in the process of social coöperation, group formation, and group action. However inconvenient they may be in the task of scientific analysis, the emotional content of these terms induces people to unite in groups and in movements for common purposes, and their ambiguity contributes to this end. People differ in their

values and objectives. Values and objectives are a function of the individual's experience and of his role and status in society, and no two people are exactly alike in these respects. Consequently efforts to define group goals with precision arouse controversy. Hairsplitting distinctions are disputed and group unity frustrated. On the other hand, people of varied conviction can get behind ambiguous symbols in the expectation that as action proceeds they can continue together step by step leaving potentialities of controversy for solution in the future.

The controversial and changeable character of these symbols permits them to persist as symbols of union and action even if policies and objectives change. Professor Lasswell has illustrated the value of ambiguity in pointing out that the goal of Marxian revolution was "the classless society," an "utterly novel social formation totally incomprehensible by means of analogies drawn from class-bound societies," thus "leaving the future open for the gratifying of the fantasies most agreeable to the individual. The old-style utopians tried to impose their private versions of heaven on mankind, and spent much of their time polishing off the celestial trumpets and refurbishing the celestial parapets, but Marx offered every man self-determination in utopias." Furthermore, Lasswell pointed out, the whole symbol system, ideology or bible of a movement which is to grow must be "ambiguous, obscure and somewhat contradictory. This facilitates the redefinition of the book to serve the purposes of the self-selected revolutionary elite." [2]

2. Unless skillfully managed, such symbols may produce indecision, conflict, and group disintegration. Because the sentimentalized connotation of a symbol has no direct relation to its objective meaning, the direction and intensity of that sentimentalization can easily change. Democracy can move from a term of contempt to a term of praise, so can monarchy, aristocracy, nationalism, and internationalism. So far as group unity is dependent upon identification of the members of the group with a symbol of plus value, the group will disintegrate when propaganda or new currents of opinion give the symbol a neutral or negative value. Even more the ambiguity in the reference of these symbols, necessary as it is, may cause trouble because of the passion of the human mind for consistency, logic, and precise definition of goals. Apparently successful movements are always on the threshold of internal argument and division upon the meaning of the key symbols which unite them. Heresies about doctrines and disagreement about ends can arise because of the ambiguity of the symbols of identification.

The ambivalent effect of ambiguous symbols, on the one hand, toward unity and coöperation and, on the other, toward division and conflict, illustrates the normal character of all human societies, movements, and policies. Ambiguity in the symbols of a society may be the source of flexibility and adaptation as it may also be of controversy and disintegration. Ambiguity in symbols maintains latent conflict in a mind or a society. This presents the opportunity to consider alternatives of action, to make choices, and thus to escape the necessity of following a single course of action to which minds and societies incapable of internal conflict are bound.[3]

3. It follows that in proportion as a political symbol identifying a group acquires among the members of the group an unambiguous meaning, ceases to be controversial, and becomes persistent in meaning and in sentimentalization, the group becomes active in the realization of its goal, incapable of adaptation to new conditions, and dangerous to the stability and peace of the supercommunity of which it is a member.

There has been much discussion on whether the difficulties of the age in which we live have arisen from the widespread rejection of absolute values or from the widespread acceptance of such values. Do we need more absolutism or more relativism? We abhor the absolutistic doctrines of Hitler and Stalin and the obedient acceptance of these doctrines by the followers of these leaders. We point out that such blind acceptance permits the justification of any means to achieve the goal set by the leader and see hope for the future only if these absolutisms are abandoned, freedom of speech, of belief, and of controversy are developed, and toleration and relativism are accepted as political values. At the same time we deplore the lukewarmness current in the West in regard to democracy, the willingness of people to tolerate the infiltration of alien ideas, the absence of a fighting faith in freedom, and the widespread opinion that values are relative, which seems to be developing in the West. We seem to fear that absolutism is strengthening our enemies and that relativism is weakening ourselves, and consequently we believe that we can defend ourselves only by adopting the very absolutism to which we object. Apparently absolutisms breed opposing absolutisms and these breed war and destruction. May it not be that only by preserving the relativism and pluralism which has been the essence of democracy, and attempting to infiltrate the absolutisms which exist with the spirit of toleration and relativism that the world can be saved from war and for democracy?

Political systems resting upon symbols which have acquired an absolute value appear to have lost the springs of progress. Absolutism asserts that all values are known, that the future cannot create new values, and that the task is to devise means to realize the goals which the value system establishes. Useful as such conviction may be to resolve ambivalences and incipient neuroses in the individual mind and to create fighting parties to achieve political tasks, they frustrate the hopes of the unconvinced within or without a community governed by such values, provide the roots of revolution and war, eliminate the opportunity to choose among values, and destroy the hope and the practice of continuous progress, in adjusting divergent attitudes and preserving unity in diversity. A relativism, which does not deny the validity of practical tests to determine that one value is better than another in existing circumstances, but does deny that the future is incapable of producing a value better than either, may have within it possibilities of both peace and progress.

It seems probable that the larger and the more diverse is a community the more dangerous is its commitment to absolute values. Large groups can achieve sufficient unity by permitting key political symbols to remain ambiguous, capable of developing in new directions as new circumstances arise, and capable of sustaining the hope of minorities that their interpretations may in time be adopted. This may sound like advocacy of political obscurantism or opposition to clarity of thought. I should rather define it as not crossing bridges until you come to them or as leaving some real choices to the future. We need political symbols that can unite groups and sustain policies but can, at the same time, preserve opportunities for future development.

4. The foregoing discussion suggests that the character of political symbols is closely related to the character of society and culture. In the tenth symposium of the Conference on Science, Philosophy and Religion I ventured the suggestion that "a culture capable of becoming universal under present conditions should be ambiguous in ultimate standards, precise in immediate procedures, scientific in methods, and tolerant of the diverse opinions and standards of its individuals and groups. Such a culture implies concern for humanity rather than for particular groups, concern for freedom rather than for conformity, reliance upon observation rather than upon intuition, and acceptance of relativity rather than of dogma." [4] Perhaps we can agree that the development of such a culture requires political symbols that are in some degree ambiguous, controversial, flexible, and sentimentalized, but not too much so. The symbols of the United Nations, such as the Charter and the Universal Declaration of Human Rights, perhaps have sufficient of that character to unite the world without straightjacketing the nations. If the people of each nation identify themselves with symbols of similarly flexible character they may be able to combine stability with progress and to remain at peace with their neighbors.

5. I hope these observations have convinced you that political symbols are important and deserve study. The measurement of their varia-

tions can be a useful guide to political and social management, and general awareness within a community of their character and social affects can have a therapeutic effect in preventing excesses either of social stagnation or of social change.

Political symbols may be studied in four relations. First, a political symbol symbolizes something. It refers to a political entity, institution, ideology, practice, procedure, ideal, myth, movement, or something else. However uncertain may be the character of that reference, the symbol serves some designative, descriptive, or informative function which may be studied. Secondly, a political symbol is related to other symbols. If it is a word it is related to other words in the sentence, paragraph, and book. If it represents an idea it refers to other ideas, in the ideology of a group or movement. If it represents a value in a community it may be superior or subordinate to other values or it may compete for attention and commitment with equal values. The relative role of political symbols can be surveyed by examining the amount of interest in and attention to them during a period in history. In the third place, a political symbol is related to the listeners, to the people on whom it impinges. Its affect can be examined by measurement of the attitudes toward it and opinions about it within a population. Finally, a political symbol is related to the speaker or leader who utilizes it. Its place in his system of values and ideas, and his purpose, method, and success in using it can be studied by political analysis of his behavior in the building of groups and the conduct of policy.[5]

Symbols of Nationalism and Internationalism

The terms, "nationalism" and "internationalism," and the other symbols associated with each of them, have been subjected to all of these kinds of analysis. A few of the results of these studies may be summarized.

The importance of these two symbols in the modern world can hardly be doubted. Historians have called the period since the Renaissance the "age of nationalism," thus asserting that nationalism has been a dominant force accounting for the political integration of some states, the political disintegration of others, for the expectation of peace within nation states and the expectation of war between them. Such symbols of nationalism as "France," "Great Britain," "United States," "Marseillaise," "Star-spangled Banner," "my country," "Constitution," "King," "fatherland," have been the subject of literature, art, and political oratory. They have won and maintained the loyalty of masses of people.

Internationalism has been recognized by historians but has usually been regarded as a less important force. Some would say that it has been of increasing importance in the twentieth century and some would say its further increase in importance would make for peace and stability under the present conditions of the shrinking material world. Others doubt whether it has increased in importance, and still others deplore it as stimulating "subversive movements." Most would recognize that symbols of internationalism such as "League of Nations," "United Nations," "collective security," "world court," "Kellogg pact," "outlawry of war," "international organization," "international coöperation," "the world community," "international law," "human rights," command less loyalty than do the symbols of nationalism. Certainly they have not been the subject of as much literature, art, political agitation, or newspaper comment.

Recent studies permit some more precise observations about these two symbols, particularly about their meaning, the attention given to them, the attitude toward them, and their political uses and consequences.

The Meaning of Nationalism and Internationalism

The object of identification or loyalty denoted by "nationalism" is ambiguous. It may be an existing state in its territorial, cultural, racial, or institutional aspect, in which case nationalism is identified with patriotism, or it may be a group seeking to become a state but now a minority within one or more states. Such a group may be regarded as distinctive by virtue of its habitat, its culture, its race, its history, its myths, or the attitudes or opinions of its members. No scientific test whether in the realm of anthropology, culture, history, geography, linguistics, or in procedures of electoral behavior, public opinion polling, or attitude measurement, has been found to determine satisfactorily to all, what is the population belonging to any "nationality," if that term is taken in any sense other than present national affiliation under law. Even the legal definition of nationality presents difficulties.[6]

This ambiguity in the designative meaning of nationalism permits rival nationalisms to claim the same people and to make the results of plebiscites often inconclusive. This ambiguity also accounts for the divergence of policies which may be stimulated by the symbol. Nationalism among the satisfied may call for defensive policies seeking to preserve the existing boundaries and status of the nations, but among the dissatisfied it may call for aggressive policies seeking independence of nationalities from imperial domination and for expansion of nations by the absorption of irredentas or even of other areas contributing to the nation's power, prestige, or prosperity.

Nationalism may be identified with isolationism or a policy of withdrawal from international contacts. On the other hand, it may be identified with interventionism or a policy or activity to preserve the balance of power or to improve the nation's position in it.

Perhaps the most to be said is that a nationalist has identified himself with a political group, larger than the local community and smaller than the world, which he regards as sharing some social and political characteristics with himself and as in some way different from other similar human groups. It also implies that he is prepared to support policies which he regards as in the interest of that group. It is clear, however, that nationalism neither defines those interests nor the group that is supposed to have them.

The symbol is usually distinguished from localism, tribalism, and parochialism, on the one hand, and from universalism, cosmopolitanism, internationalism, imperialism, and continentalism, on the other.

Even these distinctions, however, are not always clear-cut. Internationalists may characterize nationalism as localism or parochialism and when it emphasizes racial characteristics as tribalism. And nationalists, while they make the "nation" the central value, may in pursuance of that value embark upon policies of regionalism, pan-nationalism, continentalism, or even of internationalism or imperialism. The proper antinomy to nationalism is perhaps cosmopolitanism which, proclaiming the equality and brotherhood of man, seeks to reduce national differences to unimportance.

The symbol, "internationalism," is no less ambiguous. It is sometimes identified with cosmopolitanism and with imperialism, but internationalists usually emphasize that internationalism is not possible unless there are nations. Internationalists must therefore be loyal, each to his own nation, and differ from the nationalists only in recognizing the equal right of other nations and the concern of all in the international community of which they are all members. From this point of view internationalism and nationalism are both to be distinguished from cosmopolitanism which conceives humanity as a homogeneous group and also from imperialism which asserts the inequality of the nations each seeking to dominate over others.[7]

Attention Surveys

However ambiguous the meaning of nationalism and internationalism may be, the symbols themselves can be identified and the frequency of their use counted. While there may be room for difference of opinion it would usually be accepted that the names of states and such words as "patriotism," "fatherland," "self-determination," "irredentism," are symbols of nationalism, while the names of international organizations and such terms as "arbitration," "conciliation," "collective security," are symbols of internationalism. An extensive survey of the appearance of such terms in editorials of the principal "prestige" papers in the United States, Great Britain, France, Russia, and Germany since 1890 has been made by the RADIR (Revolution and the Development of International Relations) project at the Hoover Library, Stanford University.[8]

This survey indicates that in the editorials of these papers, of all general political symbols counted, fewer than one-third concerned international relations, but such symbols tended to increase, most in the case of the United States in whose prestige papers their relative frequency moved from 24 per cent before World War I, to 35 per cent in the interwar period, and to 41 per cent in the period since World War II. In France and Britain the change was from about 25 per cent before World War I to roughly 34 per cent after World War II. In Germany the relative attention to international symbols was 18 per cent both before World War I and in the Hitler period, but 39 per cent in the Weimar period. In Russia before World War I the relative frequency of such symbols was 37 per cent receding to 14 per cent in the 1930's and rising to 21 per cent after World War II. Comparison of the relative frequency of foreign geographical symbols, indicating attention to foreign affairs was roughly similar. These results suggest that during this period the United States moved away from isolationism while Russia moved toward it. They might also be interpreted as meaning that symbols of nationalism became relatively less important in the United States and those of internationalism relatively more important, while in Russia the situation has been reversed.

This interpretation, however, may be questioned. All symbols concerning international relations are not symbols of internationalism nor is interest in foreign affairs necessarily an interest in internationalism. In the United States it appears that there was a tendency for interest in foreign affairs generally to be identified with an interest in internationalism. Nationalism, isolationism, and predominant interest in domestic affairs went together and all receded as interest increased in foreign affairs, international symbols, and internationalism. In Great Britain and France there was some correlation between attention to foreign states and to general international symbols (about 66 per cent) but in Germany and Russia there was no correlation at all. Interest in foreign affairs did not mean an interest in international institutions and processes but rather in national foreign policies and the foreign policies of other nations. Nationalism was manifested not by isolationism but by an interest in national foreign policies.

If symbols concerning domestic affairs, concerning foreign nations, and concerning international situations such as "peace" and "war" are eliminated, and attention is given to symbols of international institutions and processes, which perhaps best measure interest in "internationalism," it appears that internationalism commands relatively slight attention. In Germany the proportion of the editorials counted containing such symbols was 8 per cent; in the Soviet Union since 1939 1 per cent; in France, 14 per cent; in England, 13 per cent; and in the United States, 11 per cent. These proportions were obtained from tables indicating the frequency of appearance of editorials in the prestige papers of these countries containing symbols concerned with foreign or international affairs. Except in the Soviet Union, the symbols, "war" and "peace," appeared most frequently. In the Western papers, "United Nations" was close behind. In Russia, editorials using the symbol, "fatherland—motherland," was most frequent, followed by "war," "patriotism," and "peace." "United Nations" was not among the first eleven symbols, constituting 95 per cent of all international symbols counted in the Soviet press.[9]

Although professing the doctrine of "international" Marxism, the Soviet Union appears to have the greatest interest in "nationalism" among the great powers.

Attitude Measurement

To know the amount of attention given to nationalism and to internationalism by people in the various parts of the world is important, but it helps little to predict how people will behave unless we know the extent to which they are for or against these symbols. People are interested in and give attention to the things they hate as well as those they love. Knowledge of attitudes toward nationalism, and internationalism is, therefore, important. Who are for and who are against these symbols, and how intensely?

By an "attitude" I understand a tendency to react in respect to a stimulus such as a symbol or an event. Attitudes have been measured in four dimensions: direction (for or against), intensity (much or little), continuity (persistent or changing in time) and elaboration (spontaneous or supported by argument). An attitude is a psychological phenomenon and does not necessarily correspond to the actual reaction of the individual when the stimulus occurs, as for instance when a symbol is brought to his attention in given circumstances. Apart from insincerity or conscious deception there may be many circumstances such as conflicting attitudes, the influence of surrounding persons, reasonable caution, the calculated pursuit of long-run objectives, or the representative character of the individual which induce persons to react inconsistently with their attitudes. Such reactions may be classified as symbolic or active. One may talk or one may do. A symbolic reaction is spoken of as an "opinion." Sometimes opinion is defined as the expression of attitude, but as the expression does not necessarily correspond to the attitude that definition is not altogether satisfactory. Action or behavior may differ from both attitude and opinion. Opinion is the easiest to measure, and it is often assumed that opinion measurement also provides a measurement of attitudes and a basis for predicting action. As these assumptions are frequently unjustifiable it would be desirable to make independent measurements of the attitudes toward, the opinions about, and the actions in response to given stimuli. The comparison of series respectively measuring variations in these three phenomena in a given population might provide considerable insight into the personality of individuals, the state of society, and the expectations of policy and action.

It must be emphasized that opinion and action, however they may differ from the attitudes of the people involved, are phenomena of major importance. In a society, the policy and action of governments is based more upon opinions than upon attitudes. The attitude of the policymaker may, it is true, be of some importance, but he usually knows only the opinions of the public which he serves, not their attitudes, and usually, as is evident from comparing the private letters and the public papers of political leaders, his action is more influenced by the opinions of advisers, pressure groups, and the general public than by his own attitudes. Democracy is often said to be government by public opinion, interpreted by some as government by pressure-group opinion. An attitude which is not expressed does not influence others, but an opinion, however it differs from the attitude of the speaker or writer, may be influential. It may be fashionable, prudent, or even compulsory for people to express opinions vigorously and frequently which do not correspond to their attitudes, and such expressions may snowball, giving rise to an intense public opinion inducing legislation and executive action quite contrary to the attitudes of many or perhaps most of the population. Obviously the effectiveness of legislation or executive action may be seriously impaired by such circumstances, and such circumstances may give evidence of incipient revolution within the community.

Public opinion, like private attitudes, may be measured in four dimensions: direction, intensity, continuity, and homogeneity. The latter refers to the degree in which the opinion of a given public about a given symbol clusters about a given point, or is distributed among different points and may be related to the amount of discussion in, and the cultural homogeneity of, the society. A two-party system often makes for a bimodal distribution of opinion and a multiparty system may make this dimension of public opinion multimodal. A one-party system may make public opinion homogeneous but probably tends to make it diverge radically from attitudes unless the culture is very homogeneous.[10]

There seem to have been no careful studies made of the differences between attitudes, opinions, and actions in respect to the symbols of nationalism and internationalism. The suspicion has often been expressed that the differences are greater in respect to internationalism than in respect to nationalism.

There is some evidence that attitudes toward nationalism differ considerably among persons in the same population. Studies using the Thurstone method of attitude measurement indicated that in the United States, among professional groups, salesmen and executives were most patriotic, housewives least, while labor, professional, and clerical workers were between. Middle income groups were less patriotic than high or low income groups. Political independents were less patriotic than party regulars. In general patriotism was correlated with militarism. Men were more patriotic and militaristic than women, the middle aged than either the young or the old, the poorly educated than the well educated.[11] It seems probable that opinions in regard to nationalism differ less among various classes of the population of a given nation than do attitudes.

The name of the nation, or other symbols representing it, are the most important symbols of nationalism, and studies measuring the fluctuations of public opinion in each of the great powers with reference to the symbols representing each of the others might be of considerable political importance. Such studies might provide a measurement of the variations in psychic distances between states or degrees of friendliness and hostility of each state to the others and of the fluctuations of international tension. Such measurements, if produced currently at brief intervals, might prove useful guides for statesmen or international organizations interested in preserving stability in international relations.

Studies which have been made in this field indicate that during the past fifty years the relative psychic distance of the five great powers from one another distributed them in three groups. The United States, Great Britain, and France have been relatively friendly to one another. These three powers have been moderately hostile to Russia and all four have been most hostile to Germany. These results, confirmed by different methods, were indicated in the RADIR study by the following scale: United States—Great Britain: 35; Great Britain—France: 36; United States—France: 43; France—Russia: 70; Great Britain—Russia: 70; United States—Russia: 70; Germany—United States: 82; Germany—Great Britain: 84; Germany—Russia: 88; Germany—France: 90. This study also indicated that the relative popularity of these powers, judged by the amount of criticism given and received during the sixty-year period, rank them in the following order: Great Britain, United States, France, Russia, Germany. In the postwar period Russia has fallen to the tail of the list.[12]

It is widely believed that in respect to internationalism the attitudes and actions of people are likely to diverge from their expressions of opinion. People will express belief in the United Nations but will not be emotionally thrilled on seeing its flag and will not respond to its call for contributions. Their opinions diverge from their attitudes and actions.

However that may be, content analysis of papers and Gallup polls indicate that opinions concerning internationalism have usually been favorable during the past fifty years, slightly more so in the United States than in Germany, France, and Great Britain, and least in Russia. As already noted, the amount of attention given to these symbols has been relatively small. The RADIR project found 70 per cent of editorial references to international organizations in the American paper favorable, while the figure in Germany was 69, France 67, Great Britain 64 and Russia 62. These percentages, however, varied at different times, percentages being the largest in the interwar period.[13] The figures indicated no trend favorable to internationalism during the period. They, in fact, suggest that the League of Nations operated in a more favorable atmosphere of opinion than has the United Nations. There is some ground for doubt whether the prestige papers utilized in the RADIR study adequately reflected public opinion in this regard. They certainly did not reflect public action. The United States did not join the League of Nations in spite of the favorable opinion expressed about the League in the *New York Times* and did join the United Nations although the expressions of opinion were less favorable.

The general conclusions to be reached from the studies of attitude and opinion in the prestige paper is that the Soviet Union and Germany were most nationalistic; the United States and Great Britain, least; and France intermediate during the past generation. Somewhat different results were obtained from a study made in 1933 on the basis of expert opinions on the intensity of nationalism in various countries. According to this study, in defensive nationalism France ranked first, the United States second, Great Britain third, and Germany fourth. Russia was not included in this study. In respect to aggressive nationalism, however, Germany ranked first, the others falling in the same order.[14]

Historians have generally recognized an increase in opinions favorable to the symbols of nationalism during the past few centuries but with fluctuations. Nationalism has been more intense in periods of tension and war and has been to some extent moderated by sentiments of internationalism and cosmopolitanism in periods of peace and tranquillity.[15]

Political Analysis

The symbols of nationalism and internationalism are of primary historical importance because of their influence on individual and group behavior. Doubtless the amount of attention given to these symbols, the attitudes toward and opinions about them, give some indication of the role they play in stimulating action and developing institutions. No historian questions that symbols of nationalism have been used effectively by leaders in building and sustaining modern states and shaping their policies and fighting their wars. Nationalism has been more used by some leaders than by others. Britain and France in the sixteenth and seventeenth centuries; the United States, Germany, Italy, Russia, and Japan in the nineteenth century; and China, India, the Arab states, and other Asiatic countries in the twentieth century have been unified under the symbols of nationalism. On the other hand, the Habsburgs maintained their empire for centuries by a policy of dividing the nationalities within their domain and ruling them all, as did the Turkish sultans. These policies, however, failed in the twentieth century—the Habsburg and Turkish empires fell apart.[16]

Political analysis indicates that today the symbols of nationalism are far more effective in inducing political cohesion and action than those of internationalism. A rough idea of the difference is indicated by the fact that at its maximum in 1932, when opinion toward internationalism seemed to be most favorable, the budget of the League of Nations was one part in eight thousand of the budgets of the national states. This proportion was, however, greater than that between expenditures for international organizations and national governments before World War I and less than that since World War II. During the latter period it has been estimated that the states of the world have spent a little more than one part in two thousand of their budgets for the United Nations and its specialized agencies. Political budgets have been spent in ever larger measure on international organizations during the past fifty years but the amount is still infinitesimal as compared to that spent on national governments. The personnel employed by international organizations and the range of their activities have also increased, both absolutely and relatively, but still they are small compared with the civil service and administrative activities of one large state. As a symbol of political construction and action, internationalism has been increasing in importance during the past fifty years but it still ranks far behind nationalism.[17]

In the world of today there are grave maladjustments between the areas of political autonomy and the social functions to be performed, and also between the institutions and opinions which exist and the attitudes and opinions necessary to develop institutions capable of better adjusting areas to functions. Some functions can be performed by local institutions, some by national institutions, while some require continental or universal coöperation. The problem of adjustment can be approached from many angles. Political negotiation may adjust areas, facilitate coöperation, and establish supranational organizations to perform functions beyond the capacity of national governments or diplomatic arrangements. Administrative action may improve the functioning and develop the services of regional and world organizations and increase confidence in them. It seems unlikely, however, that these processes can be adequate unless there is an important modification in the symbolic structure of public opinion and individual attitude. Attention is too exclusively focused upon the nations. A more complicated structure, abandoning absolute identifications and attributing relative values to local, national, regional, and universal institutions seems more appropriate to the shrinking world in which we live.

Such a reconstruction of attention to, and attitudes and opinions about, the symbols of nationalism and internationalism lies within the sphere of UNESCO, and indeed of all institutions and agencies dealing with the manipulation of symbols—the school, the church, the political party, and the organizations of adult education.

PART **V**

LAW AND INTERNATIONAL STABILITY

16

LAW AND

INTERNATIONAL

RELATIONS

Types of Law

A proposition may deserve the name of law because it is regularly enforced by the authorities of a society, because it is regularly verified by the observers of the phenomena with which it deals, because it has regularly proved useful as a guide to action, or because it has regularly influenced the conscience of people who are aware of it.

As illustration of the first or jural type of law I may cite the proposition that breach of contract gives an action for damages. To be accurate this proposition requires considerable elaboration of the specific meaning in a particular system of law of breach, of contract, of action, and of damages but in some sense the proposition is enforced in nearly all such systems.

As illustration of the second, or scientific type of law, I may cite the proposition that bodies are attracted to each other by a force proportional to the product of their masses and inversely proportional to the square of their distance. This proposition accounted with such remarkable precision for the motions of the planets and their satellites observed during centuries that it was considered an absolute law. A few small discrepancies were, however, observed, particularly in the motion of the perihelion of Mercury, and Einstein's theory proceeding from quite different premises, though at the first approximation it coincides with the law of Newton, has been found to account for these discrepancies.

From *Proceedings of the American Philosophical Society,* XCV (October, 1951).

For illustration of the third or practical type of law one may examine books as varied as Mrs. Lincoln's Cookbook, Culbertson on Bridge, Machiavelli on the Art of War, Wiquefort on the Ambassador, and Poor Richard's Almanac. "To make a rabbit pie, first catch your rabbit" is a rule with fewer exceptions than "Honesty is the best policy." As scientific law relates causes and effects, so practical law relates means and ends.

As illustration of the fourth or ethical type of law I may cite the proposition that promises ought to be kept. This proposition has had more influence at some times and places than at others but it appeals to the sense of justice of most men. Rules of ethics or "natural law" have a relation to the other three types of law. They constitute a source of jural law, and, in a community in which they are generally influential, constitute also rules of practical law because it is expedient in most situations to observe them. They also resemble scientific law because, if generally believed, they constitute reliable explanations of much human behavior. They have, however, this difference that scientific laws, at least those concerning physical phenomena, are valid independently of human belief, but ethical laws describe human behavior only if they are generally believed. The condition which supports the validity of scientific law is the order of nature while the condition which supports the validity of ethical law is the state of belief and opinion, or in anthropological terms, the culture of the group.

Characteristics of International Relations

Do any of these types of law have any relevance to international relations? There is no supreme power in the world that can compel nations or individuals throughout the world to observe prescribed rules. International law has, it is true, existed as a body of doctrine often cited by courts and diplomats and is the subject of a vast literature in all languages, but its devotees have found themselves somewhat on the defensive when faced by ordinary lawyers who regard reliable procedures of enforcement as the essence of jural law. Dante in the Middle Ages, like the United World Federalists today, insisted that there must be a universal empire, a world state, or a world government with power both in law and in fact to legislate, adjudicate, and execute if international law is to be "real" law.

Scientific law may seem even less relevant to the international field. There are too few states to provide a statistical base for generalization and furthermore they are so different in area, population, resources, forms of government, economy, culture, and power that they hardly constitute a class concerning which reliable generalizations might be made. If individuals are taken as the base, while more numerous and more alike in physical characteristics, their behavior in matters relevant to war and peace is so dependent on the local peculiarities of nationality, culture, and government that generalization about their behavior in general is of little value in explaining international relations. If, subordinating both nations and individuals, we regard the world as an integrated whole, each part of which is influenced by action in any other part, we are faced by the difficulty that the unique, while the essence of history, is abhorrent to science. One cannot pretend to make scientific generalizations about the world until there is another world to compare it with. However, the possibilities of science are great and it would be premature to assume that no method of analysis and measurement can contribute to predicting, and perhaps even to regulating, international relations.

Many practical laws have been asserted about international relations. "In time of peace prepare for war." [1] "Your neighbor is your enemy, your neighbor's neighbor your friend." [2] "A prudent diplomat appears to neglect those things which he most desires." [3] "Princes who have thought more of ease than of arms have lost their states." [4] "A Prince ought not to keep faith in all circumstances but he ought to appear to do so." [5] "The state which transgresses the laws of nature and of nations cuts away also the bulwark which safeguards its own future peace." [6] "War is politics carried on by other means." [7] It will be noticed that these maxims often contradict one another, that none are universally applicable, and that they are stated in such vague terms as to leave much room for interpretation in particular circumstances. In this respect they resemble general maxims of prudence and morals except that those applicable to international relations tend to have a sardonic tone. Treatises on the arts of war and diplomacy often consist of historic illustrations and rational elaborations indicating the necessary qualifications of such maxims and the conditions of their application. Except as they serve as mnemonic devices to recall such precedents, maxims may be worse than useless. Propositions in the field of international relations, relating means to ends sufficiently precisely and generally to deserve the name of law, would have to take account of so many variables that they would be too complicated for use, or they would have to state so exhaustively the conditions assumed as to be rarely applicable. However, if science can succeed in analyzing and measuring relevant variables, perhaps reliable rules of practice can be evolved.

The early international lawyers founded their systems on "natural law" or the ethical principles deemed applicable to human relations generally in the absence of organized society, and by analogy to the relations of states.[8] When the community of nations was confined to states whose peoples and rulers had a common background in classical and Christian culture, some consensus on the rules of "natural law" was possible. But when the Christian world was split by the reformation and the European community of nations extended its relations to Africa, Asia, and America and to peoples of Moslem, Hindu, Confucian, Buddhist, and Aztec religion, it was found that many rules of conduct thought self-evident were not so to people of different culture. The emphasis among international lawyers shifted from "natural law" to custom and agreement. The present movement for a universal covenant of human rights marks a new attempt to discover principles acceptable to all irrespective of culture, nationality, religion, or ideology. Through proper use of the insights of psychology, sociology, and anthropology as well as of comparative religion, ethics, and law perhaps progress can be made toward such a formulation.[9]

This review indicates that international relations are peculiarly resistant to prediction, regulation, and control by law. There have, it is true, been periods since the present system of states began five centuries ago when international law has proved reliable and useful. These periods have been characterized by a relatively stable equilibrium of power and a general increase in human welfare. They have been separated by long periods of violence and change, when statesmen could not rely on the observance of law and had no means of enforcing it, with the result that events occurred capriciously and unpredictably, and adaptation to them was accompanied by violence and disorder. Law has been a hope rather than an achieved reality in the community of nations. Today that hope is accompanied by a widespread sense of necessity because the consequences of continued anarchy and violence have become more alarming with the conquest of the air and the atom.

Jural International Law

Efforts to meet this necessity have proceeded along several lines. The easiest method for the public to understand but perhaps the most difficult to achieve is that of jural law. International organization, it is urged, must be developed into a world government with legislative, judicial, and executive organs with power to declare and enforce law. The League of Nations and the United Nations are steps in this direction, but the capacity of these bodies to make and enforce law has been limited. The demand is for a world agency dealing not with states, which like all large groups are intractable, but with individuals, thus achieving a transition, like that so lucidly described in the Federalist papers, from a League to a Federal Union.[10]

The obstacle to progress in this direction lies in the unwillingness of governments and peoples to abandon their means of self-defense until they are certain that a world federation can protect them, and the certainty that a world federation cannot protect them until the most powerful have abandoned those means. It appears that this transition cannot be made suddenly unless the great powers act on a faith which can hardly be rationally justified so long as conflicts of policy and ideology maintain the mutual suspicions and high tensions which they do today. It is also argued that the transition cannot be made gradually because a world government cannot be established with adequate power unless the great powers simultaneously renounce sovereignty, not only in the legal sense by accepting a constitution of world government, but also in the material sense by transferring their arms to that government. It is possible that the United Nations, by persistent effort in the fields of collective security, armament limitation, and international coöperation may develop, step by step, conditions of confidence which will make such a final transfer possible, but the actual course of affairs has not been in that direction. Instead, material power has tended to concentrate in rival poles. The arms race has accelerated. Mutual suspicions and tensions have increased.[11]

It is less easy to make the transition to world government in a bipolar world than in a world, such as that of the nineteenth century, when there were five or six great powers in relatively stable equilibrium. Under such conditions transfer of some power by each might create a world government with dominant power and a high probability of impartiality in law enforcement. When, however, there are only two major centers of power they must in large measure disintegrate before a world government able to enforce law against the resistance of either can be established. This each refuses to do because it fears that unless it controls that government its rival will do so. Furthermore, as the number of uncommitted states diminishes, the probability that *ad hoc* alliances or *ad hoc* collective action will be able to frustrate aggression by either of the centers of power becomes less and the deterrent influence of balance of power or collective security policies is reduced. Furthermore, each of the great powers, feeling insecure unless more powerful than the other, builds its armaments until the one against which time seems to be running precipitates war. The tendency of a bipolar world is therefore toward neither a stable balance of power nor voluntary world federation, but toward war resulting perhaps in uni-

versal conquest. This tendency is mitigated only by the universal apprehension that general war waged by modern instruments might destroy
civilization if not the human race itself. The world is in a situation in
which both the difficulty and the necessity of establishing a universal
regime of jural law are increasing.[12]

Ethical International Law

A second line of endeavor for improving international relations is that
of developing ethical law. It is hoped that, in spite of the diversity of
nationalities, ideologies, cultures, and religions in the world, certain
propositions concerning human behavior can be discovered that will
spontaneously appeal to all peoples and governments and create a world
atmosphere of opinion in which institutions to control and regulate
international relations can function. The anthropologists have discovered that continuous and abundant communication among peoples
of different culture, while initially developing conflict because of the
efforts of each to protect the peculiarities of its culture, tends in time
by a process of diffusion and assimilation to develop some common
standards of value and practice. These, in turn, develop coöperative
efforts to realize practical ends flowing from these standards, and eventually organizations to facilitate such coöperation. At this stage the previously distinct cultures become in considerable measure merged into a
single culture.[13]

Students of international relations perceive this process among na-
tions. Contact and communication between Christian and Moslem,
Protestant and Catholic, Spanish and Mexican, European and Oriental,
British, French, German, and Italian, began with war but have proceeded to acceptance of many common principles recorded in general
conventions and declarations such as the Hague convention, the Kellogg-
Briand pact, the Atlantic Charter, the United Nations Charter, the
Nuremburg Charter, and the Universal Declaration of Human Rights.[14]
It has also resulted in coöperation in numerous international organiza-
tions now in large measure coördinated in the specialized agencies of
the United Nations.

To take the first step in this process is the mission especially of the
Human Rights Commission and the International Law Commission
established by the United Nations, and of the United Nations Educational, Scientific and Cultural Organization (UNESCO). These agencies, with less confidence in the existence of a universal "natural law"
than had jurists and theologians of the Middle Ages and the Renaissance, hope to discover in psychology, sociology, anthropology, philos-

ophy, and comparative and international law the bases for a universal culture which can be developed through communication and education.[15]

There can be no doubt but that modern means of communication and education utilizing the knowledge of human nature developed by the social sciences increase the probability that common cultural standards may develop throughout the world. During earlier periods natural barriers between peoples and the assumption by each that its own standards were absolute delayed this process and effectively prevented its operation throughout the world. The process could, it is true, be observed in large areas such as Egypt, Mesopotamia, China, India, the Roman Empire, the world of Islam, and medieval Christendom originally composed of diverse cultures and warring states. Throughout this process, common cultural ideas became in considerable measure diffused and assimilated over a larger area creating what Toynbee calls a "civilization." It is to be observed, however, that in these cases the process was long and slow with many setbacks and in some cases complete failure. War and conquest were major factors in facilitating communication, destroying distinct cultures and propagandizing the ideas which triumphed. Enemies on the periphery of each "civilization," feared by all the peoples within it, also contributed to the process of assimilation and integration. And in no case was the process complete. Eventually these civilizations disintegrated before the attacks of internal barbarians who had never been assimilated or of external barbarians of different culture. These historic experiences raise a doubt whether a world culture will ever develop.[16]

Even with the advantage which modern social science and means of universal communication present, the international agencies engaged in the task have encountered serious obstacles. The first is the continued absolutism of different philosophies illustrated by the controversy in UNESCO between "scientific humanism" and "dialectical materialism" and the inability of that organization to formulate a synthetic philosophy capable of reconciling the major existing ideologies.[17]

The second difficulty lies in the practical difference in emphasis among groups pursuing common goals because of differences in social systems. This is illustrated by the Western insistence on giving priority, in the program for protecting human rights, to civil and political liberties and the Soviet insistence on giving priority to economic and social rights.[18] Although solved in a measure in the Universal Declaration of Human Rights which includes both, this difference hampers practical programs of implementation.

A third and more serious obstacle in the path of universal cultural standards lies in the artificial creation of barriers to communication. If the Iron Curtain continues to bar free and abundant communication between the communist and democratic worlds the process of diffusing and assimilating cultural standards can hardly begin. Because of the incapacity of some of the ideas and beliefs upon which the Soviet culture rests to survive among people aware of ideas and conditions outside the Soviet orbit, the Soviet rulers are likely to resist freedom of communication.[19]

Finally, the very possibility that local cultures might be assimilated in a universal culture has in recent times, as it has in the evolution of past civilizations, generated countermovements by which the leaders of local nationalities, religions, and ideologies have actively propagandized traditional doctrines, thus building up resistance to synthesis and assimilation. The new knowledge of social science and communication can be utilized as effectively in efforts to preserve differences as in efforts of the United Nations and UNESCO to accentuate similarities. Such efforts cannot in fact be entirely deplored because the competition of different cultures is essential to human progress. A uniform world would be uninteresting, static, and incapable of adapting itself to new material conditions. It is to be both anticipated and desired that universal cultural standards will always be sufficiently flexible to permit a rich variety in regional, national, functional, and local group standards. Perhaps understanding, toleration, and appreciation by each culture of the others should be the main value of a universal culture.[20]

The problem of creating a universal ethical law is, therefore, complicated, and involves the maintenance of some differences no less than the cultivation of some uniformities. The solution of this problem must perhaps be considered the consequence even more than the cause of a peaceful world. Premature efforts to communicate and propagandize among peoples whose leaders are anxious to defend the autonomy of their cultures may do more to cause than to prevent war. Yet more universal cultural understanding than exists today is undoubtedly a condition for the functioning of universal institutions able to preserve peace. The process of winning universal acceptance of ethical standards must be accompanied by a process not only of analysis but also of measurement if it is to contribute to stabilizing the world. Publicists and educators must know what standards can become universal and how to develop them in particular areas. They must also have guides to indicate how much and how rapidly it is safe to subordinate local to universal standards in each area.

Practical International Law

The third line of endeavor toward stabilizing international relations by law lies in the effort through administrative procedures to achieve practical ends which all people are assumed to cherish. Cheap postal and telegraphic communication; safe and convenient travel by rail, sea, and air; elimination of slavery, forced labor, and illiteracy; better conditions of labor, more available food, and better health; greater stability in currencies, more available developmental capital and technical skills, general increases in standards of living—these and other objectives have been formulated in generally ratified international conventions. Agencies have been established and budgets provided to facilitate coöperation toward the achievement of these goals. The jurisprudence of these organizations constitutes a body of practical law adapting means to these ends.[21]

The effort to control international relations by facilitating coöperation is hampered by several considerations. The ends assumed, in the absence of a universal culture, are not necessarily compatible with one another or with local cultures. Some states, notably the Soviet states, have in large measure refused to join any of the specialized agencies of the United Nations. This vast movement of international coöperation, therefore, while tending to draw the democratic world together, tends to widen the gap between it and the Soviet world.

Furthermore, the means adapted to advance these ends vary enormously in different areas. In densely populated areas increase in the food supply and health services may augment population more rapidly than it increases production with the result of a general lowering in the standard of living. In underdeveloped areas increase in available capital may result in cultural change and exploitation leading to unrest and instability. In illiterate areas increase of literacy may lead to the introduction of propaganda upsetting traditional patterns and stimulating violent revolution. Universal plans or precepts must be adapted to local conditions in respect both to the priority of ends and the utility of means if they are to be applied satisfactorily.[22]

Finally, the effect of coöperative activity, like that of spreading ethical standards, is to break down local cultures. Consequently the leaders of these cultures, while perhaps desiring particular advantages offered by coöperation, may react to resist modification of local autonomy and local values. International coöperation can be interpreted as a species of imperialism and may generate movements of local nationalism and autonomy. While most obvious in the case of the communist states, this phenomenon is to be observed elsewhere.[23]

Practical international law, developed through international coöperation, may fail to create stability unless its ends are integrated in a universally accepted culture and its means are geared to the local conditions of the area in which it is applied. If developed gradually and cautiously such coöperation may, by moderating economic, social, and cultural differentials and developing elements of a universal culture and a universal society contribute to the atmosphere necessary for stable international relations. But except among people that anticipate prolonged peaceful relations such coöperation is not likely to develop great effectiveness.[24]

Coöperation with the object of maintaining international peace raises a different issue. The demand for such coöperation assumes that basic oppositions exist between nations. Consequently the end is not positive, as are such ends as health, welfare, and literacy, but negative—the moderation, elimination, compromising, or sublimation of oppositions. Consequently, if practical law is to deal with peace, either peace must be given a positive content such as justice or welfare, generally deemed superior to the local objectives which have caused oppositions, or it must be conceived as a procedure to assure pacific settlement of disputes or to maintain stability and to prevent war. The first involves the development of universal ethical standards superior to local standards. The second involves the development of jural law or regulation guided by suitable measurements.[25]

Scientific International Law

Without deprecating the role of jural, ethical, or practical law in dealing with the problem of international relations, it is the object of this paper to emphasize the possibility and utility of scientific analysis and measurement of certain variables in this field. Such scientific international law might guide regulatory action by national or international agencies more effectively to stabilize international relations.

International relations have been regulated for the past few centuries by considerations of the balance of power. By that expression is meant a condition in which each of the principal states of the system pursues such policies and controls such power that no one of them has any prospect of succeeding in an endeavor to conquer another. This condition will be promoted if there are a considerable number of states in the system, if they are relatively equal in power, if each is able to resist sudden attack for a considerable time, if none is under such anxieties that it is likely to make such an attack, and if each pursues the policy of coöperating with others to prevent any one from greatly augmenting its power. On the other hand, equilibrium becomes disturbed if the number of states in the system is reduced, if great disparities in power develop, if military technology facilitates successful aggression, if high tensions make such aggression probable, and if states follow policies either of neutrality or aggression without care for the stability of the system as a whole.[26] Policies of neutrality may result from pacifism, irresponsibility or inexperience in world affairs, or from lack of a relatively invulnerable power ready to assume leadership in maintaining the balance of power.[27] Policies of aggression may result from traditional political or economic interests opposed by others, from the emergence of a dynamic leader, from acceptance of a dynamic ideology, or from conflicts within the minds of individuals or the structure of society inducing frustrations, anxieties, displacements, and high tensions.[28]

A logically organized system of propositions defining the variables involved in international relations, describing procedures for measuring them, analyzing their relationships, and describing the conditions assumed to be persistent may be called "scientific international law."

The most important variables are the power and the policies of the major human groups in world affairs. These groups include not only states, but also private and public international organizations and supranational churches and parties. At the present time, however, power is largely concentrated in a few great states. So it is with changes in the power and the policies of these "great powers" of which the United States and the Soviet Union are the greatest, that international relations is mainly concerned.[29]

International tension arises because of inconsistencies in the initiatives, policies, and opinions of different states. It tends to increase as the available power of the states increases, and as their policies become less flexible. Reciprocally, high international tension induces the rival states to augment power resulting in an arms race, and rigidifies policies by intensifying public opinion behind those which are accepted and centralizing government authority to realize them. Consequently high international tension is likely to initiate a process by which tension steadily increases until it reaches the point of war. This process is particularly likely if each of the states has large surpluses of social energy indicated by a rapid formation of capital and if each has an inflexible opinion, a condition promoted by a constitution and laws which habitually suppress dissent, forbid opposition parties, and effectively regulate the life of the people. It may be concluded that if high tension exists between two states, tension will increase within each at a rate proportionate to the product of its social energy and its resistance to change. The relation between social tension, social energy, and social resistance to change appears to be similar to that which exists in an electrical system—tension or potential energy varies with the product of current strength and resistance.[30]

International tension can also be measured by another set of variables concerning, not changes within the states, but changes in their relations. These relations may be characterized as different aspects of distance between states. Changes in the objective aspects of distance—technological, strategic, legal, and intellectual—may be roughly measured, and so may changes in the subjective aspects of distance—psychic, social, political, and war expectancy. I cannot here attempt a more precise definition of these variables or the methods of measuring them,[31] but it appears that an analysis of these relationships may provide a formula for estimating the probability of war between different pairs of states under conditions of power politics.[32] Estimates made according to such a formula in July, 1939, have been roughly verified by the order of occurrence of wars during the twelve following years.[33]

This all too brief summary of studies made in the field suggests that social science may be able to formulate relations between significant variables in international relations thus aiding, so far as these variables can be measured, in both the prediction and control of international tensions and war.

Without use of such formula, common sense has always indicated that governments with aggressive policies and increasing power to support them are likely to disturb the peace, consequently governments interested in stability have habitually used the regulatory devices available to counter such developments. They have increased their armaments or other domestic components of power, pursued compensating foreign policies of territorial or economic expansion, made alliances and guarantees, maintained neutrality, initiated preventive war, or organized collective intervention. Sometimes they have attempted diplomatic negotiations, initiated international consultations, or invoked established machinery of conference, conciliation, inquiry, or arbitration peacefully to settle controversies with the power disturbing the equilibrium.[34]

The government or international organization wishing to promote stability by use of such methods or by use of the collective measures facilitated by the United Nations would profit by information enabling it to determine as accurately as possible in a given situation the following, among other variables: (1) the degree in which each of the states of the world is involved in the situation, (2) the relative power of those principally involved, (3) their strategies and anxieties, (4) their foreign policies and public opinions.

Clearly none of these variables is susceptible of precise quantitative measurement. Each includes elements which now, and perhaps for an indefinite future, will involve qualitative judgments. Yet I believe that the social sciences are progressively discovering methods by which more of the elements of such variables can be quantified. The effects to be expected from application of regulatory methods of the type above referred to is even more difficult to deal with quantitatively. Continuous measurement of the variables noted might, however, provide a base against which "operational research" [35] could test the effect of the methods actually undertaken. Such measurements would also suggest the direction and the magnitude of the regulatory measures which should be applied at a given moment to compensate for disturbances to equilibrium.

The Degree of Interest of States in a Situation

A government or international organization desiring to initiate regulatory measures in order to maintain stability must know what states can be regarded as interested in a given situation, or, if the matter concerns "high" politics, what states can be considered within the system of states which regulate their policies by balance-of-power considerations. Up to the twentieth century only European states were in any large degree in the state system of Western civilization, and only five to eight powers normally regulated their policies by balance-of-power considerations.[36] The situation has, however, changed since Canning "called the new world into existence to redress the balance of the old," [37] and in the twentieth century both the Kaiser and Hitler erred seriously in underestimating the role of non-European powers in international politics. The League of Nations and the United Nations have increased the relative capacity of smaller states and of non-European states to influence the balance of power. Today, the submission of most major international problems to the United Nations General Assembly both indicates and augments the interest of nearly all states in those problems.

At the same time, the consequences of two world wars have been to diminish the power of several former great powers and to augment both the absolute and the relative power of the United States and the Soviet Union. Today all states tend to cluster around one or the other of these poles and, as the world shrinks in the vulnerability of each of its parts to attack from others, tensions between these poles continuously increase. The need and desire for peace on the one hand and the probability and destructiveness of war on the other, have both of them increased. It becomes ever more true to say that there is one world materially and two worlds morally.[38] Such a generalization, however, does not eliminate the need for more precise determination of both the relative interest and the relative influence of states in a particular situation.

Measurement of the different aspects of distance between states and analysis of the relation between these aspects may help in meeting this need.[39] These aspects of distances can be roughly measured by the application of judgment to the relative distance separating each pair of states in respect to each aspect. Technological and strategic distances between states, for example, have tended to decrease with inventions in the field of transportation, communication, and military destruction. That the rate has been an accelerating one is suggested if one contemplates the invention, the rapidity of utilization, and the rate of development of the printing press and the gun in the Renaissance period, of the steamboat, the railroad, the postoffice, and the telegraph in the nineteenth century, and of the airplane, the radio, and the atomic bomb in the twentieth. Yet the effect of these inventions has varied not only in time but also in space. The technological distance between the United States and Canada is today much less than that between India and China though each pair has a long frontier in common.

Psychological and social distances can also be measured by the method of comparative judgments, but the fluctuations are more radical. States can greatly alter their friendships and their acceptance of common social institutions in a short time. The psychological distance between Germany and Russia was suddenly reduced with conclusion of the non-aggression pact in August, 1939, and then suddenly increased with the German invasion of June, 1940. The influence of invention upon these distances is less predictable. Inventions which make possible more abundant and rapid communication and commerce between states tend at first to increase these distances because they are utilized much more within existing states than between them. Thus national solidarities and commitments to national values are accentuated and the distances between the societies is augmented. The long-run effect may be different.[40] Apparently factors making for a decrease in one aspect of distance may make for an increase in another. Analysis of the relations between these aspects of distance and measurement of changes in all can assist in determining the relative interest and influence of states in given structures and may in itself prove of considerable predictive and control value.

The Measurement of Power

An international regulatory body should know as accurately as possible the relative power of each nation in the system and the direction and rate at which that power is changing. Power is a complex matter, including not only armaments in being but also military potential, national morale, and national reputation.[41] The relative significance of these elements varies according to the time interval considered. Armaments in being, including military leadership, staff, mobilized forces, land, naval, and air materiel, and bases are of dominant importance in the early stages of a war, but very soon military potential, including industrial plant, management, labor, natural resources, population, wealth, inventiveness, and science become more important. Over a longer period of time national morale influenced by effectiveness of government, level of education, and national leadership play an important role. In an even longer time, which may not be granted if other elements are lacking, international reputation affecting the capacity to make allies and to gain the support of the world is of most importance. Armament in being wins the first battles but capacity to gain support of world opinion wins long wars.[42]

This complexity of the components of power, many of them incommensurable and of varying significance in time, makes it extremely difficult to measure relative power or the rate of its increase or decline even if all information which exists is available to the measurer. Much of such information is, however, kept secret within the defense departments of various governments. Consequently, statesmen have been obliged to regulate action by rough guesses. Careful analysis of the components of power and of their temporal significance, and systematic efforts to obtain and utilize such information as can be obtained, might, however, make possible continuing indexes indicating week-by-week changes in relative power. The League of Nations Secretariat published statistics of armaments in being. The United Nations has not been able to obtain the general consent of its members to do so. Resolutions seeking to require states to report information on their armed forces verified by suitable inspection have been vetoed. If such information were available and suitably analyzed, regulation of international affairs with the object of stability would be facilitated.[43]

Strategies and Anxieties

Regulatory agencies seeking to maintain stability must be aware of the state of technology and tension in the world in order to appraise the probability of sudden attacks. The influence of technological changes upon the relative advantage of the offensive and the defensive is not easy to determine. The machine gun and the trench, of great importance in World War I, seem to have increased the relative power of the defensive but the tank, the airplane, and the atomic bomb have probably increased the relative advantage of the offensive.[44] Sudden attacks are more likely to be successful if the offensive has an advantage. Consequently if the state of technology gives such an advantage aggression becomes more rational and more likely.[45]

Such attacks are also more likely under conditions of high tension. Tension, as has been noted, arises from inconsistencies in the initiatives or policies of groups and develops cumulatively from a process of power rivalry and policy rigidity.[46] Circumstances precipitating power rivalry include not only fears of external attack because of disturbed conditions of the power equilibrium, new military techniques favoring the offensive, and crusading or revolutionary ideologies and personalities, but also internal strains in government and society.[47] Such strains may spring from disharmonies, certain to arise in a maturing society, between new opportunities offered by advancing science and technology and the rigidities of traditional values,[48] between the increase in the number of the educated and the decrease in opportunities for leadership,[49] between the demand for equality and the stratifications of class and caste,[50] between the acceleration of social change and the lag of regulatory procedures.[51] Any of these disharmonies may produce parties of revolutionary character threatening social disruption. Such domestic strains can easily be converted into international tension among people accustomed by infant training and social practice to relieve ambivalences and frustrations by displacement of aggressive impulses upon a scapegoat or to project such impulses upon an opponent. By this process tensions in the minds of men can initiate tensions between two poles of a divided world.[52]

The material, social, and psychological causes of tension among nations are many and difficult to analyze, but it seems possible that changes in the intensity of these tensions can be measured by scrutinizing and analyzing the evidences of public opinion. Whether the press reflects the state of tension in the public mind, as it does in democracies with a free press, or creates that state of tension, as it tends to do in dictatorships with a controlled press, the content of the press may provide materials for an index of that state. Analysis of that content can indicate the direction, intensity, and homogeneity of opinion in regard to symbols relevant to international relations, such as the names of other nations, of international organizations, of international processes, and of ideologies and policies.[53] Rises and falls in the intensity of opinion in one nation about another as disclosed by the press or other evidences may measure the changing tension in their relations more accurately than informed guesses upon which statesmen have hitherto relied.

Foreign Policies and Public Opinion

More important than any of the factors already discussed as guides to regulatory action is information about the policies and intentions of other governments. In this field there is frequently a discrepancy between public expression and private purpose. Sources from which this information can be acquired include direct evidence from diplomatic discussion with leaders of foreign governments and espionage into their private discussions and correspondence.[54] Content analysis of official propaganda broadcasts, press releases, and speeches has on occasion given reliable information of the intentions of the government which issues them.[55] Some important evidence may be obtained from studies of the personalities, writings, experience, and contacts of political leaders.[56] Indirect evidence may be derived from the study of the traditions of the state, its foreign policies, its laws, its ideologies, the discussions in its public bodies, and the state of its public opinion.[57]

Presumptive evidence may be derived from an analysis of the apparent interests of the government and state and the means which seem most appropriate to secure these interests under the conditions which face that government.[58] The value of this evidence depends in some measure upon the similarity in values and mental processes between the analyzer and the personalities of the government analyzed. This method rests on the assumption that government "X" will act as I would act under similar circumstances. If my culture and my experience have been very different from those of "X," my appraisal, both of his interests and of the means which he will take for realizing them, may go far astray.

Evidence derived from generalized historic knowledge of the interests states have striven for and the methods they have used to achieve them in the past are far from reliable.[59] This method rests on the assumption that states are alike in their basic interests and in the means they prefer to employ. But unless "interests" refer to very general objectives such as "existence" or "security" the first proposition is not true. The peculiarities of a state's history and culture influence its interpretation of its "interests." The means which a government will use depends not only on its history and culture but on the peculiarities of the situation which is not likely to be on all fours with any historic precedent.

In utilizing any method to acquire "intelligence" about another government, the attempt should be made to see the interests of that government as it sees them, and to judge the methods it will use by its own appraisal of the situation, of its capabilities, and of the reactions to be expected from others. It is particularly important for this purpose to consider the policy of one's own government not as it is but as it is viewed by the government whose intentions are being appraised. It is to be assumed that military preparations which a government intends, or think it intends, for defense will be interpreted by its rival as intended for aggression.

The difficulty of acquiring reliable evidence in this field is obviously great and the process of acquiring it may augment international tensions, especially if espionage is resorted to. It appears, however, that the scientific analysis of much material that is available in the press and official utterances can throw light on intentions and policies of governments. The possibility of analyzing the press and other media which reflect or influence public opinion in order to measure the fluctuations in international tensions has already been referred to.[60] Analyses may also throw light on the policies which in the case of a democracy the government feels it must follow and in the case of a dictatorship the government wants its public to think it is following. Such studies should include not only quantitative variations in the intensity of opinions and attitudes concerning relevant symbols but also qualitative analyses with a view to distinguishing expressed opinions from the attitudes and intentions which they may seek to conceal. Content analysis may be able to distinguish the intent of the sender from the meaning which he expects the communication to convey to the receiver.[61]

Conclusion

The conclusion may be drawn that both the science and practice of international relations would benefit from a survey of the press and other accessible evidences of governmental attitudes and public opinion available in the principal cities of the world. Continuous, comprehensive, and systematic application to this material of the techniques of analysis and measurement which are developing might provide reliable information on changes in the intensity of international tensions, on changes in the homogeneity and intensity of national opinions about significant symbols, and in changes in the content and importance of the attitudes, policies, and intentions of the principal governments. Although more difficult, systematic effort might assemble data from which changes in the various aspects of distance between states and in their relative power could be measured.

Such measurements, continued through the years and tested by careful observation and practical application, might provide sufficient material for formulating scientific hypothesis or even scientific laws about international relations.[62] An understanding of the relations formulated in such laws and a use of statistical series indicating changes in the relevant variables week by week might make it more possible for governments to see others as they see themselves, to see themselves as others see them, to think quantitatively, and to increase the precision of regulatory action.

Such analyses and measurements might make it possible for the United States government to develop policies which would maximize defense and minimize provocation, which would maximize prospects of conciliation and minimize dangers of appeasement. They might make it possible for organs of the United Nations more adequately to relate the enforcement of its law against aggression to political action designed to localize and terminate hostilities, and more adequately to relate the application of its universal principles and objectives in economic and social matters to the distinctive needs, wants, and demands of the nations.

In the field of finance the central banks and treasuries of the principal nations, the International Monetary Fund, and the International Bank for Reconstruction and Development have been attempting to guide policies concerning credit, investment, and exchange with the object of economic stability. For this purpose they utilize information concerning national financial and commercial policies and statistical series concerning production, population, prices, income, and trade.[63] These agencies have difficulty in regulating their action by this information in the face of political pressures, and mammoth distortions arising from war, preparations for war, and national policies with ends other than stability. Yet the existence of international agencies with authority to take regulatory measures in the financial field, with knowledge of the probable effect of these measures in different situations, and with information upon the changing situation, promises to alleviate the violence of fluctuations of inflation and depression, and of exchange instability. The need for such alleviation has become increasingly apparent as industrial combinations have augmented their monopolistic or oligopolistic power, as economies have become governmentalized, as national economies have become more interdependent, and as political conditions have become less stable.[64]

The task of the foreign and defense departments of peace-loving governments and of the political organs of the United Nations is similar but the methods to be used are less understood and the information needed for regulatory action is less available. The need for effective regulation is, however, even greater as the world shrinks, as power concentrates, as tensions rise, and as peoples become more vulnerable to atomic destruction. If science can provide guides for politics, international relations may change its emphasis from national rivalries for power to regulation of the power and policy of governments.

Commitment by statesmen to such a regulatory process, although guided by consideration of the stability of the world as a whole, would not tend to eliminate the nations nor to establish a cosmopolitan society. It is not to be expected, with the great diversity of the nations and cultures that political rivalries will disappear, nor is it to be expected that any system of jural law or world government can function unless first attention is given to keeping the relative power of the nations in balance. If, however, the United Nations demonstrates its capacity, improves its procedures, and acquires greater support of world opinion, it may become an increasingly important element in the world equilibrium able to contribute to stability by both political regulation and legal enforcement.

Continuous and skillful activity on all legal fronts—jural, practical, ethical, and scientific—is essential if progress is to be made toward a more just and peaceful world, but I believe that in the immediate situation analysis and measurement of the variables of distance, power, tension, and opinion can make the greatest contribution to solving the dominant political problems of international relations. These problems increase in gravity as the world bipolarizes. The traditional methods of power politics accentuate rivalries and the traditional methods of law are ineffective. More precise guides may permit such a regulation of international tensions and relative power that an atmosphere of confidence will emerge in which jural law can be enforced, ethical law observed, and practical law administered in the world community. The emphasis of international relations might then shift from national sovereignty and power politics to international justice and the welfare of people.

17

INTERNATIONAL LAW

AND POWER POLITICS

Traditional International Law

The international law of the nineteenth century assumed the sovereignty of states and the balance of power. Each state occupied a well-defined territory within which its law was supreme, and formulated foreign policies which it was free to prosecute even by war. In time of peace the right of a state to use force was limited. Coercive methods short of war, as they were called, were only permissible by a state in the exercise of its domestic jurisdiction; in necessary self-defense, which included defense of its territory, its agencies, and its nationals; in police action within the territory of a state which had expressly consented to such use; or as a measure of reprisal after peaceful means had proved inadequate to gain reparation for an injury or to stop a continuing injury.

Every state, however, had the legal capacity to initiate a state of war, and if it did so, both it and its enemy could employ armed force subject only to the limitations imposed by the law of war. The qualifications which had been accepted in the Middle Ages and in the early modern period that war could be legally initiated only for just causes and with proper motives had been largely abandoned. Reason of state had come to be considered adequate legal justification for war.

It is therefore clear that the object of nineteenth-century international law was not to prevent armed violence, but to restrict it in time, place, and method. International law sought to restrict hostilities to the periods of time when formal war existed, thus drawing a sharp line between "time of war" and "time of peace." In the latter time, inter-

From *Measure,* II (Spring, 1951).

national law sought, as has been noted, to reduce uses of armed force in international relations to special circumstances. In time of war, on the other hand, the normal law was inoperative, and all states were either belligerents or neutrals, with special rights and duties, special powers and liabilities, pertaining to those statuses.

As the concept of war sought to limit international violence in time, so the concept of neutrality sought to limit it in space. States were free to remain neutral, unless bound to a belligerent by special alliance or guaranty, and belligerents were bound to respect that neutrality so long as the neutral lived up to its obligations of impartiality, abstention of its government from aid to either belligerent, and prevention of certain types of aid by individuals from its territory. It was assumed that a belligerent would not wish to multiply its enemies, and that, therefore, it would not declare war on neutrals unless they obviously aided its enemies or hampered its own efforts. Neutrals, it was thought, would usually prefer to observe the somewhat burdensome law of neutrality because of their interest in avoiding war and in helping their nationals to profit by trade with both belligerents, subject only to the risk of maritime capture for carriage of contraband, breach of blockade, or unneutral service. The maintenance of this balance of neutral and belligerent interest was a somewhat delicate matter, and the appropriate compromise varied with the number and character of belligerents and the prevailing military technique. Thus, the precise rules which would maintain this equilibrium were always subject to controversy. But however uncertain might be the precise law of neutrality, the concept was considered a useful device for preventing the spread of war; during the nineteenth century some wars were actually localized to the two original belligerents.

These concepts of war and neutrality came to be so favored during the relatively peaceful nineteenth century that many treaties were made to extend these time and space limitations. Thus many international boundary areas and several whole states such as Switzerland, Belgium, and Luxembourg were permanently neutralized. This meant that all states were forbidden to make war upon a state enjoying this status, or to engage in hostilities, even in time of war, in a neutralized area. Cooling off treaties also came into vogue, whereby states agreed that they would not resort to hostilities until a specified period of time had elapsed during which various procedures of pacific settlement were to be tried. The Bryan treaties made by the United States with many countries in 1913 were of this type, and the idea played a part in the League of Nations Covenant.

The methods of war which had been regulated by custom and practice since earliest times received increasing attention in national regulations and international conventions of the nineteenth century, particularly after the subject had been codified in a general order of the United States Army drawn up by Francis Lieber during the Civil War. The object of these regulations was to prevent inhumanities not justified by military necessity, and to assure certain standards of good faith mutually convenient to the belligerents, such as respect for flags of truce and armistices.

In addition to these restrictions upon the use of force, international law sought to define the rights of states in time of peace. It defined the methods for acquiring status, territory, nationals, and jurisdiction, and the precise scope and implications of each of these fundamental rights. International law also sought to facilitate peaceful methods for securing rights, forwarding policy, and settling controversies.

It was clear to international jurists that this system, while it promoted national independence and international competition and was not unfavorable to human progress under the conditions which prevailed during much of the modern period, manifested a very inchoate and primitive society. The member nations were separated by formidable barriers to international trade and communication, they recognized comparatively few moral and political standards in common, they coöperated for few common objectives which were considered important, and they were organized by institutions that were so limited in scope or membership or so decentralized as hardly to deserve the name "organization." Under these conditions, international law was sanctioned only by habit, reciprocal interest, and fear of reprisals. These sanctions were internal rather than external, moral rather than legal. While states might be influenced by a world public opinion which frowned upon illegal behavior, that opinion was so unorganized, so lacking in agencies for expression and action, that its appeal, so far as it had any, was to the conscience of peoples and statesmen, rather than to the expectation of immediate community action to remedy illegal behavior. Such fears as the law violator might have concerned not the reaction of the society of nations in response to a world opinion behind the law, but the possibility of retaliation by the state immediately injured by its illegal behavior. If that state was obviously too weak to take effective measures, this fear was unimportant unless, indeed, the injured state had more potent friends upon whom it could rely. As a consequence, international law could protect the weaker members of the society of nations only in so far as it could rely upon the operation of balance-of-power policies; that is, upon the pursuit by all important states of the policy of preventing aggrandizement by the most powerful of their number at the expense of its weaker neighbors. Such a policy might be expected because such aggrandizement could initiate a chain of events whereby the aggrandizing state, strengthened by one successful aggression, would be more likely to succeed in a second, until the existence of every state would be threatened—a possibility which all European governments had in mind through their knowledge of the course of ancient history ending in the triumph of Rome.

The principle of the balance of power, which urged states to intervene against any one of their number which threatened to become too powerful, was balanced against the principle of neutrality, which urged nonparticipation in every controversy in order to avoid and localize war. If claims were so moderate that their satisfaction would not greatly increase the power of the state which made them, neutrality was likely to be followed by states not immediately involved. But whenever a powerful state made a demand or pursued policies which if achieved would upset the balance of power, third states tended to join forces against it. If they failed to do so, the basic stability of the world society would be so shaken that a period of lawlessness was to be expected, such as occurred during the period of the Thirty Years' War, during the latter part of the reign of Louis XIV, during the period of Napoleon, and during the period of German aggression in the twentieth century. Each of these periods of war lasted for about thirty years and registered an extremely serious shock to the balance of power. The eventual overthrow in each case of the state which had grown overpowerful by successful aggressions created a certain confidence in the fundamental stability of a system which rested primarily on an equilibrium of military power. The last of these experiences, however, has aroused serious doubt whether that system can any longer be relied upon. The shrinking world, the acceleration of history, the rise of democracy, the increasing destructiveness of war, the rising capacity of the offensive compared with the defensive in military operations, and the diminution in the number of great powers present conditions which, judged both by analysis and by experience, may require the society of nations to change its law and organization, if it is to protect the states and individuals whose security and progress is its reason for being.

These circumstances account for the radical changes in international law which have been introduced by formal consent of most of the states of the world during the past generation. This new international law has not been provided with effective sanctions. It is too early to be certain that it will endure in the face of the opposition to be expected from certain nations, governments, and other vested interests. It represents the aspirations of peoples and states which their representatives have publicly declared and formally accepted, but which will require judicious accommodation to existing rights to become workable, detailed juristic analysis to become precise, and significant strengthening of international organization to become effective.

The New Concept of War

The first of these changes is in the concept of war. In nineteenth-century international law, war was a legal condition which equally permitted two or more hostile groups to carry on a conflict by armed force. War was not an outbreak of lawlessness, but a condition or institution which the law defined and regulated, and which permitted the participants to utilize armed force against one another. The most significant characteristic, however, was the equality of the parties. Third states were bound, unless they became belligerent, to treat the two sides of the conflict alike. While "benevolent" and "unfriendly" neutrality were given a certain recognition in the juristic writings and practices of the seventeenth and eighteenth centuries, nineteenth-century international law, prompted in no small measure by the attitude taken by the United States in the 1790's, and formally codified in the Hague convention of 1907, held that neutrals must be impartial except so far as they could justify discriminations or reprisals because of injuries resulting from illegal behavior by one of the belligerents. Thus the concept of neutrality defined the concept of war. The essence of war was the equality of the belligerents. Obviously, with this concept of war, discussion of the policies which the belligerents were seeking to promote or the circumstances under which the war originated were irrelevant to any legal consideration of the rights and duties of states, whether belligerent or neutral. War was a duel, the results of which determined the justice of the claims of the participants.

The change in the concept of war is to be seen in the legal elimination of the duties of neutrality, first those of abstention and then those of impartiality. The process began in the Hague convention of 1899, which recognized that all states had an interest in "obviating recourse to force" and that therefore states should "use their best efforts to insure the pacific settlement of international difficulties." States not party to a dispute were urged "on their own initiative" to tender their good offices or mediation to potential or actual belligerents. Such action was not obligatory, nor were the disputing states bound to accept the offer. Third states were not authorized to intervene in the technical sense of dictatorial interference, but there was a general recognition that every state had an interest in every war or threat of war. War had ceased to be a duel in which only the combatants were interested.

The League of Nations Covenant made more emphatic the general interest in wars and threats of wars. Such occurrences were declared a matter of concern to the whole League, which was required to "take any action that may be deemed wise and effectual to safeguard the peace of nations." This made action by the League both obligatory and authoritative. The members of the League committed themselves to collective intervention. Subsequent articles not only eliminated the disinterestedness of the neutral, but eliminated his impartiality if a resort to war had taken place in violation of the Covenant. In such circumstances all members of the League were bound to subject the aggressor "to the severance of all trade and financial relations" and to give consideration to recommendations of the Council for use of armed force "to protect the Covenants of the League."

These provisions eliminated neutrality for League members if war originated in a breach of the Covenant. Furthermore, it eliminated the conception of war as a condition in which the belligerents are equal. Under these provisions, the Covenant breaker was an outlawed aggressor, while its innocent victim was a lawful defender. There were, it is true, gaps in the Covenant as a result of which lawful war might occur, carrying with it the rights and duties of neutrality, even for League members. But these gaps were in principle closed by the almost universally accepted Kellogg-Briand pact of 1928. Under that instrument the parties condemned war, renounced it as an instrument of national policy, and agreed never to seek the settlement of any dispute or controversy except by peaceful means. Furthermore, states which violated the pact and utilized nonpacific means, that is, measures involving the use of armed force, for promoting national policy or settling disputes, ceased, according to the preamble, to enjoy the benefits of the pact, and could properly be discriminated against or attacked by any state. The unofficial Budapest Articles of Interpretation and the international discussions concerning the Manchurian invasion by Japan, the Ethiopian attack by Italy, and the German aggressions accepted the principle that states were permitted, but not obliged by the pact, to discriminate against the pact violator. It was this principle which justified the United States while still "nonbelligerent" in aiding the Allies with Lend Lease. The principle *jus ex injuria non oritur* ("rights do not arise from wrongs") was invoked to demonstrate that the pact violator acquired none of the traditional rights of a belligerent against its enemies or against "neutrals," though the defender should apply the rules of war forbidding inhumanity and perfidy even to an aggressor.

The United Nations Charter made the obsolescence of the nineteenth-century concepts of war and neutrality even more clear. The major purpose of the United Nations is "to maintain international peace and security, and to that end, to take effective collective measures for the prevention and removal of threats to the peace, and for the suppression of acts of aggression or other breaches of the peace" (Article 1). Members of the United Nations are bound "to settle their international disputes by peaceful means" and to "refrain in their international relations from the threat or use of force against the territorial integrity or political independence of any state, or in any other manner inconsistent with the purposes of the United Nations." Furthermore, members are bound to assist the United Nations "in action it takes in accordance with the Charter," and to "refrain from giving assistance to any state against which the United Nations is taking preventive or enforcement action" (Article 2). Discrimination against an aggressor is, therefore, obligatory. Impartiality is forbidden.

If these commitments are taken at their face value, war and neutrality no longer exist as legal institutions. A state that resorts to armed force is either an aggressor who should be suppressed, a defender who should be assisted, or a participant in international sanctions permitted or authorized by the United Nations. All members of the United Nations are bound by the Charter to regulate their action by these distinctions, not by the traditional concept of states of war and neutrality. The basic distinction of international law has, therefore, ceased to be that between times of war and times of peace, and it has become that between lawful uses of force and unlawful uses of force.

Sovereignty and the Individual

The sovereignty of the state meant, in nineteenth-century international law, not only that the state could initiate war at discretion, but also that it could make law applicable in its own territory at discretion. It is true that if that law and its administration denied justice to resident nationals of another state, that state could protest and demand reparation. Furthermore, the state's law must recognize certain exemptions which international law explicitly established in favor of foreign diplomats and other officials performing their functions in the state's territory. In respect to its own nationals in its own territory sovereignty was omnipotent, however, except so far as the state may have expressly consented by treaty to qualify its exercise of its domestic jurisdiction. The state could treat its nationals unjustly or even barbarously; it could deny them fair trials or execute them without trial; it could permit discrimination, starvation, or massacre, and violate no rule of international law. It is true that, during the nineteenth century, states sometimes made representations against excesses of inhumanity and brutality which shocked the conscience of mankind; and occasionally intervention was justified on humanitarian grounds, as, for example, American intervention in Cuba in 1898, the British representation against brutal treatment of natives in the Congo in 1908, and the representations made by various powers about pogroms in Russia in the early twentieth century. Such representations were made in the name of general morality and humanity, rather than as recognition of any specific rights enjoyed by the individual under international law. In theory, the individual was not a subject, but only an object, of international law. If he sometimes gained compensation for injuries which he received in foreign lands after the local courts had denied him justice, it was not in his own right but as a consequence of the rights of his state to protect him and, if it wished, to give him the reparation which it had in its own right received for the injury to its national. The individual had no access to international procedures himself, and had no power to compel his state to intercede in his behalf. His state took up his cause at discretion, and the state alleged to have been responsible for his injury could refuse to listen to the claim until the complaining state demonstrated that the individual had been its national when the injury was received and continued to be such.

There were jurists who insisted that this theory was artificial, that in fact the individual was a subject of international law, and that his state acted as his agent in protecting him. Such jurists pointed out that the individual clearly enjoyed certain exceptional rights under international law when serving as ambassador or other official agent of his country. They called attention to the principle applied by courts in some states that international law is part of national law and should be applied for the benefit of individuals in appropriate cases. They also pointed out that if an individual committed piracy or other offense against the law of nations, he was liable under that law in any tribunal that had him in custody. These views, while generally accepted by the early publicists and supported by judicial opinions of the seventeenth and eighteenth centuries, were generally rejected by nineteenth-century writers, influenced by concepts of legal positivism.

According to the positivists, who sought to save the concept of state sovereignty by judicious interpretation, piracy and other offenses against the law of nations were not acts which imposed an international liability upon the individual but acts which international law permitted, or in some cases required, any state to bring within its jurisdiction. These concepts defined, therefore, from the point of view of international law, not the individual's offense but the state's jurisdiction. If they also defined the individual's offense, it was only because they were incorporated in the municipal law of a particular state.

The positivists also asserted that the principle requiring courts to apply international law in appropriate cases was to be interpreted merely as a convenient rule of the municipal law of certain states incorporating a body of doctrine in block, and that the international law thus incorporated was always subject to overruling national legislation. The individual's rights and liabilities, therefore, were not derived from international law directly but from the rule of municipal law which incorporated certain international rules.

It is always possible to interpret the state as sovereign, protecting or punishing individuals in its own interest under such guidance as it chooses to accept from international law, but it is also possible to interpret the individual as a jural personality with rights under international law which he can pursue only through the agency of his state and with duties under international law which the society of nations can enforce only through the agency of the state having jurisdiction over him. The state, in other words, may be construed (1) as a sovereign entity valuable in itself, or (2) as an agent on the one hand of the individuals that compose it and on the other of the universal society embracing all humanity.

While nineteenth-century international law generally accepted the first interpretation, the second is more consistent with the principles which states have accepted during the past generation. The transition began with the multiplication of general treaties which specified rights of aborigines, of minorities, of workers, of women, of children, and of other classes of persons who were in danger of oppression. Such treaties were sometimes supplemented by procedures whereby violations could be brought to the attention of international agencies. Thus petitions from the inhabitants of mandated territories and from minorities protected by international treaties were submissible to appropriate organs of the League of Nations. While such petitions did not initiate a procedure, they did provide information upon which any member of the League could initiate action in the League organs.

There were also provisions in the treaties ending World War I for presentation by individuals of claims for war damages before mixed commissions and for trial in international tribunals of certain war criminals. In the latter case, the Kaiser, although indicted by the Treaty of Versailles, was not tried at all, and the jurisdiction to try other German war criminals was transferred to a German court at Leipzig, which dealt with only a few cases. A new principle was, however, in process of formation. The Permanent Court of International Justice gave its support to the tendency by cautious recognition that a treaty might make individuals subjects of international law, entitled to rights defined in the treaty, if that was the intention of the parties to the treaty.

The United Nations Charter reaffirms faith in fundamental human rights in its Preamble, and asserts as one of its purposes: "to achieve international co-operation . . . in promoting and encouraging respect for human rights and for fundamental freedoms of all without distinction as to race, sex, language, or religion" (Article 1). The General Assembly is obliged to initiate studies and make recommendations to this end (Article 13), the United Nations as a whole is bound "to promote universal respect for and observance of" these rights, and the members "pledge themselves to take joint and separate action in co-operation with the organization for the achievement" of that purpose (Articles 55, 56). The General Assembly has made a declaration of human rights; and the Human Rights Commission has progressed toward a covenant which will create specific obligations to respect certain of these rights and has discussed various international procedures enabling the individual to initiate action to assure observance of his rights. These provisions and achievements make it clear that the new international law recognizes the individual, whatever his nationality or lack of nationality, as a subject of international law with certain rights which are in principle under the protection of the society of nations, anything in the law of the state of his nationality or residence to the contrary notwithstanding.

A similar conclusion must be drawn concerning the individual's liability under international law. The charter for the trial of major war criminals of the European Axis countries described certain crimes against peace, war crimes, and crimes against humanity, for which those responsible were subject to trial and punishment by the International Military Tribunal established at Nuremberg. It was expressly recognized that the official position of the defendant, whether as head of state or as a responsible official in a government department, or the fact that he acted on orders from his government or his superior should not free him of responsibility, although the latter might be considered in mitigation of punishment.

The Nuremberg tribunal recognized the principles stated in its charter as declaratory of preëxisting international law and applied them in the trial of Göring and other high Nazi officials. It recognized that acts which had the character of piracy, brigandage, or mass murder, except that they were committed in pursuance of an "act of state" alleged to create a "state of war," reverted to their character of crimes against international law if the "act of state" authorized aggression in violation of the state's obligations under the Kellogg-Briand pact. Such an illegal act of state could not confer an immunity upon the defendants. Since the pact was ratified by Germany long before the beginning of World War II, the suggestion that the tribunal applied *ex post facto* law was not justified. The Tokyo tribunal, acting under a similar charter, quoted with approval the Nuremberg opinion on this matter. The same principle has been applied by other military tribunals, both national and international, in Europe and in the East. Furthermore, the General Assembly of the United Nations has endorsed these principles and instructed the International Law Commission, established at its third session, to prepare a code on the subject and to consider the establishment of an international criminal court for the trial of such offenses. A convention has already been opened to ratification, defining the international crime of genocide and declaring that persons committing genocide "shall be punished whether they are constitutionally responsible rulers, public officials, or private individuals."

It is clear that if these instruments and opinions are accepted as law, the sovereign state no longer has the capacity to deny human rights to persons in its control even if they are its nationals, or the capacity to grant immunity from prosecution to individuals who commit crimes against the law of nations, even if they do so in the name of the state and under its authority. Individual rights and liabilities are established directly under international law, quite apart from the law of any national state. This important development suggests that, in principle, the society of nations has acquired aspects of a true federation implying a functional division of authority over individuals between world and national governments. The principle is established, but it remains to realize it through appropriate organizations.

Interests of the Society of Nations

Traditional international law excluded the society of nations as well as the individual from the position of subject of international law. International agreements were generally bilateral, and international controversies were considered of concern to the parties alone. The facts were often otherwise. Under conditions of power politics, many treaties, the solution of many controversies, and most wars affected the stability of the equilibrium of power, and therefore were a subject of political interest to all states. The law, however, usually neglected this fact of community interest.

The multiplication of general treaties has broken down the traditional bilateralism of international law. Every party to such a treaty has a right to expect that every state party to that treaty shall, in its relations with every other party, observe its obligations; it is, therefore, entitled to intervene in controversies involving the construction of the convention, as indicated by Article 63 of the statute of the International Court of Justice.

But beyond this interest of all states in the basic principles established by general treaties to which they are parties and by customary international law, the society of nations as a unit has acquired legal interests which it can protect and promote in so far as it is organized for action. The United Nations, which is designed to serve as the organization of the society of nations, has, through appropriate organs, power to make agreements with its members on the supply of armed forces, the immunities of its officials and its headquarters, and upon other matters. It also has power to make agreements with specialized agencies establishing their relations with it. Numerous such agreements have been made. In addition to its power to make agreements, the United Nations has powers of recommendation, decision, and enforcement. The characteristics of a jural person with powers and responsibilities are more emphasized in the Charter of the United Nations than they were in the Covenant of the League of Nations. The jural personality of the United Nations and its capacity to demand reparations for injuries to its agents has been recognized by the International Court of Justice. The constitutions of the specialized agencies establish them as jural persons. The organized community of nations has been acquiring legal rights and duties, powers and responsibilities, and defining the public interests of the world society distinct from the interests of its member states. The sovereignty of those members obviously becomes qualified as this process continues.

Law and Practice

The old international law, which recognized the sovereign state to the exclusion of almost everything else, has been undergoing radical changes with the outlawing of war and neutrality, the recognition of the individual, the recognition of the public interest of the world society in many transactions, and the establishment of the jural personality of international organizations, with rights and powers embodying that public interest. The state is assuming more modest proportions in law as the positions of the individual and the world society rise in importance. This is the legal situation, but in practice some national states with their efficient controls of thought, economy, and military action appear, in fact, more independent, powerful, and dangerous than ever. Is it possible that the new principles of international law can be realized in practice? There is in fact a great gap between international law and international practice. International law, as expressed in formal documents, has accepted principles similar to those of the municipal law of civilized states. It has assumed that there is a society of men and states capable of preventing self-willed violence by its members, protecting accepted individual and national interests, maintaining its own basic standards, and forwarding its own objectives even when opposed by individual or national demands except in so far as the latter have been recognized as legal rights.

On the other hand, the past generation has witnessed two world wars which devastated important areas of the world and increased the antagonism between national groups. National states utilizing modern devices of public administration, economic control, political education, and propaganda have made more vigorous efforts to become self-sufficient and have been, in some cases, more willing to resort to violence and fraud to increase their power than ever before. The national state seems to have increased in solidarity more rapidly than has the society of nations. As a consequence of general war and of the changes in military technique, the disparity in power between great and little states has increased, smaller states have felt obliged or been compelled to seek shelter in the sphere of a great neighbor, and the world has tended to organize around two poles, the United States and the Soviet Union, between which hangs an iron curtain of suspicion, and around each of which political organization and military preparation proceed. Germany and Japan remain in undetermined status; hostilities have occurred in Korea, China, Kashmir, Indonesia, Palestine, and Greece; and economic recovery is hampered in spite of strenuous efforts by the United States to distribute the surplus of its economy. Certainly the conditions of the world bear little resemblance to the expectation set forth in legal documents.

Such a disparity between law and conditions, if long continued, may create a general contempt for international law and international institutions, encourage disorder and violence by the dissatisfied, and lead to a general deterioration of civilization out of which tyranny, whether of the extreme right or the extreme left, can grow. Such have been the consequences of similar conditions in the Chinese period of "warring states," ended by the Ts'in emperor's conquests in the third century

B.C.; in the Hellenistic period, ended by conquest of the Mediterranean area by Rome in the first century B.C.; and in the later Middle Ages, ended in the East by the vast conquests of the Ottomans and in the West by the vaster but less permanent acquisitions of the Habsburgs during the fifteenth and sixteenth centuries. Today the possibilities of conquest are extended by modern technology beyond the areas of empires of the past to the whole world. If the states of the modern world cannot consent to the development of the United Nations into an organization capable of actually maintaining its law, new wars culminating in universal conquest may occur. Can such a result be avoided? Can the new international law be made effective in spite of the discouraging condition of international politics at the moment?

The Problem of Enforcing International Law

In its broadest sense, law implies a realized generalization. In the sense in which the natural sciences use the term, the reality controls the generalization. If facts are observed contrary to existing scientific generalizations, these generalizations must be altered to accord with the facts. On the other hand, in the sense in which jurisprudence uses the term "law," the generalization is intended to control the reality. Generalizations are law if they are enforced. It is, however, recognized that enforcement may be imperfect. It is the essence of a jural law that it may be violated, whereas a scientific law cannot be violated. If a supposed scientific law is violated, that proves it was not law. Jural law does not follow the facts so closely. Nevertheless, if a supposed jural law is too frequently violated over a period of time, it ceases to be law.

The gap which always exists between jural law and social reality may become so wide that the accepted generalization ceases to be law. The suggestion that there can be such a gap indicates that the sources of jural law are not social behavior. There may be sociological laws, parallel to physical laws, which accurately reflect observed social behavior. They, however, differ from jural law, whose source lies not in the behavior of the society and its members, but in the prevailing opinion of what that behavior ought to be. The ultimate source of jural law is the public opinion within a society concerning values, but it must not be supposed that all the values which public opinion supports are law. Law includes only those values which can be discovered in accepted legal sources and which may be enforced by accepted legal sanctions.

Jural law differs from moral law by the precision of its sources and the objectivity of its sanctions. It also differs from practical law, which describes the methods for achieving particular results. Such law has its source in scientific law and its sanction in the value of its objectives. Jural law, it is true, has sometimes been conceived as a description of the means for the achievement of major social values such as peace, order, prosperity, democracy, the maximization of individual liberty, or, even more generally, "the good society" or "the good man." Such a description, however, while it may justify particular legal rules, especially new legislation, does not indicate the character of the system of jural law as a whole. A system of jural law serves many, often conflicting, ends, both social and individual. Taken as a whole, jural law seeks to do for a society what scientific law does for nature. It seeks to establish certain relatively permanent relationships which, in so far as they can be relied upon, permit prediction within a limited range of probability and thus makes rational planning by individuals and groups possible.

Jural law, therefore, involves four elements—public opinion, jural sources, jural sanctions, and actual enforcement. To be law a rule should be acceptable, just, valid, and effective. The first and last are in a sense outside the jural system, but they provide conditions under which such a system can function. Public opinion attributing a value to certain individual and social interests is the ultimate source of law in any society. Unless there is a relative consensus of opinion on some values, standards, or objectives, there cannot be a society nor can there be a legal system, but until public opinion has settled upon methods and materials (jural sources) for distinguishing relatively permanent principles of justice from the changing expressions of opinion, there can be no law. Opinion must be disciplined and controlled by jural method and by experts in its application if it is to provide generalizations which will be considered just in the society. But even if accepted sources of law yield propositions embodying justice, there is no law unless the sources, reflecting public opinion, indicate that the just rule, principle, or standard ought to be enforced by the society. Such recognition constitutes the sanction of the generalization, making it a valid rule of law. If however, in spite of such recognition, force is not sufficient, or not sufficiently organized, or not sufficiently applied to make the sanction generally effective, the generalization ceases to be law— the law becomes obsolete.

What has just been said constitutes the democratic or idealistic concept of law. Opinion creates justice, justice creates law, and law develops force for its effective maintenance. There is, however, an autocratic or realistic conception of law which starts at the other end. An authority establishes itself by effective force in a society and, having done so, finds it convenient to govern with rules of a more general application than the special order or decree. So law is born as the relatively permanent and general commands of the ruler. Law in this sense, however, is easier to enforce if it conforms to the society's sense of justice, and justice is discovered through institutions and methods permitting discussion and the generation of a public opinion.

In actual societies, both concepts of law play some part, their relative importance depending on the extent to which individual freedom and social institutions permit, or even encourage, public opinion to form outside government institutions. Where the government, controlling predominant force, also controls instruments of communication and prevents free discussion, law is largely the command of the government. Sovereignty is vested in the ruler, not in the people. Most modern legal systems have, in fact, developed by the autocratic method at first; but at a certain stage order becomes a habit, courts administer justice, individual freedom increases, public opinion develops from extragovernmental sources, and institutions are established to formulate the law. The democratic process then has greater weight. The two processes are well illustrated in the British constitution. Formally, all law proceeds from the King, who theoretically controls the army and the civil service and is merely advised by the Parliament and the Privy Council. But in fact, law proceeds from the people who elect Parliament, whose will the King must sanction. The normal sequence, under which a legal order develops through the creation first of executive authority to keep the peace, then judicial authority to settle disputes, and finally legislative and administrative authority, illustrates this process. Public opinion cannot be closely related to law in a dynamic society until "democratic" legislative and administrative procedures have been established.

International law, differing from most systems of municipal law, developed by the democratic process in its early stages, but among autocratic governments rather than among peoples. It has grown primarily from the consent of governments, manifested expressly by treaties or tacitly by custom. The opinion of the people, however, has had some influence through the conception of "natural law" and maxims of justice which formulate systems of rules, principles, and standards reflecting the general opinion as shaped by the prevailing religious, ethical, and philosophical thought. In the early history of international law, when it applied only in the society of the Christian states of Europe, "natural law" was a very important influence on its development.

The sanctions of international law have, however, been inadequate. Opinion, both popular and governmental, distinguished international law from international morality by assuming that states could in principle resort to reprisals to enforce their rights and that collective action to prevent grave breaches of international law was permissible and desirable. Yet no positive arrangements for enforcement were established by general or customary international law, and few such arrangements were established by particular treaties. There was no force of the society of nations as a whole to deal with recalcitrant states, and international law left it to the states to deal with recalcitrant individuals. It has been the objective of the League of Nations and of the United Nations to provide more adequate sanctions by organizing forces superior to those of any state.

It has, however, always been clear that the application of force against very powerful organizations, whatever may be its theory, is more likely in fact to resemble war than police action. The effectiveness of law enforcement depends upon the disparity between the force at the disposal of the legal order and the force at the disposal of the lawbreaker. If this disparity is of the order of a million to one, as it is when modern states deal with individuals within their jurisdiction, law enforcement is not difficult. When, however, the ratio is of the order of only three or four to one, the situation is very different. The victory of the legal order over the lawbreaking state is by no means certain, and resistance by that state may require the legal order to resort to hostilities which have all the material characteristics of war. When the participants approach equality in actual power, war in the material sense results, even though they differ greatly in legal position.

This situation can be observed within states as well as within the society of states. A state faced by a violation of law by a huge corporation or a huge labor union has great difficulty in law enforcement; and when a state is faced by large groups of armed rebels or insurgents, civil war may result. Consequently, it is clear that if effective sanctions are to be established for the maintenance of law, not only must there be an organization of the entire society of nations placing major forces at its disposal; enforcement must also be against individuals rather than against states. It is true that the guilty individual, if a member of a government or a chief of state, may be able to utilize the state's forces to protect himself from seizure. There is, however, the possibility that most of the population can be induced to accept the opinion that such an individual, having violated international law, has also violated the state's constitution and no longer deserves protection.

The launching of sanctions against the individual, therefore, provides a greater possibility of depriving him of the aid of the state's forces than if the sanctions were directed against the state itself. This development has been recognized in principle in the Nuremberg trials and in the Genocide Convention; but the forces of international politics, anxious to maintain the solidarity of the national state, oppose the realization of this development. The state, it is said, must be kept united at all costs in order to preserve internal order and to prevent external invasion. Thus the national legal order may be in conflict with the international legal order, and since the national legal orders have been supported by powerful sentiments of nationalism in most states, the international legal order has been weak. Do the conditions of international politics offer opportunities for modifying this situation?

The Problem of International Politics

Politics is the art of creating and maintaining groups and of achieving their policies against the opposition of other groups. Politicians who would create new national states or a world state find themselves opposed by other politicians who want to maintain their own states, the existence of which is threatened by such movements. Politicians who want to achieve the policies of their own states, whether of internal development or of external expansion, find themselves opposed by the politicians of other states pursuing conflicting policies. Such opposition becomes particularly intransigent if certain national politicians think the success of the policy of others will change the relative power position of states to their own disadvantage, and thus in the long run threaten the existence of their states.

The ceaseless play of politics in the modern world operates within a basic structure of some seventy national territorial states claiming to be sovereign in the sense of freedom limited only by international law. It concerns the creation of new states, the maintenance of old states, and the achieving of state policies. The state system which began in Europe with the elimination of the theoretically supreme power of pope and emperor in the fifteenth and sixteenth centuries has resulted in the elimination of many small states, in the extension of the system to include the world, in an increasing disparity in power between small and great states, and in a decreasing number of great states. At the beginning of this development, there are said to have been three thousand European states, and there were certainly a greater number of extra-European chieftains, tribes, kingdoms, and empires, all of them fighting occasionally, but usually locally. Now there are two great centers of power, and the remaining seventy-odd states, with the exception of a few buffer neutrals, gather around them as satellites, allies, or friends. As the tension between the two poles increases, the possibility has to be considered of a war which would, if it occurred, be world-wide and catastrophic.

During this process, there have at times been periods of relative peace and stability, separated by other periods of continuous war and partial anarchy. In so far as stability has existed, it has been because the power and the alliances of states were in such relation that no state could expand without the prospect of facing so many others opposing it that it would certainly fail. Such a condition would clearly be promoted if each state pursued the policy of balance of power, which meant that it would join with others to weaken any member of the community of nations which was getting so powerful as to threaten the balance. Stability under this system depended on skillful pursuit of such a policy, but it was always recognized that such action might require a country to violate international law. Statesmen were frequently faced by a moral dilemma: if they observed law, the equilibrium might be so disturbed that the system upon which the law rested would be shattered. If, on the other hand, they pursued policies to prevent disturbances of the equilibrium, they would often have to intervene in a manner contrary to international law and thus contribute to the weakening and perhaps the destruction of that law.

The classical writers on international law—Gentili, Grotius, Vattel—assumed that intervention or war "is only permissible in order to redress an injury received, or to protect ourselves from an injury with which we are threatened" and that "power alone does not constitute a threat of injury" because we cannot be sure it will be used wrongfully. Augmentation of the power of a state does, however, always disturb the equilibrium because of the expectation, justified by experience if not by principle, that the state will commit aggression when it has become sufficiently powerful to do so with impunity. International lawyers have discussed at length the dilemma presented by these assumptions (see chapter 4, above) as have responsible statesmen on numerous occasions. When the younger Pitt sought to justify war with France in 1793 on balance-of-power principles, Sir James Mackintosh and others of the opposition insisted that the war was not just on principles of the law of nations. On the other hand, when Neville Chamberlain 145 years later pursued a policy, deemed legally correct, of nonintervention in the affairs of Hitlerite Germany, he was attacked by Winston Churchill and others for neglecting steps necessary to prevent destruction of the balance of power.

Consideration of this dilemma illustrates the difficulty of getting out of the system of states organized by a balance of power into a system of states organized by effective law. Efforts to make such a change gradually imply that states must reach a stage when they will rely upon an international organization for the enforcement of law before they can be certain that that organization is actually strong enough or workable enough to protect their rights. Such faith may lead to their destruction, as it nearly did in the case of China in 1931, Ethiopia in 1935, and Czechoslovakia in 1938. Reliance by these states upon international law and the League of Nations proved to be more hazardous than would have been acceptance of the system of power politics, and action in accord with its precepts to increase their strength, to find allies, and to defend themselves.

But, on the other hand, efforts to make such a change suddenly by establishing a world government with adequate legal and material power to enforce law throughout the world, somewhat as the United States established its constitution in 1787, seems equally impracticable. By the act of accepting such an effective constitution, states would have to surrender the very sovereignty which it is the prime purpose of their governments to maintain. Instead of being killed by a disruption of the equilibrium of power through premature reliance upon a nonenforceable law, they would commit suicide by immolating themselves in a world state over which they would exercise only a small degree of control. Sudden establishment of world authority able to maintain law may, it is true, occur not by consent but by compulsion, and that would be likely to leave less of independence to the states than would a federation to which they consented.

States may, therefore, have to consider the following alternatives: (1) an unstable, probably increasingly unstable, balance of power sustained by cold war in a bipolar world; (2) a world federation enforcing law upon individuals in matters of world concern and thus reducing the national sovereignty of all; or (3) world empire established by conquest by that state which emerges from a world stricken by atomic war. Governments following tradition incline to choose the first alternative. The latter would probably be regarded as the worst of the alternatives. Many would say the second is the best but unachievable either suddenly or gradually. The answer to the dilemma, if there is one, cannot be found by logic, but only by history. Steps in the right direction may permit further steps until in time, objectives which seemed impossible may be realized. "Leg after leg," as the saying is, "the dog got to Dover."

Balance of Law and Politics

The difference between a world regime of law and a world regime of power politics is not that the latter rests on balance of power and the former on union of power, but rather that the latter rests on a simple balance and the former on a complex balance. National states rest on complex equilibria of power. There are balances between parties, between local and national authorities, between departments of government, between regional groups and functional groups, among businesses, churches, universities, societies, government agencies, and other organizations. Even in the most centralized despotisms, equilibria between cliques at the top and classes at the bottom can be detected. There are always local movements of incipient revolt balancing and moderating the despotism at the center. The more constitutional and democratic is the state, the more complex is the equilibrium. Simplicity, which is so dear to the hearts of the masses and so useful to the propagandists, is the road either to despotism or to social disintegration, violence, and anarchy.

The balance of power in world politics has been characterized by its simplicity, and as the number of participating states has been reduced and the great states have become vastly superior to the lesser in power, the system has become simpler and consequently less stable.

If a law-governed world is to develop peacefully from the present situation, statesmen must seek to make the balance more complicated. The building of a power of Western Europe, of the British Commonwealth, of the Middle East, of the Far East, of Latin America, and perhaps eventually of Central Europe, as offsets to the power of the United States and the Soviet Union, would help. Even more, the building of the power of the United Nations as an element in power politics would help. Practices, interpretations, and supplementary conventions may do much to reduce the frustrating influence of the veto and to increase the capacity of the United Nations to act promptly and with material force. Even if amendment of the Charter remains for a long time impossible because of the veto, even if the United Nations, for a long time or indefinitely, lacks the power to coerce the more powerful states by its own efforts, still it may, by throwing what weight it has always on the side of the law, give an assurance of predominance to that side. It can always be expected that in any emergency some of the important states will defend the law. If the United Nations itself were able to play a vigorous role in world politics, the old dilemma between supporting international law and maintaining the balance of power may be solved. By sustaining the United Nations, they will be sustaining both law and political equilibrium.

But the balance in a stable world must be more than a balance of military power. The development of the functional organizations giving service to peoples and the development of a world public opinion insistent upon the achievement of certain standards and of progress toward certain objectives may make the balance even more complex.

World political parties may also prove complicating factors. Rivalries between great religious groups and between world-wide business corporations would also reduce the relative importance of rivalries between states. With the evolution of complexity, a degree of stability may emerge within which law-maintenance institutions may be able to function with greater assurance.

If world-minded statesmen prove as skillful in building the United Nations as national-minded statesmen have been in building national states, much may become possible. But their action will be politics. Law and politics are not in opposition but coöperate as the stabilizing and the dynamic elements in a progressive society. When politics is complicated, law can predominate as long as it is not so comprehensive, so inflexible, or so unadapted to the situation as to leave no room for the progressive influence of politics. In a stable society politics must function subject to law, but also it must continually change the law. To achieve that result a delicate balance between the political and the juristic organs of society is necessary.

The situation of international law is not hopeless. The atomic bomb has driven into the minds of men everywhere the need for a more cohesive society of nations. International law has formulated these demands in new rules and standards of justice. The United Nations and its specialized agencies exist as visible organs of the world society and as mechanisms for peaceful political action. If United Nations statesmen, regional statesmen, statesmen of the great nations and of the lesser nations, statesmen of each of the functional organizations, statesmen of churches, of business corporations, of universities, of all sorts of organizations and societies all develop their groups so as to maintain a multiplicity of initiatives in the world, some coöperating, some opposing, all limited in their activity by others, the new international law may be realized in fact as well as in aspiration.

18

CONSTITUTIONALISM

AND WORLD POLITICS

An American Dilemma

"An American Dilemma" is a term used to refer to the inconsistency between American race relations and American democratic ideals. It may also apply to the inconsistency between our international relations and our democratic ideals. In this sense the American citizen has been said to face a dilemma: How to maintain a proper balance between national security and individual freedom in a continuing crisis of national defense.[1] Cold war exists and is likely to continue to exist for a long time, if indeed it does not degenerate into the more serious condition of hot war. The Soviet dictatorship needs to maintain among its population the fear of an external enemy in order to prevent revolt from its internal tyranny. There is evidence that the Politburo believes in the Marxist ideology that teaches it to expect crises of depression and decay within the surrounding capitalist countries eventually inducing attack upon the communist state while capitalism is in the last throes of dissolution. The Soviets also have a theory of revolution which urges them to be continually on the alert in order to expand their power by taking advantage of weaknesses and revolutionary conditions in other countries. This combination of necessity, fear, and ambition can be expected to keep alive Soviet pressure upon the democratic world. This will induce the democracies increasingly to fear devastating attack as the Soviet weapons improve and to intensify their defense preparations.

From University of Illinois, *Bulletin,* Institute of Government and Public Affairs, XLIX (December, 1951). Edmund J. James Lecture on Government, delivered April 12, 1951, at the University of Illinois.

273

This preparation, however, tends to convert the democracies themselves into dictatorships. Rising expenditures tend to governmentalize the economy, to centralize government—thereby reducing the degree of local autonomy and individual freedom—and to augment the position of the executive, especially that of the defense department, at the expense of the legislature and the courts. The increasing role of the military, and its consciousness of the needs of security and the dangers of subversion behind the lines, tend to reduce civil liberties, to block channels of information, to broaden the inquisitions of investigatory agencies, to reduce the influence of public opinion and parties, and to create an atmosphere of secrecy and suspicion. Freedom of communication, of science, of economic enterprise, of social relations is likely to be diminished. By this process the need for defense, if serious and protracted, tends to convert free societies into "garrison states." [2]

All states tend toward that condition in times of active and serious war, but democracies usually react to recover liberty when the war is over. The condition of continuous cold war may, however, be more corroding to democracy in that it destroys the resilience which can normally be relied upon when the tension is over. The Roman Republic gave way to temporary dictatorship and then permanent empire after a long period of hot and cold war, and its experience, according to Toynbee, has been characteristic of all transitions of civilizations from a "time of trouble" to a "universal state." [3]

From this point of view the dilemma can only be solved if the citizen and the public official are continually aware of the needs of both national security and of individual liberty, and of the incompatible tendencies of measures to meet these needs. Consequently both citizen and official must ask, in considering any defense or security measure: Does it involve taxation or inflation; centralization of government; investigation, secrecy, and reduction of civil liberties; or augmentation of the role of the military? And, if it does, as is usually the case, does its gain for defense compensate for the loss to freedom and democracy? Such a balance is clearly difficult to maintain in the face of increasing international tension. The public will demand that defense be put first.[4]

The World and the United States

Without disparaging the mode of thought which emphasizes this dilemma, I want to suggest a somewhat different approach. I would pose the question, not of adapting our necessities and our ideals to each other under the pressure of Soviet aggressiveness, but of better adapting the American constitution and the world constitution to each other under the conditions of modern science, technology, and civilization. The distinction between these two points of view was illustrated in an address by Elihu Root in 1917, soon after the United States had entered World War I. Root recognized the inconsistency between domestic democracy and effective foreign policy, which, he pointed out, had been emphasized by Alexis De Tocqueville in his classical study of democracy in America written in the 1830's. In this study De Tocqueville wrote:

> Foreign politics demand scarcely any of those qualities which a democracy possesses; and they require, on the contrary, the perfect use of almost all those faculties in which it is deficient . . . A democracy is unable to regulate the details of an important undertaking, to persevere in a design, and to work out its execution in the presence of serious obstacles. It cannot combine its measures with secrecy, and it will not await the consequences with patience. These are qualities which more especially belong to an individual or an aristocracy, and they are precisely the means by which an individual people attains to a predominant position.[5]

A similar observation was recently made by Dr. Hans Morgenthau, also looking at foreign policy from a European point of view with special reference to the United States.

> It is the peculiar quality of the conduct of foreign affairs in the United States that it maximizes the weaknesses inherent in the formulation and execution of foreign policies under democratic conditions and that it aggravates these inherent weaknesses by some unique constitutional devices and political practices.[6]

To illustrate this I need only refer to the behavior of certain senators and congressmen in the winter of 1950 in attacking the Department of State in a spirit, the partisanship of which was exceeded only by the lack of factual substantiation of the charges; nevertheless the attack had considerable public support. The result was to create a situation in which the administration, in conducting policy in an unusually critical situation of foreign affairs, had to pay more attention to the coming elections and congressional votes than to the facts of the world as disclosed by the daily cables and to the necessities of American security.

The point I want to emphasize, however, is Elihu Root's conclusion in respect to this inherent difficulty of democracy. He said:

> So long as foreign affairs were to continue as they were carried on in his day, De Tocqueville was doubtless right. It is because democracies are not fitted to conduct foreign affairs as they were con-

ducted in De Tocqueville's day that the prevalence of democracy throughout the world makes inevitable a change in the conduct of foreign affairs. Such affairs when conducted by democratic governments must necessarily be marked by the absence of those undertakings and designs, and those measures combined with secrecy, prosecuted with perseverance for which he declares democracies to be unfit.[7]

Many will say that such a change in the conduct of foreign affairs is impossible to achieve. They will note that secrecy, threat, and aggression are no less characteristic of international politics today than they were in De Tocqueville's day. Power politics, they will say, is thrust upon us, and we will have to adapt ourselves to its necessities or die.[8] Root, however, did not think so. His answer was that democracies must join together to build a regime of world law. He had expanded upon this in his address in 1915. He noted the inadequacy of the restraints of international law in the past upon policies of power and aggression, but instead of despairing he said the world must place more effective sanctions behind the law.

> Laws to be obeyed must have sanctions behind them; that is to say, violations of them must be followed by punishment. That punishment must be caused by power superior to the law breaker; it cannot consist merely in the possibility of being defeated in a conflict with an enemy; otherwise, there would be no law as between the strong and the weak.[9]

In the third of a century since Root made these remarks there have been efforts to follow his advice. The League of Nations (1920), the Kellogg-Briand pact (1928), the United Nations (1945), the Nuremberg and Tokyo trials (1946), the Universal Declaration of Human Rights (1948), and the Uniting for Peace resolution of the General Assembly (1950) have been successive steps in an effort to organize the world to support a law which outlaws war and punishes aggression—to make "the world safe for democracy" by creating a power behind international law which can redress the unstable balance of power between nations in a shrinking world.[10] This is a step toward the democratic organization of the world expressed by President Wilson in 1918, "What we seek is the reign of law, based upon the consent of the governed and sustained by the organized opinion of mankind."[11]

Must we write off the efforts of a generation to save democracy by creating a world in which it can live at peace, and resort to the policy, always destructive of democracy, of defending our state in a world of unmitigated power politics? I do not think the case is hopeless. Our difficulty is that we have not understood the complexity of the problem. We have been too much obsessed with our own culture and our own Constitution when we have thought of a law-governed world. We have tended to think of the ideal institutions of the world as our institutions made universal. We have been too prone to think that a world "safe for democracy" means a world all of which is democratic as we interpret the term.

We must think, instead, of the American society and the world society as two entities, which are distinct, though they cannot be separated because one contains the other, and which consequently must mutually adapt to one another if either is to be secure. We must ask how the world constitution may be modified to give greater assurance that international law will be just and will be observed, and how our Constitution must be modified in order that we may preserve our basic institutions and may make our appropriate contribution to the maintenance of such a world.

The World's Constitution

I will not go into the arguments among the advocates of world federation, the supporters of the United Nations, the power politicians, and the isolationists. They all have concepts of a world constitution, but, in the order I have named them, they exhibit decreasing optimism as to the possibility of modifying it to suit our particular desires.

The advocates of world federation are the most optimistic but their optimism becomes qualified as they experience the unwillingness or incapacity of the Russians, the East Europeans, the Chinese, and even the Indians, Southeast Asians, Arabs, and Latin Americans to accept and operate the American concepts of civil liberties, freedom of communication, free elections, and constitutionalism. With such experience the advocates of world federation tend to narrow the base of the society they contemplate and to be satisfied with efforts to federalize the North Atlantic community or the "free world," assuming that this quarter of the human race will, if organized, be sufficiently strong to defend itself without undue militarization from the three-quarters of the human race which is left out and which includes within it the powerful, organizing urge of the Soviet Union.[12]

The isolationists, at the other extreme, beginning with a profound pessimism about the rest of the world and a conviction that the United States must live alone and like it, cannot wholly ignore the advice of hard-headed strategists who insist that the Western Hemisphere and the off-shore islands of western Europe and eastern Asia must be incorporated in any workable defense plan for the United States. The strategists may even demand that the "rimlands" of western Europe, the Mediterranean, and Southeast Asia, be included, as first bastions of defense against aggression from the Eurasian "heartland." [13] The isolationists cannot, however, overlook the jeopardy to American institutions that such preparedness entails. Air and sea power based on "an American Gibraltar" could not indefinitely withstand attack from the remaining five-sixths of the world's population and resources if organized against it, and, if the off-shore islands and rimlands of the Eurasian continent are to be used as bases, land forces to defend them will be necessary.[14]

Neither the advocates of world federation nor the isolationists have really risen to a vision of the world as a whole. They offer no solution for the dilemma between the necessities of defense in an atomic age and the danger of becoming a garrison state. They only urge that we preserve what we can of American liberties in an almost hopeless situation. The extreme optimists and the extreme pessimists meet with a somewhat expanded American federation on the one hand and a somewhat expanded American empire on the other facing the communist enemy whom they deem beyond the range of morals or argument and in whose favor time may be running.

United Nations and International Politics

Between these extremes the students of the United Nations and of international politics attempt to look at the world as a whole. The first, believing that continued effort to influence opinion and to perfect machinery can increase the security of all under law, are somewhat more optimistic than the second.[15] Students of international politics believe that equilibrium can be stabilized by astute negotiation of agreements which will be reliable so long as their observance is in the common interest of the parties.[16] The difference between these two groups lies in the fact that the students of the United Nations give more weight to the long-run opinion of the world, and the students of international politics give more weight to the short-run interest of the nations—but each recognizes that there is both a long run and a short run, both a whole and parts, and it is neither to be expected nor desired that the world will absorb the nations or that any one nation will absorb the world.

Both of these groups appreciate the inevitability of national diversities—whether they spring from climate and geography, from population and living standards, from traditional culture and value systems, or from forms of political and economic organization. These diversities generate different and often inconsistent interests which tend to lead to tensions, conflict, and war as the world shrinks and contacts among previously separated peoples increase. But both of these groups also appreciate that all men have something in common, including the desire to live, to increase their standards of living, to enjoy their traditions and institutions and, in varied degree, to be free to live as they want. They appreciate, furthermore, that all nations and governments have something in common including the desire to serve their members and to increase their power in order to forward these interests. These desires, both individual and collective, may be frustrated by modern war. Out of these common interests a world opinion supporting world institutions may gradually develop, and more immediately, diplomacy may achieve agreements which will be observed so long as they serve those common interests.

Both advocates of the United Nations and advocates of international politics emphasize particularly the significance of time in political and constitutional change. Major political changes can hardly be achieved both rapidly and peacefully because of the important interests which they necessarily affect adversely. Such changes may, however, be achieved peacefully if sufficiently gradual to permit numerous minds to become accommodated and adjusted. Consequently, any major reconstruction of the world order, however reasonable or even necessary it may seem in the light of new technological conditions and dynamic opinions, should be conceived only as a long-run goal. So conceived it may be approached gradually and perhaps deviously by solving short-run problems on their merits but with a steady bias in the direction indicated by that goal.[17]

Experience with the operation of the United Nations suggests that its principles are not antithetic but supplementary to those by which international politics has been conducted during the past few centuries. Collective security is not world government in the sense that universal law can be declared, applied, and enforced by a world society with overwhelming power. That power does not exist and cannot exist so long as certain combinations of members of the world community rival that community in power. Under such conditions the law against aggression can be enforced by collective action only if diplomacy conducted by states or the United Nations can prevent the aggressor from gaining and holding allies, and can persuade most of the states to support the United Nations in their own interests. Collective security cannot work if every aggression is permitted to initiate a world war, but this need not happen if jural policing is accompanied by a diplomacy intent upon preserving equilibrium. Collective policing and careful diplomacy must proceed in parallel, not in sequence. The difficulty of giving proper weight to each has been illustrated in the Korean affair which began in June, 1950.[18]

In proportion as the United Nations acquires a strength of its own, by virtue of the growth of a world public opinion and of effective procedures to assure the allegiance of its members to their obligations, it may itself become an element in the balance of power always on the side of law and order. The natural tendency of states to coalesce against any of their number that is becoming too powerful and is preparing for aggression may, therefore, be strengthened and given greater preventive efficacy by the obligations and procedures of collective security. Viewed this way, collective security, far from opposing the natural tendencies of international politics, contributes to the effectiveness of that tendency and checks the opposite tendency toward universal conquest and world empire.[19]

Progress towards stabilization of the world by such a combination of law and diplomacy seems to imply widespread acceptance of certain opinions including the following:

(1) No state, even the Soviet Union, is wholly unamenable to persuasion by information and argument; consequently, negotiation on some matters is always possible if there is communication. This rests on the assumption that states act in accord with their interests, that all states have numerous interests and that some of these interests can be better forwarded by coöperation than by opposition once they are mutually understood. Even opposing belligerents negotiate with each other on exchanges of prisoners, suspensions of hostilities, and armistices.[20]

(2) Some communications between governments and some understanding by each of the interests of others is possible and desirable. Even the Soviet Union considers it worth while to communicate with others in the United Nations and occasionally to reach agreement. The Iron Curtain is undoubtedly a serious obstacle to a reduction of tensions but it may prove more penetrable to methods resting upon mutual interest than to direct assault.[21]

(3) Complete elimination of either of the great political structures of the world is unlikely, except as the result of a war which might destroy either or both. Consequently, the coexistence of these diverse systems is probable for a long future and both the United States and the Soviet Union should adjust themselves to that condition. Moderation of ideologies, postponement of objectives, and changes in domestic government

are likely to occur in time, to modify foreign policies, and to make such adjustment easier.[22]

(4) The trend toward a bipolar concentration of power with all the instability which such a system implies is not inevitable and much can be done to stem that tendency.[23]

Among efforts to modify the tendency toward bipolarity, high rank should be given to the refusal to identify communism with Soviet policy or to identify democracy with United States policy. It should be assumed that there may be communist states that are not satellites of the Kremlin, and that there may be democratic states that are not allies of the United States. The first of these identifications may be in accord with Soviet policy which seeks to strengthen itself by assuming, and persuading the world to assume, that all communist states are united under its banner. That assumption may tend to make itself true, especially if the West, because of it, seeks to "contain" all the communist states and thus to drive them together. The case of Tito, however, indicates that a communist government may act independently. The free world should continue to ask itself, might Mao Tse-Tung do the same? Premier Nehru, on the other hand, is attempting to indicate that a government, at least partially democratic, can also act independently. Such manifestations are to be encouraged.

If instead of the world polarizing into great structures centering in Moscow and Washington, cracks began to occur simultaneously in both, and a ring of states acting independently began to emerge between these two centers, a reduction of tensions could be expected.[24] A neutralized Germany, if such an arrangement could be achieved with confidence that it would endure, would probably contribute more to peace than two halves of Germany organized in each of the rival poles.[25]

In this connection it is well to realize that the low living standards of Asia may make a vigorous government leadership in economic reconstruction and a vigorous discipline of the over-abundant population, even though brutal, attractive to a people that have known little but misery. It is perhaps wise to assume, as does the United Nations Charter, that nations are sovereign and equal and to derive from that the right of each to adopt whatever ideology or form of organization it desires, so long as it makes its choice independently and adheres to its duty not to engage in aggression.[26]

If belief in reason, communication, coexistence, and decentralization of power can be spread, diplomacy may be able to alleviate tensions and to create conditions which will permit the United Nations to grow stronger and to reduce tensions still more.[27]

The American Constitution

The American constitution with its guarantees of civil liberty; its checks and balances between the Congress, the president, and the courts; its reserved powers of the states; its processes of party politics; its diverse opinions, and its protracted debates before decisions are reached, has difficulty in functioning in cold war. These characteristics of the American constitution, if observed, may lead the government to fiddle or filibuster while Rome burns; while subversives gnaw from within; while the propaganda, diplomacy, and armies of dictators take over potential allies one after another; and while the Politburo prepares snorkels and atom bombs for the destruction of its enemies. I have referred to the balance which the United States must maintain in the face of this dilemma.[28] But let us ask ourselves: Is the American constitution also unsuited for life in a stable, law-governed world community? Some current attitudes on constitutional issues suggest that it is unsuited.

Perhaps we can agree that in a law-governed world community, fundamental human rights should be respected, basic international crimes should be punished, international trade and communications should be relatively free, adequate forces should be promptly mobilized against aggression, and in general governments and their representatives should be legally and practically competent to make and to observe commitments which the consensus of world opinion deems essential for developing such a community and adapting it to new conditions.[29]

Human Rights

A respectable body of legal opinion appears to fear that a Covenant of Human Rights which did not go as far as the constitutional Bill of Rights would be unconstitutional if ratified by the United States. It is argued that such a covenant might reduce the internal effectiveness of the constitutional guarantees.[30] This argument seems to me legally unsound. Such a covenant would state a minimum standard and would not prevent any state that became a party from giving more liberty to its citizens or inhabitants. Constitutional or statutory guarantees would, therefore, be unaffected provided they were no less favorable to the individual than the covenant guarantees.

Exceptions from absolute freedom of speech and press or other civil liberties are acknowledged in all systems of law, including that of the United States. The Supreme Court has acknowledged among others, the exception of "clear and present danger to public order." [31] It is to be expected that conditions will exist in some countries which justify more government restriction on individual freedom than is necessary in the United States. The world cannot achieve the high standards of liberty maintained by the constitution of the United States at one jump —even the practice of the United States is not always up to its constitutional principles.[32] Consequently it is not likely that a general covenant on human rights can be achieved unless the standards are somewhat lower than those of the American constitution. Insistence by the United States that its standards must be accepted in such a covenant would prevent general acceptance of the covenant and furthermore would manifest a failure of the United States to appreciate that much variation in the relation of the individual to the state exists in different parts of the world, and complete uniformity is neither to be expected nor desired.[33]

On the other hand the permission given to sovereign states by the international covenant to make exceptions to individual freedoms beyond those permitted the federal government by our Constitution would not enlarge the powers of Congress. The constitutional principle that Congress can legislate when necessary and proper to implement a treaty obligation of the United States [34] does not permit Congress to legislate in violation of established constitutional guarantees. A treaty permission to the United States is not a constitutional permission to Congress nor is a treaty permission a treaty obligation.[35] Even a treaty obligation, while it may extend congressional power into the normal domain of the states, cannot permit what the Constitution forbids, such as encroachment upon the guaranteed rights of individuals.[36] The normal powers of the states are the residuum of governmental powers which remains beyond the powers, including the treaty-making power, delegated by the Constitution to the federal government. The constitutional rights of individuals, on the other hand, like the guarantees to states of territorial integrity and republican government, constitute a positive limitation upon the exercise of power by any organ of the federal government, and in most cases by the states also.[37] Legally, therefore, there seems to be no ground to fear that an international Covenant of Human Rights would impair the constitutional Bill of Rights even though its standards were lower. While the moral and political influence of such a covenant might be undesirable if it were assumed to establish an absolute standard of justice, this effect would seem unnecessary.[38] The covenant should be supported, not as an absolute standard, but as the minimum acceptable to the community of nations at the moment and subject to improvement when the standards of the less advanced nations are brought up to that level.

There has also been worry lest the international protection of human rights may impose higher standards than those required by the United States Constitution, or those actually observed in some of the states of the union. Undoubtedly the United States could properly be criticized diplomatically or in the United Nations if individuals were denied in this country rights guaranteed to everyone by a Covenant of Human Rights ratified by the United States. The United States government has not hesitated to protest in the United Nations against failure of Bulgaria, Hungary, and Rumania to observe the human rights provisions in the treaties of peace with those countries and to join in asking an opinion of the International Court of Justice concerning the obligation of those countries under the procedural provisions of those treaties.[39] It is through such processes that increasing respect for human rights may be promoted.

There seems to be some concern, however, that the courts in the United States have shown a disposition to apply the Charter provisions concerning human rights and interpretations given to them by the Universal Declaration of Human Rights approved by the General Assembly to nullify state legislation deemed to deny those rights. Article 56 of the Charter seems to pledge the United States and other members of the United Nations to observe human rights without racial discrimination. The Court of Appeals of California in the Fujii case held in 1950 that the California Alien Land Law, which in effect forbade Japanese to acquire land in that state, violated the Charter and was, therefore, null and void because of the constitutional principle declaring treaties the supreme law of the land. It has been suggested that Article 56 of the Charter, though a treaty provision, is of a political character and not judicially enforceable. There is a constitutional issue in drawing the line between treaty provisions which are self-executing and those which are not, but the courts have considered treaty provisions defining individual rights to be in the former class.[40] If the United States is to participate effectively in international legislation especially on subjects such as the protection of human rights, normally within the power of the states, the supremacy of treaties over state law should be maintained.

International Crime

Alarm has also been expressed concerning the Genocide Convention approved by the General Assembly in 1948 and now in force among many states but not yet ratified by the United States. It seems to be feared that the crime of genocide which the parties commit themselves to punish might apply to Americans guilty of lynching, that it might subject Americans to the jurisdiction of an international tribunal, and that the United States might be obliged to use armed force to compel observance of the convention by other states. These fears are, to say the least, premature.[41] Like all treaties dealing with criminal matters, under the American constitution, the Genocide Convention, if ratified, could not be applied by federal courts until Congress had interpreted it and given the courts jurisdiction over the offenses it describes. It has long been held that federal criminal jurisdiction is statutory and consequently that treaty provisions in this field are not self executing.[42] No international tribunal exists with jurisdiction over the crime of genocide. The convention, while suggesting the possibility of such a court, does not establish it. Consequently until a new agreement establishing such a court has been negotiated speculation about its jurisdiction is premature.

If the Genocide Convention is ratified, Congress should, of course, give appropriate courts jurisdiction to punish the offense as intended by the convention but it could properly insert clarifying restrictions which would prevent unintended extensions which might be deduced from an unduly liberal construction of the terms of the treaty. It is clearly the purpose of the convention to assure that the crime of genocide shall be punished wherever committed. It may be that an international court to deal with cases not prosecuted in any national court will be found to contribute to this end and the convention foresees this possibility. The convention also opens the way to diplomatic protest or action in the United Nations to assure observance of obligations undertaken by the convention. It does not, however, require the United States or any other state to engage in military or other intervention to compel observance by other parties. Only if toleration or encouragement of genocide in a state reached such magnitude as to threaten international peace and security, and appropriate action by the United Nations had recognized that threat, might a situation calling for the use of armed forces by the United States arise.

Freedom of Trade and Information

The efforts to establish an International Trade Organization and to increase freedom of information across national boundaries have also been subjects of concern, the first mainly on the ground that it may give too much freedom of trade and the latter mainly on the ground that it may not give enough freedom of information.

As has been pointed out ratification of a convention concerning transnational communication could not legally reduce American constitutional guarantees of freedom of speech and press in this country.[43] Whether compromises with the desire of many governments to control such communications have to be so serious as to render the convention worthless is a political question.[44] Half a loaf may be better than none particularly in view of the fact that customary international law recognizes an almost absolute right of states to censor or prohibit both outgoing and incoming information and propaganda.[45]

Ratification of the ITO charter and the functioning of the organization it would have set up, might have contributed to removing barriers to international trade and might have interfered with extreme American protectionism. That was its objective, as it is the objective of the United States expressed in the Recipocal Trade Agreements policy accepted and applied by Congress since 1934 and affirmed in the Atlantic Charter, the Lend Lease agreements, and other policy declarations made since.[46] If the United States is to live peacefully and prosperously in a world in which it is the greatest creditor, produces nearly half of the world's goods, and maintains its people at a standard of living which now varies from twice to fifty times that of other peoples,[47] it must contribute to general expansion of trade and a greater equalization of living standards. It cannot permanently profit from its foreign credits unless it imports more than it exports in normal commercial transactions. It cannot contribute to the equalization of living standards unless the government supports large-scale programs extending technical aid and capital to assist in the economic development of underdeveloped areas.[48]

The Use of Armed Forces

More vigorously expressed in Congress has been the fear that the obligations of the Charter and the North Atlantic pact might permit the president to use American forces in Europe or elsewhere without specific congressional authority. This, indeed, was done in the Korean operation. The issue is an old one and presidents since Washington have assumed that the commander-in-chief is responsible for carrying out obligations of treaties and for protecting American citizens abroad as well as American territory and is, therefore, permitted, even obliged, to use the forces which Congress provides for those purposes. This position is not only sanctioned by practice but has been amply supported by the courts.[49] The question of whether the president should wish to have Congress share responsibility for large-scale movements of forces such as maintaining several divisions in Europe for a long time, is a political, not a legal question.[50]

It is clear, however, that the certainty and speed of military coöperation, essential if the system of collective security established by the United Nations Charter and the North Atlantic pact is to work, cannot be realized unless the president has broad discretion in the use of force to fulfill the obligations of these treaties. Congress only can provide the budget and may thus limit the size of forces available and the magnitude of operations, but the president must be able to use the forces which Congress has provided promptly and automatically when the occasion arises. Congressional debate on the expediency of fulfilling the obligation in a particular emergency would destroy the preventive effect of collective security arrangements and encourage aggression.[51]

International Commitments

Fears have been expressed that the representatives of the United States in the United Nations and in the specialized agencies, may, without Senate or congressional support, commit the United States in resolutions or agreements. Such commitments by executive authority are supported by ample practice and precedent.[52] Again the problem of when Congress should be consulted is political. Effective American participation in international organization has a tendency to enlarge the practical influence of informal executive agreements in comparison with formal treaties, and thereby to augment the relative position of the president in the United States government.[53]

These issues are symptomatic of the larger issue already envisaged by some advocates of world federation: Are the qualifications of national sovereignty, essential to a world organization able to maintain peace and law, possible for the United States without radical constitutional amendment?[54] It has perhaps not been sufficiently stressed that this issue, like those I have discussed, is primarily one of opinion and politics rather than of law. To this point, President Lincoln addressed himself:

> Public sentiment is everything. With public sentiment nothing can fail; without it nothing can succeed. Consequently, he who molds public sentiment goes deeper than he who enacts statutes or pronounces decisions. He makes statutes and decisions possible or impossible to be executed.[55]

Neither the text of the Constitution, practice under it, nor judicial interpretation presents serious obstacles to the United States assuming obligations by treaty which modify the exercise of sovereignty or even sovereignty itself, provided that the treaty deals with a topic of international importance and that guaranteed rights of individuals and the procedures of constitutional action are not impaired.[56] The president externally and the courts internally have power to implement such obligations in so far as the Congress has provided the president with funds and weapons, and the courts with jurisdiction.[57] Even the problem of appeal from national courts to an international tribunal or the problem of the functioning of agencies of the United Nations with power to deal with individuals within the territory of the United States could be solved, within the orbit of existing precedents by appropriate treaties.[58]

Constitutional obstacles can, however, spring up like mushrooms if public sentiment opposes the action proposed. This is not to say that careful thought should not be given to gearing American legal and administrative institutions into the requirements of good membership in the United Nations. There is a technical task to be accomplished, but if public opinion approves, it can be accomplished without constitutional amendment. The proposal of an amendment might, it is true, be a useful method for ascertaining public opinion and perhaps for stimulating public approval of such modifications of national sovereignty, as may be essential if we are to have a law-governed world.[59] The amendments proposed in 1952 by Senator Bricker of Ohio had the opposite objective of increasing the rigidity of national sovereignty. Their effect would be to increase the power of Congress to obstruct the making and enforcement of treaties and executive agreements, thus upsetting the balance of the Constitution and hampering effective participation by the United States in the United Nations.[60]

Conclusion

We live in a critical age and will continue to do so. World government is premature and isolation is obsolete. Neither will solve our problems. We are in a small world, from which we cannot escape, and it contains shipmates such as Stalin and Mao with a capacity to scuttle it. We cannot progress toward a greater security for our way of life unless we accept this world as it is, seek to live and let live, encourage others to do likewise in its narrowing confines, and coöperate with all in trying to improve it.

If the public understands these fundamentals, the government can do much to lessen tension by skillful negotiation. While we would prefer to negotiate from superior strength, so would our opponents, and if negotiations are delayed until each has superior strength to the other, the arms race will continue and tensions will rise above the danger point. If the object of negotiation is not victory, but accommodation, and if the influence of time on relative power positions is uncertain, the reason for delaying negotiation is not obvious.

If diplomacy can initiate the easing of tensions, the United Nations may do much to stabilize the balance of power by strengthening its machinery and developing a more favorable world opinion supporting its operations. As the power of the United Nations increases, it can contribute to stabilizing the equilibrium and creating conditions favorable to the application of law. The law of the Charter then may become more reliable, and men and nations may live in increasing confidence that the date for realization of dangerous ambitions has been postponed and that aggression is not likely in the near future.[61] In such an atmosphere the American democracy will need neither to commit suicide by becoming a garrison state nor to die heroically defending itself from the attacks of its enemies.

We cannot be sure that the world can be made safe for democracy, but we are certain it cannot be unless the democracies see it steadily, see it accurately, and see it whole.

PART **VI**

TECHNOLOGY AND INTERNATIONAL STABILITY

19

AVIATION AND

WORLD POLITICS

The development of aviation has thrust upon each of the politically active inhabitants of the globe, in a more peremptory manner every succeeding year, the task of reconciling his opinions as a human being with his opinions as a citizen. These conflicts in the opinions of men and groups will not, however, be reconciled simultaneously in one direction throughout the world. Reconciliation will tend to be in one direction in some countries and in the other direction in other countries, and in many there will be no reconciliation at all. In some there will be no appreciation that conflicts exist. Group opinions are certain to lag behind changes of conditions. Man is a rational animal and a social animal, but in the mass he perceives inconsistencies slowly and broadens the area in which he is a good neighbor reluctantly.

Optimists who believe that men in the mass ultimately act in accord with their interests and ultimately formulate their interests in accord with human considerations will foresee the emergence of a world commonwealth assuring peace and justice.

Pessimists, on the other hand, who believe that man in the mass is a beast, do not expect him to act consistently in support of his interests as he formulates them, or to formulate them in terms requiring vision beyond the horizon of the traditional social group. Consequently they look forward to a continuance of world anarchy terminating perhaps in a world empire which would be even worse. They recall in support of this gloomy prediction that past civilizations have moved from periods of relatively stable equilibrium among their states to periods of increasing instability and war terminating in conquest of all by one, fol-

From *Air Affairs,* I (September, 1946).

lowed by corruption of the government and decay of the civilization after a short period of oppressive tranquillity under this universal empire.[1]

This article does not attempt to settle the issue between optimists and pessimists, nor to predict what is going to happen in the generations to come. It proposes the more modest task of indicating the nature of current conflicts of opinion, the tendencies of aviation since its invention, the course of recent world politics, and the relations, if any, between opinion, aviation and world politics.

Conflicting Opinions

The most superficial consideration suggests that it is becoming more and more difficult for the average man to ignore the frequent inconsistency of his opinions as human being with his opinions as citizen. I assume that as human beings most men want to live securely, freely, and prosperously, and in lesser degree want all other men to enjoy the same privilege. In other words, as human beings, men want to maximize the security, the freedom, and the welfare of all human beings and to consider all organizations, societies, and communities including the state as means to this end. They want to consider the state for man, not man for the state. As citizens, on the other hand, I assume that most men want first of all the state of their allegiance to be secure, independent, and prosperous. Furthermore, they are willing to conform their wants as human beings to what the constitution, laws, and customs of the state permit. The good citizen is even ready to ignore the wants of other peoples, nations, states, and governments if his state refuses to admit them, and to assist his state at the risk of his life and property in utilizing resources, technology, science, administration, and the art of war to destroy other governments, states, nations, or peoples who persist in demands opposed by his state.

While action to promote the economic and social needs of individuals often conflicts with action to promote the political and military needs of the state this is not always the case. The individual in pursuing his private ends may be convinced that he is acting for the good of the state, and in forwarding national policies he often thinks he is serving his private ends. Thus his opinions as man and as citizen are reconciled. Furthermore, one cannot assume that because an individual thinks in terms of individual needs he is necessarily interested in those needs of the entire human race. By limiting his horizon to his fellow citizens he may believe that he reconciles his opinions as man and as citizen. In emergencies, however, he will often find that such recon-

ciliations do not free him from the necessity of choosing between human
and national interests.

This conflict is in fact but an aspect of the perennial problem of the
individual and the group. Anthropologists have observed that even the
rigorous mores of the primitive tribe do not entirely suppress the individualism of human nature. Sociologists, while insisting that personality and culture continually interact, and that consequently the
dichotomy of individual and group is a fiction, have not been able to
evade the problem latent in all societies, and occasionally emerging in
violent revolts against established laws and customs, under the banner
of individual rights and human freedom.

International lawyers from Victoria, Suarez, and Grotius down to
the present time have discussed the question of whether international
law should protect only the rights of states, including the "rights" to
tyrannize over its nationals and to conquer its neighbors, or should also
protect the rights of man against both foreign states and his own. It
has been suggested that international law though primarily designed
to protect the independence of states, imposes limits upon the exercise
of that independence in the interest not only of other states but also of
individuals and of the human race. The civil law of the state, as Grotius
pointed out, springs from the authority of natural law which imposes
on all men and institutions respect for human personality.[2]

Constitutional documents—the English Magna Carta, the French
Declaration of the Rights of Man and Citizen, the American Bill of
Rights—have faced the same dilemma and have sought a reconciliation
by the theory that constitutions must require the government to respect fundamental rights of both alien and citizen. Yet the insufficiency
of this reconciliation is indicated by the French document of 1789
which states:

> Men are born and remain free and equal in rights. . . . The
> aim of every political association is the preservation of the natural
> and imprescriptible rights of man. . . . The source of all sover-
> eignty is essentially in the nation; no body, no individual can
> exercise authority that does not proceed from it in plain terms.
> . . . The law has the right to forbid only such actions as are in-
> jurious to society. . . . Law is the expression of the general will.

What if the "general will" as expressed in law declares it to be injurious to society that men should speak freely or write freely, that men
should question summary arrests or incarceration in concentration
camps, or that men should object to violation of international obligations or mobilization for total war? Germs of the totalitarian state lurk

in the "sovereignty of the nation" and the duties of the citizen, unreconciled with the "rights of man" in the famous French declaration.

These inconsistencies have been discussed by philosophers and occasionally faced by common men in all periods of history. But the shrinking world and the totalitarian state have today drawn the attention of almost everyone to the difficulty. Everyone is aware that the United Nations Charter, ratified by governments representing a great majority of the world's population, declares that a major object of the United Nations is:

> To achieve international cooperation . . . in promoting and encouraging respect for human rights and for fundamental freedoms for all without distinction as to race, sex, language or religion.

The next article, however, denies to the U.N., with a single exception, authority

> . . . to intervene in matters which are essentially within the domestic jurisdiction of any state.

The conflicts between the rights of man and the power of the state are no more reconciled in the U.N. Charter than in the French Declaration. They are, in fact, emphasized. We are today aware that sovereignty can subject the human being to its will at home, and subject him to its destructive power abroad in a manner unsuspected in the eighteenth century. We are also aware of the helplessness of international law and natural law in a shrinking but anarchic world when faced by the Leviathan of the totalitarian state. We perceive the threat to human rights in the strength of the state and the weakness of the world order. We perceive that men as citizens loyal to their states are destroying men as human beings. Men as citizens are being required to serve the state alone and to build its power above that of other states, but in doing so they are preventing the strengthening of the world community without which, as human beings, they are becoming impoverished and insecure. It is more necessary and more difficult than ever before for men to be at the same time citizens of the state and citizens of the world. As a result the world is advancing in opposite directions at the same time. It is moving toward one world and toward none. Complacency in the face of such contradictions becomes difficult.

Tendencies of Aviation

What has the airplane to do with all this?

The airplane was invented and first flown in 1903. In forty-three years the trend of development has been regular and continuous for most indices with some temporary aberrations resulting from two world wars. Among these indices the following may be mentioned.

(1) The number of airplanes in the world increased from one to a maximum of over a quarter of a million at the end of World War II. This number diminished after hostilities ceased but increased as the cold war became serious and hostilities broke out in Korea. The number of nonmilitary planes is continually and rapidly increasing.

(2) The average weight of planes has increased from less than half a ton to more than ten tons. While this average will probably decrease as the proportion of "personal" and "feeder" types of aircraft becomes greater, the weight of transport and bombing planes will continue to increase.

(3) The average speed of planes has increased from thirty to over two hundred miles per hour, of military planes to almost four hundred miles per hour and jet planes have achieved supersonic speeds. The average speed will undoubtedly continue to increase.

(4) The safety of transport planes has increased from fatalities of twenty-seven to fatalities of under two per hundred million passenger-miles of travel. Even greater safety may be expected.

(5) The number of passengers carried in the United States increased from none to a rate of more than six million per year. Further increases may be expected.

(6) The number of passenger-miles flown on regular routes in the United States has increased from none to four billion a year. Further increases can be anticipated.

(7) The cost of passenger travel has decreased from twelve cents to less than five cents per mile. Further decreases are expected.

(8) The quantity of mail and express carried has increased from nothing to hundred million ton-miles a year. Further increases are to be anticipated.

(9) The length of commercially feasible hops has increased from nothing to over three thousand miles.

(10) The number of types of planes has increased from one to hundreds specialized for peace and war. Nonmilitary planes are specialized for speed, safety, water and ground landing, long and short hops, commercial and personal use. Military planes specialized for transport, bombing, attack, reconnaissance, and water, ground, and carrier landing have proliferated in many types. The helicopter and other types for slow-speed landing in limited space have developed, as have types for greater speeds, higher flights, and longer flights.

(11) The number of regular operative routes has increased from none

to a world network. Further routes are being continually opened.

(12) The number of airports in the world has increased from none to thousands. A large program of further airports is planned in the United States and in other countries.

(13) The equipment of airports and airways has improved with the development of means for providing accurate weather information, radio beacons, radar control, and other facilities for minimizing the influence of weather or regularity of schedules, and particularly safety of landing.

(14) The schedules of commercial planes have increased in regularity, reliability and frequency.

(15) The number of nations participating in the production of planes, the organization of airlines, and the licensing of pilots and routes has increased though the major commercial business is still conducted by companies or governments of less than a dozen states.

(16) Civil aviation has tended to be controlled by national governments in domestic commerce through government operation or regulation, and in international commerce through government owned or controlled "chosen instruments."

(17) While military aviation has predominated in number of planes used, the relative importance of civil aviation has tended to increase.

(18) As a military arm, aviation has tended to increase in relative importance as compared with armies and navies. This has been manifested by the establishment of departments of air coördinate with the army and navy and by the recognition of the independent mission of the air arm. This mission is the attack on enemies' industry and morale, distinct from airplane coöperation with ground or sea forces in reconnaissance and attack. This independent mission of the air arm has proved increasingly important in comparison with the navy's basic mission of blockade and the army's basic mission of territorial occupation, and even in comparison with the mission of all these arms in destroying the enemies' armed forces in being. That military air power equipped with atomic weapons may assume a dominant role in the latter activity is suggested by the magnitude of the destruction and damage to naval vessels and animals on board those vessels in the Bikini atoll and other experiments.

(19) The military characteristics of the airplane in performing its independent mission have developed steadily in all the elements which contribute to an efficient weapon, mobility, striking power, protection, and holding power. Speeds of the bomber have increased to 400 miles per hour. Striking power has increased from comparative equality in man-hours cost and man-hours destroyed (characteristic of nearly all

weapons of the past) to a ratio of 1 to 50 (1 to 6 for damage of strategic importance) for bombers with chemical explosives in the raids over Germany and Japan in 1945, and to a ratio 10 to 100 times greater with the atom bomb at Hiroshima and Nagasaki.[3] A ratio many times greater is in prospect as the cost of atomic weapons decreases and the hydrogen bomb is perfected. Protection has increased not only through armor and machine guns, radar, and observation bubbles but also through increased speed. Holding power has increased through the development of airborne troops and through the massive striking power of the atom bomb, destroying all opposition over large areas.

(20) Use of the air arm in war has tremendously increased the power of the offensive compared with that of the defensive, particularly since the invention of the atom bomb greatly augmented the plane's striking power. This increase can be measured by the ratio of the cost of the weapon to its destructiveness in terms of man-hours, which with the atom bomb borne by airplane or rocket may rise to an order of a thousand man-hours of life and property destroyed to one man-hour expended in constructing and operating the weapon. The increase of offensive power can also be indicated by considering the influence of the extremes of mobility and striking power now possible through use of the plane. Mobility and protection are in general inversely related because protection, such as armor, interferes with mobility. But when mobility surpasses a certain threshold, it becomes invulnerable without special protection as did the Germans' V-2 weapon. Striking power and holding power are also usually inversely related, because high striking power ordinarily exhausts its ammunition and must retire unless a line of transport is maintained. When, however, striking power surpasses a certain threshold, it becomes invincible because it has destroyed all opposition. When the mobility and striking power of a weapon pass these thresholds, the offensive power of the weapon approaches the absolute. There is no defense except the fear of reprisal and even that defense may diminish as the power of the weapon becomes so great that the first attack by the aggressor may destroy its enemies' capacity to retaliate. In such circumstances the advantage of the initiative becomes tremendous. The war of surprise and pounce supersedes the war of momentum, of maneuver, and of attrition.[4] While in the past, defensive methods have usually caught up with the offensive and war has again reached a stalemate, there has been no experience with situations where weapons approached an absolute protective and holding power because of their extreme mobility and striking power. The consequences of changes in these relations have been studied among animals,[5] and among civilizations of the past [6] but further examination might throw

light on the prospects of the future. Pending such further examination, it is safe to say that the new relation of offensive and defensive power is of an order unheard of in the history of war and revolutionary in its implications upon the stability of a military balance of power.

(21) Aviation has greatly increased the area over which government can exercise effective power to maintain order and justice. Estimates have been made of the average size of empires under different conditions in world history. These estimates made without knowledge of the atom bomb indicated that land forces alone could never have been adequate to implement world government. Sea power at its rate of advance might have been adequate for this purpose in some eight hundred years. Air power, however, had advanced so rapidly that it might be sufficient by 1950.[7] Detailed studies have suggested that by a suitable distribution of bases and the organization of a relatively small policing force of reconnaissance, combat and bombing planes, international government could today prevent aggression and maintain justice and order throughout the world. The problem of world order has ceased to be primarily technical and has become almost entirely political.[8]

In summary, the trend of the airplane has been toward increasing efficiency and increasing use as an instrument of transport, of communication, of commerce, of cultural diffusion, and of offensive war. This trend has progressively reduced technical and strategic distances in the world. It has diffused techniques and cultures, and has tended to reduce the differences of civilization in the world. It has increased the vulnerability of peoples everywhere to attack and has reduced the value of distance or geographic barriers as defenses against military attack, cultural penetration, or economic competition. It has created the technical possibility of a world police force capable of preventing aggression.

Condition of World Politics

What has been the condition of world politics in this period?

(1) War has been more frequent, widespread, and destructive than in any period of similar length, at least since the seventeenth century and probably in all human history.

(2) Centers of major military and political power have decreased in number and these centers have tended to exercise influence over the smaller states in their regions, thus augmenting the differential between the few "great powers" and the other states.

(3) The balance of power has become less stable, international law has been less observed, and confidence in peace and order has declined.

(4) The governments of national states have tended to become more

centralized and to plan economy and control opinion more completely and efficiently than ever before.

(5) War and preparation for war has tended to absorb a larger proportion of the population and the economic activities of countries than ever before.

(6) Persecutions and massacres under public authority or public tolerance have occurred with a barbarity and on a scale unprecedented in human history.

(7) International organization in the technical, economic, humanitarian, and political fields have been more generally accepted, more comprehensive, and more active than ever before.

(8) International legislative treaties have been more abundant, more comprehensive and more generally ratified than ever before.

(9) Institutions and procedures of international adjudication, conciliation, consultation and inquiry have been accepted and used more widely than ever before.

(10) Declarations by governments, individually and collectively, have professed greater devotion to universal peace, to international justice, to human welfare and to human rights than ever before.

These conditions, so obvious as to require no elaboration, manifest the extreme and conflicting developments, on the one hand, of government policies and actions supported by national sentiments oblivious to consideration of humanity, liberty, justice, and peace in the pursuit of national security, sovereignty, and power. On the other hand, they manifest sentiments expressing the determination of all nations to promote the welfare and liberty of mankind, to pursue international peace and justice, and to develop a stable and orderly community of nations. There has been no general trend but two contradictory tendencies. Barbarities in the service of national power and expressions of allegiance to the most universal ideals have occurred simultaneously. If there has been a trend, it has been toward more extreme and more widely distributed contradictions as history has progressed from the Spanish-American War and the Hague conferences, through World War I and the League of Nations, to World War II and the United Nations. Man as citizen supporting his state has more and more spoken and behaved in contradiction to man as human being.

Civilization's Problem

While aviation has manifested a continuous and consistent trend toward greater efficiency and wider utilization, world politics has been characterized by ever-greater confusion, inconsistency and violence, and men's thinking has become more self-contradictory.[9] Such extreme contradictions have in the past often characterized the declining days of a civilization.[10]

The course of science and of civilization in the past forty years is but an epitome of their course in world history. In general the history of science and technology from earliest times has been cumulative and progressive while the history of culture and civilization has been oscillating and unpredictable. Civilizations have risen and fallen. Each has had periods of uncertainty, of progress, of confusion, and of decline. Frequently, when science and technology have progressed the most rapidly as in the sixteenth and seventeenth centuries world politics has been the most chaotic and bloody. Our own period illustrates such a relation. Is this relation accidental or causal? This problem cannot be adequately analyzed in this article, but a causal relation is suggested by the following considerations.

A civilization is a people's effort on the one hand to realize the ideas and beliefs inherent in the philosophies and religions which they predominantly accept, and on the other, continuously to adapt their practices and institutions to the requirements of life under changing conditions. The changes in conditions which most insistently demand such adaptation are scientific discoveries and technological inventions, represented in our age particularly by aviation and the inventions supplementary to and accompanying it such as radio, radar, rockets, and the atom bomb.

The development and utilization of discoveries and inventions afford the opportunity to realize some social ideas, novel or hitherto latent in the civilization, but at the same time such development and utilization is almost certain to create conditions which frustrate the realization of other ideas and beliefs, some of which may have been considered the core of the civilization. Thus opinion becomes divided between the desire for rapid adaptation of ideas, beliefs, institutions, and practices in order to utilize advancing science and technology for human welfare, and the desire to preserve the institutions, strengthen the faiths, and realize the ideas of the past in spite of the obstacles presented by new conditions. Often both opinions remain unreconciled in the same mind though they may become the bases for partisan contention or international conflict. Today man as human being, anxious to utilize the airplane for human welfare, is in conflict with man as citizen ready to sacrifice everything that his state may prevail.

The airplane has been a powerful influence in the crisis of opinion, of world politics, and of civilization through which the world is struggling. Gunpowder, the printing press, and the mariner's compass steadily developed in efficiency and use during the fifteenth and sixteenth centuries, creating conditions to which medieval feudalism, ecclesiasticism, and cosmogony found it continually more difficult to adjust themselves. The diversities of opinion which resulted led to the chaotic politics and savage wars of the Renaissance and the Reformation. From these wars emerged the modern political order with the national state, international trade, and ideas of a universal family of nations.

Similarly today the airplane, the radio, and the atom bomb, steadily progressing in efficiency and use, are creating conditions to which the nationalism, the territorial sovereignty, and the power equilibrium of modern civilization find it difficult to adjust. Fortunately modern civilization has also developed ideas of humanism, liberalism, toleration, and scientific method better adapted to these new conditions. Emphatic and inconsistent opinions, however, have arisen, and have again produced chaotic world politics and bloody wars. From experience with these wars, men as rational and social animals, but always inhibited by their varying loyalties from the past, are trying to create, select, and develop common ideas, beliefs and institutions under which they can live in the age of the airplane, the Hertzian wave, and the nuclear fission. Can men reconcile their opinions as men and their opinions as citizens of the state by subordinating both to their opinions as citizens of the world? That is the problem which aviation has presented to world politics.

20

THE ATOMIC BOMB

AND WORLD POLITICS

Five atom bombs were exploded in the world before March, 1947. The first explosion, at Alamogordo, New Mexico, on July 16, 1945, was known only to a few scientists and military men. It doubtless influenced the strategy of the Allied operations against Japan and the character of the Potsdam declaration of July 26, 1945, stating terms of surrender to that country. It also stimulated intensive thought by a number of scientists and others on the subject of world organization.

The second and third explosions at Hiroshima and Nagasaki on August 6 and 9, 1945, destroying those cities and 150,000 persons, precipitated Japanese acceptance of the Potsdam terms [1] and induced President Truman to state on August 9, 1945, that "We must constitute ourselves trustees of this new force—to prevent its misuse, and to turn it into the channels of service to mankind." Furthermore, statesmen and scientists throughout the world were stimulated to think intensively on the problem of control. This resulted in international declarations by United Nations statesmen during that autumn,[2] and in unanimous acceptance by the General Assembly of the United Nations on January 24, 1946, of a resolution creating a commission to make specific proposals "with the utmost dispatch,"

> for control of atomic energy to the extent necessary to insure its use only for peaceful purposes; for the elimination from national armaments of atomic weapons and of all other major weapons adaptable to mass destruction and for effective safeguards by way of inspection and other means to protect complying states against the hazards of violations and evasions.

From *Air Affairs,* I (March, 1947).

This commission composed of representatives of the states represented on the United Nations Security Council and Canada began its work on June 14, 1946, with a proposal by the American representative Bernard Baruch. In the meantime in the United States the May-Johnson Bill providing for strict military control of atomic energy had been introduced in Congress and then superseded by the McMahon Bill as a result of intensive agitation by atomic scientists.[3] The latter bill providing for civilian control and contemplating eventual international control became law on August 1, 1946. Before passage of this act the State Department had set up a committee under David Lilienthal to study the problem of international control and the report of this committee, which provided the basis of the Baruch proposal, was published on March 28, 1946.[4]

The fourth and fifth explosions at Bikini atoll in July, 1946, resulted in reports by an Army-Navy commission "that vessels within a mile of an atom bomb air burst would eventually become inoperative due to crew casualties." A civilian evaluation commission reported:

> The Bikini tests strongly indicate that future wars employing atomic bombs may well destroy nations and change present standards of civilization. To us who have witnessed the devastating effects of these tests, it is evident that if there is to be any security or safety in the world, war must be eliminated as a means of settling differences among nations.[5]

These observations undoubtedly had important effects on the planning of United States naval development, and some effect on public thinking, though apparently the import of the experiment—that the bomb was more effective than had been anticipated—was not at first clear to the public. These explosions, however, and the intensive study given to the problem by a technical subcommittee [6] of the United Nations Atomic Energy Commission in September, 1946, may have contributed to the acceptance in principle of the Baruch plan of control by that commission and its transmission to the Security Council on December 31, 1946. In this the commission acted unanimously with abstention of the Soviet Union and Poland.

Precise analysis of the political consequences of an invention has been difficult even decades or centuries after the invention has first proved successful.[7] It is perhaps rash to attempt to predict the political consequences of the atom bomb with more precision than to say that these consequences will be important. Even on that there have been some differences of opinion. There have been public statements by scholars [8] and statesmen [9] suggesting that predictions of revolutionary political effects may have been exaggerated. The majority, however, have been convinced that the atom bomb would have revolutionary effects.[10] Such effects have been anticipated (1) on world opinion and national policies, (2) on the art of war and the localization of political power, (3) on international law and international organization, and (4) on the future of civilization.

Opinion and Policy

The impact of the atom bomb upon opinion varied considerably in different groups. The atomic scientists in the United States were probably most convinced of any group that the atom bomb would, if used by both sides, make war unbearably destructive; that within a decade nuclear fission could be developed into far more destructive weapons than the Nagasaki bomb; that Russia and other countries would be able to develop atomic weapons independently within a period variously estimated at three to twenty-five years; that if effective controls were not established war would be likely in fifteen to twenty-five years; and that no control would be adequate except an international system of control so far-reaching as to constitute a limited world government.[11]

American opinion tended to follow the views of the scientists with a lag in time, with less intensity, and with some inconsistencies. An examination of American opinion polls in December, 1946, disclosed opinions ranging from 80-90 per cent that in another war bombs more powerful than those dropped in Japan would be used against American cities, that there was no real defense against such bombing, and that a large share of the city residents of the earth would be killed. Further, 70 per cent expected another war within twenty-five years, over 90 per cent of them thought that Russia would be the enemy, and 66 per cent thought Russia would have atom bombs within three years.

In spite of this fatalistic attitude, opinion generally favored international organization to prevent war and to control the atom bomb. Thus, 80 per cent wanted the world organization to have power to send inspectors throughout the world, 75 per cent wanted legislative and executive power over atom-bomb making throughout the world, and 60 per cent were ready to have the United States destroy all its atom bombs if required by such legislation.

Rather inconsistently, however, a majority wanted the United States to keep the secret of making atom bombs even if an international control is set up, to keep up its military preparedness and, if war becomes inevitable, to launch an atomic attack first.

Majorities, therefore, thought both that war was inevitable and that steps should be taken to prevent it, that effective international control should be established and that the United States should keep its secret, that international organization should be established to prevent war and control atomic energy and that the United States should be prepared to launch a preventive atomic attack in case war becomes inevitable. These inconsistencies indicate that the public mind was unstable and could be easily moved one way or another by argument. Speakers reported that they had experienced this fluidity of opinion in their audiences. Furthermore opinion polls indicated considerable changes in time. Thus, according to the Denver poll, the expectation of war in twenty-five years which stood at only 40 per cent before Hiroshima, rose to 44 per cent in September, 1945; reached a high of 68 per cent in March, 1946; and receded to 63 per cent in September, 1946. Another poll indicated the same changes but found the expectation of war 75 per cent in the autumn of 1946.[12]

British polls were similar. The expectation of war in twenty-five years rose from 45 to 70 per cent during 1946, and 75 per cent were convinced in the spring of 1946 that atom bombs would be used, though this number declined to 50 per cent after the Bikini experiments because of the "extremely misleading initial reporting" of those experiments suggesting that the destructiveness of the bomb had been exaggerated. The British reporter of this poll added, "The results of the experiment are revolutionizing naval design in America, a fact which is too little realized here" and "there has been nothing done here comparable with the effort of the scientists in the United States both to awaken and inform public opinion as to the dangers and potentialities of the new power now in our hands." British opinion was strongly committed to the United Nations but confidence in it and desire to increase its strength by eliminating the veto vote and by giving it an embodied police force declined from 65 per cent to 50 per cent after the winter of 1946.[13]

Polls of opinion elsewhere in the world were not available but observers believed sentiment was much less disturbed in continental Europe and Asia than in America and Britain. In countries which had been devastated by the war this may have been due to the feeling that nothing could be much worse than what they had recently suffered, and in dictatorial countries the absence of information probably contributed to that opinion. Russian papers devoted little attention to the bomb, and on September 24, 1946, Premier Stalin said:

> I do not believe the atomic bomb to be as serious a force as certain politicians are inclined to regard it. Atomic bombs are intended for intimidating weak nerves, but they cannot decide the

outcome of war, since atomic bombs are by no means sufficient for this purpose. Certainly monopolist possession of the secret of the atomic bomb does create a threat, but at least two remedies exist against it: (a) monopolist possession of the atomic bomb cannot last long, (b) use of the atomic bomb will be prohibited.[14]

It is perhaps significant that in his statement of a month later, after Soviet scientists had intensively discussed the bomb and its control with other scientists in the Technical Subcommittee of the United Nations Atomic Energy Commission, Stalin replied to the question "How in your opinion can atomic power best be controlled? Should this control be created on an international basis, and to what extent should the powers sacrifice their sovereignty in the interest of making control effective?" by a brief statement: "A strong international control is needed." [15]

Opinion, while unconvinced that atomic war could be avoided, appeared to have been increasingly convinced that such a war would be a disaster and that every effort should be made to develop international institutions to control the bomb and to prevent war.

Policies in accord with this opinion developed. American policy, which at first President Truman suggested should be one of monopoly control and secrecy, was revised under the influence of the Truman-Attlee-King meeting of November, 1945; the Moscow foreign ministers meeting of December, 1945; the United Nations resolution of January, 1946; the Lilienthal report of March, 1946; and the congressional adoption of the McMahon Bill in August, 1946. The United States policy embodied in the Baruch proposal contemplated thorough-going international control not only through inspection but through operation by a United Nations atomic development authority of all production of fissionable material including the mining of ores. This policy also involved effective international sanctions through the United Nations unhampered by the veto vote in the Security Council. This plan was accepted in principle by all the members of the Atomic Energy Commission except Russia and Poland which abstained from voting. The outright rejection of the Baruch plan by Gromyko, speaking for the Soviet Union on July 24, 1946,[16] was modified after the informal discussion among scientists in the Technical Subcommittee. In the General Assembly meeting Soviet Foreign Minister Molotov accepted the principle of international inspection and control, and recognized that the operations of any inspection and control commission defined in a special treaty need not be hampered in their exercise by the veto vote applicable in the Security Council. He also suggested that the atomic energy problem be related to other aspects of armament regulation.[17]

These ideas were embodied in the resolution of the General Assembly of December 13, 1946.[18]

The Soviet government's final attitude on the problem of sanctions in case an atomic or other armament treaty is violated was not disclosed. The Baruch proposal contemplated the most extensive subordination of national sovereignty to international authority and the most far-reaching reliance upon international agencies for security contemplated in any negotiation among great powers in modern history.

Whether the United States and the other states which accepted this policy will continue to do so and whether they will continue to be supported by public opinion remains to be seen.

That governments did not unequivocally commit themselves to this policy is evident from their military policies. In his budget message of January 11, 1947, President Truman, while expressing confidence that the United Nations would achieve world peace, proposed a national defense budget of over eleven and a quarter billion for 1948 as "a proper balance between security and economy." He said any cut "would immediately weaken our international position." While this defense budget was three and a half billion below that of 1947 and only one-eighth of the war peak in 1944, it exceeded the defense budget of 1941 by five billion. The president also continued to urge universal training in time of peace. The newspapers of January 12 that reported this message also reported a speech of General Omar Bradley that security could only be maintained by international action; a House of Representatives subcommittee recommendation that the United States hold and develop as bases numerous distant Pacific islands; and a Russian proposal to Norway that the Bear Island and Spitzbergen arrangement of 1920 be modified to permit Soviet establishment of bases in that area within bombing distance of Chicago and Detroit. Mention was likewise made of United States efforts to obtain bases in Iceland and of the United States "Operation Frostbite" in Greenland.

Government policy as well as public opinion was clearly in a process of transition, but the trend toward viewing with skepticism the hope of national security through national armament, a trend evident since World War I, was augmented by the atom bomb.

A continuance of this trend, however, was not certain. The monopoly of the bomb by the United States did not create great anxieties abroad apparently because of general conviction of the war weariness and the pacific intentions of the American government. While other countries strove to discover the secret of atomic energy, they did not moderate their foreign policies because of fear that the United States might use the weapon against them. It seems in fact probable that there was more anxiety about the bomb in the United States itself than in any other country. What effect would it have on American opinion and policy if, before effective international controls are in operation, authoritative information were received that Russia had the secret and was about to make a bomb? Would it increase efforts to strengthen the United Nations and to give it effective power to prevent war? Would it augment military preparedness? Might it even precipitate a preventive war? It is not impossible to imagine that conditions of tension approaching panic might develop. The alarm of states located between the two great rivals might augment such a condition.

War and Power

Experience with the atom bomb in Japan, and especially under the controlled conditions of Bikini, convinced military men that the air- and rocket-borne atom bomb of the types already used could rapidly visit unparalleled destruction upon an enemy separated by oceans; that its costs in proportion to the losses it could visit on the enemy were much less than of any other weapon which had been used; and that there was no direct defense against it.[19]

Those on the inside of atom-bomb making believe those exploded are only a beginning. A former assistant secretary of war wrote:

It is certainly possible to increase the quantity of the fissionable material in the bomb. We talk today of the bomb in terms of the equivalent of twenty thousand tons of TNT. From first-hand information given to me by the scientists whose prophecies were uncannily accurate during the course of the war, there can be little doubt that within the next ten years, to be conservative, bombs of the power equivalent of one hundred thousand to two hundred and fifty thousand tons of TNT can be made, something over ten times more powerful than the bomb dropped on Hiroshima. And if we can move to the other end of the periodic table and utilize hydrogen in the generation of energy, we would have a bomb somewhere around one thousand times as powerful as the Nagasaki bomb. I have been told by scientists who are not mere theorists but who actually planned and made the bomb which was exploded in New Mexico that, given the same intensive effort which was employed during the war toward the production of that bomb, we were within two years' time at the close of the war of producing a bomb of the hydrogen-helium type, i.e., a bomb of approximately one thousand times the power of the present bombs.[20]

Scientists themselves suggested that the blast destruction from such bombs might not be their most serious effect:

> Ten or fifteen years from now giant bombs which disperse radio-active substances into the air may be set off far away from our cities. If such giant bombs were used against us the buildings of our cities would remain undamaged but the people inside of the cities would not remain alive.[21]

Calling attention to the harmless but detectable radioactive materials swept by the westerly winds to California from Bikini atoll, scientists said:

> If the activity liberated at Bikini were multiplied by a factor of a hundred thousand or a million, and if it were to be released off our Pacific coast, the whole of the United States would be endangered. That the enormous amounts of activity just mentioned can in actuality be released at some future date is by no means an established fact; but it is much more than a fantastic possibility. If such great quantities of activity should become available an enemy could make life hard or even impossible for us without delivering a single bomb into our territory.[22]

In military terminology the airplane- or rocket-borne atom bomb increased the power of the offensive over that of the defensive in war to a degree far beyond that achieved by any other invention. When both sides in a war have these weapons there is no defense for either other than mutual fears of retaliation. According to General of the Army H. H. Arnold:

> . . . against this future of increasing range, speed, and destructiveness of the weapons of air power, adequate protection by pure defense seems unlikely. Our defense can only be a counteroffensive; we must be prepared to give as good as we take or better.[23]

There was much discussion as to whether in this situation states would actually be deterred from using the weapon because of this fear. Doubtless each side by distributing and protecting its atom bombs, the plants to make them, the planes or rockets to carry them, and the sites from which to launch them would make it improbable that a sudden attack would destroy its power of retaliation. Some thought that if retaliation were made certain, neither side would initiate such an attack; they cited the nonuse of poison gases in World War II in support of this opinion. Poison gas, however, was never so decisive a weapon as is the atom bomb.[24]

It seems likely that atom bombs would be used in the following circumstances: (1) if an aggressive government convinced itself that by sudden atomic attack in time of peace it could paralyze its enemies' powers of effective retaliation, (2) if such a government were so intensively bent upon achieving its aim that it was prepared to sacrifice its own great cities if necessary for victory, (3) if during a war or in time of peace any government became convinced that its actual or potential enemy was about to use the bomb and that a priority in use would give an advantage even though slight, and (4) if a war initiated with other weapons had reached a condition of military stalemate and of intense hatred of the enemy by each side. It is not unlikely that one or the other of these circumstances would occur during a long period of armed peace in which several countries had atomic weapons and it seems practically certain that one or the other would occur if war should develop between great powers.

Fear of retaliation seemed a slender reed to lean upon, and even if it were adequate during a period of time, it was pointed out that "a world in which two or more states were sitting on powder kegs powerful enough to destroy every major city on earth will be a world of half peace at best." [25]

Military history suggests that in the past when military invention has given an advantage to the offensive, the equilibrium of power has become less stable, wars have been more frequent, conquests have been more rapid, and the size of states has increased. In the Renaissance period the increasingly effective use of gunpowder produced all these effects. Napoleon's improved methods of logistics and propaganda, Bismarck's use of railroads, and Hitler's use of airplanes, temporarily augmented offensive power and expanded empires.[26] Such conditions have frequently been terminated through the invention of countervailing defensive measures, but no such measures have been suggested against the atom bomb.

During the twentieth century the inventions of the airplane and the tank have tended to increase the power of the offensive, to augment the disparity in power between small and large states, to eliminate some small states, and to reduce the number of great powers.[27] What will be the effect of the atom bomb upon this trend?

The opinion has been expressed that because of the considerable dispersion of uranium and thorium and the relative cheapness of bomb manufacture small powers might by making a few bombs acquire a capacity to make aggression costly even to the greatest power and thereby improve their relative power position.[28] I do not share this opinion. There are in fact only a few small powers with considerable supplies of the basic minerals. The making of fissionable materials is a large and expensive operation. It is unlikely that a great power would permit a small state in its vicinity to embark upon such a manufacture unless the large state were certain of controlling the products. Furthermore, to become weapons, atom bombs require planes and rockets whose manufacture is only possible in highly industrialized countries. It, therefore, seems unlikely that under conditions of power politics any small state would have both the capacity and the opportunity to equip itself with atomic weapons. But if a small state did possess such weapons, the threat implied by such possession might prove ineffective and the small state might be invaded. If this happened and the small state decided to use atom bombs against the invader it would almost certainly cease to exist. A small state has little capacity to protect itself by dispersion of its atomic weapons and plants. Consequently it is more likely than a great state to be rapidly deprived of its powers of retaliation. Small states in a jungle world would assume suicidal risks if they attempted to defend themselves by atom bombs. They are, therefore, more likely to put themselves under protection of a great neighbor than to assume such risks.

Modern inventions in the fields of communications, transport, and military attack have contributed to the reduction of the number of great powers in the world to two or three, to a practical elimination of the capacity of small states to defend themselves from the great, and to a decrease in the strategic distances between states. These conditions make it unlikely that the instability of the balance of power, consequent upon the superiority of the offensive in war, can be remedied by political means. They reduce the possibility of rectifying disturbances of the equilibrium by alliances and diminish the time available for diplomatic maneuvers. A bipolar balance of power is certain to break down in war as soon as one party becomes convinced that time is running against it, that it can be attacked, and that war eventually is inevitable or highly probable. The latter expectation always exists in greater or less degree in a system of power politics. The air-borne atomic weapon launched from the territory of any of the great powers can reach major cities of any of the others in a few hours and attack can be coördinated throughout the world by radio. With these considerations in mind it seems wise to assume that an equilibrium of military power between the major states will remain extremely unstable.

Apart from the direct influence of the atom bomb on power politics, the invention of atomic energy may provide new causes for international controversy. Interest in Antarctica seems to be promoted in part by the possibility of uranium deposits in that area. Other areas may become objects of rivalry among the powers for this reason. In the past the development of the military importance of resources such as petroleum or the discovery of resources of military importance in new areas has often precipitated international controversy. The use of atomic energy for industrial purposes may also precipitate political problems. Areas such as eastern Siberia, central China, and Brazil, without easily available coal or water power and hitherto of little industrial or military importance, may become important through the use of atomic energy as a source of power.

By increasing the destructiveness of war, by increasing the instability of the balance of power, by changing the relative importance of different areas of the world, the invention of atomic fission will tremendously affect the future of international politics. In the absence of a world organization which creates general confidence that world politics will act within legal limits, it is to be expected that the probability of war will rapidly increase after the shock of the recent war has subsided and the secret of the atom bomb has become known to all the great powers.

Law and Organization

International law has been developed in theory since World War I toward the outlawry of aggressive war and the modification of the status of neutrality, toward a greater recognition of the human rights and criminal liabilities of individuals, toward the subjection of the sovereignty of states to international institutions enforcing these principles, and toward a recognition of general principles of justice as a source for interpreting and applying international conventions and customs. These principles were given a certain sanction in the League of Nations Covenant and the statute of the Permanent Court of International Justice after World War I. They were developed by judicial opinions, international declarations, and general treaties such as the Pact of Paris during the interwar period. The Charter of the United Nations and the Charter of the International Military Tribunal explicitly accepted these principles and provided an institutional framework which it was hoped would make them effective.

These principles, however, have in fact been imperfectly honored in practice. In truth they are hardly compatible with an international system based upon an equilibrium of military power. In such a system the state must reserve the rights of war and neutrality as the exigencies of power politics suggest, must control the individuals subject to its law, must insist on its sovereign authority in domestic and foreign policy, and must limit international law to those rules which it has accepted or habitually acquiesced in. The new principles of international law look toward a federalistic world constitution which can maintain a regime of law upon which states and peoples can rely for security. They contemplate that world politics, instead of being unlimited in the methods which it can use, shall be limited by rules of law and procedure eliminating violence except for the enforcement of law.[29]

Will the atom bomb accelerate or retard such a development? As already pointed out, the atom bomb has contributed to weakening the prospect for a stable balance of power. The natural trend toward bringing the smaller states into regional arrangements dominated by one or the other great power would, by promoting bipolarity, make the equilibrium even less stable. If, however, statesmanship should succeed in increasing the power of Britain, France, and China relative to that of the United States and the Soviet Union, of decreasing the dependence of lesser states upon one or another great power so that they would occupy buffer positions, of solving the major issues between Russia, the United States, and the other great powers, and of habituating the powers to the procedures of the United Nations, the conditions for a stable equilibrium of power might be improved even if the atom bomb remains uncontrolled.[30] But with the danger of atomic war such an equilibrium could hardly be maintained unless the states kept themselves in continuous preparedness for such a war by placing essential industries underground, by dispersing the population of cities, and by regimenting the population to follow orders for seeking shelter at a moment's notice. The regimentation required for such preparedness would probably prove incompatible with the maintenance of civil liberties and democracy. An equilibrium of power in a world of uncontrolled atom bombs would, as Lasswell has pointed out, require all states to become "garrison states." Lasswell, it is true, conceived the possibility of such a condition gradually ameliorating.

> If actual warfare is deferred from one year to the next, the expectation of imminent violence will gradually recede into the background, save for occasional scares (perhaps engineered by the ruling groups to maintain internal discipline). Should the ruling groups in both zones succeed in maintaining a comparatively low level of internal tension (obviating any sort of revolution), eventually they may feel secure enough to expand a thin trickle of contact between the "two worlds." As the area of contact and confidence gradually extends, a movement toward "one world" would

gradually get under way. (Institutions like the United Nations, however anemic today, would be available to implement a new trend toward world organization.) [31]

While such a development is conceivable, it seems more likely that a peace so intensely armed would move toward war. From twelve years' experience as economic advisor of the United States State Department, Herbert Feis sees little hope for peace in a world of neurotic garrison states.

> The whole world thus lives with a sense of constant exposure to hostile influence. This is quickened with greater alarm because of the deathly character of the new weapons of war. The jet plane, the rocket projectile, and the atomic bomb have left all countries more exposed to attack. They seem to promise advantage to the ruthless, to offer better opportunities to any who may be ready to attack. This means, and of this the grim Economic Advisor is certain, that no diplomatic arrangement and no form of international organization can bring prolonged peace unless the production and use of these weapons are brought under drastic international control. No people will dare to be trustful as long as they may be destroyed by a brief rain from the clouds. The growing generation will not be able to live satisfactorily with the lurking image of the 'supernatural mushroom' in its brain. Unless control is certain, control supported as completely by the whole world as against the plague, expect both old and young to be neurotic. Expect them to go to the devil in a desperate effort to forget the devil in wait. [32]

It is to be expected that under the conditions of uncontrolled atomic weapons, the lesser garrison states will seek protection of the greater [33] —two great feudal garrisons will face each other as did Rome and Carthage in antiquity and Christendom and Islam in the Middle Ages. Crusades of one against the other would move rapidly with the technology of plane, rocket, and atom bomb. While civilization would in large measure be destroyed, one world empire might emerge. The prospect of one world by conquest, however, would not augur better for liberal democratic civilization than the equilibrium of garrison states. Either result would be almost unrelieved disaster.

Civilization

According to the foregoing analysis, the continuance of civilization as it has developed since the various parts of the world came into continuous contact with one another at the Renaissance, requires world control of atomic energy and of war. It cannot be expected that the use of atom bombs will be avoided, whatever the control, if great powers get into war. Consequently, control of the atom bomb will not be effective unless war itself is prevented. The path toward these objectives has been indicated in the United Nations and the Atomic Energy Commission. The atom bomb has stimulated public opinion, national policies, and United Nations policies to move more rapidly in the course outlined by the League of Nations Covenant and the United Nations Charter. Even the latter instrument, completed before the atomic age began, was widely recognized to need supplementation and for this reason the Atomic Energy Commission was created.

Clearly the effect of the atom bomb on world politics depends upon the success of these policies. If the effort at world control fails the consequence to civilization for a long future will be very different from what they would be if the effort succeeds. It must be emphasized that success depends on the development of a world public opinion no less than upon formal negotiations and institutions. The latter can hardly be effective unless the major groups of people in the world are willing to subordinate their particular customs and ideologies to a world order able to prevent war.

The organization of world authority and the development of a world opinion are not independent of one another. Effective authority and supporting opinion may each reciprocally aid the other, in a spiral of increasing confidence and security. There is, however, the danger that people upset by fear of the atom bomb may overcentralize civilization leading to tyranny and stagnation.

For a satisfactory constitutional development of the world order, only the minimum of authority necessary to assure security should be transferred to world institutions. Coöperation in economic, social, educational, and cultural matters may well develop voluntarily in full recognition of the values of individual liberty and of national autonomy. The world public is still but imperfectly informed of the nature and potentialities of atomic energy. Unless information is increased— an important task of UNESCO—so that understanding will moderate and control fear, success may prove impossible.

There has been no military invention, parallel to the atom bomb, the historic consequences of which might be compared with the projection here suggested on the basis of present trends and analysis. Gunpowder is, perhaps, the nearest parallel. It destroyed the invulnerability of feudal castles in the Middle Ages and, with the printing press, contributed to building the modern age of nation-states. The process, however, was slow. It took three centuries of development before firearms became decisive weapons. The atom bomb took less than three years. After gunpowder was used effectively in war the *idea* of a world community under international law developed but sovereign national states in a system of fluctuating power equilibrium formed the *reality*.[34] The atom bomb with other modern inventions has probably made absolutely sovereign nations as obsolete as feudal baronies, but it remains for modern man to develop sufficient solidarity in the world community to assure himself a modicum of security, justice, and progress. The airplane and the radio have created the potentiality, the emerging world institutions may provide the procedures, and the atom bomb may develop the will and determination to move steadily toward this achievement.

21

POLITICAL

CONSEQUENCES

OF THE SOVIET

ATOM BOMB

Three years ago I wrote in AIR AFFAIRS:

> What effect would it have on American opinion and policy if,
> before effective international controls are in operation, authorita-
> tive information were received that Russia had the secret and was
> about to make a bomb? Would it increase efforts to strengthen the
> United Nations and to give it effective power to prevent war?
> Would it augment military preparedness? Might it even precipitate
> a preventive war? It is not impossible to imagine that conditions
> of tension approaching panic might develop. The alarm of states
> located between the two great rivals might augment such a condi-
> tion.[1]

On September 23, 1949, President Truman announced "We have
evidence that within recent weeks an atomic explosion occurred in
the U.S.S.R." This statement did not say that the explosion was controlled, but it was popularly thought to mean that the Soviet government had the secret of the bomb, and this opinion was officially confirmed, with reference to later explosions.

From *Air Affairs*, III (Spring, 1950).

Opinions and Policies

The questions which I asked in 1947 may be made the basis for considering the consequences of the president's announcement. The impression prevailed through 1949 that these consequences were not momentous. Life went on as before. No "conditions of tension approaching panic" developed and there was no talk of "preventive war." The president, in his announcement, said "The eventual development of this new force by other nations was to be expected. This probability has always been taken into account by us." Similar soothing statements were made by high political and military officials of the government. Secretary of State Acheson said "This event makes no change in our policy." General Bradley, chairman of the joint chiefs of staff, said "We have anticipated it for four years, and it calls for no change in our basic defense plans." General Eisenhower said "I see no reason why a development that was anticipated years ago should cause any revolutionary change in our thinking or in our actions." General Groves, who managed the Manhattan project that made the first bomb, said he "would not lose any sleep over the announcement because this country was certainly in the lead in any atomic race." General Bedell Smith, former ambassador to Russia, thought "that it will take Soviet Russia at least ten years to get to the point of mass production that we have now reached." David Lilienthal, chairman of the Atomic Energy Commission, felt now precisely as he had felt before he knew Russia had the bomb. . . . "This country must do everything necessary to establish atomic leadership." [2]

Some scientific analysts played down the importance of the atomic bomb in war, thus giving support to Stalin's suggestion, quoted on page 307, that atomic bombs are more useful for intimidating weak nerves than for deciding the outcome of wars. Professor P. M. S. Blakett expressed such an opinion in his book *Fear, War and the Atomic Bomb,* published before the Soviet bomb was announced.[3] Since that time Admiral Radford, commander in chief of the Pacific fleet, Rear Admiral R. A. Ofstie, and other naval officers have minimized the military value of strategic bombing and emphasized its inhuman and impolitic effects in their testimony before the Congressional committee dealing with the inter-service controversy concerning unification.[4] Mr. Vannevar Bush, director of the Office of Scientific Research and Development and the Advisory Committee on Uranium during the war, has analyzed the effects of modern science on war and democracy with cautious conclusions somewhat minimizing the decisive influence of the atom bomb and suggesting that defensive measures are in process of development. He wrote:

> A new great war would not end the progress of civilization, even in the days of the riven atom, even with the threat of disease marshaled for conquest. It is even possible that defenses may become tightened, not made absolute, but competent to halt the full flood of death from the air. As science goes forward it distributes its uses both to those who destroy and to those who preserve. A great war would be terrible; it would not utterly destroy. It need not destroy democracy, for the organization of free men tends to become refined under stress . . .[5]

The public at first accepted these reassuring statements and interpretations; on the other hand, some students of international politics were astonished at this complacency.

Professor Hans Morgenthau rated the attention given in the American press to episodes of importance to American foreign policy from 1945 to 1949 in the following order: (1) Communist seizure of Czechoslovakia, 1948, (2) Trial of Cardinal Mindszenty in Hungary, 1949, (3) Berlin blockade, 1948, (4) Shooting of American aviators in Yugoslavia, 1946, (5) Greek civil war, 1947, (6) Soviet occupation of northern Iran, 1946, (7) Chinese communist revolution, 1949, (8) Hostilities in Palestine, 1948, and far below any of these the Russian explosion of an atomic bomb in 1949.[6]

This list suggested that American opinion was more interested in evidences of the opinion and intentions of other states and in abstract issues, factors which Bismarck called "imponderable" although they may not be insusceptible of measurement, than in evidences of change in the material elements of the power equilibrium. All of the events noted, except Palestine and the atomic explosion, were considered significant because they gave evidence of the spirit, opinion, and intentions of communist regimes, even though, with the possible exception of the communist revolution in China, they had little immediate effect on the power position of the Soviet Union. Each of them, with the exception of the atomic explosion, actually occasioned the crystallization of world public opinion on an abstract issue, the importance of which was deemed to extend far beyond the immediate circumstances.

Professor Morgenthau rated the acquisition by Russia of an atomic weapon "as an event of greatest importance. In comparison with it all the great issues of the postwar period fade into insignificance. Certainly in the short run, and probably for the foreseeable future as well, it overshadows even the passing of China into the Soviet camp." [7] To support this conclusion, he called attention to "the decisive change in the world balance of power" which Soviet possession of the bomb entailed. It "not only removes the counter-weight to the superior Russian military establishment, constituted by the American monopoly of the atomic bomb" but "now the superior industrial plant of the United States is as exposed to destruction by atomic bombs as has been the inferior Russian industrial plant." He continued with the gloomy prognostication, "Before the initial phase of the war is over, the superior American industrial plant will have been wiped out as well as the inferior Russian one. The atomic bomb is no respecter of technological achievements, and before it all industrial plants are equal. Thus the main potential source of American military superiority will have been eliminated." [8]

This change, Professor Morgenthau believed, destroyed the assumption on which American policy toward Russia has been based. He accepted Winston Churchill's analysis made at the Massachusetts Institute of Technology in March, 1949: "It is certain that Europe would have been communized and London under bombardment sometime ago, but for the deterrent of the atomic bomb in the hands of the United States." [9] General Vandenberg, chief of staff of the United States Air Force, expressed the same view in opposition to the position taken by the Navy in October, 1949. He thought the concept of strategic bombing with atomic weapons had served as "the one greatest equalizing factor in the balance of military power between a potential enemy and the Western democracies." General Bradley, chairman of the joint chiefs of staff, expressed the same opinion. [10] Assuming that Russia could not make a bomb before 1951, the date which military authorities usually considered the minimum, [11] Professor Morgenthau thought the United States calculated on time enough to revive and re-arm Western Europe sufficiently to resist a Soviet armed invasion while Russia was still checked by the American monopoly of the bomb supported by a sufficient air force to carry it to Russian cities. The Marshall plan, the North Atlantic pact, and the European Rearmament Program were, in his opinion, based primarily on this assumption. In the new situation, Professor Morgenthau believed the United States was confronted by the alternatives of "war with the Soviet Union" or "a negotiated peace." Favoring the latter alternative he identified the major Soviet interest as domination of eastern Europe and thought the Soviet Union might be willing to evacuate central Europe in exchange for Western recognition of this interest. [12]

While other analysts differed considerably from Professor Morgenthau in estimating the bases of agreement, many of them shared the opinion that Soviet possession of the atom bomb was an event of major importance which called for re-appraisal of American foreign policy.[13] Advocates of world government wrote, "Alarm must ring!" [14] Atomic scientists characterize the reassuring official comments as "whistling in the dark" and, while denying any intent to create public hysteria, said: "We do not advise Americans that doomsday is near and that they can expect atomic bombs to start falling on their heads a month or a year from now; but we think they have reason to be deeply alarmed and to be prepared for grave decisions." [15] A group of atomic scientists said the opinion expressed by General Bedell Smith that "It will take Soviet Russia at least ten years to get to the point of mass production that we have now reached" has "no basis in fact." [16]

It was evident after 1950 that public complacency was evaporating. Not only was there alarm over actual and imagined Soviet aggressions and inadequacy of defense preparations, but irrational excitement over domestic Communism was manifested by public support of congressional inquisitions, conducted without regard for probable cause, reasonable evidence, or traditional civil liberties.

The complacency in the public utterances of the political and military leaders seemed not to be entirely reflected in their actions, nor was it reflected in the considered judgments and proposals of political, military, and scientific experts either official or unofficial. As Bernard Brodie remarked "A good deal of the sober and intensive strategic thinking demanded by the times, which has been going on either not at all or at much too leisurely a pace, must now really get up steam." [17] In their professional addresses, high staff officers called attention to the sweeping advances which Soviet land forces are now in a position to make to the British Channel, the Pyrenees, the Mediterranean, the Middle East, and Southeast Asia through resistances which would hamper them for only a few weeks. Such officers called for a careful reassessment of the position with the implication that perhaps the answer is to be found rather in the political than in the military field.

Let us reflect on some of the new emphases in American foreign policy which were considered. These fall under the heads: (1) International Atomic Energy Control and Strengthening of the United Nations, (2) Military Preparation and Alliances to Strengthen the Power Position of the United States, and (3) Conciliation of Russia Without Appeasement.

Strengthening the United Nations

President Truman said in his announcement of September 23: "This recent development emphasizes once again, if indeed such emphasis were needed, the necessity for that truly effective and enforceable international control of atomic energy which this government and the large majority of the members of the United Nations support." [18] The official position of the United States and most of the other members of the United Nations was not changed during the meeting of the fourth assembly. Andrei Vishinsky asserted that the Soviet Union was utilizing atomic energy for economic purposes such as "razing mountains," "irrigating deserts," and "cutting through the jungle and the tundra" so as "to spread life, happiness, prosperity, and welfare in places where the human footstep had not been seen for thousands of years." He admitted, however, if "unfortunately and to our great regret, [war] were necessary, we would have as many of these [bombs] as we should need —no more and no less." Assistant Secretary of State John D. Hickerson countered for the United States implying some skepticism about the Soviet pacific uses of atomic energy and pointing to the distribution of isotopes for medical and research purposes by the United States.

After these pleasantries, the states on the two sides of the Iron Curtain reaffirmed the position on atomic control which they had been taking for the past years. The General Assembly passed by a vote of 49 to 5, with Israel, South Africa, and Yugoslavia abstaining and the Soviet group in opposition, a resolution introduced by France and Canada which requested the sponsoring powers (Canada, China, France, U.S.S.R., U.K., and U.S.) to continue their conversations "exploring all possible avenues and examining all concrete suggestions," and recommended that "all nations join in mutual agreement to renounce the individual exercise of such rights of sovereignty in the control of atomic energy as . . . are incompatible with the promotion of world security and peace." An interim report made to the General Assembly on October 24 indicated no progress toward agreement.

New ideas were, however, thrown into the debate by General Romulo of the Philippines, president of the General Assembly. He spoke with great emotion saying "Atomic energy is too serious to be treated as an incidental phase of the battle of propaganda. This is one problem before which all mankind stands equally interested and equally defenseless." He continued: "If the horrors of atomic war should ever be visited upon this planet, the pitiful survivors of blasted and ruined cities will take little consolation in the thought that the representatives of the United Nations made brilliant and witty speeches about atomic energy. They will ask just one question: why did you not stop this before it happened?" [19] General Romulo proposed four lines of possible action in a letter to the six sponsoring powers in which he referred to the control of atomic energy as "the paramount problem before mankind": (1) A short-term armistice on bomb production accompanied by an inspection system, (2) an interim prohibition of the use of atomic weapons with adequate safeguards, (3) the possibility of further compromises between the majority (United States) and minority (Soviet) plans for atomic energy control, especially modification of the provision in the majority plan for ownership and management, and (4) a new approach to the fundamental problems of control through appreciation that the quantity of atomic energy at present needed for legitimate purposes and research is small and will remain so until power reactors are perfected, a development unlikely in less than ten years.[20]

Besides the idea of an interim agreement, the idea of a very simple agreement not to use the bomb in war, except in retaliation for use by another, was widely discussed in the autumn of 1949. Such an agreement would not limit the manufacturing or possession of bombs or of fissionable materials and would not involve any problem of inspection or international control. It would be sanctioned only by the mutual right of retaliation against use of the bomb. Such an agreement was said to be supported by the precedent of the poison gas convention of 1925, though the analogy was imperfect because poison gas is a much less decisive military instrument than is the atom bomb. It was argued against this proposal that it might lull peace loving democracies such as the United States into a sense of false security inducing them to relax in the atomic armament race while dictatorships like the Soviet Union forged ahead. It was also suggested that the outlawry of the use of the atom bomb, if observed, would change the balance of power unfavorably to the United States because the relative importance of mass armies would be augmented and in these the Soviet Union excelled. The same argument, however, could be made against the United States (Baruch) proposed for effective international control of atomic energy and elimination of its use for warlike purposes. The Argentine proposal calling for renunciation of the use of atomic weapons for purposes of aggression was defeated in the General Assembly by a vote of 15 to 20 with 23 abstentions.[21] It may be, however, that more careful consideration of such a simple arrangement would indicate that it would have some value in stilling anxieties while providing the way for a more extensive agreement.

Defense Preparation

Defense preparation accelerated in the United States after President Truman's announcement of September 23, 1949, in spite of the fact that a reduction in the size of the army by some 30,000 was announced on October 25 and a reduction in the air force and in naval vessels in commission, by some 20 per cent, was announced on October 30 and November 18. These reductions, said to be motivated by budgetary cuts,[22] were more than compensated by the step-ups in appropriations for foreign aid and atomic development and in the progress of defense unification and North Atlantic strategic planning. Sudden changes of position in Congress on some of these matters indicate the important influence of the president's announcement.

Early in October the charges of naval officers that the Department of National Defense was pursuing policies which reduced naval morale, precipitated extensive congressional hearings in which defense policies were reviewed. The result was a strengthening of the Department of National Defense above the three services and an understanding that the air force concept of strategic bombing would be given adequate weight.[23]

The Mutual Defense Assistance Act, authorizing military aid to Western Europe, which had lagged before the president's announcement, was acted upon by the Joint Congressional Committee on Atomic Energy on September 26, 1949, passed the House and Senate on September 28 by large majorities and was signed by the president on October 6. The foreign Economic Recovery Act was passed on September 29 and signed by the president on October 6. The House approved on October 14 the military-aid appropriations which the president had requested on October 10. The Senate approved on October 17 and the measure was signed by the president on October 28. On October 18 Congress approved national-defense appropriations of $15\frac{1}{2}$ billion dollars for the year and the bill was signed by the president on October 29.

During October Congress repealed the rider which had limited Atomic Energy Commission expenditure and on October 20 President Truman stated that Congress would be asked to approve an expansion of the atomic energy program. On October 25 the Atomic Energy Commission stated that it was planning to spend 300 million on expansion. According to one commentator writing in the autumn of 1949 "the desire to assure United States pre-eminence in atomic weapons is Washington's primary response to the Asiatic explosion. The next impulse has been: perfect civilian defense. The Joint Committee expects to hold hearings on this subject next year." [24]

The problem of atomic energy development in the United States received public attention through the congressional investigation of the commission which had been begun before the president's announcement. The majority report declared "Russian ownership of the bomb is a monumental challenge to American boldness, initiative, and effort." [25]

A statement on November 1 by Senator Johnson of Colorado, a member of the Joint Congressional Committee on Atomic Energy, precipitated discussion of a hydrogen bomb, one thousand times more powerful than the Nagasaki bomb, on which the United States was said to have made "considerable progress." Senator Johnson, in publicly referring to this, to American possession of a bomb six times as powerful as the Nagasaki bomb, and to a defensive device that will detonate an enemy's atomic weapon before it reaches its target, aroused discussion of the need for more secrecy in the Atomic Energy Commission and among congressmen informed of its activities. Opinions were sharply divided on the problem of secrecy. Senator Johnson's utterance may have been designed to "intimidate weak nerves." On November 29 plans for new atom bomb experiments in Eniwetok Atoll in the Pacific were announced by the Atomic Energy Commission and the Department of National Defense.[26]

Another direction of defense preparation was evident in the rumors which developed during the autumn of a policy for rearming Western Germany. On October 17, 1949, the United States replied to the Soviet note of October 1 rejecting charges of militarism in Western Germany and accusing the Soviet Union of rearming the Eastern Zone through paramilitary police forces. On November 16 Secretary Acheson denied that he or any of his staff had discussed the possibility of raising a German army and the next day President Truman denied that the formation of a Western German army was being considered. On November 27 General Bradley in Paris said, "We do not favor rearmament of Germany at this time." Senator Thomas, Chairman of the Senate Armed Services Committee, however, told a press conference in Paris that he favored provision of some German divisions. Field Marshall Montgomery, chief of staff of the Brussels powers, on his visit to the United States at the end of November to confer on Western Union defense problems was reported to have said that the defense of Western Europe required the rearmament of Germany, particularly as Eastern Germany was being rearmed under communist auspices. Public opinion, he was reported to have thought, must be prepared for this development. Field Marshal Montgomery had met with the Defense Committee on the Brussels powers in London on November 23 and decisions had been made perfecting defenses and setting up measures of coördination with the North Atlantic Committee.

These defense preparations by the United States were paralleled by defense activities of the Soviet Union. The arms race accelerated and acrimonious discussions went on between the two countries both inside and outside the United Nations. These discussions concerned particularly Germany and atomic energy control. The Soviet Union tightened its ideological control in its zone in Europe with the exception of Yugoslavia, and communism won in China. Finally, President Truman announced American intention to proceed with the construction of the hydrogen bomb.

Conciliation of Russia

New consideration was given in many quarters to the possibility of conciliation with Russia after the September 23 announcement. Opinion both official and unofficial appears to have been sharply divided whether further preparedness, or more active efforts for conciliation, or both were called for by the new situation. Even the military strategists on some occasions expressed doubt whether military superiority in atomic weapons as well as in other weapons, which it is their business to establish, can yield a high degree of security. Some of them called for international control or better political relations.[27]

A quaker proposal on American-Russian relations was given publicity during the autumn. It called for recognition that both "communist" and "democratic" societies would coexist in the world for a long time, for conciliation of attitudes and opinions, for more trade between the halves of the world, and for unification and neutralization of Germany.

Among the atomic scientists, Harold Urey insisted on the need to develop the North Atlantic powers into a true federation [28] and Leo Szilard proposed neutralization not only of Germany but of the whole of Western Europe. He suggested that France and the Low Countries might come to doubt the capacity of the North Atlantic pact to defend them as the Soviet stock of atom bombs increased, and might come to consider neutrality as a safer course. Professor Szilard proposed neutralization, demilitarization, and unification of Germany perhaps including Austria and some former German territories under Polish occupation. He also proposed that France and the Low Countries form a neutral bloc with a unilateral United States guarantee to make war on the Soviet Union if it violated that neutrality. The plan called for a Western European customs union, including Germany, and for general disarmament, including atomic weapons, sanctioned by a system of inspection.[29]

The abundance of ideas looking toward conciliation as well as toward defense and the honest efforts to rethink the problem and to break the deadlock, indicated the seriousness with which officials and thinkers viewed the problem of an atomic arms race in the bipolar world. From these discussions several points seem to emerge.

1. While some elaborate and comprehensive plans were proposed, thinking tended to doubt the feasibility of large settlements and to look toward a long process of negotiation, each step of which would deal with one matter ripe for agreement.

2. In line with this thought, attention was particularly directed to the possibilities of a short-run or interim agreement for atomic energy control leaving the elaboration of a permanent comprehensive system of control for the future.

3. Political sanctions such as fear of mutual retaliation and recognition of mutual interest were given more weight than legal or collective sanctions.

4. The concept of absolute security was coming to be recognized as utopian. The question was being asked: In what direction can most relative security be found?

5. From this point of view, the opinion grew that a race for military superiority offers less prospect of security than do political efforts directed toward reduction of tensions and conciliation.

6. Finally, there was a growing impatience with reiteration of positions which had for a long period of time offered nothing but frustration, and a demand for constructive thinking. According to one observer:

> The one hopeful element in the present Washington picture may lie in the intrinsic contradictions in our policies. The State Department professes to look to international control for a solution, at the same time it treats negotiation as hopeless. The Department of Defense relies upon a military strategy which centers upon the atomic bomb without being at all clear under precisely what circumstances the nation can or will use it. The Atomic Energy Commission—entrusted with Civilian control—seems to be forced more and more into the limited role of munitions maker. There are some reports that top officials here and there are privately beginning to notice these paradoxes. Sooner or later the paradoxes may cause enough strain to produce some new developments and some new ideas.[30]

Since that statement was written in December, 1949, rising tensions in American opinion have become obvious. The public discussion of the destructiveness of the H-bomb, the speculations whether Russia is already razing mountains with it, and the president's decision to con-

tinue work on it divided opinion between those who put power position first and those who put conciliation first. Acrimonious discussion
concerning China which had come largely under communist control
resulted in a split between the president and Congress and between
Democrats and Republicans on whether the Nationalists should be
aided in Formosa. The Soviet's withdrawal of all representation in organs of the United Nations where Nationalist China continued to be
represented, removed the United Nations for the moment as a forum
for debate with the Soviet Union. There were Soviet threats of a new
blockade of Berlin and congressional demands for new negotiations
with Russia, especially a proposal by Senator McMahon to combine
extensive atomic and conventional disarmament supported by adequate international inspection with large-scale programs of economic
rehabilitation from the money thus saved. After this, the secretary of
state suggested that since the Soviet Union resembled a river which
would flow down unless diverted by material barriers, treaties with that
country were worthless unless they merely recorded a state of facts. The
public was unconvinced, but further frustrated. The Soviet acquisition
of the atom bomb resulted in an increase in anxiety and tension on
the American side of the Iron Curtain, in many demands that something
be done, but in no crystallization of opinion on what that should be.

In my opinion the invention of the atom bomb, the airplane, and
the rocket are likely in the long run to revolutionize civilization. As
I said in *Air Affairs* for March, 1947, "In the absence of a world organization which creates general confidence that world politics will
act within legal limits, it is to be expected that the probability of war
will rapidly increase after the shock of the recent war has subsided
and the secret of the atom bomb has become known to all the great
powers." [31]

While the fear of retaliation is an important deterrent, it may not
suffice to prevent war if power political rivalries continue with mounting tensions. I pointed out in the article referred to the circumstances
under which the atomic bombs would probably be used, doubted the
possibility of a stable balance of power or the desirability of a universal
empire, and emphasized the need for world control both of atomic
energy and of war. "Absolutely sovereign nations," I suggested, have
become as obsolete as feudal baronies." [32]

Since writing this nothing has happened to modify my opinion that
efforts to achieve national security by exclusive reliance on either military superiority or a military balance are likely to achieve ruin for all.
Relative security must be sought in political processes for changing
opinions and conciliating differences. The "imponderables" of which

Bismarck spoke must be considered and if possible measured, a procedure which modern social science brings into the realm of the possible. Perhaps American opinions have manifested an instinctive wisdom in paying more attention to events giving evidence of the opinion in, and intentions of, the Soviet Union and of the world community than to those giving evidence of changes in power position. Such attention, however, will be fruitful only if it is directed also to events giving evidence of our own opinions and intentions as others see them, and to the peaceful means of education, discussion, and negotiation for modifying the opinions and intentions of both Russians and Americans so that they will better relate their needs to the changing conditions of the world.

NOTES

NOTES TO CHAPTER 1

1 See Talcott Parsons, *The Social System* (Glencoe, Ill.: Free Press, 1951); W. F. Ogburn and Meyer F. Nimkoff, *Sociology* (New York: Houghton-Mifflin, 1940), p. 557; Walton H. Hamilton, "Institutions," *Encyclopedia of the Social Sciences.*

2 F. M. Thrasher, *The Gang* (University of Chicago Press, 1927); Louis Wirth, *The Ghetto* (University of Chicago Press, 1928).

3 See chap. 16, below.

4 Robert Redfield, "The Primitive World View," *Proceedings, American Philosophical Society*, XCVI (February, 1952), 30 ff.

5 W. F. Ogburn, *Social Change* (University of Chicago Press, 1934), p. 247; Quincy Wright, *A Study of War* (University of Chicago Press, 1942), pp. 403 ff., 1284 ff.

6 Quincy Wright, "Fundamental Problems of International Organization," *International Conciliation* (April, 1941), no. 369, pp. 468 ff.

7 Lester F. Ward, *Pure Sociology* (New York: Macmillan, 1903), pp. 76 ff.

8 Sophinisba P. Breckenridge, "Institutions, Public," *Encyclopedia of the Social Sciences.*

9 George Kennan, "The National Interest of the United States," *Illinois Law Review* (February, 1951); *American Diplomacy, 1900–1950* (University of Chicago Press, 1951), pp. 95 ff.

10 John U. Nef, *War and Human Progress* (Cambridge: Harvard University Press, 1950), pp. 412 ff.

11 Harold D. Lasswell, "Interrelations of World Organization and Society," *Yale Law Journal*, LV (August, 1946), pp. 889 ff.

12 See address of Congressman John T. Wood of Idaho, "The Story of the United Nations," *Congressional Record* (October 15, 1951).

13 Florence Allen, *The Treaty as an Instrument of Legislation* (New York: Macmillan, 1952).

14 Quincy Wright, *A Study of War*, p. 1065; Ithiel de Sola Pool, *Symbols of Internationalism* (Stanford University Press, 1951), p. 57.

15 David Riesman, *The Lonely Crowd* (New Haven: Yale University Press, 1951).

16 W. F. Ogburn, *Social Change;* James B. Conant, *Science and Common Sense* (New Haven: Yale University Press, 1951), pp. 37 ff.

17 Henry Adams, *The Degradation of Democratic Dogma* (New York: Macmillan, 1919).

NOTES TO CHAPTER 2

1 Art. 1, par. 1; art. 2, par. 3.

2 Art. 1, par. 3.

3 Art. 2, pars. 1, 7; art. 27, par. 3.

4 Art. 2, pars. 4, 5; arts. 55, 56; arts. 24, 25, 39–42, 48.

5 Quincy Wright, "Measurement of Variation in International Tensions," in Lyman Bryson, Louis Finkelstein and R. M. MacIver, eds., *Learning and World Peace*, Eighth Symposium, Conference on Science, Philosophy and Religion (New York: Harper, 1948), pp. 54 ff.

6 James B. Conant emphasized the important role of curiosity, speculative concepts, and accident in the advance of fundamental science in contrast to the predominant role of practical aims, empirical knowledge, and directed thought in the advance of technology. *Science and Common Sense* (New Haven: Yale University Press, 1951), pp. 11 ff., 47 ff., 108 ff.

7 Speech in House of Commons, December 12, 1826; Canning, *Speeches* (London, 1836), VI, 111.

8 Psychology and Sociology may provide bases for criticizing the prevailing assumptions of international politics and such criticism may suggest practices modifying the existing conditions of international politics.

9 Quincy Wright, *A Study of War* (University of Chicago Press, 1942), pp. 1025 ff., 1045 ff., 1084 ff.

10 *Ibid.*, pp. 1240 ff., 1466 ff.; Ithiel de Sola Pool, *Symbols of Internationalism* (Stanford University Press, 1951).

11 Quincy Wright, *A Study of War*, pp. 1276 ff., 1284 ff., 1484 ff.

12 Note 5, above, and chaps. 8 and 10, below.

13 Chap. 16, below.

14 Elihu Root, "A Requisite for the Success of Popular Diplomacy," *Foreign Affairs*, VII (September, 1922), 3 ff.

15 Quincy Wright, *A Study of War*, pp. 839 ff.

16 *Ibid.*, pp. 1347 ff.

17 Harold D. Lasswell discusses the problem of education in, and propaganda for, the ideology of "world loyalty" to prepare the world for universal political institutions by developing its "political miranda," "political doctrine," "political formulae," and "political applications." Quincy Wright, ed., *The World Commnity* (University of Chicago Press, 1948), pp. 200 ff. See also Harold D. Lasswell, *World Politics and Personal Insecurity* (New York: McGraw-Hill, 1935), "In Quest of a Myth, the Problem of World Unity," p. 237 ff. Some advocates of world government assume that a world constitution, more centralized than that which now exists, must be established before this educational process can begin. But it is not explained how this can be done unless opinions and attitudes are in some degree prepared. Some advocates of world loyalty prefer to approach the problem by an exposition of desires in respect to the good world, others by an exposition of the trends toward a more united world. *The World Community*, pp. 1 ff., 227.

18 P. B. Potter discusses the problem of institution building in *The World Community*, pp. 259 ff. The problem of institutionalizing the world has been analyzed into interdependent processes developing cultural uniformity, social solidarity, material unification, and institutional integration (*ibid.*, pp. 5 ff.) through propaganda, politics, law, and administration (Quincy Wright, *Study of War*, pp. 1021 ff.). On "fruitful ambiguity" see *The World Community*, pp. 193, 227.

19 These are illustrated in Hans Kelsen's treatise, *The Law of the United Nations* (London: Stevens, 1950).

20 Sir Charles K. Webster, *The Art and Practice of Diplomacy* (London School of Economics and Political Science, 1952), pp. 17 ff.

21 Kelsen, *op. cit.*, pp. xiv–xv and *Supplement,* 1951, pp. 911, 985.

22 Chap. 4, below.

23 W. E. Rappard, "The United Nations as Viewed from Geneva," *American Political Science Review*, XL (June, 1946), p. 549.

24 O. W. Holmes, *The Common Law* (Boston, 1881).

25 This flows from the principle, sometimes referred to "natural law," that no one should be judge in his own case. Hobbes, *Leviathan*, chap. 15; Locke, *Second Treatise of Civil Government*, chap. 2; *Dr. Bonham's Case* (1600), 8 Coke Rep. 107a, 114a. See also Vattel, *Le Droit des gens*, I, Bk. 2, chap. 17, sec. 265.

26 J. L. Brierly, *The Law of Nations* (4th ed., Oxford University Press, 1949), pp. 295 ff.

27 Charter, art. 92.

28 *Ibid.*, art. 94.

29 International Court of Justice, *Statute*, art. 36.

30 For example the question of what constitutes a "republican form of government" guaranteed to the states (Constitution, art. 4, sec. 4), *Luther v. Borden* (1848), 7 How. 1; *Texas v. White* (1868), 7 Wall. 700; *Pacific States Telephone and Telegraph Co. v. Oregon* (1912), 223 U.S. 118.

31 The advisory opinions on article 4 of the Charter may have increased the difficulty of expanding the membership of the United Nations.

32 H. Lauterpacht, "Restrictive Interpretation and the Principle of Effectiveness in the Interpretation of Treaties," *British Year Book of International Law*, 1949, pp. 48 ff.

33 *McCulloch v. Maryland* (1819), 4 Wheat 316.

34 Charter, art. 103.

35 *Ibid.*, art. 39.

36 *Ibid.*, art. 34.

37 These terms, while suggesting less immediacy of hostilities than the terms "breach of the peace" or "act of aggression" (art. 39), suggest more immediacy than the expression "questions relating to the maintenance of international peace and security" (art. 11) and situations "likely to impair the general welfare or friendly relations among nations" (art. 14).

38 This has been especially notable in the attitude of the General Assembly and of the Union of South Africa on the question of the treatment of Indians in South Africa.

39 Wimbledon case, Permanent Court of International Justice, 1923, Series A, No. 1, p. 25; *World Court Reports*, I, 175.

40 Note 39, above.

41 Charter, art. 25.

42 Florence E. Allen, *The Treaty as an Instrument of Legislation*, (New York: Macmillan, 1952).

43 Quincy Wright, "Congress and the Treaty Making Power," *Proceedings, American Society of International Law*, 1952, pp. 43 ff.

44 Charter, art. 33.

45 General Assembly, Resolution, November 14, 1947, U.N. Doc. A, p. 459, *American Journal of International Law*, XLII (January, 1948), p. 17.

46 Herman Pritchett, *The Roosevelt Court* (New York: Macmillan, 1948).

47 As for example in the Munich agreement of September, 1938, in which the rights of Czechoslovakia were sacrificed by agreement of Great Britain, France, Italy, and Germany to appease Hitler. Quincy Wright, "The Munich Settlement and International Law," *American Journal of International Law*, XXXIII (January, 1939), 12 ff.

48 Quincy Wright, "The Problem of Establishing and Maintaining a Stable World Society," in Bryson, Finkelstein, and MacIver, eds., *Perspectives on a Troubled Decade*, 10th Symposium on Science, Philosophy and Religion (New York: Harper, 1950), p. 286.

49 After Director Julian Huxley's pamphlet, suggesting "evolutionary humanism" as a philosophy of UNESCO, had been attacked by the advocates of "dialectical materialism" and of Christianity in the first conference, 1946, he came to see that "efforts to draw up such theoretical principles might be actively harmful, for attempts at precise formulation would almost certainly provoke exacerbating conflicts of ideology." UNESCO, Report of the Director General for 1947, p. 11.

50 *Human Rights, Comments and Interpretation*, A Symposium prepared by UNESCO, with an Introduction by Jacques Maritain (London: Allan Wingate, 1948).

51 Quincy Wright, "National Courts and Human Rights—The Fujii Case," *American Journal of International Law*, XL (January, 1951), 76 ff.

NOTES TO CHAPTER 3

1 Peter Duponceau, *Jurisdiction of the Courts of the United States* (Philadelphia: 1824), p. 3; Quincy Wright, *The Control of American Foreign Relations* (New York: Macmillan, 1922), p. 58.

2 Tyler Dennett, *Americans in Eastern Asia* (New York: Macmillan, 1922), pp. 677 ff.

3 Senator Elbert Thomas, *Congressional Record*, Senate, February 22, 1937.

4 John E. Stoner, *S. O. Levinson and the Pact of Paris* (University of Chicago Press, 1943), pp. 191 ff.

5 Quincy Wright, "Neutrality Following the Pact of Paris," *Proceedings, American Society of International Law*, 1930, pp. 81 ff.; "Meaning of the Pact of Paris," *American Journal of International Law*, XXVII (January, 1933), 59 ff.; "The Law of the Nuremberg Trial," *ibid.*, XLI (January, 1947), 64.

6 Sara R. Smith, *The Manchurian Crisis, 1931–1932* (New York: Columbia University Press, 1948).

7 Cordell Hull, *Memoirs* (New York: Macmillan, 1948), p. 666. See Department of State, *Peace and War, United States Foreign Policy, 1931–1941* (Washington: 1943), p. 3.

8 Hull, *op. cit.*, p. 545.

9 Quincy Wright, *A Study of War* (University of Chicago Press, 1942), pp. 1065, 1251.

10 *United Nations Bulletin*, IX (October 15 and November 15, 1950), 348, 508; Commission to Study the Organization of Peace, *Sixth Report, Collective Self-Defense Under the United Nations* (New York: May, 1948); U.S. Congress, Senate, 81st Cong., 1st sess., Con. Res. 52, introduced July 8, 1948, by Senator Thomas of Utah and Senator Douglas of Illinois; discussion of this resolution in the Senate, *Congressional Record*, July 13 and 18, 1949, and in hearings before the subcommittee of the Senate Committee on Foreign Relations on "Revision of the United Nations Charter," February 2, 15, 1950, pp. 1–71, 415–427, 743–753.

11 Edmund Burke, "Speech to the Electors of Bristol, 1774," *Burke's Speeches*, Everyman's ed., pp. 72 ff.

12 C. Wilfred Jenks, "Some Legal Aspects of the Financing of International Institutions," *Grotius Society*, XXV (London: Longmans, 1943), 87 ff.; Commission to Study the Organization of Peace, *Independent Sources of Revenue for the United Nations* (mimeographed; December, 1948). On the proposal for the organization of a United Nations Postal Administration, see U.N. General Assembly, Resolution 342, (IV) October 20, 1949 and Report of the Secretary General, September, 1950.

13 Quincy Wright, *Control of American Foreign Relations* (New York: Macmillan, 1922), pp. 284 ff.; "Constitutional Procedure in the United States for carrying out Obligations for Military Sanctions," *American Journal of International Law*, XXXVIII (October, 1944), 678 ff.

14 J. Reuben Clark, *Right to Protect Citizens in Foreign Countries by Landing Forces* (3d rev. ed.; Washington: Government Printing Office, 1934).

15 *The Prize Cases* (1862), 2 Black 635.

16 Paul Douglas, Ill., *Congressional Record*, Senate, July 5, 1950.

17 Emory Upton, *The Military Policy of the United States*, 62d Cong., 2d sess., S. Doc. 494 (1912), pp. 96 ff. Quincy Wright, "A Report on the Military Department of the State of Illinois," from *Report of the Efficiency and Economy Committee, State of Illinois* (Chicago: Windermere Press, 1915), p. 897.

18 Commission to Study the Organization of Peace, *United Nations Guards*, September, 1948; *United Nations Guards and Technical Field Services*, September, 1949.

19 David Hunter Miller, *The Drafting of the Covenant* (New York: Putnam, 1928), I, 19.

20 Assembly Resolution C, "Uniting for Peace," November 2, 1950, *United Nations Bulletin*, IX (November 15, 1950), p. 509.

21 Quincy Wright, et al., *The World at the Cross Roads, The United Nations* (Chicago: World Citizens Association, 1946), pp. 37 ff.

NOTES TO CHAPTER 4

1 Georg Simmel, "The Sociology of Conflict," *American Journal of Sociology,* IX (1904), 490; R. E. Park and Ernest Burgess, *Introduction to the Science of Sociology* (2d ed., University of Chicago Press, 1924), p. 582; W. F. Ogburn and M. F. Nimkoff, *Sociology* (New York: Houghton Mifflin, 1940), pp. 844 ff.; Quincy Wright, *A Study of War* (University of Chicago Press, 1942), p. 957.

2 Wright, *op. cit.,* pp. 1015 ff.

3 W. F. Ogburn, *Social Change* (University of Chicago Press, 1934); Wright, *op. cit.,* p. 1284.

4 T. P. Wright, *Aviation's Place in Civilization,* Wilbur Wright Memorial Lecture (London, 1945), p. 4.

5 Eugene Staley, *World Economy in Transition* (New York: Council on Foreign Relations, 1939), pp. 51 ff.

6 Frances DeLaisi, *Political Myths and Economic Realities* (New York: Viking Press, 1927).

7 Karl Mannheim, *Ideology and Utopia* (New York: Harcourt, Brace & Co., 1936); Quincy Wright, *op. cit.,* pp. 358, 1032.

8 Wright, *op. cit.,* pp. 975 ff.

9 Wright, *op. cit.,* pp. 1240 ff.

10 George Sarton, *Introduction to the History of Science* (Washington: Carnegie Institution, 1927), introductory chapter.

11 Wright, *op. cit.,* pp, 169 ff.

12 Arnold Toynbee, *A Study of History* (1st edition; London: Oxford University Press, 1934).

13 Franz Alexander, *Our Age of Unreason* (New York: Lippincott, 1942), p. 339; Quincy Wright, *op. cit.,* pp. 403–405.

14 Wright, *op. cit.,* pp. 103–119, 678.

15 *Ibid.,* 1456.

16 *Ibid.,* pp. 757, 1493.

17 Franciscus de Victoria, *De Jure Belli* (Washington: Carnegie, Bate's trans., 1917), par. 13, See also Balthazar Ayala, *De Jure et Officiis Bellicis et Disciplina Militari* (Washington: Carnegie, Bate's trans., 1912), chap. 2, par. 11.

18 Alberico Gentili, *De Jure Belli* (London: Carnegie, Rolfe's trans., 1933), chap. 14, p. 66.

19 Hugo Grotius, *De Jure Belli ac Pacis* (London: Carnegie, Kelsey's trans., 1925), chap. 22, par. 5.

20 Samuel Pufendorf, *De Jure Naturae et Gentium,* 1688 (London: Carnegie ed., 1934), VIII, chap. 6, par. 5.

21 Christian Wolff, *Jus Gentium Methodo Scientifica Pertractatum,* 1749 (London: Carnegie ed., 1934), chap. 6, pars. 617, 646–652.

22 E. de Vattel, *Le Droit des Gens,* 1758 (Washington: Carnegie ed., Fenwick's trans., 1916), III, chap. 3, par. 44, pp. 248–249.

23 *Ibid.,* par. 49, pp. 251–252.

24 *Ibid.,* par. 50, pp. 252–253.

25 See L. Oppenheim, *International Law,* (5th ed., London: Longmans, 1935), II, par. 136; G. G. Wilson, *International Law* (3d ed., St. Paul: West, 1939), p. 64.

26 Quincy Wright, "Peace and Political Organization," *International Conciliation* (April, 1941), no. 369, p. 457.

27 Quincy Wright, *A Study of War,* pp. 1169–1172.

28 Whether technological changes have rendered obsolete the opinion which has sustained free enterprise economy is highly controversial. See F. A. Hayek, *The Road to Serfdom* (University of Chicago Press, 1944), pp. 43 ff.

29 Quincy Wright, "The Historical Circumstances of Enduring Peace," *Annual Report, American Historical Association* (1942), II, 361.

30 The worst wars of the century were the Taiping rebellion in China (1850–1864), the Lopez war of Paraguay (1865–1870), and the American Civil War (1861–1865). The Crimean (1854–1856), Italian (1859), Austro-Prussian (1866) and Franco-Prussian (1870) wars occured in Europe during the same period but were much less costly in life and property. *Ibid.*, p. 365.

31 Quincy Wright, *A Study of War*, pp. 298–300, 758–766.

32 W. E. Rappard, *The Quest for Peace Since the World War* (Cambridge: Harvard University Press, 1940), pp. 474 ff.

33 Quincy Wright, "The Outlawry of War," *American Journal of International Law* XIX (January, 1925), 76; *idem*, "Neutrality and Neutral Rights Following the Pact of Paris," *Proceedings, American Society of International Law*, 1930, p. 79; *idem*, "The Meaning of the Pact of Paris," *American Journal of International Law*, XXVII (January, 1935), 39; *ibid.*, "The Present Status of Neutrality" XXXIV (July, 1940), 391; Quincy Wright, *A Study of War*, pp. 891–894; International Law Association, "Budapest Articles of Interpretation," *Report*, 38th Conference (1934), p. 66; Research in International Law, Harvard Law School, "Draft Convention on Rights and Duties of States in Case of Aggression," *American Journal of International Law, Supplement*, XXXIII (1939), 823; Attorney General Robert H. Jackson, "Address," Habana, Cuba, *American Journal of International Law*, XXXV (April, 1941), 348, 354; International Military Tribunal, *Trial of the Major War Criminals . . .* (Nuremberg: 1947), I, 218 ff.

34 E. H. Carr, *The Twenty Years' Crisis, 1919–1939* (New York: Macmillan, 1939), pp. 39, 277, 298; Rappard, *op. cit.*, pp. 486 ff.; E. Benes, R. Coulborn and A. Feiler, *International Security* (University of Chicago Press, 1939); Quincy Wright, *A Study of War*, pp. 1055 ff.

35 Hans J. Morgenthau, ed., *Peace, Security and the United Nations* (University of Chicago Press, 1946); H. H. Arnold, J. R. Oppenheimer, W. Lippmann, H. Urey *et al.*, *One World or None* (New York: McGraw-Hill, 1946).

36 The transitions from the Period of Warring States to the Ts'in emperor in China (221 B.C.) and from the hellenistic period to the Roman Empire (31 B.C.) illustrate the development of this condition. See Toynbee, *A Study of History* (1st ed., London: Oxford University Press, 1934), I; Quincy Wright, *A Study of War*, pp. 117, 463, 575 ff., 760–766.

37 Wright, *op. cit.*, pp. 382, 755, 763.

38 Wm. T. R. Fox wrote, however, "Since the centers of greatest power are more widely separated than heretofore, the new military situation makes it enormously difficult for one super-power to defeat another. Wars between the powers of first rank will necessarily be protracted, far-flung, and indecisive. All ought, therefore, to be anxious to avoid such a conflict. . . . Relatively small variations in military power will not jeopardize the military security of any of the super-powers. The possibility of settling disputes by compromise or by reference to the merits of the dispute ought correspondingly to be enlarged." *The Super-Powers* (New York: Harcourt, Brace & Co., 1944), pp. 22, 23. This was written before Hiroshima, and since that event Dr. Fox [B. Brodie, ed., *The Absolute Weapon* (New York: Harcourt, Brace & Co., 1946), pp. 1–78, 196–197] seems to have less faith in an equilibrium dependent on retaliation than some of his colleagues (*ibid.*, pp. 16, 76, 134).

39 Clarence Streit, *Union Now* (New York: Harper, 1939); Emery Reves, *The Anatomy of Peace* (New York: Harper, 1945).

40 A. Wolfers in Brodie, ed., *The Absolute Weapon* (New York: Harcourt, Brace & Co., 1946), p. 116.

41 Quincy Wright, *A Study of War*, pp. 982–986.

42 *Ibid.*, pp. 117, 963, 969.

43 Quincy Wright, "International Law and the World Order" in Laves, ed., *The*

Foundation of a More Stable World Order (University of Chicago Press, 1941), pp. 107 ff.; *A Study of War*, pp. 907–916, 935–952.

[44] J. F. Dulles, "Thoughts on Soviet Foreign Policy and What to Do About It," *Life*, (June 3, 1946), p. 112, (June 10, 1946), p. 118.

[45] Quincy Wright, *A Study of War*, pp. 117, 963, 969. But see F. Alexander, *Our Age of Unreason* (New York: Lippincott, 1942), p. 331.

[46] Quincy Wright, *A Study of War*, pp. 1087–1089, 1207–1211, 1466–1481.

NOTES TO CHAPTER 5

[1] See Preamble and Article 1 of the Charter.

[2] *New York Herald Tribune*, August 16, 1948.

[3] *Public Opinion Quarterly* XII (Summer, 1948), 354, 360, 369.

[4] United Nations, *Annual Report of the Secretary-General on the Work of the Organization* (1948), p. 115.

[5] *Public Opinion Quarterly*, XII (Summer, 1948), 368.

[6] United Nations, *op. cit.*, pp. xvii–xviii. See also Commission to Study the Organization of Peace, *Recommendation on United Nations Guards* (September, 1948).

[7] It is also interesting to notice that the Supreme Court of the United States in refusing to allow judicial aid for the enforcement of restrictive covenants referred to a brief before it relating the problem to the human-rights articles in the Charter, although it actually rested its opinion upon the provisions of the fifth and fourteenth amendments to the Constitution. *Shelley v. Kraemer* (1948), 68 U.S. 836, 849–850.

[8] U.N. Doc. A/578 (July 15, 1948).

[9] Commission to Study the Organization of Peace, *Sixth Report, Collective Self-Defense under the United Nations* (New York: May, 1948).

[10] A. Loveday, "An Unfortunate Decision," *International Organization*, I (June, 1947), 279.

[11] See Article 55 of the Charter.

[12] United Nations, *op. cit.*, p. 114 f.

[13] "We must never forget that it is a constitution we are expounding. . . . Let the end be legitimate, let it be within the scope of the constitution, and all means which are appropriate, which are plainly adapted to that end, which are not prohibited, but consist with the letter and spirit of the constitution, are constitutional." *McCulloch v. Maryland* (1819), 4 Wheat. 316. See also *Gibbons v. Ogden* (1824), 9 Wheat. 1, 187–189.

[14] Quincy Wright, *A Study of War* (University of Chicago Press, 1942), p. 1332.

[15] Chap. 4, above.

[16] Wright, *op. cit.*, pp. 1332–1362.

NOTES TO CHAPTER 6

[1] "For the first time in history, the nations who want peace have taken up arms under the banner of an international organization to put down aggression. Under that banner, the banner of the United Nations, they are succeeding. This is a tremendous step forward in the age old struggle to establish the rule of law in the world. . . . Today as a result of the Korean struggle, the United Nations is stronger than it has ever been. We know now that the United Nations can create a system of international order with the authority to maintain peace." President Truman, address in San Francisco, October 17, 1950, *Department of State Bulletin*, XXIII (October 30, 1950), 683.

[2] "The truth, as I see it, was demonstrated by the League of Nations and is now, I believe, confirmed in Korea. It is that a universal society cannot enforce peace by collective action and will be destroyed if it tries. The reason collective security is an unworkable principle was expounded by Alexander Hamilton in the fifteenth of the *Federalist Papers:* 'Every breach of the laws must involve a state of war; and military

execution must become the only instrument of obedience.' " Walter Lippmann, *New York Herald Tribune*, January 15, 1951.

3 *United Nations Bulletin*, IX (November 15, 1950), 508 ff.

4 I have discussed the legal, political, psychological, and technical aspects of collective security in "The Outlawry of War," *American Journal of International Law*, XIX (January, 1925), 96 ff.; "The Present Status of Neutrality," *ibid.*, XXXIV (July, 1940), 346 ff.; "Peace and Political Organization," *International Conciliation* (April, 1941), no. 369, pp. 454 ff.; "Fundamental Problems of International Organization," *ibid.*, pp. 468 ff.; *A Study of War* (University of Chicago Press, 1942), pp. 1043–1076; "International Law and the Balance of Power," *American Journal of International Law*, XXXVII (January, 1943), 97 ff.; "National Security and International Police," *ibid.*, pp. 502 ff.; "Peace Problems of Today and Yesterday," *American Political Science Review*, XXXVIII (June, 1944), 516 ff.; "Enforcement of International Law," *Proceedings, American Society of International Law*, 1944, pp. 77 ff.

5 *United Nations Bulletin*, IX (July 15, 1950), 65 ff. See also United Nations Department of Public Information, *Korea and the United Nations* (October, 1950), and Department of State, *United States Policy in the Korean Crisis* (July, 1950).

6 Biweekly reports by General MacArthur, beginning July 25, 1950, were transmitted by the United States representative to the Security Council in accord with its resolution of July 7, 1950. The special report of November 8, 1950, indicating Chinese intervention was published in *United Nations Bulletin*, IX (November 15, 1950), 534 ff. For debate on this, see *ibid.*, IX (December 1, 1950), 594 ff.

7 Note 5, above.

8 Hans Kelsen, *The Law of the United Nations* (London: Stevens, 1950), pp. 239 ff.; F. B. Schick, "Videant Consules," *Western Political Quarterly*, III (September, 1950), 311 ff.; Leo Gross, "Voting in the Security Council: Abstention from Voting and Absence from Meeting," *Yale Law Journal*, LX (February, 1951), 209 ff.

9 Myres S. McDougal and Richard N. Gardner, "The Veto and the Charter: An Interpretation for Survival," *Yale Law Journal* LX (February, 1951), 258 ff.; Jiménez Aréchega, *Voting and the Handling of Disputes in the Security Council* (New York: Carnegie Endowment for International Peace, 1950), pp. 17 ff.; Leland Goodrich and Edvard Hambro, *Charter of the United Nations, Commentary and Documents* (Boston: World Peace Foundation, 1949), p. 223.

10 Each principal organ is authorized by the Charter to make its own rules of procedure and the determination of the validity of credentials of representatives has been provided for in these rules.

11 Quincy Wright, "Some Thoughts on Recognition," *American Journal of International Law*, XLIV (July, 1950), 553.

12 Goodrich and Hambro, *op. cit.*, pp. 547 ff. An interpretation of any article given by the International Court of Justice in an advisory opinion or judgment should undoubtedly have great weight, *ibid.*, pp. 21, 549.

13 McDougal and Gardner, *op. cit.*, pp. 289 ff.; Goodrich and Hambro, *op. cit.*, pp. 169 ff.

14 Note 6, above.

15 *United Nations Bulletin*, X (February 15, 1951), 151.

16 A study of the activities of the League of Nations Assembly suggested that it had an important function to perform in emphasizing principles, but that it was not as well adapted as the Council to "the delicate process of negotiation," and that disputes should not be referred to so large a body except as "an extraordinary measure." Margaret E. Burton, *The Assembly of the League of Nations* (University of Chicago Press, 1941), p. 381.

17 Quincy Wright, "Constitutional Procedures in the United States for Carrying Out Obligations of Military Sanctions," *American Journal of International Law*, XXXVIII (October, 1944), 678; *Control of American Foreign Relations* (New York: Macmillan, 1922), pp. 305 ff.; U.S. Congress, Senate, "Power of the President to Send Armed Forces Outside the United States," *Report to the Committee on Foreign Rela-*

tions and Committee on Armed Services, 82d Cong., 1st sess. (February 28, 1951).

18 Department of State, *Korea and the United Nations* (July, 1950), p. 89.

19 Statement of U.S. Representative Harding Bancroft, *Department of State Bulletin,* XXIV (March 19, 1951), 462.

20 Note 5, above. See also *United Nations Bulletin,* X (February 15, 1951), 160; Brookings Institution, *Current Developments in United States Foreign Policy,* IV (January, 1951), 452.

21 See statement by Sir Gladwyn Jebb, U.K. representative, Security Council, January 31, 1951, *United Nations Bulletin,* X (February 15, 1951), 160. The General Assembly finally did place the question of Chinese Communist intervention on its agenda on Dec. 1, 1950, after the Soviet veto of the Security Council resolution which was supposed to deal with this question on November 30; *ibid.,* IX (December 15, 1950), p. 658.

22 *United Nations Bulletin,* IX (November 1, 1950), 449; *International Organization,* V (February, 1951), 231 ff.

23 *United Nations Bulletin,* IX (December 15, 1950), 672.

24 *Ibid.,* X (January 1, 1951), 4 ff.; *International Organization,* V (February, 1951), 233.

25 *United Nations Bulletin,* X (February 1, 1951), 106 ff.

26 *Ibid.,* X (February 15, 1951), 151. See also pp. 146 ff. See address before the Political Committee of the General Assembly by U.S. Representative Austin, January 18, 27, 1951, *Department of State Bulletin,* XXIV (January 29, February 5, 1951), 166 ff., 206 ff. The U.S. House of Representatives and Senate passed resolutions on January 19 and 23, 1951, urging the United Nations to declare the Chinese Communists aggressors. The Senate resolution added the opinion that Communist China should not be admitted to represent China in the United Nations, *ibid.,* pp. 168, 208. In an address of May 1, 1951, Ambassador Austin distinguished the military objectives of the United Nations to repel aggression and restore international peace and security in the area of South Korea from the political objective to establish a unified independent and democratic government in the sovereign state of Korea. "The United Nations," he said, "has not declared, nor has it ever been asked to declare, that the political objectives must be achieved by military means. . . . The policy of the United Nations has been—and should always be—to achieve its political objectives by pacific settlements." In his address of April 11, 1951, President Truman said, "We do not want to widen the conflict. We will use every effort to prevent that disaster." *Department of State Bulletin,* XXIV (April 16, 1951), 605.

27 This situation was referred to immediately after Chinese Communist intervention in the High Command's report of November 6 and December 27, 1950, Department of State, *United Nations Action in Korea,* 8th, 9th and 10th reports to the Security Council, pp. 12, 22. See also 15th and 16th reports, February 15, 28, 1951, *Department of State Bulletin,* XXIV, (April 16, 1951), 626, 633.

28 Discussion by the High Command of such issues as extending operations across the 38th parallel, bombing bases in Chinese territory, and the matters which should be dealt with in peace negotiations might easily have been taken by the Chinese Communists as evidence of United Nations or United States political intentions. See Brookings Institution, *Current Developments in United States Foreign Policy,* IV (March, 1951), 40 ff.

29 See radio broadcast by President Truman, April 11, 1951, relieving General Mac-Arthur of his commands "so that there could be no doubt as to the real purpose and aims of our policy." *Department of State Bulletin,* XXIV (April 16, 1951), 605.

30 This purpose is hardly served by the provision for the appointment by the secretary-general with approval of the Collective Measures Committee of a panel of military experts to give technical advice to members on the organization, training, and equipment of earmarked units for prompt service with the United Nations. See *United Nations Bulletin,* IX (November 15, 1951), 509. See also statements by Harding Bancroft to Collective Measures Committee, March 5, 1951, *Department of State Bulletin,* XXIV (March 19, 1951), 461.

31 Note 2, above.

32 In his address of May 1, 1951 (note 26, above), Ambassador Austin, with General MacArthur's statement "there is no substitute for victory" in mind, said: "The fight to stop aggression in Korea is a fight to prevent it everywhere else in the world. The aim is not to settle political issues by force, but to prevent the aggressor from imposing a settlement by force. The aim is not conflict without limit, but peace without appeasement. That is the victory we seek."

33 Quincy Wright, "American Policy Toward Russia," *World Politics*, II (Summer, 1950), 464; see chaps. 4, 5, above; chap. 8, below.

34 The Collective Measures Committee established by the Uniting for Peace resolution might function in this way.

35 Note 33, above.

36 George F. Kennan, "America and the Russian Future," *Foreign Affairs*, XXIX (April, 1951), 351 ff.

37 Quincy Wright, "Freedom and Responsibility in Respect to Transnational Communication," *Proceedings, American Society of International Law*, 1950, pp. 95 ff.; "International Law and Commercial Relations," *ibid.*, 1941, pp. 30 ff.

38 Quincy Wright, *Control of American Foreign Relations*, pp. 360 ff.

39 Note 17, above.

40 Quincy Wright, *A Study of War* (University of Chicago Press, 1942), pp. 893 ff.; note 38, above.

NOTES TO CHAPTER 8

1 Quincy Wright, *A Study of War* (University of Chicago Press, 1942), pp. 16, 681 ff., 1358 ff.

2 *Ibid.*, pp. 43, 68, 74 ff., 379.

3 *Ibid.*, pp. 217, 379, 402 ff., 1332 ff.

4 *Ibid.*, pp. 743 ff.

5 Quincy Wright, "The Historic Circumstances of Enduring Peace," *Annual Report, American Historical Association*, III (1942), 364 ff.

6 Quincy Wright, "The Balance of Power," in H. W. Weigert and Vilhjalmur Stefansson, editors, *Compass of the World* (New York: Macmillan, 1944), p. 53 ff.

7 Chap. 4, above.

8 Quincy Wright, *A Study of War*, pp. 1316, 1328.

9 The Constitution of UNESCO declares: "Since wars begin in the minds of men, it is in the minds of men that the defenses of peace must be constructed."

10 Chap. 10, below.

11 Quincy Wright, *A Study of War*, p. 73.

12 *Ibid.*, pp. 956 ff., 1103 ff., 1218 ff.

13 *Ibid.*, p. 972 ff.

14 Hague Regulations of Land Warfare, 1907, arts. 32–40; U.S. War Department, *Basic Field Manual, Rules of Land Warfare*, arts. 215–270.

15 George Kennan, "Is War With Russia Inevitable?", *Readers Digest* (March, 1950), p. 6; Quincy Wright, ed., *A Foreign Policy for the United States* (University of Chicago Press, 1947), p. 41.

16 E. R. Stettinius, Jr., *Roosevelt and the Russians* (New York: Doubleday, 1949), pp. 140, 295.

17 Quincy Wright, *A Study of War*, pp. 380, 776, 969, 1018, 1043 ff., 1072, 1284 ff.; chap. 5, above.

18 Charles E. Merriam, *The Making of Citizens* (University of Chicago Press, 1931).

19 Quincy Wright, *A Study of War*, p. 975; *The World Community* (University of Chicago Press, 1948), p. 5 ff.

NOTES TO CHAPTER 9

1 Quincy Wright, *A Study of War* (University of Chicago Press, 1942), pp. 699, 956.

2 *Ibid.*, pp. 8, 341, 891. See also Quincy Wright, "Neutrality and Neutral Rights Following the Pact of Paris," *Proceedings, American Society of International Law*, 1930, p. 86; chap. 17, below.

3 Quincy Wright, *A Study of War*, pp. 9, 685.

4 Kurt Singer, "The Meaning of Conflict," *Australian Journal of Philosophy* (December, 1949); *The Idea of Conflict* (Melbourne University Press, 1941), pp. 13 ff.

5 Majid Khadduri, *The Law of War and Peace in Islam* (London: Luzac, 1940), p. 20.

6 Naval War College, *International Law Documents* (Washington: Government Printing Office, 1917), pp. 17, 220.

7 George Fort Milton, *The Eve of Conflict: Stephen A. Douglas and the Needless War* (New York: Houghton Mifflin, 1934), p. 608. "There is no scientific validity in the phrase 'inherent contradiction' and 'inevitable conflict.' In so far as they are not just untrue, they merely express a pessimistic conviction that human beings will always fail to find a sensible method of resolving a dangerous situation." R. H. Crossman, "Reflections on the Cold War," *The Political Quarterly*, XXII (January, 1951), 10.

8 Chap. 10, below.

9 Quincy Wright, "Measurement of Variations in International Tensions," in Bryson, Finkelstein, and MacIver, eds., *Learning and World Peace*, Eighth Symposium, Conference on Science, Philosophy and Religion (New York: Harper, 1948), p. 54.

10 Quincy Wright, *A Study of War*, p. 959. On factors making for extreme tensions, see pp. 1107 ff.

11 *Ibid.*, pp. 684 ff.

12 *Ibid.*, pp. 1410 ff. This process is illustrated in various forms of the duel.

13 *Ibid.*, p. 1439. See also R. E. Park, and E. Burgess, *Introduction to the Science of Sociology* (University of Chicago Press, 1924), pp. 574 ff.; W. F. Ogburn and M. F. Nimkoff, *Sociology* (New York: Houghton Mifflin, 1940), pp. 346, 369. Kurt Singer defines conflict as "a critical state of tension occasioned by the presence of mutually incompatible tendencies within an organismic whole the functional continuity or structural integrity of which is thereby threatened." "The Resolution of Conflict," *Social Research*, XVI (December, 1949), 230.

14 Quincy Wright, *A Study of War*, pp. 42 ff., 497 ff.

15 *Ibid.*, pp. 11, 36 ff.

16 *Ibid.*, pp. 277, 1198. John M. Fletcher, "The Verdict of Psychologists on War Instincts," *Scientific Monthly*, XXXV (August, 1932), 142 ff.

17 Quincy Wright, *A Study of War*, p. 145.

18 Henri Bergson, *Creative Evolution* (New York: Holt, 1911), p. 267.

19 Quincy Wright, *A Study of War*, pp. 517, 957; Georg Simmel, "The Sociology of Conflict," *American Journal of Sociology*, IX (1903), 490; Park and Burgess, *op. cit.*, pp. 1, 583; Robert Waelder, *Psychological Aspects of War and Peace*, Geneva Studies, X (May, 1939), 17 ff.

20 Kurt Singer, "The Meaning of Conflict," *Australian Journal of Philosophy* (December, 1949), pp. 5, 21 ff.; Park and Burgess, *op. cit.*, p. 578.

21 Kurt Singer, *The Idea of Conflict* (Melbourne University Press, 1941), p. 14.

22 Quincy Wright, *A Study of War*, p. 698.

23 *Ibid.*, pp. 720 ff., 1227 ff., 1332 ff.

24 Harold D. Lasswell, "The Garrison State," *American Journal of Sociology*, XLVI (1941), 455; *National Security and Individual Freedom* (New York: McGraw-Hill, 1950); see also Quincy Wright, *A Study of War*, p. 306.

25 Quincy Wright, *A Study of War*, pp. 307 ff.; John U. Nef, *War and Human Progress* (Cambridge: Harvard University Press, 1950), p. 464.

26 Harold D. Lasswell, "The Interrelations of World Organization and Society," *Yale Law Journal*, XV (August, 1946), 889 ff.

27 Chap. 8 above, chap. 10, below.

28 Quincy Wright, *A Study of War,* p. 317.

29 John U. Nef, *op. cit.,* p. 464; Hoffman Nickerson, *Can We Limit War?* (New York: Stokes, 1934).

30 Kurt Singer, "The Meaning of Conflict," *Australian Journal of Philosophy* (December, 1949); "The Resolution of Conflict," *Social Research,* XVI (1949), 230 ff.

31 In a communication to the author dated January 12, 1951, Kurt Singer writes: "I am in fact inclined to emphasize the dangers of identifying conflicts within the mind and within a society still more than you do. . . . But even a modern democracy organized in an 'agnostic' state must be based on decisions—it requires a consensus and a common fund of values and norms, and even the 'agreement to disagree' on the rest and on the mode of settling such differences requires a decision of a very high order. . . . On the other hand I would not equate the individual personality with a monolithic structure and its decision with rigid centralization. In the richest personalities of our culture, Dante, Shakespeare, Goethe, unity (*Gestaltung*) harbours more differences (e.g., Antique and Christian values) than any democracy could hope to manage and which are never reconciled once forever." Singer emphasizes the differences of "decisions" in a complex situation with respect to explicitness rather than with respect to duration. The latter distinction is also important. It may be the essence of science, as of democracy, to accept any solution only tentatively. Scientists know that in time new observations will force reconsideration of the best verified "laws"; and politicians know that in time new opinions will force legislation superseding established "laws."

32 Singer suggests that conflicts may be resolved by (1) integration and constructive action, (2) by sublimation and withdrawal, (3) by resolute contention and fighting, and (4) by regression and yielding. ("The Resolution of Conflict," pp. 230 ff.); Commission to Study the Organization of Peace, 8th Report, *Regional Arrangements* (New York: June, 1953).

33 Arnold J. Toynbee, *A Study of History,* (Oxford University Press, 1935), I, 129 ff.; III, 167.

34 Dewitt C. Poole, "Balance of Power," *Life* (September 22, 1947), 76 ff. Compare with methods of political, legal, physical, and ideological conflict, discussed pp. 149, 152, above.

NOTES TO CHAPTER 10

1 Quincy Wright, "Measurement of Variations in International Tension," in Bryson, Finkelstein, and MacIver, eds., *Learning and World Peace,* Eighth Symposium, Conference on Science, Philosophy and Religion (New York: Harper, 1948), p. 54. See also Harry Stack Sullivan, in Sargent and Smith, eds., *Culture and Personality* (New York: Viking Fund, 1949), p. 175.

2 Lecomte du Noüy, *Human Destiny* (New York: Longmans, 1948), p. 10.

3 Professor Louis Wirth suggests that the problem could be looked at the other way around. Tensions within the larger constellation may produce tensions among the constituent groups and individuals and within the minds of individuals. The group may define the issues for the members. Doubtless the whole and the parts continually interact upon one another, but, from the point of view of controlling the whole, understanding of the influence of the parts upon it may be more useful.

4 A. L. Kroeber, *Anthropology* (New York: Harcourt, Brace & Co., 1922); Robert Lowie, *Culture and Ethnology* (New York: D. C. McMurtrie, 1917), chap. 1; David Bidney explained and criticized this point of view in "Towards a Psycho-cultural Definition of the Concept of Personality," (*Culture and Personality,* pp. 31 ff.) and in "Culture Theory and the Problem of Cultural Crisis," (Bryson, Finkelstein, and MacIver, eds., *Approaches to Group Understanding,* Sixth Symposium, Conference on Science, Philosophy and Religion [New York: Harper, 1947], pp. 553 ff.)

5 Most cultural anthropologists now recognize that personalities within a culture,

especially those of important status, can change cultural traits, some more easily than others. See L. M. Hanks, Jr., and Ralph Linton, in *Culture and Personality*, pp. 107 ff., 163 ff.

6 Erich Fromm and Abram Kardiner point to the influence exerted by the necessities of the society under changing conditions, as interpreted by parents and educators, continually to modify character traits and to develop a "social" or "basic" character adapted to the culture. If conditions change too radically and rapidly, the "social" character may become so incapable of satisfying individual requirements that the educational process can no longer sufficiently inculcate it, and the culture breaks down. *Culture and Personality*, pp. 4 ff., 59 ff.

7 Arnold J. Toynbee, *A Study of History* (Oxford University Press, 1935), III, 232; V, 29.

8 Vilfredo Pareto, *The Mind and Society* (New York: Harcourt, Brace & Co., 1935); Gaetano Mosca, *The Ruling Class* (New York: McGraw Hill, 1939).

9 Anna Freud's experience in educating small children, removed from their homes during the bombing in London during World War II, convinced her of the serious psychic results of depriving children of the security of a single personal protector. (Manuscript, UNESCO, Tensions Study.)

10 Gardiner Murphy refers to the implications of the "field theory," which has superseded atomic theory in the study of electromagnetism, and calls for a new terminology which will not even conceptually separate culture and personality, but will indicate that they constitute two aspects of the same phenomenon. Everyone, he says, has a chameleonlike disposition to conform to conditions and also a beaverlike disposition to keep gnawing whatever happens. *Culture and Personality*, pp. 13, 16, 22. See also notes 1, 2, above.

11 Franz Alexander, "The Psychiatric Aspects of War and Peace," *American Journal of Sociology*, XLVI (January, 1941), 526; "Peace Aims," *American Journal of Orthopsychiatry*, XIII (October, 1943), 575; E. F. M. Durbin and J. Bowlby, *Personal Aggressiveness and War* (New York: Columbia University Press, 1939).

12 Quincy Wright, *A Study of War* (University of Chicago, 1942), pp. 73, 373, 958, 973; Bronislaw Malinowski, "War and Weapons among the Natives of the Trobriand Islands," *Man* (January, 1920), p. 33; W. C. McLeod, *The Origin and History of Politics* (New York: John Wiley, 1931), pp. 112, 218.

13 F. Alexander, "Peace Aims," p. 576; Quincy Wright, *A Study of War*.

14 William James, "The Moral Equivalent of War," *International Conciliation* (February, 1910), no. 27; F. Alexander, "Peace Aims," p. 575.

15 Quincy Wright, *A Study of War*, p. 1011.

16 John Dollard, *Frustration and Aggression* (New Haven: Yale University Press, 1934); F. Alexander, "Peace Aims," p. 574.

17 Gardiner Murphy, ed., *Human Nature and Enduring Peace* (Boston: Houghton Mifflin, 1945), p. 27; Sylvanus M. Duvall, "War and Human Nature," *Public Affairs Pamphlet*, no. 125 (New York: 1947).

18 Walter Lippmann, *Public Opinion* (New York: Harcourt, Brace & Co., 1922), p. 79 ff.; S. I. Hayakawa, *Language in Action* (New York: Harcourt, Brace & Co., 1941); Quincy Wright, *A Study of War*, p. 1288 ff.

19 Gunnar Myrdal, *An American Dilemma* (New York: Harper, 1943).

20 Robert Waelder, "Psychological Aspects of War and Peace," *Geneva Studies* (May, 1939), X, 20 ff.

21 Durkheim noted the tension between the psychobiological ego with which an individual is endowed by nature and the sociocultural ego which he acquires through participation in a given society and culture. See "Le dualisme et la nature humaine" in *Scientia*, XV, 206 ff., cited by Bidney, in *Culture and Personality*, p. 41.

22 Even if propaganda does not operate, literacy eventually creates greater awareness of the economic differences which exist and this may lead to unrest and tension. Such tension may be an essential condition of reform. Thus the values of peace and of human welfare may be to some extent in conflict with one another.

[23] S. Chandrasekhar, "Population Problems and International Tensions," UNESCO, *International Social Science Bulletin,* I (1949), 54. These relationships do not mean that health measures should be abandoned but that they should be preceded by birth-control education and technological improvements.

[24] The problem of introducing technological skills and capital into underdeveloped areas under conditions which will avoid these difficulties has been studied by the United States and the United Nations in connection with the Point Four program proposed by President Truman in January, 1949.

[25] Richard McKeon, ed., *Democracy in a World of Tensions, A Symposium Prepared by UNESCO* (University of Chicago Press, 1951).

[26] Lewis F. Richardson, "Generalized Foreign Politics," *British Journal of Psychology Monograph Supplements,* XXIII (Cambridge, 1939), 83; Quincy Wright, *A Study of War,* p. 1483.

[27] This statement results from an analysis of the list of wars in Quincy Wright, *A Study of War,* p. 636 ff.

[28] The study of this problem has been proposed by UNESCO.

[29] Otto Klineberg, "The UNESCO Project on International Tensions," *International Social Science Bulletin,* I (1949), 11 ff.

[30] Quincy Wright, letter, *International Social Science Bulletin,* I (1949), 22.

[31] M. M. Willey and S. A. Rice, "The Agencies of Communication," in W. F. Ogburn, ed., *Recent Social Trends* (New York: McGraw-Hill, 1933), I, 217; Harold Lasswell, *World Politics and Personal Insecurity* (New York: McGraw Hill, 1935), p. 203; Quincy Wright, *A Study of War,* p. 174; "Modern Technology and the World Order" in W. F. Ogburn, ed., *Technology and International Relations* (University of Chicago Press, 1949), p. 182; Karl W. Deutsch, *Nationalism and Social Communication* (New York: Wiley, 1953), pp. 155 ff.

[32] Quincy Wright, ed., *The World Community* (University of Chicago Press, 1948), p. 6; W. F. Ogburn, ed., *Technology and International Relations,* p. 174.

NOTES TO CHAPTER 11

[1] Quincy Wright, *A Study of War* (University of Chicago Press, 1942), pp. 1087, 1472.

[2] Harold D. Lasswell, *World Politics and Personal Insecurity* (New York: McGraw Hill, 1935), pp. 203–206; Wright, *op. cit.,* pp. 175, 380.

[3] Wright, *op. cit.,* p. 169 ff.

[4] *Ibid.,* p. 1082 ff.

NOTES TO CHAPTER 12

[1] "The Meaning of Unity Among the Sciences," *Philosophy and Phenomenological Research,* VI (June, 1946), 493, 495.

[2] "Education—and Its Modifiers," *Philosophy and Phenomenological Research,* VII (December, 1946), 259.

[3] R. N. Montgomery, ed., *The William Rainey Harper Memorial Conference* (University of Chicago Press; 1938), p. 32.

NOTES TO CHAPTER 14

[1] *Foreign Affairs,* XXVI (October, 1947), 40–42.

[2] *Ibid.,* pp. 19 ff.

[3] Arnold Toynbee, *A Study of History* (New York: Oxford University Press, 1934).

[4] *Life* (September, 1947), p. 76.

[5] James F. Byrnes, *Speaking Frankly* (New York: Harper, 1947).

[6] *Foreign Affairs,* XXV (July, 1947), 566 ff. Reprinted in George Kennan, *American Foreign Policy, 1900–1950* (University of Chicago Press, 1951).

[7] "National Defense and National Reputation," *Department of State Bulletin,* XVI (February 2, 1947), 202 ff.

8 James Burnham, *The Struggle for the World* (New York: John Day Co., 1947).

9 Leo Szilard, "Letter to Stalin," *Bulletin of the Atomic Scientists,* III (December, 1947), and "Comment," *ibid.,* IV (March, 1948). See also news column by Eleanor Roosevelt, March 12, 1948.

10 Cord Meyer, Jr., *Peace or Anarchy* (Boston: Little, Brown & Co., 1947).

11 Clarence Streit, *Freedom and Union,* II (August–September, 1947), 4, and Harold Urey, *ibid.,* II (July, 1947), 12.

12 C. W. de Kieweit, in Quincy Wright, ed., *A Foreign Policy for the United States* (University of Chicago Press, 1947), pp. 18 ff.

13 Walter Lippmann, *The Cold War* (New York: Harper, 1947).

14 *Life* (September, 1947), p. 76.

15 Note 6, above.

16 Address at Des Moines, February 13, 1948, *Department of State Bulletin,* XVIII (February 22, 1948), 231.

17 P. W. Bridgman, H. C. Urey, W. F. Ogburn, *et al.,* "Scientists and Social Responsibility," *Bulletin of the Atomic Scientists,* IV (March, 1948).

NOTES TO CHAPTER 15

1 Harold D. Lasswell, *The World Revolution of Our Time,* Hoover Institute Studies (Stanford University Press, August, 1951).

2 Harold D. Lasswell, *World Politics and Personal Insecurity* (New York: McGraw-Hill, 1935), pp. 134, 219.

3 Chap. 9, above.

4 Quincy Wright, "The Problem of Establishing and Maintaining a Stable World Society" in Bryson, Finkelstein, MacIver, eds., *Perspectives on a Troubled Decade,* Tenth Symposium, Conference on Science, Philosophy and Religion (New York: Harper, 1950), p. 287.

5 Charles Morris distinguishes signs as designators or identifiors, as formators, as prescriptors, and as appraisors to indicate respectively the predominance of these four relations. (*Signs, Language and Behavior* [New York: Prentice-Hall, 1946], pp. 60 ff.) He also uses the words, "semantics" and "syntactics," to refer respectively to the study of signs in the first two relations and "pragmatics" to refer to their study in the last two relations (pp. 217 ff.).

6 Quincy Wright, *A Study of War* (University of Chicago Press, 1942), pp. 991 ff.

7 Quincy Wright, "Specialization and Universal Values in General International Organization," in Bryson, Finkelstein, MacIver, eds., *Approaches to Group Understanding,* Sixth Symposium, Conference on Science, Philosophy and Religion (New York: Harper, 1947), pp. 207–217.

8 Ithiel de Sola Pool, *Symbols of Internationalism,* Hoover Institute Studies. (Stanford University Press, 1951).

9 *Ibid.,* pp. 36, 41–44, 46, 47, 53, 54. The percentages of editorials mentioning international organizations were: France 10, Germany 8, Great Britain 6, United States 6, Russia 3. The number of symbols on which these percentages were based, was, however, small. Only 3 per cent of all general symbols counted referred to international organizations, of which the largest number were in American and the least in Russian papers (p. 57).

10 Harold D. Lasswell, *Public Opinion in War and Peace* (Washington: National Education Association, 1943), pp. 7 ff.; Quincy Wright, *A Study of War,* pp. 1079, 1087 ff., 1203, 1208 ff.

11 Wright, *ibid.,* p. 1203.

12 Ithiel de Sola Pool, *op. cit.,* pp. 4, 18; Quincy Wright, *A Study of War,* pp. 1253, 1471.

13 Ithiel de Sola Pool, *op. cit.,* p. 57.

14 Quincy Wright, *A Study of War,* p. 1000.

15 *Ibid.,* pp. 999, 1002.

16 Charles E. Merriam edited a series of studies on *The Making of Citizens,* indicat-

ing the devices of civic education used in the principal countries and their success or failure in building national sentiment. (University of Chicago Press, 1931).

17 Quincy Wright, *A Study of War,* pp. 1005, 1251.

NOTES TO CHAPTER 16

1 Washington.

2 Choiseul.

3 Wicquefort.

4 Machiavelli.

5 *Ibid.*

6 Grotius.

7 Clausewitz.

8 E. D. Dickinson, *The Equality of States in International Law* (Cambridge: Harvard University Press, 1920), chap. 1.

9 Quincy Wright, "Human Rights and the World Order," *International Conciliation,* no. 389 (April, 1943), pp. 238 ff.; H. Lauterpacht, *International Law and Human Rights* (London: Stevens, 1950), pp. 73 ff.

10 *The Federalist* (Hamilton), No. 15; Quincy Wright, "Fundamental Problems of International Organization," *International Conciliation,* no. 369 (April, 1941), pp. 468 ff.; Clarence Streit, *Union Now* (New York: Harper, 1939), chap. 1.

11 Chap. 4, above.

12 Chap. 4, above, chap. 19, below; Quincy Wright, *A Study of War* (University of Chicago Press, 1942), pp. 382, 763; "American Policy Toward Russia," *World Politics,* II (Summer, 1950), pp. 463 ff.; W. T. R. Fox, "The United States and the Other Great Powers," in Quincy Wright, ed., *A Foreign Policy for the United States* (University of Chicago Press, 1947), pp. 3 ff.; H. D. Lasswell, "Interrelations of World Organizations and World Society," *Yale Law Journal,* LV (August, 1946), 889 ff.

13 Robert Angell, Lloyd Warner, Margaret Mead, *et. al.,* in Quincy Wright, ed., *The World Community* (University of Chicago Press, 1948), pp. 145 ff.; M. M. Willey and Stuart A. Rice, in "The Agencies of Communication," W. F. Ogburn, ed., *Recent Social Trends* (New York: McGraw-Hill, 1933), I, 217; Harold D. Lasswell, *World Politics and Personal Insecurity* (New York: McGraw-Hill, 1935), p. 203; Quincy Wright, *A Study of War,* p. 174; W. F. Ogburn, ed., "Modern Technology and the World Order" in *Technology and International Relations* (University of Chicago Press, 1949), pp. 174 ff.

14 Quincy Wright, *A Study of War,* pp. 975 ff.

15 *Human Rights, Comments and Interpretation,* a symposium by UNESCO with an introduction by Jacques Maritain (London: Allan Wingate, n.d.); *Democracy in a World of Tensions,* a symposium prepared by UNESCO, edited by Richard P. McKeon with the assistance of Stein Rokkan (University of Chicago Press, 1951). Modern social science emphasizes the obstacles which infantile conditioning by the culture presents to intercultural understanding. See Nathan Leites, "Psychocultural Hypotheses about Political Acts," *World Politics,* I (October, 1948), 102 ff.

16 Arnold J. Toynbee, *A Study of History* (Oxford University Press, 1939), V, 58 ff.; Quincy Wright, *A Study of War,* pp. 103 ff., 166 ff., 357 ff.

17 Julian Huxley, *UNESCO: Its Purpose and Its Philosophy* (Washington: Public Affairs Press, 1947), UNESCO Conference, First Session, Paris, November 20–December 10, 1946, UNESCO C/30, Paris, 1947, 37 ff.

18 See colloquy between Ribnikar of Yugoslavia and Malik of Lebanon, United Nations Human Rights Commission, February, 1947, *U.N. Weekly Bulletin,* II (February 25, 1947), 170.

19 Quincy Wright, "Freedom and Responsibility in Respect to Transnational Communication," *Proceedings, American Society of International Law,* XLIV (1950), 98 ff.

20 Margaret Mead and Robert Angell in *The World Community,* pp. 47 ff., 152 ff.

21 Linden A. Mander, *Foundations of Modern World Society* (Stanford University

Press, 1947); Louis B. Sohn, *Cases and Other Materials on World Law* (Brooklyn: Foundation Press, 1950).

[22] T. W. Schultz, ed., *Food for the World* (University of Chicago Press, 1945), pp. 66 ff., 335 ff.; Phillips Talbot, ed., *South Asia in the World Today* (University of Chicago Press, 1950), especially Kingsley Davis, "The Economic Demography of India and Pakistan," pp. 86 ff.

[23] *South Asia in the World Today*, part iv, on political forces in South Asia.

[24] Hans J. Morgenthau, in *The World Community*, pp. 273, 286.

[25] Quincy Wright, *A Study of War*, pp. 1089 ff., 1310, 1326 ff.

[26] *Ibid.*, pp. 743 ff.; Hans J. Morgenthau, *Politics Among Nations* (New York: Knopf, 1948), pp. 125 ff.

[27] Quincy Wright, *A Study of War*, pp. 758 ff., 783 ff., 1258 ff., 1329 ff.; idem, "The Present Status of Neutrality," *American Journal International Law*, XXXIV (July, 1940), 391 ff.; *ibid.*, "Repeal of the Neutrality Act," XXXVI (January, 1942), 8 ff.

[28] Chaps. 8, 10, above; Quincy Wright, *A Study of War*, pp. 760 ff., 814 ff., 1235 ff., 1311 ff.

[29] W. T. R. Fox, *The Super Powers* (New York: Harcourt, Brace & Co., 1944); Hans J. Morgenthau, *Politics Among Nations;* Quincy Wright, *A Study of War*, pp. 220 ff., 239 ff., 268, 848 ff.

[30] Chap. 10, above.

[31] Quincy Wright, *A Study of War*, pp. 1240 ff., 1466 ff. The rank order of distances among the great powers was established by answering the following questions:

1. Technological distance (T)—With which of the six other great powers does X have most contact? Second most? Third most? Fourth most? Fifth most? Least?
2. Strategic Distance (St)—Which can X most easily attack? Etc.
3. Legal Distance (L)—Which does X treat most equally? Etc.
4. Intellectual Distance (I)—Which does X most resemble intellectually? Etc.
5. Social Distance (S)—With which does X share the most institutions? Etc.
6. Political Distance (P)—With which is X most politically united? Etc.
7. Psychic Distance (Ps)—With which is X most friendly? Etc.
8. War Expectancy Distance (E)—Which does X least expect to fight? Etc.

[32] *Ibid.*, p. 1489. The formula arrived at for determining the probability of war between a pair of states (a and b) utilizing the above symbols for distance was as follows:

$$\frac{dx}{dt} = \frac{dE}{dt} + \left(\frac{2dPs}{dt} - \frac{dT}{dt} \right) + \left(\frac{dS}{dt} - \frac{dI}{dt} \right) + \left(\frac{d(E_{ab} - E_{ba})}{dt} + \frac{d(St_{ba} - St_{ab})}{dt} \right)$$
$$+ \left(\frac{d(P_{ab} - P_{ba})}{dt} + \frac{d(L_{ba} - L_{ab})}{dt} \right)$$

[33] The probability of war and the rank order of these estimates followed by the date and rank order of the actual occurrence of wars were as follows (*ibid.*, p. 1491):

Japan-U.S.S.R.	.96	1	11	8-8-1945
Germany-U.S.S.R.	.86	2	5	6-22-1941
Germany-France	.82	3	1	9-3-1939
Italy-France	.82	4	3	6-11-1940
Germany-Great Britain	.68	5	2	9-3-1939
Japan-Great Britain	.60	6	8	12-7-1941
Germany-U.S.	.60	7	9	12-11-1941
Japan-U.S.	.58	8	7	12-7-1941
Italy-Great Britain	.56	9	4	6-11-1940
Italy-U.S.S.R.	.56	10	6	6-22-1941
Italy-U.S.	.50	11	10	12-11-1941
U.S.-U.S.S.R.	.38	12		
Great Britain-France	.38	13		
Japan-France	.32	14		

U.S.-France	.32	15
U.S.-Great Britain	.28	16
Germany-Italy	.26	17
Great Britain-U.S.S.R.	.24	18
France-U.S.S.R.	.12	19
Japan-Italy	.12	20
Germany-Japan	.08	21

The most serious error was in the failure to foresee the Soviet-German Nonaggression Pact of August, 1939. This postponed war between those countries for nearly two years and was probably responsible for postponing war between the Soviet Union and Japan for six years although minor hostilities were taking place between these countries when the estimate was made in July, 1939. Hostilities have occurred in the twelve years since the estimate was made between all the pairs estimated at 50 per cent probability and rank order less than twelve, and none between pairs where the estimate indicated less probability, although Vichy France had minor hostilities with Great Britain in Syria during May and July, 1941 and with Japan in Indochina in September, 1940; and Italy changed sides after the defeat of Mussolini and engaged in hostilities with Germany in 1945 (pp. 1280 ff.). China and other states not considered "great powers" in 1939 were not included in the estimates. Another method of estimating the probability of war between pairs of states, applied in January, 1937, to many small states as well as to the great powers, gave roughly parallel results and indicated a probability over 60 per cent that China, Czechoslovakia, Yugoslavia, Poland, Belgium, Hungary, Rumania, and Lithuania would be involved in war (p. 1479).

[34] Quincy Wright, *A Study of War*, pp. 796 ff.

[35] Herbert Solow, "Operation Research," *Fortune* (April, 1951), p. 105; Marshall Stone, "Science and Statecraft," *Science*, CV (May 16, 1947), 507 ff.; note 43, below.

[36] For list of the states regarded as "great powers" at different periods since 1500 see Quincy Wright, *A Study of War*, pp. 220 ff., 649; Brookings Institution, *Major Problems of United States Foreign Policy, 1950–1951* (Washington: 1950), pp. 47 ff.

[37] *Speeches of the Right Honorable George Canning*, (London: Ridgway and Sons, 1936), VI, 107 ff., quoted in Hans J. Morgenthau, *Politics Among Nations*, p. 140.

[38] Quincy Wright, *A Study of War*, pp. 357 ff., 402 ff., 766, 860, 1284 ff.

[39] Note 31, above.

[40] Note 13, above.

[41] Quincy Wright, *A Study of War*, pp. 278, 746, 753; Hans J. Morgenthau, *Politics Among Nations*, pp. 80 ff.; Harold and Margaret Sprout, *Foundations of National Power* (Princeton University Press, 1945), pp. 28 ff.

[42] In the balance-of-power wars of the past three centuries the militarily best prepared country has been the aggressor in about nine-tenths of the wars, and in about half of these wars that state, though winning the early battles, eventually lost the war, largely because its less prepared enemy had gained allies. This has been true in two-thirds of the fifteen major balance-of-power wars, that is, wars involving most of the great powers, beginning with the Thirty Years' War of the seventeenth century and ending with World War II. Balance-of-power wars refer to wars between states which utilize modern military techniques, thus excluding civil wars where one side is not a state, and imperial wars where one side is a people or state which does not employ modern military techniques. The tendency, however, of the better prepared aggressor to lose the war has been less marked in the twentieth century than in the nineteenth century, probably because the development of military technique has given an advantage to the offensive over the defensive. The use of aircraft, rockets, and atomic bombs in war may further augment this advantage of the offensive. Thus unless collective security is well organized and the agency of collective action has adequate information and military material at its disposition, it may very well be that in the future militarily prepared aggressors will have a better chance of conquest than they had in the past. Quincy Wright, *A Study of War*, pp. 636 ff.

[43] "Operational Research" such as that conducted by the Rand Corporation in be-

half of the United States Air Force attempts to estimate the capabilities of potential enemies in particular situations with a view to United States weapon development. See John McDonald, "The War of Wits," *Fortune* (March, 1951), pp. 99 ff., and note 35, above.

44 Quincy Wright, *A Study of War*, pp. 291 ff., 792 ff., 805 ff.

45 *Ibid.*, pp. 80 ff., 144 ff., 313 ff., 324 ff., 797 ff.

46 Chap. 10, above.

47 Note 28, above.

48 Quincy Wright, *A Study of War*, pp. 402 ff.

49 *Ibid.*, p. 1107.

50 *Ibid.*, pp. 1108 ff.

51 *Ibid.*, pp. 1284 ff.

52 *Ibid.*, pp. 132, 287, 1456 ff.

53 *Ibid.*, pp. 1473 ff. Polling of the opinions of experts and of samples of the population has also been used. *Ibid.*, pp. 1253, 1471, 1480; The Radir Project at the Hoover Library, Stanford University, has engaged in a study of the comparative importance of national and international symbols. See chap. 15, above.

54 The important governments have increasingly organized intelligence agencies utilizing all of these sources. The Rand Corporation has sought to ascertain the intention as well as the power of potentially hostile governments. Note 43, above.

55 Bernard Berelson and Sebastian de Grazia, "Detecting Collaboration in Propaganda," *Public Opinion Quarterly* (Summer, 1946), pp. 244 ff. Studies by the Rand Corporation have indicated positive results in this field.

56 Biographical studies and analysis of the writings of Hitler and Stalin have been used as guides respectively to German and Russian policy.

57 George F. Kennan, "The Sources of Soviet Conduct," *Foreign Affairs* (July, 1947); *idem,* "Is War with Russia Inevitable?," *Reader's Digest* (March, 1950); *idem,* "America and the Russian Future," *Foreign Affairs* (April, 1951); *idem,* " 'Historicus,' Stalin on Revolution," *Foreign Affairs* (January, 1949).

58 This is a common method of newspaper speculation.

59 This method has often been used by academic writers on international politics.

60 Note 53, above.

61 On method and application of "content analysis" see Harold D. Lasswell, Nathan Leites, and Associates, *Language of Politics* (New York: G. W. Stewart, 1949) and note 55, above.

62 Chap. 4, above. Any operative project in this field should be accompanied by a checking project to test its reliability and validity under changing conditions. Methods of social measurement and hypotheses about social relations require continuous modification in the dynamic conditions of modern life.

63 The principal types of information used are listed in chap. viii, section 5, of the Articles of Agreement of the International Monetary Fund.

64 W. Riefler, in *The World Community*, p. 138. A less optimistic view was expressed in 1951 by Charles P. Kindelberger, "Bretton Woods, Reappraised," *International Organization*, V (February, 1951), pp. 32 ff.

NOTES TO CHAPTER 18

1 Gunnar Myrdal, *An American Dilemma* (New York: Harper, 1943); Harold D. Lasswell, *National Security and Individual Freedom* (New York: McGraw-Hill, 1950), p. 1.

2 Harold D. Lasswell, "The Garrison State," *American Journal of Sociology,* XLVIII (1941), 455. See also Lasswell, "The Interrelations of World Organization and Society," *Yale Law Journal,* LV (August, 1946), 889 ff.

3 Arnold J. Toynbee, *A Study of History* (Oxford University Press, 1939), IV, 3 ff.

4 Robert E. Cushman considers it possible to have both freedom and security if the best minds of the country plot out proper policies and procedures. These he suggests might be guided by the following principles. "We must resist the intrusion of military

authority into the areas in which the professional soldier in a democracy does not belong. . . . We must resist the further extension of secrecy in scientific research and in government affairs, except in cases of clearest necessity, and we should rescue from official secrecy many things which ought to be open to public scrutiny and criticism. . . . We must protect the public security without establishing a program of thought control which violates freedom of opinion, freedom of expression, and freedom of association." *Bulletin of the Atomic Scientists,* V (March, 1949), 72. See also Walter Gelhorn, *Security, Loyalty, and Science* (Ithaca: Cornell University Press, 1950).

⁵ E. Root, *Proceedings, American Society of International Law* 1917, p. 9, quoting De Tocqueville, *Democracy in America* (New York: 1862), I, 254. All governments in which there is not complete centralization of authority face some inconsistency between the international responsibility of the representative authority and the domestic responsibility of the legislative, executive, and judicial organs. International responsibilities cannot be discharged without action by the latter organs whose powers are defined by the constitution and exercised under the influence of domestic opinion likely to be inadequately informed on international affairs. The difficulty increases as power is decentralized and influenced by domestic opinion through constitutional establishment of separation of powers, federalism, and democracy. See D. C. Heatley, *Diplomacy and the Study of International Relations* (Oxford University Press, 1919), pp. 55 ff.; Quincy Wright, *Control of American Foreign Relations* (New York: Macmillan, 1922), p. 3 ff.; idem, "Domestic Control of Foreign Relations," in C. P. Howland, ed., *Survey of Foreign Relations* (New York: Council on Foreign Relations, 1928), pp. 83 ff.; Quincy Wright, *A Study of War* (University of Chicago Press, 1942), pp. 273 ff., 824 ff., 1045 ff.

⁶ "Conduct of American Foreign Relations," *Parliamentary Affairs,* III, no. 1 (1949). To similar effect see George Kennan, *American Diplomacy, 1900–1950* (University of Chicago Press, 1951), pp. 73, 93 ff.

⁷ Root, *op. cit.*

⁸ Hans J. Morgenthau, *Politics Among Nations* (New York: Knopf, 1948), pp. 125 ff.; Kennan, *op. cit.,* p. 95.

⁹ *Proceedings, American Society of International Law,* 1915.

¹⁰ In his address of April 2, 1917, calling for war with Germany, Wilson left the purport of this phrase ambiguous. On the one hand he referred to "the rights of nations, great and small, and the privileges of men everywhere to choose their way of life and of obedience" implying that they might not choose democracy; but on the other hand he said, "the peace must be planted upon the tested foundations of political liberty" and "a steadfast concert for peace can never be maintained except by a partnership of democratic nations," implying that all nations must be democratic. See J. B. Scott, ed., *Official Statement of War Aims and Peace Proposals, December, 1916 to November, 1918* (Washington: Carnegie Endowment for International Peace, 1921), pp. 89, 91.

¹¹ *Ibid.,* p. 351. Wilson's concept of the League of Nations became increasingly insistent upon the democracy of its members and increasingly antipathetic to the balance of power and special alliances as he abandoned the concept of neutrality and neutral rights with which he had confronted the belligerents at first. See address, September 27, 1918, *ibid.,* pp. 399 ff., and Edward H. Buehrig, "Wilson's Neutrality Reexamined," *World Politics* (October, 1950), III, 1 ff. In his address to the Senate on January 22, 1917, Wilson attempted to reconcile "government with the consent of the governed," neutrality, freedom of the seas, the Monroe Doctrine, and opposition to entangling alliances and balancing of power with a "League for Peace," "a community of power," and a "peace made secure by the organized major force of mankind." Scott, ed., *op. cit.,* pp. 50 ff.

¹² See Clarence Streit, *Union Now* (New York: Harper, 1939); the monthly periodical, *Freedom and Union,* edited by Streit; and statements by Streit, Owen Roberts, Will Clayton, and others on Senate Concurrent Resolution 57 for Atlantic Union Federation, February, 1950, in *Hearings,* 81st Cong., 2d sess., on *Revision of the United*

Nations Charter, pp. 227 ff. Certain world federalists continue to believe in universal federation; see statements by Cord Meyer, Jr., James Warburg, Alan Cranston, Senators Pepper, Morse, Graham, and others on Senate Concurrent Resolution 66, *ibid.*, pp. 317 ff.; *Common Cause*, a periodical published by the Committee to Frame a World Constitution, and Stringfellow Barr, *Let's Join the Human Race* (University of Chicago Press, 1950).

[13] These terms have figured in the strategic ideas of geopoliticians like Sir Halford Mackinder, Karl Haushofer, and Nicholas Spykman.

[14] See Herbert Hoover, "A Cause to Win," *The Freeman* (New York: 1951), including five addresses, especially that of December 20, 1950. See also statement by Representative Clare E. Hoffman, in Hearings (note 12, above), p. 479.

[15] See statements by Clark E. Eichelberger, Arthur Holcombe, H. F. Armstrong, Quincy Wright, Clyde Eagleton, Mrs. Allen Mitchell and Senators Paul Douglas and Homer Ferguson on Senate Concurrent Resolutions 52 and 72, in Hearings (note 12, above), pp. 2 ff., 348 ff., 472 ff.

[16] Hans J. Morgenthau, "The Policy of the U.S.A.," *Political Quarterly*, XXII (January–March, 1951), 43 ff.; Quincy Wright, "American Policy Toward Russia," *World Politics* (Summer, 1950), II, 463 ff.; W. T. R. Fox, *The Superpowers* (New York: Harcourt, Brace & Co., 1944).

[17] Chap. 15, above.

[18] See especially the debate preceding passage by the Political and Security Committee of the General Assembly of a resolution on January 13, 1951, proposing a cease fire to the Chinese Communist government, and on February 1, 1951, finding that government guilty of aggression. Summary in Brookings Institution, *Current Developments in United States Foreign Policy*, IV (January, 1951), 39–52; chap. 6, above.

[19] Collective security does, however, differ from traditional international politics in certain respects. Collective security relies on permanent rather than ad hoc organizations and thus gives more weight to the status quo and less to change. It also operates against any state guilty of aggression rather than against a state that is becoming overpowerful and thus reduces the tendency of international politics toward bipolarization and eventual universal conquest. See chap. 4, above.

[20] Chap. 8, above. Writers on diplomatic practice generally point out that skillful negotiation may be successful even in the most inauspicious circumstances. See François de Callières, *De la manière de négocier avec les Souverains* (Paris: 1716), chap. 2, quoted by Heatley, *op. cit.*, p. 239. Winston Churchill has frequently affirmed his hope that negotiations may bridge the "gulf which yawns between the two worlds now facing each other, armed and arming, reaching out for agencies which might eventually destroy the human race." *Parliamentary Debates* (March 28, 1951), 5th series, CDLXXIII, 203 ff. According to Hans J. Morgenthau (*Politics Among Nations*, p. 444), "When nations have used diplomacy for the purpose of preventing war, they have often succeeded."

[21] Quincy Wright, "Freedom and Responsibility in Respect to Transnational Communication," *Proceedings, American Society of International Law*, 1950, pp. 95 ff.

[22] George F. Kennan, "America and the Russian Future," *Foreign Affairs*, XXIX (April, 1951), 351 ff., reprinted in *American Diplomacy, 1900–1950*, pp. 125 ff. Quincy Wright, "American Policy toward Russia," *World Politics*, II (July, 1950), 463 ff.

[23] *Ibid.*

[24] Dewitt C. Poole, "The Balance of Power," *Life* (September 22, 1947), 76 ff. Commission to Study the Organization of Peace, *Regional Arrangements and the United Nations* (New York: June, 1953).

[25] James P. Warburg, *You Can Still Act for Peace, Speak up Now or Never* (New York: Current Affairs Press, 1950); *Victory Without War* (New York: Current Affairs Press, 1951).

[26] Stringfellow Barr, *op. cit.*

[27] Chap. 4, above; Charles Easton Rothwell, "International Organization and World Politics," *International Organization*, III (November, 1949), pp. 605 ff.

28 Note 4, above.

29 This at least is the assumption of the United Nations. The more fundamental psychological and sociological conditions underlying such a rule of law are discussed in Quincy Wright, ed., *The World Community*, Harris Foundation Lecturers (University of Chicago Press, 1948), and *Foundations for World Order*, Social Science Foundation (University of Denver Press, 1949).

30 American Bar Association, *Report of Committee on Peace and Law through the United Nations*, September 1, 1951, pp. 26 ff.

31 J. Holmes in *Schenk v. U.S.* (1919), 249 U.S. 47 and dissenting in *Abrams v. U.S.* (1919), 250 U.S. 616 and *Gitlow v. New York* (1925), 260 U.S. 652. See also *Thomas v. Collins* (1945), 323 U.S. 516; *Dennis v. U.S.* (1951), 341 U.S. 494, 503; and Herman Pritchett, *The Roosevelt Court* (New York: Macmillan, 1948), pp. 275 ff.

32 The Report of the President's Committee on Civil Rights, "To Secure these Rights" (Washington: Government Printing Office, 1947), pp. 13 ff.

33 Margaret Mead in *The World Community*, pp. 51 ff., 58 ff., 66 ff.

34 *Missouri v. Holland* (1920), 252 U.S. 416.

35 Quincy Wright, *Control of American Foreign Relations*, pp. 55, 71.

36 Secretary of State Marcy in the Dillon case, J. B. Moore, *Digest of International Law* (Washington: Government Printing Office, 1906), V, 167; Quincy Wright, *Control of American Foreign Relations*, p. 81.

37 Wright, *ibid.*, pp. 76 ff., 86 ff.

38 See note 44, below.

39 International Court of Justice, *Reports 1950*, pp. 65 ff., 221 ff.; *American Journal of International Law*, XLIV (January, 1950), 742 ff. and comments by Manley O. Hudson XLV (January, 1951), 4 ff.

40 *Fujii v. California* (1950), 217 Pac.2d, 481; 218 Pac.2d, 595; Manley O. Hudson, *American Journal of International Law*, XLIV (July, 1950), 545 ff.; Quincy Wright, "National Courts and Human Rights, The Fujii Case," *ibid.*, XLV (January, 1951), 62 ff. The Supreme Court of California sustained the Court of Appeals, but on the ground that the Fourteenth Amendment of the U.S. Constitution, not the U.N. Charter, forbade the discriminatory land law.

41 American Bar Association (see note 30), pp. 51 ff.; U.S. Congress, Senate Committee on Foreign Relations, Subcommittee, *The Genocide Convention*, Hearings, 82d Cong., 1st sess. (February 8, 1950), pp. 155–255. In refutation see Adrian Fisher, legal adviser to Department of State, *ibid.*, pp. 256 ff.; Resolution of the Association of the Bar of New York, March 8, 1949, and Myres S. McDougal and Richard Arens, "The Genocide Convention and the Constitution," *Vanderbilt Law Review*, III (June, 1950), 683 ff.

42 *Ex parte Bollman* (1807), 4 Cranch 75; *U.S. v. Hudson* (1812), 7 Cranch 32; *U.S. v. Coolidge* (1816), 1 Wheat. 415; Quincy Wright, *Control of American Foreign Relations*, pp. 196 ff.

43 Notes 35, 36, 37, above.

44 See Carroll Binder, "United States Representative on United Nations Committee on Freedom of Information," January, 1951, *Department of State Bulletin*, XXIV (January 29 and February 5, 1951), 194, 232.

45 Note 21, above.

46 Clair Wilcox and Herbert Feis, in Quincy Wright, ed., *A Foreign Policy for the United States* (University of Chicago Press, 1947), pp. 257 ff.; Harold H. Hutchin, "The United States and World Trade," *Foreign Policy Reports*, XXV (January 1, 1950), no. 16; Quincy Wright, "International Law and Commercial Relations," *Proceedings, American Society of International Law*, 1941, pp. 30 ff.

47 See United Nations report on national and per-capita incomes of seventy countries, 1949, giving figures of $1450 per capita for the United States, $870 for Canada, $849 for Switzerland, $773 for the United Kingdom, $482 for France, $346 for Argentina, $320 for Western Germany, $308 for U.S.S.R., $300 for Poland, $102 for Brazil, $100 for Egypt, $57 for India, $27 for China and $25 for Indonesia. *United Nations*

Bulletin, IX (December 15, 1950), 720. The General Assembly on November 20, 1950, adopted a resolution calling for statistics on the volume and distribution of national incomes of underdeveloped countries. *Ibid.*, IX (December 1, 1950), 610.

48 Willard L. Thorp, Assistant Secretary of State for Economic Affairs, "Basic Policy in Economic Development," *Department of State Bulletin*, XXIV (January 15, 1951), 94 ff.

49 *Martin v. Mott* (1827), 12 Wheat. 19; *The Prize Cases* (1862), 2 Black 635; *In re Neagle* (1889), 135 U.S. 1; U.S. Congress, Senate, Committee on Armed Services, Hearings, 82d Congress, 1st sess., Con. Res. (February 8, 1950), especially the statement by Secretary of State Acheson, pp. 88 ff.; *Background Information on the Use of United States Armed Forces in Foreign Countries*, 82d Congress, 1st sess., H. Rept. 127 (February 20, 1951); Quincy Wright, "Constitutional Procedures in the United States for Carrying Out Obligations of Military Sanctions," *American Journal of International Law*, XXIII (October, 1944), 678 ff.; Quincy Wright, *Control of American Foreign Relations*, pp. 1, 92–94, 293–310.

50 The Senate, in a resolution on April 4, 1951, approved the sending of four divisions to Europe hoping that the President would obtain its consent before sending more. This was not a resolution of legal effect and did not deny the legal right of the President to act independently. See Hearings (note 49, above), especially statements by former president Hoover (p. 729), Secretary Acheson (pp. 96 ff.), Senator Taft (p. 606), Senator Paul Douglas (p. 814), and speech of latter in Senate, July 5, 1950.

51 See Hearings (note 49, above), especially remarks by General Eisenhower (pp. 5 ff., 11 ff.), Secretary Acheson (pp. 82 ff.), and General Bradley (pp. 128 ff.).

52 *U.S. v. Belmont* (1937), 301 U.S. 324; *U.S. v. Pink* (1942), 315 U.S. 203; Quincy Wright, "The United States and International Agreements," *American Journal of International Law*, XXXVIII (July, 1944), 341 ff.; Quincy Wright, *Control of American Foreign Relations*, pp. 234–248.

53 This was one reason for the Senate's reservations on, and eventual rejection of, the League of Nations Covenant in 1920. See Quincy Wright, *Columbia Law Review*, XX (February, 1920), 124 ff.

54 *Common Cause*, II (June, 1948), 401 ff.

55 Quoted by J. W. Dafoe in Quincy Wright, ed., *Public Opinion and World Politics*, (University of Chicago Press, 1933), p. 3.

56 *Geofroy v. Riggs* (1890), 133 U.S. 258; *Missouri v. Holland* (1920), 252 U.S. 416; Quincy Wright, *Control of American Foreign Relations*, pp. 76 ff., 124.

57 *Missouri v. Holland;* Quincy Wright, *Control of American Foreign Relations*, pp. 57, 87.

58 Wright, *ibid.*, pp. 110–118, 312 ff., 334.

59 Note 53, above.

60 Quincy Wright, "Congress and the Treaty-making Power," *Proceedings, American Society of International Law*, 1952.

61 Chap. 16, above.

NOTES TO CHAPTER 19

1 Arnold J. Toynbee, *A Study of History* (London: Oxford University Press, 1934), I; J. S. Lee, "The Periodic Recurrence of Internecine Wars in China," *China Journal* (March, 1931), p. 111, (April, 1931), p. 159; Quincy Wright, *A Study of War* (University of Chicago Press, 1942), pp. 117, 463, 594.

2 Hugo Grotius, *De Jure Belli ac Pacis*, Progelomena, sec. 16.

3 General H. H. Arnold, "Air Force in the Atomic Age," in Dexter Masters and Katherine Way, eds., *One World or None* (New York: McGraw-Hill, 1946), p. 27.

4 Wright, *op. cit.*, p. 792.

5 *Ibid.*, p. 504.

6 *Ibid.*, pp. 81, 144, 291, 573.

7 Hornell, Hart, *Can World Government be Predicted by Mathematics?* (Durham,

N.C.: the author, 1943), p. 12. See also W. F. Ogburn, ed., *Technology and International Relations* (University of Chicago Press, 1949).

8 Commission to Study the Organization of Peace, Fourth Report: "Security and World Organization," *International Conciliation*, no. 396 (January, 1944), pp. 56 ff.; T. P. Wright, *Aviation's Place in Civilization*, 33d Wilbur Wright Memorial Lecture, London, May 31, 1945 (London: Royal Aeronautical Society, 1945), p. 29.

9 Quincy Wright, *op. cit.*, pp. 357 ff.

10 *Ibid.*, pp. 64, 370, 386.

NOTES TO CHAPTER 20

1 Henry L. Stimson, secretary of war at the time, stated that these were the only two atom bombs the United States then possessed, and the military leaders thought unless they were used and induced Japan to surrender, major fighting would continue until the end of 1946 with an anticipated cost of a million casualties to the United States alone. "The Decision to Use the Atomic Bomb," *Harper's Magazine*, CXCIV (February, 1947), 97–107.

2 Declaration by President Truman, Prime Minister Attlee, and Prime Minister King, November 15, 1945; declaration by Foreign Ministers Conference, Moscow, December 27, 1945.

3 Cf. Senator Brian McMahon, "Atomic Bomb," *Air Affairs*, I (March, 1947), 400 ff.

4 The basic documents have been brought together in: Department of State Publication 2702, *The International Control of Atomic Energy: Growth of a Policy* (Washington: Government Printing Office, 1946).

5 "Bikini Tests—Radiological Effects," *Bulletin of Atomic Scientists*, II (August 1, 1946), 26.

6 United Nations, Department of Public Information, *Scientific and Technical Aspects of the Control of Atomic Energy* (Lake Success, N.Y.: 1946). Reprinted in *International Control of Atomic Energy*, pp. 261–278.

7 Bernard Brodie discussed the political consequences of the major naval inventions in his *Sea Power in the Machine Age* (Princeton University Press, 1941); William F. Ogburn discussed the political effects of the invention of the airplane in his *The Social Effects of Aviation* (Boston: Houghton Mifflin, 1946); I have examined the effects of gunpowder and other military inventions in *A Study of War* (University of Chicago Press, 1942), pp. 291 ff. See also W. F. Ogburn, ed., *Technology and International Relations* (University of Chicago Press, 1949).

8 Jacob Viner, "Implications of the Atomic Bomb for International Relations," *American Philosophical Society, Proceedings*, XC (January 29, 1946), 53; James T. Lowe, "Aviation and War," *Air Affairs*, I (September, 1946), 67.

9 See note 14, below.

10 University of Chicago Round Table no. 386, *Atomic Force, Its Meaning for Mankind*, a radio discussion by Robert Hutchins, Reuben Gustavson, and William F. Ogburn (August 12, 1945); Joseph E. Willets, James T. Shotwell, and Irving Langmuir, *American Philosophical Society, Proceedings*, XC (January 29, 1946), 48, 59, 65; Harold C. Urey, "Atomic Energy, Aviation and Society," *Air Affairs*, I (September, 1946), 21–29; J. Oppenheimer, H. H. Arnold, Irving Langmuir, Harold C. Urey, Albert Einstein, *et al.*, in Dexter Masters and Katherine Way, eds., *One World or None* (New York: McGraw-Hill, 1946); Bernard Brodie, ed., *The Absolute Weapon: Atomic Power and the World Order* (New York: Harcourt, Brace & Co., 1946).

11 See articles by Urey and Oppenheimer (note 10, above) and statements by McCloy, Szilard, and Teller, quoted below.

12 I have used the summary on *Public Opinion in the United States* presented to the Conference on Atomic Energy in Chicago, December 10–15, 1946, by Harrison Brown; and *Opinion News: A Fortnightly Digest of Outstanding Polls and Surveys* (Denver: National Opinion Research Center, especially the issue for January 7, 1947. Summaries of reports of more refined polls presented to the American Statistical

Association at its meeting January 25, 1947, by R. Likert and Richard Crutchfield confirmed these conclusions about the inconsistencies in American opinion, but indicated less anxiety about the occurrences of another war, less conviction of its destructive effect if it does occur, less willingness to accept international control of atomic energy, and greater desire to maintain the secret in the United States. These reports indicated that some knowledge about the atom bomb was almost universal in the United States. Many who had never heard of the United Nations knew about the bomb and its destructive force. The lack of great anxiety was attributed to imperfect capacity or inclination of many to think ahead at all, or to blind faith that means of defense against it would be found. These reports indicated that the elements of the population less informed on international affairs were more certain that war would occur in 25 years, were more favorable to "isolationist" policies, and were less anxious to maintain friendly relations with Russia. The degree of information on international affairs, however, made little difference in respect to anxiety about an atomic attack on the United States. About one-third in all classes thought this danger "very or fairly great" and two-thirds, "slight or none."

[13] "World Organization and the Future: A Mass Observation Survey," *The New Commonwealth,* VIII (London; November, 1946), 381–383.

[14] "The Text of Premier Stalin's Statement" in reply to written questions by the correspondent of the *London Sunday Times,* September 24, 1946. *Foreign Notes, Chicago Council on Foreign Relations,* XXIII (October 10, 1946), 4.

[15] "Stalin's Views on Foreign Policy" in reply to questions by Hugh Baillie of the United Press, October 28, 1946, *Foreign Notes,* XXIII (November 8, 1946), p. 3.

[16] *The International Control of Atomic Energy* (note 4, above), pp. 220, 239.

[17] Statements in Political Committee, December 4, 1946, and in Disarmament Subcommittee, December 6, 1946: Royal Institute of International Affairs, *Chronology of International Events and Documents* (London: The Institute, 1946), II, 759, 761.

[18] *Department of State Bulletin,* XV (December 22, 1946), 1137–1138.

[19] H. H. Arnold, *One World or None;* Bernard Brodie, *The Absolute Weapon.* . . .

[20] "McCloy Predicts Super-Atomic Bombs within Decade," *Bulletin of the Atomic Scientists,* III (January 1, 1947), 5. (Extract of an address to the National Association of underwriters.) On November 16, 1952, the United States Atomic Energy Commission announced satisfactory experiments on "thermo-nuclear" research, understood to refer to the hydrogen bomb.

[21] Leo Szilard, address before Foreign Policy Association, Cincinnati, Ohio, January, 1947.

[22] Edward Teller, *Bulletin of the Atomic Scientists* (January, 1947).

[23] H. H. Arnold, *op. cit.,* p. 31; see chap. 19, above, and Quincy Wright, "Comment," *Air Affairs,* I (December, 1946), 242–245. Even before the atomic bomb Prime Minister Baldwin of Great Britain could say that against air attack "the only defense is offense, which means you have to kill women and children more quickly than the enemy if you want to save yourselves." See Quincy Wright, *A Study of War,* pp. 315–316.

[24] See discussion by Bernard Brodie, *The Absolute Weapon,* p. 86; and H. H. Arnold, *loc. cit.*

[25] W. T. R. Fox in Bernard Brodie, *The Absolute Weapon* . . . , p. 196.

[26] Quincy Wright, *A Study of War,* pp. 292–300, 760–766, 792–797.

[27] William F. Ogburn, *The Social Effects of Aviation,* pp. 702 ff., 719 ff. Quincy Wright, *A Study of War,* pp. 303, 322, 763, 778, 1343. During the first year of World War II it was still uncertain whether these inventions produced conquest or stalemate among equally equipped states. *Ibid.,* pp. 313–316, chap. 19, above.

[28] Jacob Viner, *op. cit.,* p. 55.

[29] Quincy Wright, *A Study of War,* chaps. 23, 24, 40. Chap. 17, above.

[30] Commission to Study the Organization of Peace, *Regional Arrangements and the United Nations* (New York: June, 1953).

[31] Harold D. Lasswell, "Interrelations of World Organization and Society," *The Yale Law Journal,* LV (Summer, 1946), 897–898.

32 Herbert Feis, *Seen from E. A.* (New York: Knopf, 1947), p. 290.

33 William F. Ogburn, *The Social Effects of Aviation,* pp. 702 ff., 719 ff.

34 The influence of military invention in some past civilizations is considered by Quincy Wright, *A Study of War,* pp. 324–328, 760–766.

NOTES TO CHAPTER 21

1 Chap. 20, p. 310, above.

2 Quoted from *New York Times* by Hans J. Morgenthau, *Bulletin of Atomic Scientists* (hereinafter cited *B.A.S.*), VI (January, 1950), 21 ff.

3 New York: 1949; first published in England under the title *Military and Political Consequences of Atomic Energy* (London: 1948). See analysis by Carl Kaysen, *B.A.S.,* V (December, 1949), 340. Senator Brian MacMahon refers to Blakett as "an apologist for the Kremlin" and E. M. Shils calls Blakett's book an "ingeniously argued and more or less well documented apologia for the Soviet behavior in the United Nations Atomic Energy Commission." Philip Morrison, an atomic scientist, on the other hand, deplores the intemperate attacks on the book "in spite of its moderate and reasoned air and its by no means extreme conclusions." *B.A.S.,* V (February, 1949), 34, 40, 43.

4 Brookings Institution, *Current Development in United States Foreign Policy,* IV (October, 1949), 4; *B.A.S.,* V (December, 1949), 327.

5 *Modern Arms and Free Men* (New York: Simon and Schuster, 1949), p. 263.

6 *B.A.S.,* VI (January, 1950), 21.

7 *Ibid.,* p. 24.

8 *Ibid.,* p. 25.

9 Brookings Institution, *op. cit.* (March, 1949), p. 6.

10 *Ibid.* (October, 1949), pp. 5, 6.

11 Bernard Brodie, *B.A.S.,* V (October, 1949), 268. General Bradley said on October 12, 1949: "Estimates by our staff on when the Russians would have the atomic bomb ranged from 1950 to 1952. The 'atomic explosion' preceded the earliest of these estimates by several months." *B.A.S.,* V (December, 1949), 244.

12 *Ibid.,* VI (January, 1950), 26.

13 Vera M. Dean, "Should the United States Re-examine its Foreign Policy," *Foreign Policy Reports,* XXV (December 15, 1949), 178.

14 *Common Cause,* V (December, 1949), 225.

15 Eugene Rabinovich, *B.A.S.,* V (October, 1949), 273.

16 Statement by Harrison Brown, James Franck, Joseph E. Mayer, Leo Szilard, and Harold Urey, October 1, 1949, *ibid.,* p. 264.

17 *Ibid.,* p. 268.

18 *Ibid.,* p. 261.

19 *Ibid.,* VI (January, 1950), 20.

20 *Ibid.,* V (December, 1949), 345.

21 *Ibid.,* p. 19.

22 Brookings, *op. cit.* (October, 1949), p. 8; (November, 1949), p. 4.

23 *Ibid.,* pp. 3–4.

24 Anne Wilson Marks, *B.A.S.,* V (December, 1949), 327.

25 *Ibid.*

26 *Ibid.* (November, 1949), pp. 4, 5. See also chap. 20, note 20, above.

27 Statements by General Groves and Frederick Osborn, *B.A.S.,* V (October, 1949), 267.

28 *B.A.S.,* V (October, 1949), 283.

29 *B.A.S.,* V (October, 1949), 269; VI (January, 1950), 9.

30 Anne Wilson Marks, *B.A.S.,* V (December, 1949), 328.

31 Chap. 20, p. 314, above.

32 Pp. 312, 315, 316, 318, above.

INDEX

(*c* = cited, *q* = quoted)

361